D1783667

Men, Money and Markets
The elements of economics

John Molyneux MA

The English Universities Press Limited

ISBN 0 340 12395 8

First printed 1971

Copyright © 1971 J. Molyneux
All rights reserved. No part of this publication may be reproduced or
transmitted in any form or by any means, electronic or mechanical,
including photocopy, recording, or any information storage and retrieval
system, without permission in writing from the publisher.

The English Universities Press Ltd,
St Paul's House, Warwick Lane, London EC4P 4AH

Printed and bound in Great Britain by
Hazell Watson & Viney Ltd, Aylesbury, Bucks

Preface

This book was written in the hope that it would satisfy not only the basic wants of students fairly new to the subject but also the slightly more advanced requirements of those preparing for examinations leading either to university entrance or to professional qualification.

Part A, accordingly, is a general introduction, which describes the field of study, defines essential terms, and outlines the application of some fundamental principles. Part B is a more detailed analysis of the chief sectors of the field of study.

My thanks are due most sincerely to Mark Dowling, who, at all stages of the book's preparation, willingly gave much invaluable advice and time to improving the raw typescript. Roger Stone, also, made many suggestions for improving the book, and George Jamieson read the typescript; I thank them both. Those faults which remain are, of course, entirely my own responsibility. Above all, however, and for many reasons, I wish to express profound gratitude to Sheila, my wife.

In conclusion, I acknowledge with thanks the sources of the photographs (Pilkington Bros, Camera Press, British Enkalon, Barnaby's Picture Library, The Stock Exchange and United Press International) and of the selection of examination questions (Cambridge Colleges' Joint Examination; Institute of Bankers; Joint Matriculation Board; Oxford and Cambridge Schools Examination Board; and University of London School Examinations Department).

J.E.M.

Contents

Part A
General Introduction

Section 1
The field of study

1A Definition

No one should ignore economics.

Taxes may be raised or unemployment created in its name. We may be exhorted to 'export or die' in its name. We may be restricted to a £50 travel allowance in its name. Politicians make and break promises in its name.

We should all have some idea of the reasons for these things; we should at least know what economics is about.

In the past, because of its preoccupation with scarcity, economics was described as the 'dismal science'. Nowadays, it is more happily described as one of the social sciences. It is social in that it is concerned with some aspect of the behaviour of society; it is a science in so far as it is concerned with the collection of data and the formulation and application of laws and theories based on those data. It is, in fact, the particular social science which is concerned with the investigation of man's efforts to satisfy his material wants. Some people now call it the science of wealth.

Material wants (e.g., for food, clothing, shelter) are satisfied by using various resources. Such resources exist in differing quantities in the world, but in order to qualify for study by economists there must be less of them than people would like to have. In other words, resources are **scarce**. There is normally enough air, for example, to satisfy everyone, and so it is not studied by economists; it is not scarce. On the other hand, even though there is a great deal of oil in the world there is still less than people would like (i.e., it is scarce), and so people have to be 'economical' in using it. Other examples of scarce resources include not only raw materials but also labour and organising ability. Apart from being scarce, resources also have **alternative uses**. This means that they may be used for different purposes; however, if they are used for one purpose then they cannot be used for another. For example, a particular ton of coal may be used either to produce electricity or to power a ship or to provide domestic warmth, but it cannot be used for all these purposes; they are alternative uses, and whichever is chosen involves the sacrifice of use for the other purposes. Such sacrifice is called the real or **opportunity cost** of production.

It is therefore possible to define economics as the study of man's adaptation of scarce resources to alternative uses.

1B Methods of analysis

However discrete any economic actions appear to be there is usually some link between them. The link may be simple, such as that between a person buying a woollen cardigan in England and a farmer shearing his sheep in

Australia, or it may be complex, such as that between the establishment of fruit canneries at Nîmes in the south of France and the retraining of a Welsh miner for work in a washing machine factory at Merthyr Tydfil—the link in this case being: fruit canneries are needed to handle the large quantities of fruit produced near Nîmes as a result of the Rhone irrigation project, which in turn was made possible by the demand in France for hydro-electric power, which was itself partly necessitated by the increasing cost of coal imports. Some of the imports used to come from Wales, because of the coastal location of its main coalfield, but exhaustion of the cheaper and more accessible seams in Wales inevitably put up the price of its coal, and so markets were lost to other sources of power. As less coal was mined there was unemployment among Welsh coal miners, which British governments have to some extent offset by encouraging other industries, such as washing machine manufacturers, to establish factories in the area.

However simple or complex the chain of events is in any instance, it usually reveals a train of causal relationships when investigated. The methods of economic analysis aim to establish such relationships and to provide the justification for valid generalisations based upon apparently discrete phenomena. The first step is to collect facts (by observation, interview, questionnaire survey, etc.) and then see if any particular patterns emerge. If they do, it becomes possible to formulate theories related to the facts. A theory based on collected facts in this way is called an empirical or inductive theory, and it forms a useful basis for analysis and prediction. However, it is not enough on its own; an essential second step is to test the theory by collecting more facts and by checking predictions against events. This second step is called deductive analysis. It is quite possible that new facts—sought deductively—may cause the initial empirical theory to be modified; economic analysis thus proceeds on the twin basis of proposition and verification. Bear in mind that new facts can only either disprove or support a theory; they can never prove it to be right.

1C Problems

Economics, then, is concerned overall with the investigation of causal relationships in the sphere of man's adaptation of scarce resources to alternative uses in the satisfaction of his material wants. Such a concern gives rise to problems, which are divisible into those of purpose, choice and method.

The problems of purpose are related primarily to a search for efficiency, which means obtaining the best (sometimes called 'optimum') combination of scarce resources to satisfy the particular wants of the community, expressed either individually or collectively. It is difficult to define exactly what is meant by 'best', but in most countries of the world it means 'most profitable'. In some of the most advanced countries, it is beginning to mean also achieving the highest quality of life without destroying the environmental balance. Secondary, but cognate, concerns of the economist relate to the recommendation of ways by which a steadily increasing amount of wealth may be produced annually, and the suggestion of means whereby that wealth may be distributed equitably throughout the community.

The problems of choice are related to those of purpose, in that the search for the optimum combination of scarce resources necessarily involves selection of those resources (as to both type and quantity), and also in that the particular wants of the community are likely to exhibit some order of priority. Such problems are also matters of concern in other fields of study, notably politics. A fundamental decision to be made by politicians is whether they plan the economy or not, but since different political parties have different ideas about the extent of planning, and since in a free democracy the different political parties have to persuade the electorate to put them into power, then ultimately the problem of economic choice comes back to us all.

The problems of method arise from the complex overall concern of economics, the complexity being epitomised in the words *causal relationships*, *adaptation*, and *alternative*. It is risky, but occasionally profitable, to draw analogies, and accordingly economic theory may be likened to a web with many interconnected strands; touch (or study) one strand and the whole web reacts. Full understanding can come only from comprehension of the whole web—the *Gestalt**—but it is difficult to investigate the *whole*. There is a methodological necessity to analyse, or break down, the whole, and then study the separate strands in detail. Such an approach involves problems in its turn, since it is difficult to deal with one strand fully without considering the relationships it has with the rest of the web. In reality there are so many complex interconnections that the task is a formidable one. It is equally difficult to produce a final synthesis, or putting together, of the strands. If the analysis is successful the integrated final synthesis follows automatically; there is an awareness in the student of the Gestalt, of the complex interconnectedness of the strands.

---

* *Gestalt* is a German word meaning 'standing together' or 'frame'; it was applied by German psychologists in the early years of the century to a theory of perception (understanding), which rested on the concept that the whole is greater than the sum of its parts. The word is widely used now to indicate a frame of relationships which conforms with the Gestalt concept.

Section 2
Definitions of essential terms

2A Goods and services

We noted in section 1 that economics is concerned with the investigation of man's efforts to satisfy his material wants. Such wants may be satisfied by either goods or services, or, in the totality of wants, by both goods *and* services. The investigation of transport, medical and entertainment services, for example, is just as much part of the field of study as is the investigation of the production and consumption of coal, oil and shoes; entertainment services have to be produced and paid for just as do shoes. Scarce resources in the form of labour, time, organising ability and so on have to be adapted to the provision of services just as much as they do to the provision of goods. It is useful at the outset, therefore, always to link goods and services together; never think of one without thinking of *both*.

The generation of goods and services to satisfy man's material wants is called economic production. Its indivisibility is illustrated by cigarettes: workers in tobacco plantations produce the leaf; transporters take it and produce it at the factory; manufacturers use it to produce cigarettes; transporters distribute the cigarettes via wholesalers to retailers, who produce them off the shelf for customers; the cigarettes themselves then produce satisfaction for the customers. Under such circumstances it is impossible to distinguish between the production of goods and the production of services in the satisfactoin of the ultimate want. Both are essential in the complete chain of production.

2B Utility

The capacity of a good or service to satisfy a want is called its utility. From the use of cigarettes as an example it is obvious that a good or service does not possess any intrinsic utility; many people dislike cigarettes and accordingly derive no utility whatsoever from them. A good or service acquires utility only as it is wanted, and since the amount of wanting varies from time to time and from person to person utility is clearly difficult to measure. In fact, there is no measure for it. If you have just eaten a good meal then another one will not have much utility for you (i.e., it will not give you much satisfaction), but it might have great utility for someone else—or it might acquire utility for you in a few hours' time. Obviously the meal has no intrinsic utility; it acquires utility only to the extent that people want it. And there is no known scale against which people's wants may be measured (though you can bear in mind that the price people are prepared to pay for the good or service gives a very rough indication of the extent of people's wants).

A distinction should be drawn between utility and usefulness. A good or service which satisfies a want has utility; it may or may not also be useful. For example, a cigarette has utility to a smoker, but it is rarely useful to him. If the good or service is a definite nuisance it is said to have disutility, but it might still be useful—such as being conscripted into the armed forces.

2C The margin

The margin is what divides the occurrence of something from its non-occurrence. If you consume six beers and then stop, you have reached your margin of consumption; if you produce 55 runs in a cricket match and then stop, you have reached your margin of production. The marginal unit is the one on either side of the point at which you stop, i.e., either the sixth or the seventh beer, either the 55th or the 56th run. It is not necessarily any different from the other units; it is merely the last occurrence or the next possible occurrence of whatever units are under consideration.

The words *margin* and *marginal* may be applied widely; they may be used to describe production, rates of taxation, utility, firms, consumption, or indeed almost any other topic of economic study. If you stop reading this book now then you have reached the margin of reading (this book), and either this or the next sentence is the marginal one for you. We shall come across the words frequently in the following pages, and so it is well that you know exactly what they mean. A couple of examples taken from common usage will help fix the concept in your mind:

1 Marginal costs of production
A firm produces, say, 1000 television sets at a total cost of £50 000. It will cost the firm a little more to produce 1001 sets, because the firm will have to pay for an additional tube and cabinet as well as another 30 or so valves, and it will also have to pay a few workers a small amount of extra money to assemble the extra set. Let us assume that all this extra cost amounts to £40. Such a sum represents the marginal cost of producing the additional 1001st unit. If we determine to regard the 1000th unit (i.e., the *last* one) as the marginal unit, then we can assess the marginal cost of its production only by ascertaining how much it would have cost in total to produce 999 sets and subtracting such a figure from £50 000, which is the known cost of producing 1000 sets. In either case you will appreciate that a certain amount of close guesswork is required to calculate the marginal cost, because a comparison is being made between a known figure and an estimated one. Note carefully that the marginal cost is not necessarily the same as the average cost, which is here £50 per television set.

2 Marginal utility
A person consumes, say, 10 cream cakes at a party, and derives a certain (but unknown) amount of utility from each. At the 10th cake he feels sick and so does not want another; he has reached the margin of consumption for that particular occasion. Marginal utility is the satisfaction he has gained from the 10th cake; in the case of the unconsumed 11th cake

marginal utility is either zero or negative, since it will probably make him sick. If the person is buying cakes instead of being given them at a party, and if he could well enjoy more than 10 but can afford to buy only 10, then marginal utility is still the satisfaction he derives from the 10th cake —but in the case of the 11th cake it is the satisfaction he undoubtedly would derive from it if he could afford to buy it.

The location of the margin is not fixed. If, and when, you stop reading this book, then the marginal sentence is the last (or next) one that you read (or would have read); the margin therefore moves along with you. In economic matters, the location of the margin is determined largely by prices, and as prices fluctuate so does the margin. For example, if the price of cream cakes rises then the person in our example may be able to afford to buy only six, in which case the marginal cake is the sixth or seventh and marginal utility is the utility derived from consumption of the marginal cake.

2D Real and nominal

The word *real* has already been used (section 1A), in relation to cost of production. You doubtless appreciated that its meaning is different from a monetary (or *nominal*) assessment of cost. The television sets noted in section 2C had an average monetary or nominal cost of £50 each; their real cost is incalculable, since it is the range of potential products which could have been produced had the resources not been employed in making television sets. And who can assess what other products might have been made instead? The word *real* therefore implies actual goods and services, i.e., the various resources and works of production. We shall return to this topic later.

Like marginal, real is often applied to many different topics. For example, real income is not the amount of money a person earns (that is his nominal or monetary income), but the actual amount of goods and services he can obtain in exchange for his money. Thus, real income is food, travel, accommodation and the like.

2E Laws and frictions

There are many types of laws: some tell you to do this or not to do that; others tell you that if *x* happens then *y* will inevitably follow. And there are economic laws. They tell you merely what is likely to happen under certain circumstances, when one condition changes and other things remain the same. The law of demand is an example; it tells you that provided other things remain the same when the price of a good changes then people tend to buy less of the good as it gets dearer and more of it as it gets cheaper. The law is empirical, being based on the observations of common action; it is employed as part of the framework for subsequent analysis. The purpose of inserting the conditional clause *provided other things remain the same* (the *ceteris paribus* clause, as it is often called) is to facilitate analysis; if more than one factor changes then it becomes immensely difficult, because of the 'web' character of economics, to isolate the effects of changes in a single factor. In order properly to analyse the effects of changes in one factor we must rigidly exclude the possibility of simultaneous changes in other factors. Such an approach lends a superficial artificiality to the study of economics, since, in practice, it is highly unlikely that only one factor will change while the rest of the economic system remains stable. However, as an introductory method of study, such an approach is the only one possible.

Even though we restrict our analysis to changes in one factor only, we still cannot guarantee that the law will 'work'; the law describes merely what is likely to happen. In a perfect world the law would not need to be qualified in this way, but in the imperfect reality of the present world the law is hindered in its operation by all sorts of **frictions**. These are any factors which prevent the full and smooth operation of the law. In the case of the law of demand, smooth operation may be hindered by such frictions as habit, laziness and ignorance: people may buy a good at a certain shop simply because they have always done so; because they are too lazy to try elsewhere; or because they are ignorant of the opportunities somewhere else, despite the possibility that the good in the certain shop is more expensive than elsewhere. Because of the operation of economic frictions there are nearly always exceptions to economic laws. The customary approach to economic study is to ignore the frictions at first and to treat the economic system as perfect, only subsequently investigating the imperfect—and more complex—real conditions.

2F Wealth

Economic wealth consists of those various goods and services which have a value. However much you may personally value something (sentimental value, etc.) its economic value is determined solely by what (in real or nominal terms) you can exchange it for. Economic value, therefore, equals exchange (or market) value, and is acquired by the goods and services in question:

> having (or promising) utility to someone else;
> being scarce; and
> being marketable.

Wealth may be possessed privately, socially and nationally. Private wealth is owned by individual persons or private groups of persons; social wealth is owned by society as a whole (parks, schools, roads); national wealth is a summation of all the private and social wealth possessed by the citizens of the country, whether domestically or abroad. Wealth may also be categorised as material, personal and representative. Material wealth is real things, such as farmland, tools and cars; personal wealth is the ability of a person to provide a service; and representative wealth is merely pieces of paper giving entitlement to real wealth, in the manner of property deeds and share certificates.

2G Welfare

There is occasional confusion about the meaning of welfare. Britain is described as a welfare state, and most people probably take this to mean the provision of a great many 'free' services—health, education, etc.—by the state. Such services are valuable, and, of course, have a cost of production. Doctors and teachers do not just come into being—they have to be trained and paid for; hospitals and schools have to be built; ancillary services have to be provided. Britain organises the production of its welfare services by the adaptation of its scarce resources to these ends by means of taxation and government spending. Welfare is not, in fact, a lot of 'free' services, but a state of mental well-being induced by lack of worry about expenditure on necessary services on the part of the individual citizens in Britain.

An increase in real wealth will clearly facilititate an increase in welfare; if more hospitals and schools can be built, then there is likely to be more mental well-being among the population. The relationship is not, however, automatic, since the additional wealth may be gained at the expense (i.e., real cost) of health, comfort and leisure, thus reducing the level of mental well-being.

2H Factors of production

Production is the *process* of making goods and services available to the consumers. A factor of production is anything that assists this process. The factors are traditionally classified by economists into four groups: land, labour, capital and enterprise.

Land comprises all the natural resources of an area. It includes: position in relation to other areas; size; topography; climate; mineral wealth; rivers; forests; soil fertility; etc. It indicates the complex of fundamental qualities that reside in an area irrespective of man's occupance of that area.

Labour consists of the services of all those who work in economic production, i.e., in producing goods and services which have an economic value. Thus a doctor, a singer, a writer and a civil servant are each as much part of the labour factor as are a coal miner and a steel worker.

Capital (see figure 2.1) constitutes the variety of things that help labour make the most economic (i.e., most efficient) use of land.

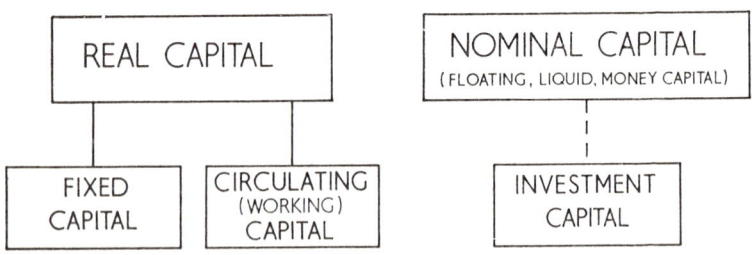

FIG 2.1   Types of capital.

There are two basic types of capital: real and nominal. Real capital is goods such as machinery, factories, roads, ports, hospitals and schools. It may be subdivided into fixed capital (i.e., goods which are used repeatedly, such as a factory) and circulating or working capital (i.e., goods which are used once only, such as a ton of coal). Nominal capital is money, which represents a potential claim on real wealth. If a person holds money, then he can, of course, buy machinery—provided the machinery (the real wealth) is produced. Nominal capital is often also called floating or liquid capital, since it can fairly easily be diverted—or made to flow—in any desired direction (i.e., towards this or that item of real wealth). A special type of nominal capital is investment capital, which is money set aside for the particular purpose of creating additional or replacement real capital—for, say, building a new and additional factory or for replacing one which is falling down.

Enterprise means the skill and initiative needed to organise the other factors into actual productive channels. The person providing the skill and initiative is called the **entrepreneur**; increasingly nowadays the functions of the entrepreneur are being assumed by governments.

Section 3
A general view

3A Equilibrium price theory

Equilibrium denotes the most efficient balance which it is possible to obtain between any two economic factors. In perfect conditions, without frictions, it is possible to conceive of perfect equilibrium; in the real imperfect world, however, perfect equilibrium is unattainable, though it is nevertheless a goal towards which the economic system strives.

Price is the most fundamental aspect of an equilibrium analysis. In essence, price is the product of a balance between the two economic factors of demand and supply, and accordingly we must first briefly examine the nature of these factors.

Demand is the expression in the market of the desire for a good or service together with the willingness and ability to purchase it. If a person has the desire for, say, a book, but neither the willingness nor the ability to purchase it, then he has no demand for the book. He may lack the willingness because he would rather spend his scarce money on some other good; or he may lack the ability to purchase at all. The starving millions in the world create no economic demand for food; however much they desire it they lack the ability to pay for it.

We have already noted the existence of a law of demand (section 2E), and we shall have more to say about it later; however, for the moment, let us accept the law as it stands. It states that as prices fall people will tend to buy more of a good (i.e., demand will *extend*) and as prices rise people will tend to buy less of a good (i.e., demand will *contract*), other things being equal. The relationship thus formulated between price and the quantity of demand is usually expressed in the form of a demand curve (see figure 3.1), which is strictly applicable to one sort of good only and then for only one moment of time—the demand for cars, for example, being different from the demand for potatoes, and even just for cars the demand for Aston Martins being different from the demand for Minis, and for Aston Martins alone the demand being different at different times.

The existence of economic demand for a good tends to draw forth a supply to satisfy that demand. Supply is defined as the willingness and ability of suppliers to put a good on the market. If the prevailing market price for the good is considered by the suppliers to be too low they will (if possible) hold back the good from the market until such a time as the price rises, i.e., they will be unwilling to put the good on the market until they have the chance of an improved profit. If the prevailing price rises, then suppliers will be encouraged by the expectation of increased profits to put even more goods on the market (provided they are able). The law of supply, collocating these

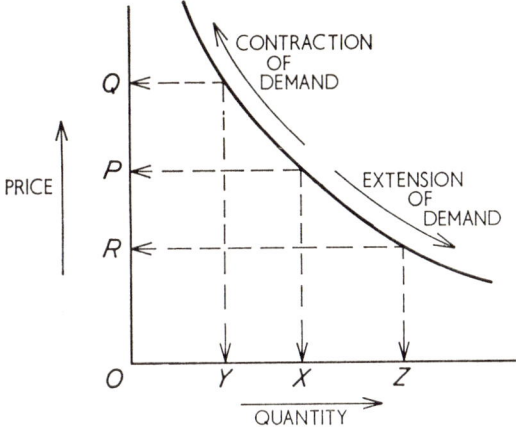

FIG 3.1   A normal demand curve.
NOTES:
1   At a price of *OP* the quantity demanded is *OX*.
2   If the price RISES to *OQ*, demand CONTRACTS to *OY*.
3   If the price FALLS to *OR*, demand EXTENDS to *OZ*.

tendencies, states that a rise in price produces an extension of supply and a fall in price a contraction of supply, other things being equal. The relationship is usually illustrated in a supply curve (see figure 3.2), which has the same restricted application to one sort of good at one moment of time as has a demand curve.

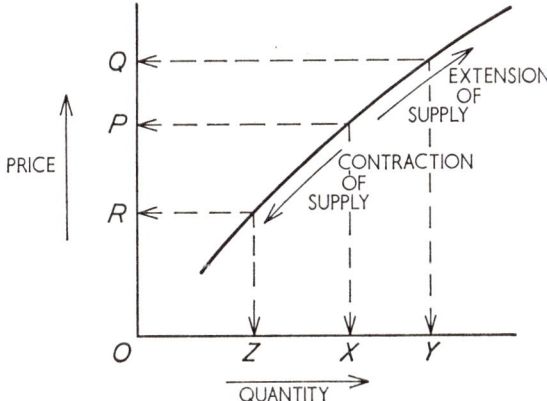

FIG 3.2   A normal supply curve.
NOTES:
1   At a price of *OP* the quantity supplied is *OX*.
2   If the price RISES to *OQ*, supply EXTENDS to *OY*.
3   If the price FALLS to *OR*, supply CONTRACTS to *OZ*.

If both the demand and supply curves for the same good are plotted on the same graph and to the same scale, then the intersection of the two curves (see figure 3.3) will yield both the equilibrium price and the quantity of goods exchanged on the market.

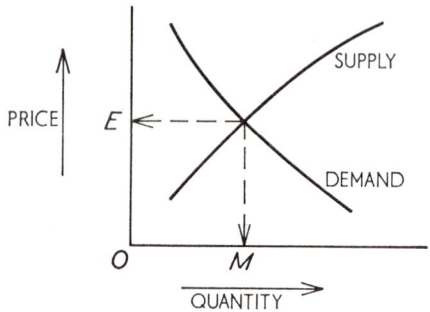

FIG 3.3   Equilibrium price.
NOTES:
1   The equilibrium price is *OE*.
2   The quantity exchanged is *OM*.

Both demand and supply curves must be plotted to intersect before an equilibrium price can be illustrated. It is possible to think of goods and services for which this cannot be done—time-travel, for example, may be demanded, but (as yet) there is no supply, and so there is no price; a floating town in the middle of the North Sea could undoubtedly be supplied (see plate 2), but (as yet) there is no demand for it, and so there is no price.

Despite the ultimate simplicity of an equilibrium price graph, the price itself is the product of complex bargaining. When a completely new good is produced for the market there are six factors which help to influence the ultimate equilibrium price. Three of these factors operate on the demand side, and three on the supply side.

The demand factors are:

1   The preparedness, but unwillingness, of some demanders to pay a high—but restricted—price for the good. This imposes a price 'ceiling', called the **marginal demand price**, i.e., that which separates the occurrence and non-occurrence of any demand at all.

2   The hopes held by demanders of obtaining the good very cheaply. The demanders are usually optimistic in this, and accordingly think in terms of a price well below the marginal demand price.

3   The prices of other goods which demanders could well buy instead of buying the new good. Such goods satisfy the same general want as the new good and are called **substitute** goods. Thus, a very high price for tea compared with the price for coffee would lead consumers to buy more coffee and less tea.

The supply factors are:

1   The desire of suppliers to cover their long-term costs of production. This imposes a supply price 'floor', called the **marginal supply price**, i.e., the price which separates the occurrence and non-occurrence of any supply at all.

2   The hopes held by suppliers to get as much money as they can for the good. The suppliers are usually optimistic in this, and accordingly think in terms of a price well above the marginal supply price.

3   The reasonable expectations of suppliers. These are influenced by market research, which gives suppliers an initial idea of a reasonable price to expect.

If there is to be any trade at all, then the marginal supply price must be below the marginal demand price—otherwise the good would cost more to make than people were prepared to pay for it. Between such a floor and ceiling there will be a point of eventual compromise between the hopes of both suppliers and consumers, based on considerations of 'reasonable expectations', and also on the price levels of substitute goods. The process of bargaining between floor and ceiling is illustrated in figure 3.4.

3B Optimum production

We noted the word *optimum* in section 1C, and related it to the search for the best or most efficient combination of scarce resources to satisfy the particular wants of a community. We also outlined the resources available, in section 2H on production factors. Optimum production is accordingly the most efficient combination of production factors necessary to satisfy a community's wants.

All four groups of production factors (land, labour, capital and enterprise) are necessary to actual production, but not always in the same proportions. If more fertiliser (capital) is used in farming, for example, then the same quantity of food can almost certainly be produced from less land (thereby releasing it for such alternative uses as housing, factories, new roads, parkland, etc.); if more machinery (capital) is used, then almost certainly the same quantity of food can be produced by less labour; and so on.

The possibility of one factor being used as a partial replacement for another in production is called **factor substitution**; the degree to which it is done depends partly upon the stage of technological achievement by the community and partly upon the relative prices of the different factors. Within the limits imposed by technological possibilities, economics is concerned to analyse the operation of the price mechanism with regard to factor substitution for the purpose of obtaining the cheapest or most efficient combination of factors for actual production. If the price of labour (wages) is low in relation to the price of real capital, then there is a tendency for labour rather than real capital to be used. This is probably the case now in China; labour is so cheap that it is not worth employing at least that part of real capital which can be replaced by labour. Conversely, if the price of labour is high relative to that of real capital,

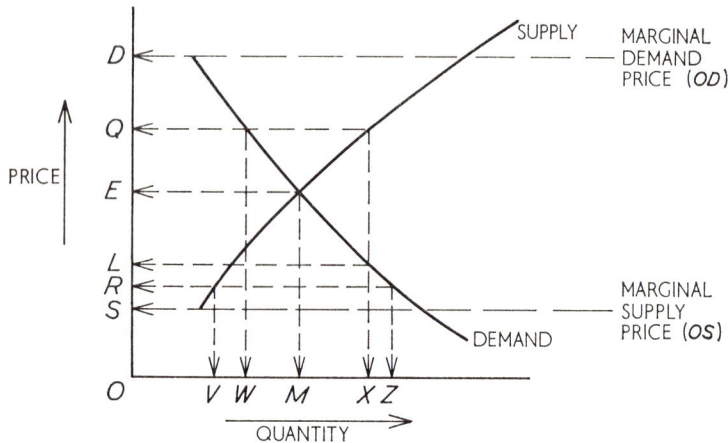

FIG 3.4   The equilibrium price mechanism.

NOTES:

1   There is no demand above the marginal demand price and no supply below the marginal supply price.

2   If the initial price (for any reason whatsoever) is OQ, then supply at OX outstrips demand at OW. Suppliers have to reduce the price in order to sell the excess quantity, and as the price is reduced demand extends until eventually an equilibrium situation (price OE, quantity OM) is reached.

3   If the initial price is OR, then demand at OZ outstrips supply at OV. Consumers bid up the price in order to obtain what supply there is, and suppliers put more goods on the market as the price rises in order to achieve higher profits. Eventually, an equilibrium situation (price OE, quantity OM) is reached.

then industry tends to use real capital rather than labour to the extent that substitution is possible. This is the case now in the United States.

We are not concerned at this early stage to investigate the reasons for the different prices of land, labour and capital, but let it be noted that—in perfect conditions—the prices are obtained through the equilibrium price mechanism by the interaction of demand and supply. If the demand for labour outstrips the supply ($OZ > OV$ in figure 3.4), then the consumers of labour (i.e., the entrepreneurs) will bid up the price in order to obtain what supply there is, and, because of the rising wages so caused in a certain area, there will be an extension of supply through immigration—and, in the longer term, possibly through a higher birth rate consequent upon both generally increasing economic optimism and the influx of vigorous immigrants. For example, Australia and Canada, receiving European immigrants, both show not only higher rates of annual population increase but also higher birth rates than the

European countries supplying much of that migration (Australia and Canada both have annual rates of population increase of about 2% and birth rates of 19·3/1000, whereas the comparable figures for the UK are 0·6% and 17·9/1000, for Italy 0·7% and 18·5/1000, and for Greece 0·7% and 17·9/1000). Eventually, an equilibrium situation will be reached. The converse proposition is equally valid; if the supply of labour outstrips the demand for it ($OX > OW$ in figure 3.4), then the suppliers (i.e., the workers) have to accept both a lower price (wage) and a contraction of supply. There will probably be any, or all, of unemployment, emigration and a falling birth rate, until eventually an equilibrium situation is reached.

The existence of frictions (section 2E) in the imperfect real world prevents the smooth working of the price mechanism, but it does not destroy the mechanism. For instance, in real life, workers are rarely likely to accept a lower price for their labour than formerly; if you apply the mechanism illustrated in figure 3.4 to this, you will see that if the demand for labour relative to its supply *falls* from an initial position of OQ wages (price) and OX employment (quantity) then there are three possibilities:

1   The *perfect* solution of a compromise to an equilibrium situation of OE wages and OM employment, i.e., lower wages and less employment.

2   An *imperfect* solution of maintained wages and considerable unemployment. If wages were to be maintained at OQ, then demand for labour at that price would fall from OX to OW. This is a bigger fall than from OX to OM, and represents a degree of 'frictional' unemployment greater than the 'frictionless' unemployment under perfect equilibrium conditions.

3   An *imperfect* solution of maintained employment (OX) and greatly reduced wages (OL). The practical expression of this solution is short-time working (e.g., a 'four-day' week); so that all the workers can be kept on, but for reduced earnings.

3C   State action

Governments have interfered throughout history with the smooth working of the price mechanism under perfect economic conditions; there are numerous instances at various times in Britain's history of trade acts, navigation acts, factory acts, labour regulations, restrictions on liquid capital, price controls, and so on. Today the British government is responsible for organising about 50% of the country's production and consumption. The proportion varies from country to country, being higher in Communist societies and lower in North America, but in all countries there is some degree of government interference with the perfect price mechanism.

The reasons for such government interference are many and varied; among them we may note:

1   The desire of governments to maintain the existence and operation of industries which are suffering from the effective competition of more

popular substitute industries (i.e., those with alternative products more satisfying to the individual citizens in the nation). The suffering industries are marginal ones, in the sense that competition from generally preferred substitutes has brought them to the limit of 'occurrence' and the prospect of 'non-occurrence'. British Rail is an example of an industry whose existence and operation have been maintained by the government, despite increasingly effective competition from road transport. The facts of such a situation mean that scarce resources are being diverted to a marginal use and away from possibly more profitable alternative uses. Governments do this chiefly because they regard the marginal industries as serving a fundamental social or strategic need, irrespective of profitability.

2   The desire of governments to prevent exploitation of the public by firms in natural monopoly positions. In Britain it would be unpractical to have, say, two or more competing telephone services (i.e., operating in the same area and seeking the custom of the same consumers) or two or more London Undergrounds. In such circumstances an independent firm would have little or nothing to fear in the way of competition from substitutes, and so could charge excessively high prices.

3   The desire of governments to appropriate for the benefit of the general public the rewards of enterprise. This is the basis of many of the arguments for nationalisation, socialism and communism.

4   The desire of governments to secure public control over what they consider to be nationally important and/or strategic sectors of the economy. Government control of the armed services is an obvious example; less obvious examples are government control of, say, broadcasting, international airlines, newspapers, education and medical services.

5   The desire of governments to organise land use for social, aesthetic or strategic reasons rather than for purely economic reasons.

The list gives merely an indication of the extent and causes of government action; it is by no means exhaustive—for example, the apparently trivial restrictions on licensing hours and on what types of food can be sold on Sundays have been omitted.

In addition to variations in the amount of government interference, and in the motives for it, there are also variations in the type of interference. Governments may assume the running of whole industries, establishing either special civil service departments (as for pension services) or special boards with responsibility to parliament (as for electric power generation). In either case, large sectors of the economy are brought under influences which frequently override the price mechanism, thereby restricting its operation to the rump of the circumscribed private sector. On the other hand, governments may merely select parts of industries for public control, thus allowing a certain amount of competition from the private sector remaining in those industries. Cases in Britain are the steel industry (not wholly nationalised) and civil aviation. Even so, governments may (and do) control and influence activity in the private sector—for example, government control of civil aviation is exerted through licensing arrangements for both aircraft and flight routes. Other methods of control and influence include direct participation in share ownership (sometimes referred to as 'backdoor nationalisation'), tax and grant incentives, tax disincentives, and the offer of awards and honours for firms and people deemed by the government to be serving the national interest (Queen's Prizes and peerages may be so awarded).

Planning is another method whereby governments attempt to influence the private sector. Socialist and communist states have long used planning as an alternative to the price mechanism, determining their resource allocation and production by reference to social and strategic needs rather than to purely economic considerations. In free enterprise economies such as those of the western world, planning is coming to be regarded by entrepreneurs as an unpleasant necessity—chiefly because they have generally been persuaded that otherwise there might be recurring unemployment, poverty in old age, uncured sickness, restricted educational opportunities, and so on. Planning does not of itself prevent these things; it merely enables governments to replace the singular dominance of the price mechanism with a more varied group of considerations. The net result of planning is estimated quantification of future production and consumption, i.e., so much land will be used for this or that purpose, so much steel will be produced for this or that purpose, so much electricity will be consumed in this or that market; in other words, the effects of planning are not necessarily any different from the effects of the price mechanism. The difference rests in the factors that are taken into account in the first instance. The estimated (planned) future quantities may be set as targets, with appropriate penalties for failure, or as guidelines. The British National Plan of 1965 set guidelines for industry, but because of an imperfect assessment of the prevailing economic situation the plan went badly awry. Its failure was not a condemnation of planning as such, but of the preparation of the 1965 plan.

An interesting extension of government interference has grown in Britain during the present century—exhortation. Various 'Buy British' (1930s) and 'Back Britain' (1960s) campaigns have been interspersed with exhortations to 'Dig for Victory' (1940s) and to 'Export or Die' (1950s). In 1967 the British government embarked on a new—and rather special—type of exhortation through the agency of the Industrial Reorganisation Corporation (IRC). The Corporation was established with state finance and private-sector members. The idea behind its establishment was that a great part of private-sector industry was not operating at its most efficient level, and that private-sector entrepreneurs would respond better to advice and financial help if these came from other private-sector (and successful) entrepreneurs rather than from a government department. The IRC's first report in May 1968 underlined the need for this sort of approach to the private sector; many firms sought the IRC's help voluntarily, but the IRC noted that there was 'still timidity and unwillingness to change in several important industries . . . too often local prejudices and family and personal interests stand in the way of effective reorganisation.' Nevertheless, the IRC was instrumental in its first year of operation in prompting and backing some major industrial mergers and rationalisation schemes, such as the Leyland and British Motor Holdings merger and the GEC take-over of AEI. It promised to be an effective instrument for industrial efficiency in Britain, until it was dismantled in 1971.

Part B

Sectors

Section 4
Demand, the motive for production

4A Human wants

People have greatly varied wants. Some of the wants may be satisfied freely and without effort, such as the want for air to breathe and the want for companionable conversation. Others, such as the want for a car to drive and the want for a house to live in, can be satisfied only with the expenditure of effort and the use of scarce resources (see section 1A); such wants are called **economic wants**, and their satisfaction is the motive for the production of goods and services.

The chief characteristics of human wants are that:

1. They may be ineffective or effective. Ineffective wants are those unsupported by money or effort, such as the wants of the Amazon Boro for more food. Effective wants are those supported by both money and willingness to purchase, such as the wants of American tourists for hotel accommodation. Effective wants are called demand.

2. Their satisfaction may cause competition among several commodities. Thirst, for example, may be satisfied by the consumption of tea, coffee, cocoa, beer, lemonade, wine, water, etc. At any one time, following the maxim about not mixing one's drinks, only one of these alternative commodities will be used to satisfy the want of thirst. All could be used, but the likelihood is that only one of them will be. Goods which compete with one another in this way in order to satisfy a single want are called substitute goods (see section 3A).

3. They may be satisfied in the present or in the future. The satisfaction of future wants, such as your next holiday, is a stimulus to saving, which may accordingly be regarded as the sacrifice of some satisfaction of present wants for the sake of greater satisfaction of future wants. If you are now reading this book in order to help yourself pass an examination in the future, then you are almost certainly sacrificing the satisfaction of some immediate wants in order to gain even greater satisfaction when you pass the examination—you are, in fact, saving your time at the present for the purpose of examination-passing in the future. If the word *saving* seems unusual in this context, try substituting the word *investing*. We shall have more to say about this later, but for the time being it will be useful to you to remember that saving is the key to investment.

4. They are unlimited in variety, even though some of them may be ineffective. Doubtless you can think immediately of hundreds of things you would like to have or to do; many of the things you think of will remain

merely dreams and unfulfilled ambitions—your wants may be unlimited, but your *effective* wants are only a small part of them. Even if you are a millionaire, then your unlimited total wants will still not all be satisfied— because you have only so much time. And time is one of the scarce resources (with alternative uses) which we noted in section 1A.

5 They are limited in their capacity for satisfaction. For example, one car gives great utility to its owner, a second even more, a third perhaps no more, while a fourth may even provide disutility (see section 2B). This is a general tendency, and applies to all goods and services other than money and 'habit' goods; it is called the **law of satiable wants**. The time factor is a necessary qualification to the law; for example, if you have just had a meal a second one *now* would probably provide you with great disutility, but another one shortly will no doubt provide you with great utility. The time scale obviously varies from one type of good or service to another; so use your common-sense when applying the law. Since, under normal conditions and beyond a certain stage of consumption, it is the *additional* unit which gives less utility (and not the units already held or consumed), the general tendency of satiable wants is also often refererred to as the **law of diminishing marginal utility** (see section 2C). In other words, beyond a certain stage of consumption, the more you consume of a good or service the less utility you derive from each additional unit of consumption. The reasons for the exclusion of money and 'habit' goods should be obvious to you—few people can have enough money, and addicts can rarely get enough of whatever it is they are addicted to.

6 They are variable in their degree of intensity. Some wants are generally regarded as more pressing than others. The traditional classification of wants into

> necessities
> comforts
> luxuries

has been attacked by many economists on the valid grounds that what is a luxury for one person may be a necessity for another. Alternative classifications have been suggested, such as

> necessities for existence
> necessities for efficiency
> luxuries

and

> basic necessities
> conventional necessities
> luxuries

but all these alternatives are open to the same fundamental criticism that what is a luxury for one person may be a necessity for another. And, of course, the concepts of luxury and necessity vary from time to time and from place to place. Television receivers, for example, were probably regarded as luxuries in England in 1939; they were certainly generally regarded as necessities in 1969, whereas even in 1999 they might still be regarded as luxuries in, say, Mongolia.

4B Equi-marginal utility

A normal consumer cannot buy all he wants to; his income is limited, i.e., it is a scarce resource. What he tries to do, therefore, is so distribute his expenditure as to derive maximum utility from his overall expenditure pattern. This means that he will rarely buy any good or service up to the point where, in isolation, its marginal utility is reduced to zero. For example, if he likes beer he will buy it, but he will probably not keep on buying it up to the point where another beer gives him no satisfaction at all (zero utility) because before he reaches that point he will almost certainly think that he would rather spend the money on something else instead. The point at which he actually ceases buying beer—the margin of consumption—is the point where the utility of the marginal beer equals the utility of its money cost (the money cost represents other goods which he could buy instead of the marginal beer, i.e., it represents the alternative uses of the scarce resource, money income). If the consumer were to go beyond this point of consumption, then the tendency (law) of diminishing marginal utility would take the utility of additional beers below the utility of money, and this would produce a nonsensical situation for the consumer (since, by definition, he would prefer to have the money rather than the beer). He could, of course, be drunk—but then he would be beyond the scope of rational economic analysis.

Figure 4.1 illustrates a possible marginal utility curve for beer consumption, and compares it with a possible marginal utility curve for money. Remember that the marginal utility of money does not diminish according to the law of diminishing marginal utility (section 4A, characteristic 5), and so its

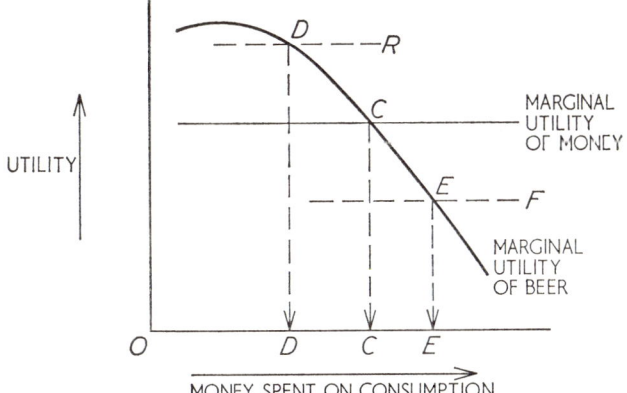

FIG 4.1   Marginal utility curves for money and beer.

curve is drawn as a straight line. When we examine the situation graphically, it is obvious that up to point *C* (the margin of consumption) the consumer derives more utility from consumption of beer than he does from holding money. Beyond point *C* the money has more utility to him, and so he ceases buying beer at that point, preferring to keep his money for some other expenditure. Similar graphs can be plotted for any items of consumption, irrespective of the quantities consumed or their cost in money-per-unit terms. Eventually, for any item of consumption (except 'habit' goods) a point is reached where the consumer begins to prefer holding his money rather than spending it on any additional consumption of that item. In all cases, therefore, the margin of consumption occurs at the point where the utility of the marginal item of consumption equals the utility of its money cost (see figure 4.2).

The tendency for a consumer to distribute his expenditure so as to gain equal amounts of utility at the margin of consumption of each item is called the **law of equi-marginal utility**, or—sometimes—the **law of equi-marginal returns**. It operates whatever the level of the marginal utility of money curve; whether the curve is raised or lowered is immaterial since it will still intersect the marginal utility curves of the separate items at an equal level.

If the marginal utility of money curve falls, then the effect is to increase

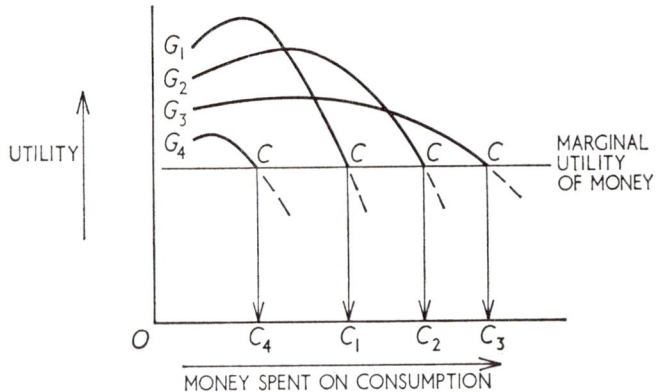

FIG 4.2 Marginal utility curves for four items of consumption compared with the marginal utility of money.

NOTES:

1   The initial utility may vary (G_1, G_2, G_3, G_4).

2   The marginal utility of the items may diminish at different rates.

3   The amounts of money spent on consumption of the items may differ (C_4, C_1, C_2, C_3).

4   In each case the margin of consumption (C) is at a point where the marginal utility of the item equals the marginal utility of money.

spending on consumption; conversely, a rise in the marginal utility of money curve will result in a decrease in the amount of money spent on consumption. Figure 4.1 illustrates the principle (which can be applied to figure 4.2)—notice how expenditure is increased from OC to OE when the marginal utility of money curve falls to level F, and how it is decreased to OD when the curve rises to level R. Now, the marginal utility of money curve derives its origin from the utility of money; in other words, the level of the non-diminishing marginal utility curve is determined by its starting point on the left side of the graph.

Consequently, the marginal utility curve rises or falls as the utility of money rises or falls. We can now move to an additional—and slight—expansion of the concept of saving introduced in section 4A: income is limited, and is either spent on consumption or not; if not, it is saved. Accordingly, if the amount of money spent on consumption increases (because of a fall in the utility of money), then it usually does so at the expense of saving, other things being equal, thus reducing the amount of money set aside for capital investment (see section 2H). Conversely, a rise in the utility of money will reduce expenditure on consumption and encourage saving. If a government, therefore, wishes to encourage saving it must attempt to increase the utility of money (i.e., make it more satisfying to hold). How can it do this? We shall return to this topic again.

Meanwhile, let us note the two qualifications to the law of equi-marginal utility:

1 The consumer must be assumed to be 'normal', i.e., have no pattern of abnormal consumption such as with drug-addition.

2 Goods and services must be assumed to be available in minutely divisible quantities. This is a perfect qualification, incapable of operation in the imperfect real world—for example, a consumer may be forced to pay £5 weekly rent because there is nothing else available, despite his wishes to pay, say, only £3. In such cases a consumer (unconsciously) applies the law of equi-marginal utility over only that part of his expenditure pattern which is free of such restrictions.

4C Consumer's surplus

Consumer's surplus is very simply the difference in money terms between what a consumer is prepared to pay up to the margin of consumption and what he actually pays. Figure 4.1 has shown that up to the margin of consumption a consumer derives more (though marginally diminishing) utility from consumption of a good than he does from holding its cost in money; this can be represented as a willingness on the part of the consumer to pay more for the good than it actually costs. Beyond the margin of consumption, of course, the good—with its constant price—becomes dearer than the amount the consumer is prepared to pay for it. Let us assume that a consumer is prepared to pay

£
20 for one raincoat,
15 for a second raincoat,
10 for a third raincoat,
5 for a fourth raincoat, and
0 for a fifth raincoat

and that when he gets to the shop he finds that the price of the raincoats he wants is £10 each. Under these conditions he buys three raincoats at a total cost to himself of £30; he does not buy a fourth because the raincoats are £10 each and he is prepared to spend only £5 on a fourth raincoat. He actually pays £30, but he was prepared to pay £45 (£20 + £15 + £10); so he has acquired a consumer's surplus of £15. Had the raincoats been £20 each, he would have bought only one—and acquired no surplus. At a price higher than £20 each he would not have bought one at all. Consumer's surplus accrues, therefore, only when the utility of consumption exceeds the utility of the money cost of the item consumed. A rise in the utility of money will clearly reduce consumer's surplus, and vice versa.

4D The law of demand

Demand, you will remember (section 3A), is the expression in the market of the desire to have a good or service, together with the ability and willingness to purchase it. It implies that the consumer has made a choice; that he is willing to purchase one good or service rather than another.

Utility is clearly the essence of demand. The consumer must derive equal or greater utility from his purchase than from holding the money, otherwise there is no demand (because there is no willingness to purchase). The consumer must also prefer the utility he can derive from one good or service to that he can derive from another, otherwise again there is no demand (because there is no willingness to purchase).

The law of demand has already been noted (sections 2E and 3A). It is quite explicit: that demand contracts with a rise in price and extends with a fall in price, other things being equal. It is based on the observed phenomenon that as prices rise marginal purchasers (i.e., those near the dividing line between purchase and non-purchase) cease buying and regular purchasers buy less, and the corollary that as prices fall sub-marginal purchasers (i.e., those who had not previously purchased because the good was too expensive) start buying and regular purchasers buy more. Regular purchasers buy less or more as the price rises or falls because of the rising or falling level of money utility in relation to the marginal utility of the good or service in demand (see section 4B). Remember that the level of money utility is determined by the possible alternative expenditure on other goods and services; if the price of a good rises, everything else remaining the same, then the possible alternative expenditure rises too, and of necessity so does the level of money utility. Figure 4.1 shows that if the level of money utility rises to R (reflecting a price rise for the good in question), then the margin of consumption contracts to OD, and that if the level of money utility falls to F (reflecting a price fall for the good in question), then the margin of consumption extends to OE.

We must also remember that a consumer's income is limited and that he distributes his expenditure of it to conform to the principle of equi-marginal utility. If, in conformance to this principle, a consumer decides that out of his limited income he should spend, say, £2 per week on clothing, and then the price of clothing rises, he will clearly buy less clothing—but probably still to a total expenditure on it of £2 per week, otherwise his equi-marginal utility balance will be upset. Conversely, if the price of clothing falls, the consumer will tend to buy more of it, possibly still up to his £2 per week allowance for clothing—though there is also the possibility that he might divert some of his new spending capacity to some other form of expenditure for which he was previously sub-marginal.

The relationship between price and a consumer's demand for a good can be illustrated either by an individual demand schedule (see the raincoat example in section 4C) or by an individual demand curve (see figure 4.3).

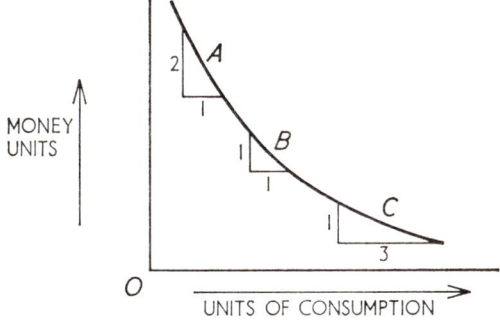

FIG 4.3   An individual demand curve.

The concave shape of the curve is caused by diminishing marginal utility. At an early stage in the sequence of purchases the consumer derives much utility from a marginal purchase; as he purchases more units the utility of each successive unit diminishes and he is less willing to sacrifice money for additional units. The situation gradually changes, therefore, from one where the good is preferable to the money it costs to one where the money is preferable to the good. At A on figure 4.3 the consumer is prepared to yield two money units in order to gain one unit of the good, i.e., the good is preferable to the money. At B the utility of the money and the utility of consumption are equal at one unit each. At C, however, as marginal utility diminishes, the consumer wants three units of the good in return for one unit of money, i.e., the money is now preferable to the good. The consumer therefore wants the price of the good to fall before he is willing to continue buying—at A the price is $\frac{2}{1}$ money units, at B it is $\frac{1}{1}$, and at C $\frac{1}{3}$. Any shape other than concave fails to fulfil the diminishing marginal utility requirement; a straight line would indicate a constant willingness on the part of the consumer to exchange one unit of money for one unit of the good (i.e., constant marginal utility), whereas a convex curve would indicate increasing marginal utility.

Market demand is the aggregate of individual consumers' demands, and market demand curves are obtained by aggregating the individual consumers' demand schedules (table 4.1) and plotting the ensuing totals on a price-quantity graph (figure 4.4).

	number of goods purchased by consumers					
market price	1	2	3	4	5	total market demand
100p	20	2	—	—	4	26
90p	21	3	—	—	5	29
80p	22	4	1	—	7	34
70p	24	7	2	—	9	42
60p	26	11	4	1	11	53
50p	30	15	6	3	14	68

TABLE 4.1 Individual and market demand schedules.

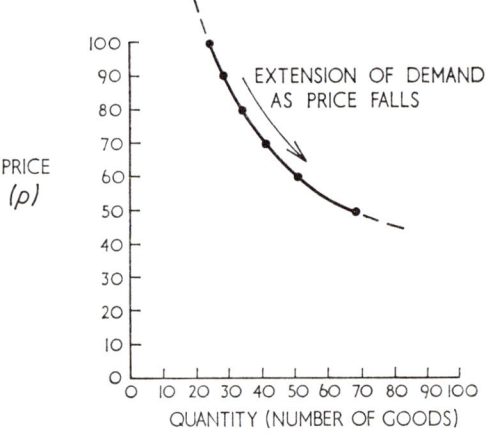

FIG 4.4 A market demand curve.

Market demand curves also have a concave slope *down* to the right (i.e., they are concave *negative* curves). This is because:

1 They are composed of the aggregate of a number of such curves.

2 The distribution of wealth and income in a country is usually such that *few* people have much and can thereby exercise demand at a relatively high price, whereas *many* people have little and can thereby exercise demand only at a relatively low price. In the schedule quoted in table 4.1, consumers 3 and 4 exercise no demand at the higher prices. They are sub-marginal at prices of 100p and 90p, entering into purchase only

when the price falls to 80p (consumer 3) and to 60p (consumer 4). Meanwhile, the regular purchasers buy more as the price falls.

It is important to note the following points:

1   A market demand curve properly refers to only one sort of good. There is no proper market demand curve for, say, cars—merely for one particular make, model and year. Other cars require their own market demand curves.

2   A market demand curve is properly plotted for only one moment of time. The market demand for, say, tennis balls varies considerably from time to time throughout the year, even at a constant price. A proper market demand curve can be drawn for only one particular time; other times require their own market demand curves.

3   A market demand curve illustrates the *potential* range of demand at a variety of *possible* price levels for one good at one moment of time. For example, if the price in figure 3.1 (section 3A) falls to *OR*, demand will extend to *OZ*, and if the price rises to *OQ*, then demand will contract to *OY*, and so on.

4   A market demand curve can be tested against reality only in the zone of prevailing market price for the good. This is done by market research, which is strictly limited in accuracy to a very narrow zone of price fluctuation; projection of the curve (extrapolation) beyond this zone is pure guesswork.

4E Elasticity of demand

Market demand varies according to the market price; if the price rises people buy less, if the price falls people buy more. Elasticity of demand is a measure of how much less or more people buy as the price rises or falls. Thus if a small change in price causes a large change in demand, the demand is said to be **elastic**; and if a large change in price is necessary to cause any marked change in demand, the demand is **inelastic**. The demand situation may be likened to a length of elastic, which is said to be very elastic if it responds easily to a small pull (small price change) and very inelastic if it needs a large pull (large price change) to change it.

There are three possible ways of obtaining an indication of the nature of elasticity. Since they give indications only, the methods are not exactly comparable.

1   Percentage changes. This is the simplest method, and is based on the formula

$$\text{elasticity of demand } (E_d) = \frac{\% \text{ change in quantity demanded}}{\% \text{ change in price}}$$

Thus, if a 5% price rise produces a 5% contraction of demand then elasticity is 1 (i.e., unit elasticity). If a 5% price rise produces a 10% contraction of demand then elasticity is 2 (i.e., demand is elastic). And if a

5% price rise produces a 2·5% contraction of demand then elasticity is 0·5 (i.e., demand is inelastic).

2   Total amount of money spent. The total amount of money spent at any price-demand combination may be obtained by multiplying the price per good by the total number of goods demanded. It is accordingly possible to compare the total amounts of money spent at any two or more different price levels. If the total amount of money spent after a (possible) price rise is greater than that spent at the starting price then demand is inelastic, i.e., people are not buying proportionately fewer goods despite the price rise. If the total amount of money spent after a price rise is less than formerly then demand is elastic, i.e., a price rise puts a relatively large number of buyers out of the market. Note carefully that the opposite is true in both cases if the price falls—elastic demand produces an increased total amount of money spent and inelastic demand a decreased total.

3   Marshall's formula (point elasticity). This is a graphic method of obtaining the elasticity of demand at any point on a plotted demand curve. Figure 4.5 shows a demand curve for which elasticity is required at point P. A tangent to the demand curve is drawn touching the curve at P, and produced to intersect both axes. Elasticity at P is then merely the proportion obtained from the following equation:

$$E_d = \frac{PT}{Pt}$$

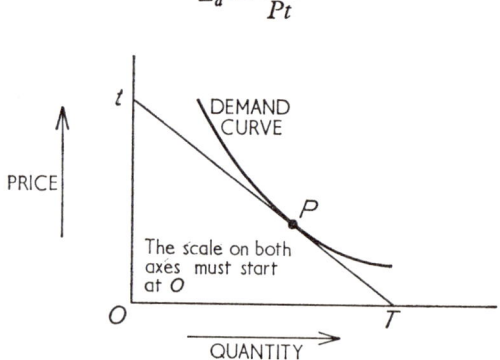

FIG 4.5   A point elasticity graph.

NOTE:

The ratio $\dfrac{PT}{Pt}$ is here $\dfrac{1}{2}$; so elasticity of demand at P is 0·5, i.e., a price rise or fall of $x\%$ at that point would contract or extend demand by $0·5x\%$. Demand is therefore inelastic.

Elasticity varies. Not only does it vary slightly according to the method of measurement, but it differs even throughout a single demand curve and its accompanying schedule. For example, if we take a simple case and apply the same quantitative changes to both price and quantity we see that the elasticity varies:

	price	quantity	elasticity
starting point	20p	100	—
first change	25p	80	$\dfrac{20\%}{25\%} = 0.8$
second change	30p	60	$\dfrac{25\%}{20\%} = 1.25$

Note that at the second change the percentage changes are calculated from the level existing after the first change, and not from the starting level.

There is, in fact, only one case where elasticity is constant (at unity) throughout a demand curve; that is where the demand curve is in the shape of a rectangular hyperbola (i.e., where the curve is supported by any number of rectangles of equal area), so that since total amount of money spent is a product of the two co-ordinates (price × quantity) and the area of a rectangle is also a product of the two co-ordinates then the area of a rectangle equals total amount of money spent. Since the rectangles are equal in area, then so are the total amounts of money spent, i.e., demand elasticity is constant at unity. Figure 4.6 shows a rectangular hyperbola; it can readily be seen that rectangles *ODKW*, *OCLX*, *OBMY* and *OANZ* are equal in area, and that therefore the total amounts of money spent at points *K*, *L*, *M* and *N* on the demand curve are also equal.

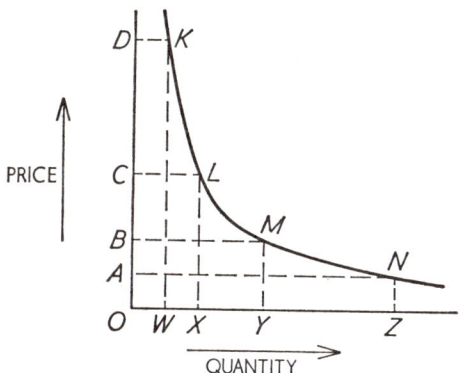

FIG 4.6   A rectangular hyperbolic demand curve.

It is an accepted custom to generalise about the shapes of demand curves, despite the facts that elasticity varies throughout most demand curves, that market demand curves are aggregated from individual consumers' demand curves, and that the accuracy of the curves can be tested against reality only in the zone of the prevailing market price. Between the theoretical possibilities of perfect elasticity and perfect inelasticity there is an infinite variety of possible slopes of demand curve, indicated in figure 4.7. Line *A–A* shows a constant price with an infinite variation in quantity of goods demanded, i.e., perfect elasticity. Line *B–B*, conversely, shows a completely fixed quantity demanded at any price, i.e., perfect inelasticity. Line *X–X* is a more realistic shape, showing a high degree of elasticity of demand, while line *Y–Y* shows highly inelastic demand. Remember which is which with the aid of a mnemonic: try *HOPE FLED (HOrizontal Perfect Elasticity, FLat curve Elastic Demand)*— if you are desperate!

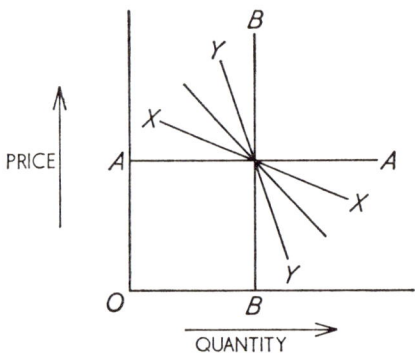

FIG 4.7 Possible demand curve slopes.

Why does elasticity vary? There are several reasons:

1 The degree of need for the good. Quite plainly, any good which is a necessity of life (such as salt) will be demanded in a particular quantity at almost any price, i.e., demand for it will be highly inelastic, whereas a luxury good (such as cream cakes) will be demanded in widely varying quantities as its price changes, i.e., demand will be highly elastic.

2 The availability of substitute goods. If there are closely substitutable goods (such as beef and lamb), then a price rise for one will tend to switch a considerable amount of demand to the other. If there are no acceptable substitutes (such as for photographic film), then demand will be fairly inelastic, subject to the degree of need for it. Note very carefully, however, that even though total demand for photographic film may be inelastic, the demand for any one make of photographic film will be elastic, simply because one make of film is highly substitutable by another.

3 The relationship between the price of the good and the spending ability of the consumer. If the price of the good is only a small proportion of the spending ability of the consumer then even relatively large changes of price are unlikely to make much difference to the consumer. A doubling of the price of paper clips would not, on its own, cause much change in the demand for paper clips. However, a doubling of the price of cars would have a considerable effect on demand; the very rich might continue to buy cars as usual, but the poor would probably stop buying altogether. In general as a person becomes richer so his demands become

more **price-inelastic**, because the prices of all goods form a progressively diminishing proportion of his spending ability. Conversely, the poor tend to have relatively **price-elastic** demands for most goods.

4 The existence of economic frictions (see section 2E). Knowledge, however derived, makes people aware of the possibilities of substitution, and so tends to produce demand elasticity. Ignorance, on the other hand, predisposes habit, and consequently demand inelasticity. Habit and demand inelasticity may, of course, be produced by factors other than ignorance; advertising, for example, aims to produce demand inelasticity by achieving product or brand loyalty.

Knowledge of elasticity of demand—at best, remember, a 'guesstimate'—is useful to the following:

1 Suppliers of goods and services, who, in their search for maximum profits, need to be able to assess fairly accurately whether or not a rise in price will bring in greater total revenue. If demand is inelastic, then prices can be raised safely; elastic demand, however, will cause a decrease in total revenue if prices are raised.

2 Governments, which need to be able to assess fairly accurately the effects of their fiscal (tax) policies. An increased tax on a good is similar to a price rise as far as the consumers are concerned; if the demand for the good is elastic then the total amount of money spent on the good will decrease, and so may tax revenue. If governments wish to increase tax revenue then they should tax goods which are in inelastic demand—which is why beer and tobacco are so frequently the objects of increased taxation in Britain.

4F Changes in demand

Changing quantities of goods are demanded either because of changes in price or because of changes in any one or more of a series of underlying **demand conditions**.

Demand changes caused by price changes alone are called extensions or contractions of demand as the case may be, and are always plotted on a single demand curve (see figure 3.1).

Demand changes caused by changes in the underlying demand conditions, irrespective of price, are called shifts, rises, falls, increases or decreases of demand as the case may be, though the convention of using different terms to distinguish the different types of change is not always observed in practice. The chief demand conditions are:

1 The season of the year. As summer changes to winter then the demand for, say, tennis balls *decreases* and that for, say, fur coats *increases*, irrespective of price changes.

2 The general conditions of trade, i.e., boom or slump. During boom times, demand will *increase* simply because people are generally more optimistic, irrespective of whether prices rise (as they probably do) or fall.

3   Fashion. As fashions or tastes change, so people buy more or less of certain goods, irrespective of price changes.

4   Advertising. Most advertising aims at *increasing* demand for a particular good, regardless of any price changes which may or may not occur.

5   The availability of credit buying. If credit is easy to obtain, then people tend to buy more goods at existing prices (or even at higher prices).

6   The size of the population. As the total population expands, so demand for goods *increases* irrespective of price changes.

7   The age structure of the population. If the average age of the population moves progressively lower as the birth rate rises, then there will be an *increased* demand for toys, baby carriages, etc., irrespective of price changes.

8   Anticipation of future price changes. If prices are expected to rise in the future there is likely to be an *increase* in demand at existing prices. This happened in England after the 1967 devaluation, in anticipation of the 1968 tax increases. Conversely, if prices are expected to fall in the future, people will hold off buying at current prices, thus causing a *decrease* in demand.

9   New inventions. The invention and subsequent widespread availability of cars, for example, has *decreased* the demand for railway passenger services, irrespective of railway fare changes. Television has had a similar effect on the demand for cinema seats.

10   Changes in consumer spending ability. If consumers earn more they are likely to spend more, thereby *increasing* demand at existing prices. The degree of demand shift caused by such variation in consumer incomes is called the **income-elasticity of demand,** and is given by the formula:

$$\text{income-elasticity of demand} = \frac{\%\text{ change in quantity demanded}}{\%\text{ change in income}}$$

A 5% increase in income, producing a 5% *increase* in demand, is called unit income-elasticity of demand. Other points about increased spending ability are that it is likely to produce increased price-inelasticity (see section 4E) as well as positive demand shift.

11   Prices of other goods
(a) joint demand. Cars and petrol, for example, are in joint demand. A price rise for cars will tend to *contract* demand for them and accordingly *decrease* the demand for petrol, irrespective of the price of petrol.
(b) derived demand. For example, a *contraction* of demand for cars will inevitably *decrease* demand for the goods of which cars are made, e.g., steel, rubber, plastic.
(c) competing demand (i.e., substitute goods). A rise in the price of electricity could, for example, *increase* the demand for gas. The degree to which demand is shifted to a preferred substitute good is called the **elasticity of substitution** or the **cross-elasticity of demand,** and is measured by the formula:

$$\text{cross-elasticity of demand} = \frac{\%\ \text{change in quantity of } X \text{ demanded}}{\%\ \text{change in price of } Y}$$

where X is the substitute good and Y the good from which demand is shifted because of its increased price. Accordingly, a price change for Y causes demand *shift* to or from X—i.e., a change in demand for X when its price is unchanged.

Demand shifts require the construction of two or more demand curves on the same graph. Figure 4.8 illustrates the market demand for tennis balls on June 21st 1999; it represents the potential sales of tennis balls at a variety of possible prices. Thus, if the price were x, then a tennis balls would be sold; if the price were y, then b tennis balls would be sold. The purpose of the demand curve is to indicate these possibilities, and not to indicate what the price actually is—remember anyway that price is not a function of demand alone. Let us assume that the price is p; the number of tennis balls actually sold is therefore s.

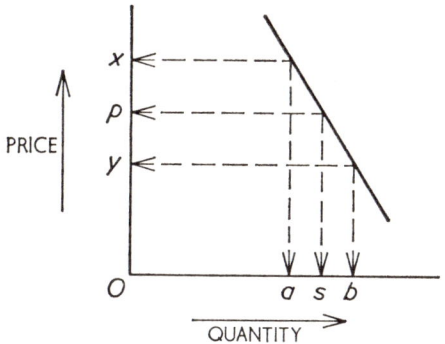

FIG 4.8   Market demand curve for tennis balls.

On June 21st 1999 the various demand conditions are stable. On the great majority of days we can regard the demand conditions as stable; even if they are in the process of change, the process is usually slow. With time, however, the conditions do change: fashions change, population size changes, season of year changes, the prices of other goods change, consumer spending ability changes, and so on. By December 21st 1999 the season for tennis has ended. The ball manufacturers maintain the price at p, but people buy fewer balls than they did in June. The negative shift in demand is illustrated in figure 4.9.

At the maintained price of p, the market demands only m balls on December 21st; a reduced price of w would be needed to maintain the quantity demanded at s. Note that the two curves on figure 4.9 are both of the same type; they both show potential sales at a variety of possible price levels. Thus, if the price fell to v on December 21st, then d balls would be sold.

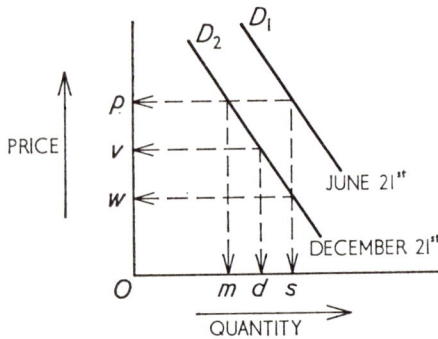

FIG 4.9 Demand shift diagram for tennis balls.

4G The Giffen paradox

Sir Robert Giffen noticed that in the nineteenth century the poor bought more bread as its price rose and less as its price fell; a situation in apparent conflict with the (empirical) law of demand. Rather than accept it as an exception to the law, modern economists prefer to regard the Giffen case as an example of negative income-elasticity of demand for 'inferior' goods.

In the nineteenth century bread was considerably cheaper than meat and vegetables, and so was often eaten as a substitute. As the price of bread rose, the poor could not afford so much meat and so many vegetables, and accordingly had to fill up their diet with even more bread; conversely, a fall in the price of bread liberated extra money from the very scarce income of the poor for the purchase of more desirable meat and vegetables, and so people bought more of them at the expense of bread. A certain amount of bread was a necessity, and variations in its price correspondingly caused fluctuations in the *real income* of the poor. A rise in its price was tantamount to a reduction in the real income of the poor (they had less money left for turning into other goods and services); so that when the price of bread rose the poor became poorer, and could afford only more bread!

4H Preference

Demand analysis so far has been based primarily on the concept of utility. However, as we noted at the beginning of section 4D, the use of the word *demand* implies that a choice has been made—that a consumer has chosen to purchase one good or service rather than another. So, even though utility may be immeasurable in absolute terms (i.e., there are no known units of satisfaction with which to measure utility), it *is* possible to assess it in relative terms. This is done by an analysis of the *revealed preference* of the consumer, itself made possible by the element of choice inherent in the nature of demand. It is possible, therefore, to assert that the consumer derives more utility from one good or service than another, simply because he chooses one in preference to the other; it is not possible to assert how much more utility is derived.

4I Indifference

Faced with the choice implicit in demand, a consumer may initially prefer one good to another, e.g., he may prefer one whisky to one beer. However, if the quantities of the alternative goods are varied, a consumer will probably eventually reach a stage where he is not really bothered which choice he makes, e.g., he may prefer one whisky to two beers and subsequently to three beers, but if the choice is between one whisky and four beers he will probably not be bothered which he takes. He is *indifferent* to the choice before him, i.e., both alternatives offer him equal utility.

If the choice is between a number of whiskies (instead of merely one) and a number of beers, then our consumer may derive equal utility from (i.e., be indifferent to) a variety of possible combinations. Let us assume that he has a real income of five whiskies and that beer is available to him as an alternative; his indifference schedule is as shown in table 4.2.

5 whiskies and 0 beers (combination *A*)
or 4 whiskies and 4 beers (combination *B*)
or 3 whiskies and 8 beers (combination *C*)
or 2 whiskies and 14 beers (combination *D*)
or 1 whisky and 20 beers (combination *E*)
or 0 whiskies and 30 beers (combination *F*)

TABLE 4.2 A consumer's indifference schedule.

Such a schedule means that the consumer is just as satisfied with a combination of five whiskies and no beers as he is with one of two whiskies and 14 beers or one of three whiskies and eight beers. It also means that he is prepared to yield only one of his whiskies in return for four beers, and all five whiskies in return only for 30 beers. Figure 4.10 shows an indifference curve based on the schedule; it is important to note that the consumer derives equal satisfaction from all points on the curve—that he is as satisfied with combination *B* as he is with combination *E*, and so on, and that therefore there is no incentive to trade.

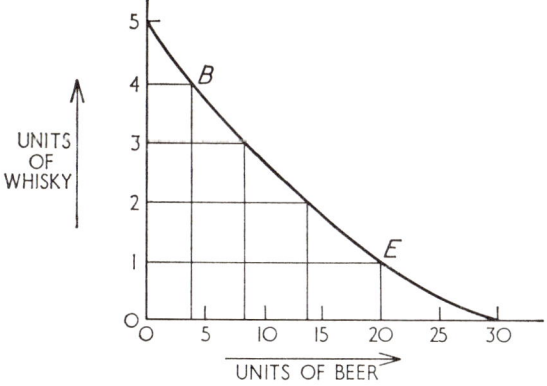

FIG 4.10 An indifference curve.

If the output of beer increases, our consumer will probably be able to obtain more beer in exchange for his whiskies (for example, a combination of four whiskies and *five* beers might become possible), thus affording him greater *total* utility. If, as well, he earns a real income of more than five whiskies, then both sides can obtain an increase in total utility (for example, if our consumer earns six whiskies he might willingly barter one of them for four beers, producing a combination of five whiskies and four beers, which, when compared with the original combination of five whiskies and no beers, shows the whisky owner to be better off by four beers and the beer owner to be better off by one whisky). It is possible, therefore, to produce a series of indifference curves on one graph, each one representing the plotted indifference schedules for combinations of different quantities. As either or both quantities increase, so the indifference curves are plotted farther and farther from the origin of the graph (*O*); so that any curve to the right of another represents combinations which offer greater total utility. In figure 4.11, curve

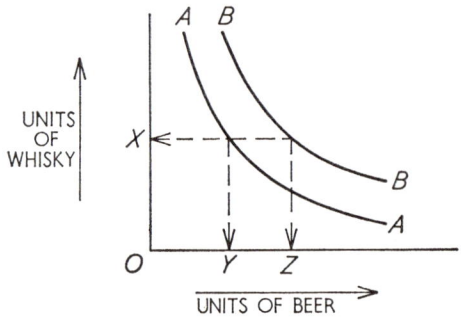

FIG 4.11   A series of indifference curves.

B–B represents combinations of greater total utility than does curve *A–A*; a combination of *OX* whisky and *OZ* beer, for example, is preferable to a combination of *OX* whisky and *OY* beer. And remember: all points on a single curve are equal, so that any point on *B–B* is preferable to any point on *A–A*.

So far, we have treated the consumer and his indifference schedules as existing in a vacuum. They do not; there is, in fact, an external rate at which the rest of the society normally exchanges whisky for beer. Our consumer must accept this rate; it exists irrespective of his personal wishes in the matter. If it is one which will not yield a combination of whiskies and beers at least as satisfactory as one of the combinations on his own personal indifference schedule, then he will not trade, i.e., the 'price' of beer is too high for him (he cannot get sufficient beer to satisfy him for giving up his whisky). For example, if the external rate is one whisky for three beers then at no time will an exchange of whisky for beer yield as satisfactory a combination as any on his original indifference schedule; so he will not trade. If the great majority of whisky-earners were to think like this, then the beer-owners would not readily be able to dispose of their beer (assuming that they wanted to). The beer-owners would therefore have to offer more beer in exchange for whisky, i.e., the price of beer would fall, because a unit of whisky would buy more of it.

The situation is different if the external exchange rate is, say, one whisky for five beers. Faced with such a rate, our consumer will mentally juggle the various possible combinations of whisky and beer until he finds the one which is most satisfactory to him. This can be done by comparing his original indifference schedule with the actual combinations possible under an externally established rate (table 4.3).

Original indifference combinations					Combination possible under an exchange rate of one whisky for five beers		
whisky		beer			whisky		beer
5	and	0	..	combination A ..	5	and	0
4	and	4	..	combination B ..	4	and	5
3	and	8	..	combination C ..	3	and	10
2	and	14	..	combination D ..	2	and	15
1	and	20	..	combination E ..	1	and	20
0	and	30	..	combination F ..	0	and	25

TABLE 4.3 Comparison of combinations under indifference and exchange conditions.

The comparison reveals that the combinations possible under an exchange rate of one whisky for five beers are worse at combination F, as satisfactory at combinations A and E, and better at combinations B, C and D. The largest consumer surplus (see section 4C) occurs at combination C, where the consumer is better off by two beers. This, therefore, will be the point of exchange for him. Figure 4.12 illustrates the process graphically; note how the point of exchange occurs on the budget line (the line representing the actual exchange rate) at its greatest distance to the right of the indifference curve. In order to avoid too many consumers deriving a surplus, the beer-owners will clearly try to keep the actual exchange rate at as much of a tangent to the generality of indifference curves as possible. This is a difficult task, because the beer-owners can only guess at the generality of indifference curves, supporting their guesswork with experience and some market research in the zone of contact between the budget line and the modal indifference curve.

As a method of interpreting the law of demand, the theory of indifference provides an alternative to the concept of diminishing marginal utility. Consumer incomes in money terms can be held to replace whisky, and any other good or service under investigation to replace beer. If the price of the good is high (i.e., not much of it in return for a unit of income), then the exchange rate is such that it provides combinations of money and the good in question satisfactory to merely a few consumers. As the price falls (i.e., the exchange rate moves in the direction of more of the good for a unit of money), then more and more consumers find that a satisfactory combination is possible on their individual indifference schedules, while existing purchasers derive more

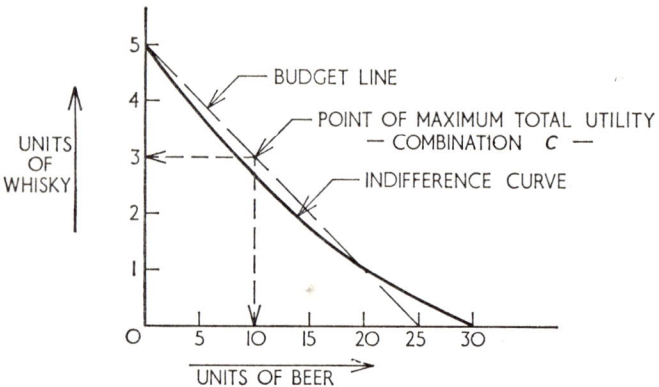

FIG 4.12   Indifference curve, budget line and point of exchange.

and more surplus. Demand for the good, therefore, gradually extends. Conversely, as the price rises (i.e., less of the good in return for a unit of money), fewer and fewer consumers find a satisfactory combination and demand accordingly contracts.

Section 5
Supply, the response of production

5A The law of supply

A supply of goods and services is drawn to the market in response to demand; the supply is the quantity of goods and services that suppliers are both willing and able to put on the market at a particular price.

The law of supply (see section 3A) states that supply extends with a rise in price and contracts with a fall in price, other things being equal. It is based on the observed phenomenon that as the price of a good rises sub-marginal suppliers (i.e., those who had not previously supplied because the price was too low) enter into supply and regular suppliers supply more, and the corollary that as the price of a good falls marginal suppliers (i.e., those near the dividing line between supply and non-supply) cease supply and regular suppliers supply less.

The explanation of this phenomenon rests in the *expectation of profit* on the part of suppliers. As the price of a good rises sub-marginal suppliers enter into supply because they see the chance of gaining some profit, and regular suppliers supply more because they see the chance of increasing their profit. Conversely, as the price of a good falls, marginal suppliers cease supply because they see their profit vanish, and regular suppliers supply less because they see their profit dwindle.

As a motive to economic action, therefore, expectation of profit by suppliers is the equivalent of expectation of utility by demanders. And just as demanders seek to derive maximum utility from their expenditure, so suppliers seek to gain maximum profit from their supply. Profit is a complex topic, to be returned to later; for the moment, however, let us just regard it as consisting of two parts—**normal** profit and **excess** (or surplus) profit. Normal profit is the cost of inducing an entrepreneur to supply a good or service; without it there would be no supply, and it is therefore one of the essential costs of production. Excess profit, on the other hand, is any profit which accrues to an entrepreneur over and above his normal profit; it is therefore not one of the essential costs of production. Excess profit may accrue to an entrepreneur if the price of a good rises when he is *already* producing and selling it and taking his normal profit. Under such new conditions he derives even greater (excess) profit, and is thereby induced to produce more goods. In this way, a rise in price causes an extension of supply.

But by how much? For an indication, let us examine the cost-price-profit relationship for an individual firm. A firm's costs of production can be investigated in several different ways, but for the purpose here in hand we need to know something about both average and marginal costs. Average cost is obtained quite simply by dividing total cost (including normal profit) by the number of goods produced. Thus, if the total cost is £50 000 and the number of goods produced is 1000, then average cost is £50. Marginal cost has already been noted (section 2C)—it is the cost of producing either the last or the next good in a series, and it is not necessarily the same as average cost. For most types of production, total cost includes some money spent on fixtures (which are used repeatedly) and some money spent on consumed items (which are used once only); the money spent on fixtures, called **fixed cost**, is spent whatever the level of actual production, while the money spent on consumed items, called **variable cost**, varies with the level of actual production. For example, an entrepreneur owning a shoe factory incurs some costs (such as rent, rates, depreciation of machinery, etc.) whether he produces shoes or not; these are fixed costs, irrespective of the level of production. If he produces shoes, he will then also incur the costs of leather, power supplies, labour, transport, etc.; these are variable costs, varying in amount with the total number of shoes produced. If he produces *more* shoes, then the variable costs will rise, since he needs more leather, more power, more labour, more transport, etc. Marginal cost—the cost of producing *one more* pair of shoes—is clearly part of the variable cost structure. But variable cost itself is only *part* of the total cost structure; the other part is fixed cost. And whereas marginal cost is related only to variable cost, average cost is related to total cost; so marginal cost is not necessarily the same as average cost.

In the early stages of production a firm will find that its marginal costs fall rapidly. The additional (marginal) output is gained fairly cheaply by using the existing men and machinery just a little bit harder. A firm has already met its biggest costs when it has obtained its initial supply of men and machinery; it costs relatively little more to use the men and machinery a bit harder to turn out a few additional goods. In other words, a firm's additional (marginal) costs of production are diminishing. It is only when a firm has to hire more men and buy more machinery that its additional (marginal) costs begin to rise. Average cost, meanwhile, continues to fall; it keeps on falling so long as the marginal additions to total cost are less than average cost itself. However, once marginal cost rises above average cost, then average cost begins to rise too—though more slowly than marginal cost (see table 5.1).

number of goods	(£) total cost	(£) marginal cost (addition)	(£) average cost
1	840	—	840
2	1240	400	620
3	1560	320	520
4	1860	300	465
5	2150	290	430
6	2460	310	410
7	2800	340	400
8	3200	400	400
9	3690	490	410
10	4300	610	430

TABLE 5.1   Total, marginal, and average costs for a firm.

You can see that marginal cost is lowest at an output of five goods, but that average cost continues to fall until, at an output of eight goods, marginal cost has risen to equal it. As marginal cost thereafter rises above average cost, so average cost begins to rise too, though much more slowly. Figure 5.1 illustrates the principle graphically, and also shows two possible price levels. It is obvious that at a price of *OP* this particular supplier is sub-marginal; his own lowest average costs are above the market price and he cannot profitably supply. It is only as the price rises to *OQ* that the supplier can think of entering production, since it is just at this price level that his lowest average costs of production are covered. This minimum price level necessary to ensure production is called the marginal supply price (see section 3A); it corresponds with the point of optimum production, i.e., the cheapest possible combination of production factors (see section 3B). At the price *OQ* output is *OV*; in table 5.1 we can calculate the marginal supply price as £400 and the output at that price as eight goods. In this way, we can get an initial idea of the relationship between price and supply.

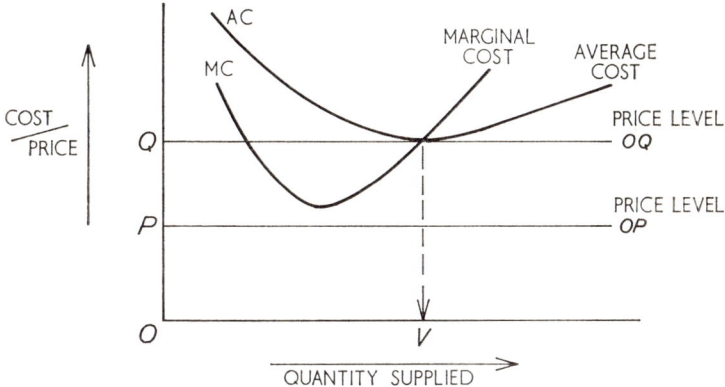

FIG 5.1   Price, average cost and marginal cost.

In a perfect (and unreal) world we should stop our analysis of supply at this point; the factors of production have been mobilised into supply in their most efficient combination (i.e., lowest average cost), the price per good produced is the lowest possible and includes only the normal profit, and supply is capable of extension only through other firms entering production under the same conditions (i.e., at a level where marginal cost = average cost = price). However, even perfect economics is not that perfect; price, as a function of supply *and* demand, is an important variable.

And as price rises, supply extends. We have just seen how a minimum price level is necessary to bring any supply at all to the market; let us now examine how a price rising above that minimum level causes supply to extend. Figure 5.2 shows us that at a price of *OR* there is a zone of excess profit between points *A* and *B*; in other words, by selling his goods at a price of *OR*

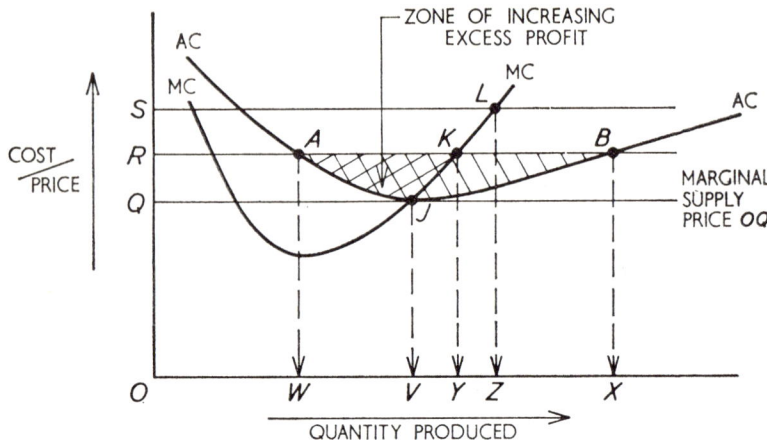

FIG 5.2 A price, cost and profit graph.

the supplier is obtaining a revenue in excess of his average costs (which—don't forget—include normal profit). The range of output which yields excess profit to the supplier is from *OW* to *OX*; within this range the entrepreneur seeks the point which will yield *maximum* profit. It is fairly clear that profit will keep on increasing in total only so long as the revenue from an extra sale (marginal revenue) exceeds the cost of making an extra good (marginal cost). When—eventually—the point is reached where it costs the supplier more to make the additional good than he gains in revenue by selling it, he will cease production. Profit increases, then, so long as marginal revenue exceeds marginal cost. Note that it increases at a decreasing rate beyond the point of optimum production (point *J*), and that it stops increasing at the point where marginal cost equals marginal revenue. Assuming a constant price, marginal revenue is the same as average price, and at the price level *OR* the point of equality is therefore *K*, giving an output of *OY*. Continued production beyond this point (at a price of *OR*) will still yield excess profit, but, under conditions where marginal cost is rising more rapidly than average cost and where marginal cost exceeds marginal revenue (i.e., additional goods cost more to make than they produce in revenue), such excess profit will decrease at an increasing rate, until eventually (at point *B*, output *OX*) there will not be any excess profit at all; at point *B*, output *OX*, the firm will be operating at a normal profit level only. An entrepreneur seeking to maximise profits at a price level *OR* will clearly push production up to point *K*, but not beyond it. However, if the price were to rise to *OS* it would be worth extending output to *OZ*, since marginal cost would then equal marginal revenue at point *L*. We could thus build up a series of situations where, as price rose, output (supply) extended—from *OV*, through *OY*, to *OZ*. Figure 5.3 shows us how the supply from an individual firm is caused to extend by a rising price. You can see that the supply curve is positive (i.e., it slopes *up* to the right), and that it corresponds

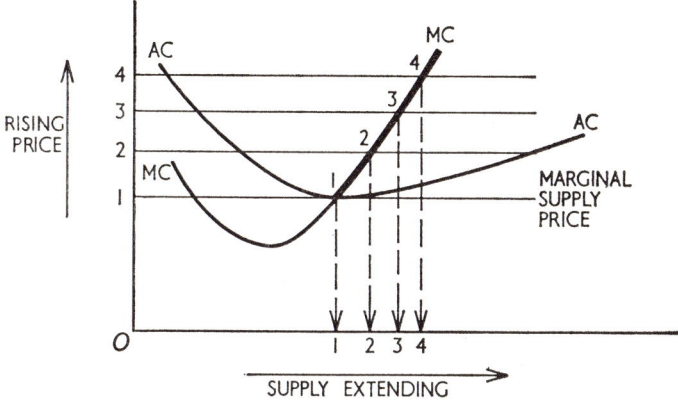

FIG 5.3 Supply curve for an individual firm.

with the firm's marginal cost line beyond the point of optimum production and up to the price level.

Total, or market, supply consists of the aggregate of a number of supply schedules for different firms, and market supply curves are obtained by aggregating the individual firms' supply schedules (table 5.2) and plotting the ensuing totals on a price-quantity graph (figure 5.4). The method is similar to that used for obtaining market demand curves (see section 4D).

market price	number of goods supplied by producers					total market supply
	1	2	3	4	5	
100p	30	15	6	3	14	68
90p	26	11	4	1	11	53
80p	24	7	2	—	9	42
70p	22	4	1	—	7	34
60p	21	3	—	—	5	29
50p	20	2	—	—	4	26

TABLE 5.2 Supply schedules for five firms.

A market supply curve, like a market demand curve, properly relates to only one sort of good at one moment of time; it is also comparable in its quality of illustrating the *potential* range of supply at a variety of *possible* price levels—e.g., referring to the schedule in table 5.2, if the price were 100p, then supply would be 68 goods, but if the price (for any reason whatsoever) fell to 60p, then supply would contract to 29 goods (producers 1, 2 and 5 cutting back production, and producers 3 and 4 ceasing production altogether).

5B Elasticity of supply

If the supply of a good or service on the market changes considerably in response to price changes, then it is said to be **elastic**; if only slightly, then **inelastic**. Supply elasticity is measured according to the formula:

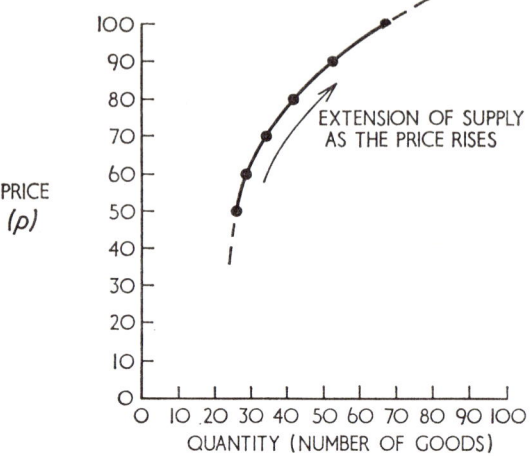

FIG 5.4 A market supply curve.

$$\text{Elasticity of supply } (E_s) = \frac{\% \text{ change in quantity supplied}}{\% \text{ change in price}}$$

If $E_s = 1$, then supply elasticity is at unity, and a 5% rise in price will extend supply by 5%; if $E_s < 1$, then a 5% rise in price will extend supply by less than 5%, and supply is said to be inelastic; and if $E_s > 1$, then supply is elastic, and a 5% rise in price will extend supply by more than 5%. Figure 5.5 illustrates the various possibilities in the shapes of supply curves.

Differences in supply elasticity are caused by:

1   The ease with which the good can be stored. Note that supply is not exactly the same as production; production is the overall generation of goods and services to satisfy consumer wants, whereas supply is merely

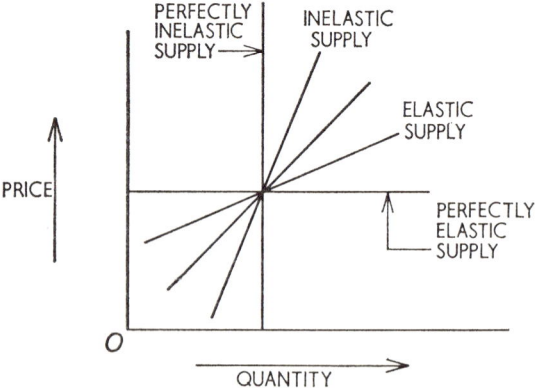

FIG 5.5 Possible supply curve slopes.

the end of the process—the last stage in bringing the goods and services to market. If the producers (or suppliers) regard the prevailing market price as unsatisfactory they might—if they are able—hold back the supply from the market in an attempt to force up the market price; they may equally stockpile some of the goods in order to be able to extend the supply at once if the price is forced up by increasing demand. In either case, the possibility of storing the good allows the suppliers to respond quickly and easily to price changes. If the good (e.g., freshly cut flowers) cannot be stored, then we can regard the supply—once it is on the market —as perfectly inelastic; the supply can be neither extended if the price rises nor contracted (save by destruction) if the price falls. Most goods, however, are capable of being stored, even though sometimes only with technical help (e.g., canning, refrigeration, freeze-drying); there is therefore some degree of price-elasticity in the supply of most goods.

2   The extent to which the supplier is specially equipped. This reflects the ease with which the factors of production can be moved in or out of the supply of a particular commodity, and is determined by the degree of mobility conferred on a factor by its substitutability. If an employed factor is highly substitutable in alternative production, then it is likely to move to that alternative production if the price of its initial employment falls. Factors which have a high degree of substitutability tend to be *general* rather than *specific* in character; for example, unskilled labour is a general factor and may transfer fairly easily from one type of unskilled work to another, whereas a concert pianist is a specific (highly specialised) factor and may not transfer easily to a different type of work. The same considerations apply to the other factors of production also; a shipyard, for example, is much more specific than a typewriter, and may therefore be less easily turned to alternative work. The more mobile the factors are, the greater the ease with which they can move into or out of the supply of a commodity; and the greater the ease with which the factors can move into or out of supply, the greater the elasticity of supply.

3   The number of different markets open to the supplier. If a supplier can sell in many different markets (e.g., different countries), then the supply in any *one* will be elastic, since the supplier can readily transfer goods to or from other markets. Thus, if the price of tomatoes were to rise in England, suppliers in other countries could fairly easily switch their supplies to the English market. It is not necessarily equally easy with all goods, however; there may be serious transport problems involved (as with steel and oil) as well as possible contractual agreements.

4   Time. In our examination of demand changes (sections 4E and 4F) we rigidly excluded time as a determinant of demand elasticity, referring it solely to the complex of demand conditions. Supply, however, is different from demand in this respect; whereas demand may be regarded as 'instantaneous', supply—apart from the existence of stocks—is merely the end link in a lengthy chain of production. Of necessity, it takes time

for supply to adjust to new price levels. Higher prices will extend supply, but not—apart from the existence of stocks—immediately; conversely, lower prices will contract supply, but not—apart from the possibility of either creating stocks or destroying the product (to avoid the costs of storage)—immediately. Most economists distinguish three levels of time in relation to supply analysis: market term, short term, and long term. Market term is the time during which the goods are actually on the market and the supply is fixed—apart from the possibilities of storage and destruction. In the market term, then, supply is highly inelastic; indeed, for highly perishable goods it is perfectly inelastic. The short term is the time during which the supply may be extended or contracted by more or less intensive use of the existing production factors only; neither more nor fewer factories, neither more nor fewer workers, but overtime or short-time, full-capacity or half-capacity. In a short term, supply is fairly inelastic; the more so with a fall in price than with a rise in price, since the suppliers tend to maintain production in the hope of improvements to come. The long term is the time during which productive capacity itself has chance to adjust to the new price, i.e., more or fewer factories, more or less land under cultivation, etc. In the long term, supply is elastic; by definition, the long term *is* the length of time required to permit supply to adjust to price changes. Any single supply curve, as we have already noted, is related to a particular moment of time; regard it now, in the light of the time qualification, as illustrating a 'still' out of a changing elasticity pattern.

5C Changes in supply

Supply changes may occur because of changes in price, other things remaining the same, and are then called extensions or contractions of supply and are plotted on a single supply curve. The quantity of goods supplied may also change—regardless of price—because of a change in one or more of the underlying **supply conditions**. Such changes are called shifts, rises, falls, increases or decreases of supply as the case may be, and, like demand, require the construction of two or more curves on the same price-quantity graph.

The chief supply conditions are:

1 The sources of supply. Existing sources may cease production (e.g., a mine may become exhausted), thus decreasing supply irrespective of price changes. Or new sources of supply may be developed—sometimes under the stimulus of higher prices, but often just as the result of happy discovery.

2 The weather. Manufacturing industry is little affected (e.g., it is rarely too cold, say, to cause the temporary closure of a factory; though it does happen), but farming is greatly affected. Great variations in output can occur because of favourable or unfavourable weather, absolutely regardless of price.

3 Technical progress. Better machines, new inventions, more efficient

organisation, better education and new methods all help to increase the supply of commodities, irrespective of price.

4　Production costs. Many factors influence average costs of production: not only technical progress, but also such things as government taxation policies, wage bargaining with workers' unions, the availability and cost of credit for financing expansion schemes, the general conditions of trade (boom or slump), and the interest rates on borrowed capital. If the costs of production *rise,* then clearly (see figure 5.6) those firms which were previously taking only the normal profit (i.e., the marginal firms) will cease production, and the supra-marginal firms will cut back production closer to the optimum—though still maximising their profits and perhaps still taking some excess profit.

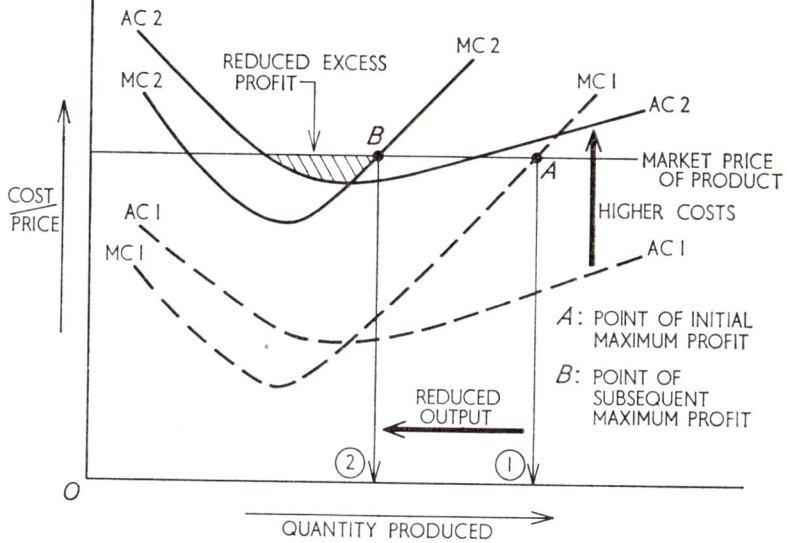

FIG 5.6　The effect of rising production costs on output and excess profit.

5　Joint supply. Just as cars and petrol are in joint demand, so petrol and fuel oil are in joint supply. The one cannot be produced without the other. Until the 1950s, vast supplies of natural gas were obtained with oil, and wasted or burnt simply because no one realised its potential; its supply was great, without any stimulus from price. Similarly, the Bolivians mine lead and tin, and obtain silver from the same ores; the supply of silver is thus increased without any stimulus from a high price. The supply of coke is (or has been) dependent on the volume of coal-gas required, irrespective of the price of coke.

Supply shift is illustrated in figure 5.7; it can be seen that as supply shifts from the first to the second set of conditions, a constant price of *p* results in a

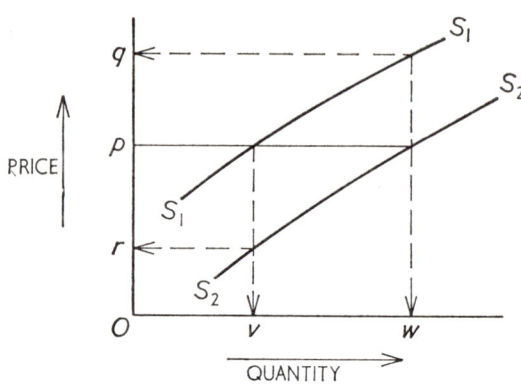

FIG 5.7   A supply shift graph.

rise of supply from *v* to *w*. If the higher supply of *w* had been required under the first set of supply conditions, then the price necessary to draw forth that supply would have been high, at *q*. And, conversely, if the initial supply of *v* were all that was required under the second set of supply conditions, then the low price of *r* is all that would be needed to ensure it.

5D The interaction of supply and demand

The relationships between supply and demand may be expressed in a number of laws, bearing in mind that in each case *other things remain equal*:

1   The lower the price of a good, the greater the demand and the smaller the supply.
2   The higher the price of a good, the smaller the demand and the greater the supply.
3   The greater the demand for a good, the higher the price and the more extensive the supply.
4   The greater the supply of a good, the lower the price and the more extensive the demand.
5   The price tends to equalisation of supply and demand.

Price, of course, expresses the interaction of supply and demand. We have already examined (section 3A) the price mechanism under static conditions of supply and demand in both equilibrium and disequilibrium situations; let us now see what happens when the conditions change.

If we make the assumption, illustrated in figure 5.8, that supply conditions remain stable while demand conditions change, then we can see clearly that—in conformance with law 3—an increase in demand from D_1 to D_2 produces both a higher price ($OB > OA$) and, as a consequence of the higher price, an extended supply ($OZ > OX$). The degree to which price is raised and supply extended depends on the elasticity of supply; parts (b) and (c) of

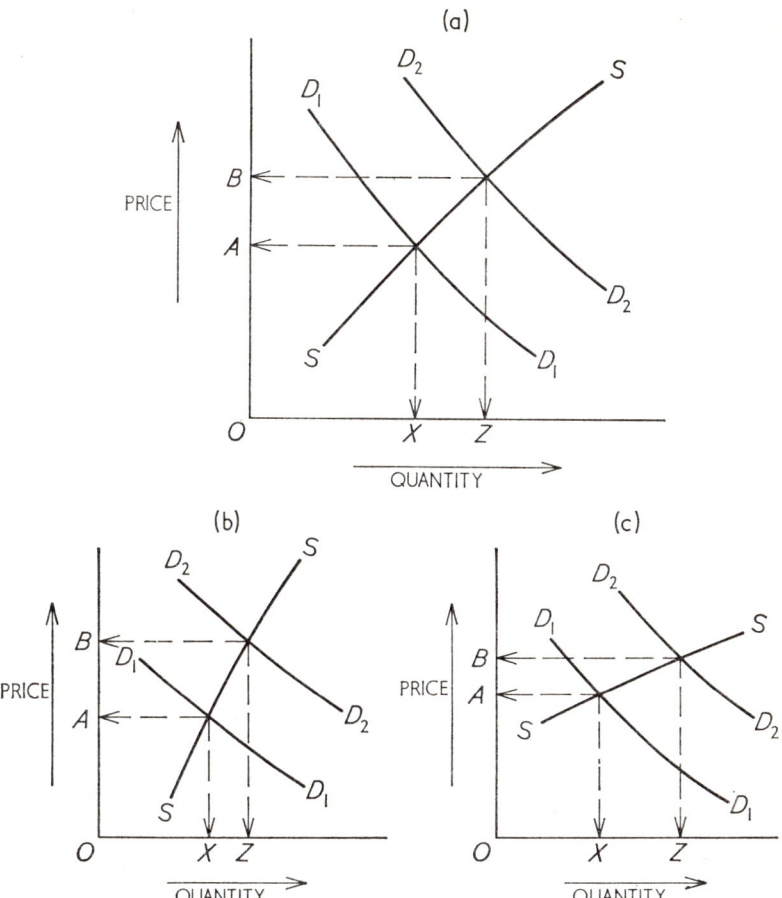

FIG 5.8   The market effects of demand shift.
NOTES:
(i) In part (a), a decrease in demand from D_2 to D_1 will lower the price to OA and contract the supply to OX.
(ii) In part (b) $AB > XZ$
(iii) In part (c) $XZ > AB$

figure 5.8 show two different cases—in (b), with inelastic supply, the price rises very much more than the supply extends, whereas in (c), with elastic supply, the supply extends very much more than the price rises. Remember, in either the market term or the short term, supply is—by definition—inelastic; so the more common state of affairs is that shown in inset (b). However, in the long term, the situation shown in part (c) will prevail.

Figure 5.9 illustrates the fourth law quoted: that an increased supply of a good (demand conditions remaining stable) lowers its price and extends demand for it. We can see that as supply shifts from S_1 to S_2 price falls from OA to OB, and demand extends from OX to OZ. On this occasion, the extent of change in both price and quantity depends on the elasticity of demand. Part (b) shows that with inelastic demand the price falls very much more than the demand xtends; part (c) shows that with elastic demand the demand

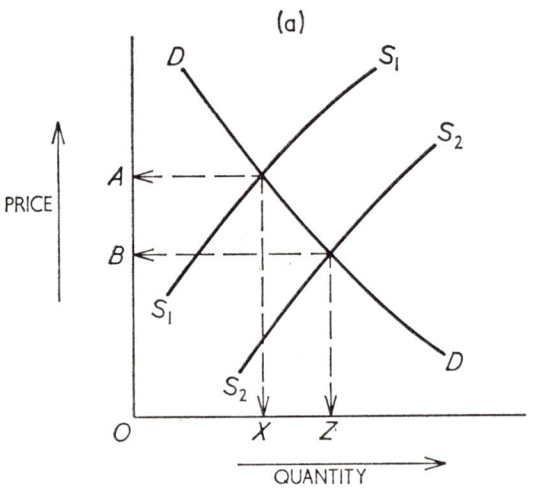

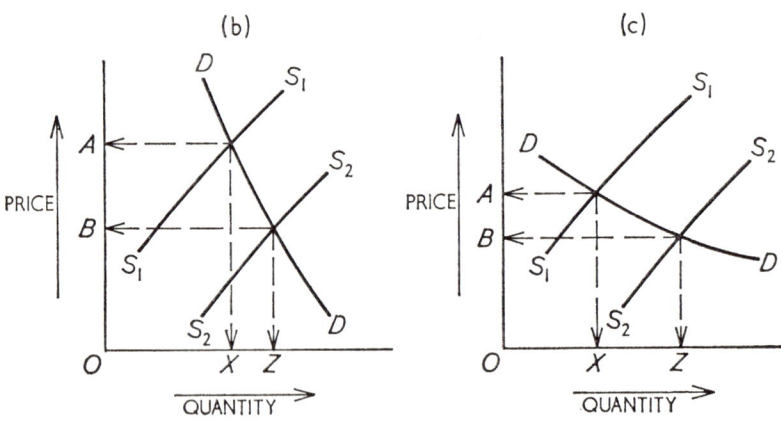

FIG 5.9   The market effects of supply shift.
NOTES:
(i) In part (a), a decrease in supply from $S2$ to $S1$ will raise the price to OA and contract the demand to OX.
(ii) In part (b) $AB > XZ$
(iii) In part (c) $XZ > AB$

extends very much more than the price falls. In the market, demand elasticity is quite varied; so both situations are common.

The occurrence of changes in both supply *and* demand conditions opens up a variety of possibilities. If supply and demand both shift positively (see figure 5.10), then the quantity of goods supplied will certainly increase; the price, however, may fall, rise or remain stable. The behaviour of price depends on the relative degree of shift involved. If the joint change of supply and demand is negative rather than positive, then the quantity supplied will certainly decrease; the price, again, however, may fall, rise or remain stable, depending upon the relative degree of shift involved.

Opposed shifts of supply and demand create different possibilities. If supply *in*creases while demand *de*creases, the only certainty is a large fall in price; the quantity exchanged may decrease, increase or remain stable (see figure 5.11). On the other hand, if supply *de*creases while demand *in*creases,

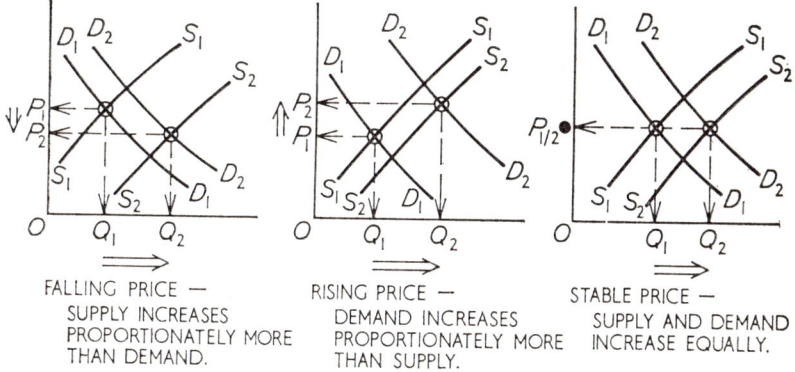

FALLING PRICE —
SUPPLY INCREASES
PROPORTIONATELY MORE
THAN DEMAND.

RISING PRICE —
DEMAND INCREASES
PROPORTIONATELY MORE
THAN SUPPLY.

STABLE PRICE —
SUPPLY AND DEMAND
INCREASE EQUALLY.

FIG 5.10 The possible market effects of increased supply and increased demand.

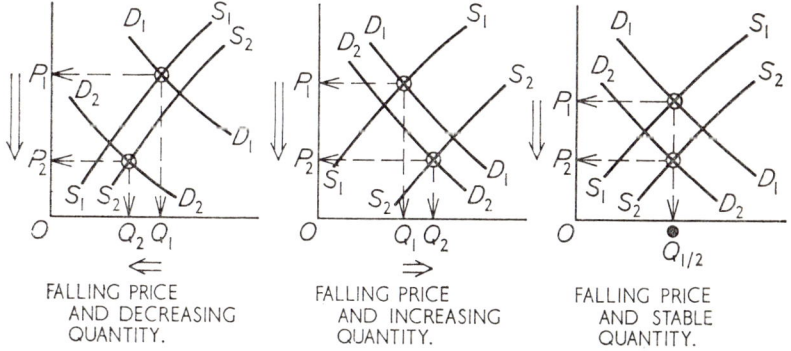

FALLING PRICE
AND DECREASING
QUANTITY.

FALLING PRICE
AND INCREASING
QUANTITY.

FALLING PRICE
AND STABLE
QUANTITY.

FIG 5.11 The possible market effects of increased supply and decreased demand.

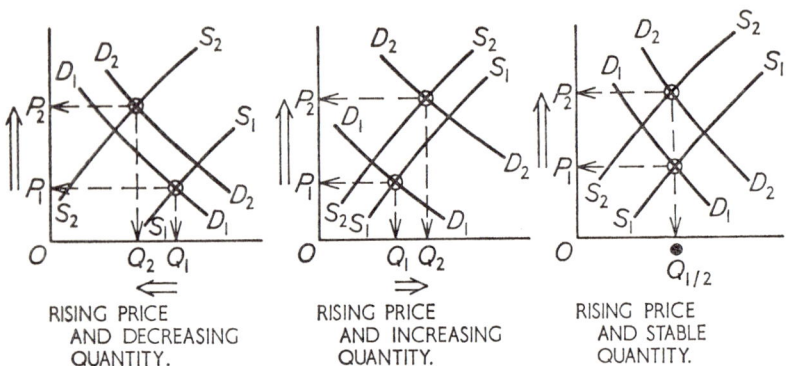

FIG 5.12   The possible market effects of decreased supply and increased demand.

prices will inevitably rise, and the quantity exchanged may, again, decrease, increase or remain stable (see figure 5.12).

Having outlined the great variety of possible price determinants in situations where the supply and demand conditions are changing, either singly or jointly and either together or contrarily, let us now return to the static conditions. In section 3A we examined the operation of the equilibrium price mechanism; we noted that excess supply causes suppliers to contract supply until an equilibrium point is reached, and that excess demand causes demanders to bid up the price until an equilibrium point is reached. The assumption underlying this examination was that both suppliers and demanders would somehow know where the equilibrium point was, and would be able to cease creating any excess or deficit supply or demand at the very moment the point was reached. On frictional grounds alone, that is not an entirely reasonable assumption to make, especially in the short term; in the long term, no doubt, both suppliers and demanders become aware—through experience—of the existence of an equilibrium zone, even if not of a precise point. In the short term, however, it is more likely that the market price—with its related levels of supply and demand—will oscillate about the theoretical equilibrium point. The *cobweb theorem* is an attempt to relate these oscillations to the attainment of an equilibrium position.

To understand the cobweb theorem, we again need to make certain assumptions: that supply and demand conditions remain stable; that supply in the short term is inelastic; and that supply in the market term is perfectly inelastic. These are assumptions which we can reasonably make.

We start (see figure 5.13) with a disequilibrium situation—supply S_1. At this position the perfectly inelastic supply of goods *on the market* is Q_1, and demand is D_1 at a price of P_1. On the next occasion that the suppliers put a (perfectly inelastic) supply of goods on the market they will expect to receive a price of only P_1, and will accordingly take up a supply position S_2, delivering only Q_2 goods to the market. However, the level of demand for Q_2 goods

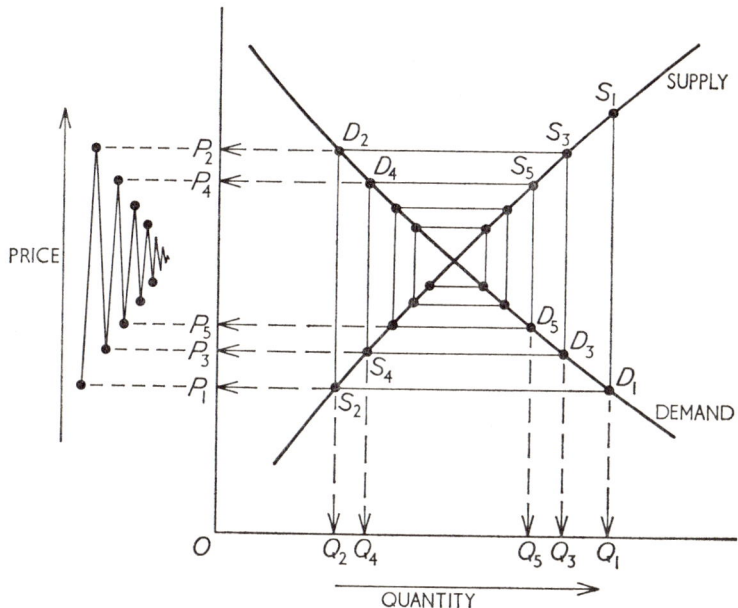

FIG 5.13 Illustration of the cobweb theorem.

is D_2, and the price therefore is bid up to P_2. Expecting this price on the next delivery, the suppliers assume position S_3 and deliver Q_3 goods to market. The demand for Q_3 goods is D_3 at a price of P_3, which consequently encourages ensuing positions of S_4, Q_4, D_4 and P_4, and so on. Eventually, equilibrium is approached at the intersection of the supply and demand curves.

Section 6
The factors of production

6A The meaning of production

Production is the generation of goods and services to satisfy human wants (see section 2A); it is a process which remains incomplete until the goods and services are ultimately made available to consumers. Since the purpose of production is to provide utility to consumers, we can accordingly further define production as the process of utility-creation.

Utility can be created in different ways. The utility of form is that created by changing the form of a material, e.g., changing a tree into furniture, changing sand into glass; the utility of place is that created by changing the place of a material, e.g., transporting wool from Australia to Britain, bringing oil from under the ground to the surface; the utility of time is that created by making a material available at a time when it would not normally be available, e.g., by freezing fish, by canning fruit; and the utility of service is that created by producing the services needed to facilitate the creation of form, place and time utilities, e.g., the provision of financial and marketing services. Actual production usually involves some combination of these different utilities; for example, the sale of a tin of corned beef in a London supermarket has involved changing the form of the material (from a live cow to a processed hash), changing the place of the material (from the Argentine or the US corn belt—possibly the reason for calling the hash 'corned' beef—to Britain), changing the time of the material (from fresh meat at slaughter to preserved, i.e., 'corned', meat after slaughter), and also the provision of numerous services, especially those of merchants and bankers.

Production is often further classified into three stages: primary, secondary and tertiary. **Primary production** refers to the direct use of largely- or wholly-natural resources and the consequent production of basic raw materials, such as iron, wool, oil, coal, wheat, timber and fish. **Secondary production** relates to the processing of the primary products into finished or semi-finished goods, such as the turning of iron into steel (semi-finished) and then into machines or cars (finished), and the turning of timber into paper or furniture. The secondary stage of production is often also called the 'manufacturing' stage; it is a widely varied stage, containing everything from complete processes (such as turning raw cotton into cloth in one fully integrated process) to interlocking but separate processes (such as turning iron, lead, oil, aluminium, rubber and a range of petrochemicals into a car). **Tertiary production** consists of the provision of essential services, and includes transport, finance, marketing, insurance, construction and education, as well as the whole attenuating line of all the other services you can think of.

Remember that however production is classified, and of however many separate processes it consists, it is still an integrated and indivisible unity; think of the cigarette example in section 2A again.

6B Classification of the factors of production

Think also of the *Gestalt* concept noted in section 1C, and remember the methodological necessity to break down—or analyse—the *whole* unit of knowledge. Production is a major theme in economics, and can be comprehended only through analysis; so we classify.

Having established a need to classify, we now meet the problem of how to classify. However, if you think about it you will realise that that is not a very important problem; the classification is more or less arbitrary anyway, and certainly for our immediate purpose the matter requires a brief review only.

The factors of production are all the various means used in the creation of wealth (see section 2F); traditionally, they have been classified into land, labour, capital and enterprise (see section 2H). A great deal of criticism has been levelled at the traditional classification, and alternative classifications have been suggested. The chief points of criticism are:

1 That none of the factors is of uniform quality. In fact, that land is variable in quality, that workers are unequal in efficiency, that capital is not all uniformly productive, and that enterprise is unevenly enterprising. The validity of the criticism is self-evident, but do not forget that the same criticism can be equally validly levelled at *any* system of classification— not all flowers are roses, and not all roses are red, and still less are all red roses equally red, for example. The truth is that all factors are individually unique, and any grouping of them will produce differences within the group. But that qualification does not destroy the validity of the criticism; it merely tempers it.

2 That the factors are not mutually exclusive. In other words, that they may be substituted for one another at the margin—for example, an increase in production may be gained by the application of a bit more land *or* labour *or* capital. The possibility of substitution was noted in section 3B; note now that substitution is possible only at the margin. Additional farm output, for example, is possible from the application of more labour to a given area of land, or, using the same amount of labour, from more land; either way, a degree of substitution is possible between land and labour. Nevertheless, a certain amount of land and a certain amount of labour have to be used; it is only the additional units that provide substitution possibilities, i.e., substitution is possible only at the margin. The existence of substitution possibilities is certainly a valid point of criticism of the factor classification; it is indeed a valid criticism of any system of classification that it does not provide a mutually exclusive series of classes. However, provided we bear in mind the general indivisibility of production, and treat the classification as an analytical tool only, then the criticism ceases to be so dangerously pointed.

3 That the terms *land, labour, capital* and *enterprise* form a mixed scheme of classification, rather like a classification of animals according to a series of classes headed brown, four-footed, dogs and size. The justification for this view is that land is a 'gift of nature' insofar as it exists irrespective of labour and capital and therefore has no cost or supply price, unlike labour and capital; that labour cannot be separated from its suppliers, unlike land and capital, and, therefore, if unused, creates problems of quite a different order from those created by the non-use of land and capital; that capital does not exist instantaneously, like land and, to a lesser extent, labour, but has to be created in time out of surplus production; and that enterprise is distinct from land, labour and capital in that it is 'active' whereas the others are 'passive', merely there waiting to be organised and used.

The existence of criticism is accompanied (as it should be) by suggestions of alternative systems of classification. One of the most widely accepted of these alternative systems is the classification of production factors into *specific* and *general*. Specific factors are those which—in their application—are limited to particular purposes, so that an oil rig may be used only in oil drilling, a balance wheel only in watch-making, a blackboard only in teaching, and a loom only in weaving. General factors are those which can be used in a variety of applications and for many different purposes, so that money is a general factor, along with unskilled labour and a great deal of land. Another suggested system of classification divides production factors into *work* (i.e., all sorts of human effort, whether made by labour or enterprise) and *property* (i.e., all sorts of natural resources and already-produced goods). And yet another system is based on the division of factors into *human* and *non-human* groups.

Throughout this book the traditional classification will be used; it is both widely accepted and understood, and it is the basis of most established theory.

6C Characteristics of land

Land is everything which exists naturally. It is seas, oceans and waterfalls as much as sunshine and winds; and sunshine and winds as much as forests, minerals and soils. Because land has been occupied and used by man for centuries, the naturalness of much of it is now often difficult to distinguish in practice; for example, forests may be the result of afforestation projects as well as of purely natural growth, and soil qualities may be the product of careful cultivation and fertilisation as well as of natural development. For the purposes of theoretical analysis, however, the distinction must be made; the natural element and the artificial element are conceptually different—the natural element is land whereas the artificial element is a product of labour and capital.

The chief characteristics of land are:

1 It is immobile. It must therefore be used where it exists. The fixed position of land confers quite random economic advantages and—

equally—inflicts numerous penalties; and it does so in many different ways. On a global scale, for example, Britain receives—as a permit, if not as a stimulus, to economic activity—the great benefit of the Gulf Stream Drift, whereas northern Canada suffers the penalty of a rampant polar climate; and there is nothing to be done to change the situation. Neither can mountains be removed to make available more flat land for farming or factories or towns, nor coal or oil deposits be shifted from their fixed locations. Rubber trees and cotton plants grow in certain parts of the world only; salmon can be caught in certain rivers only; softwood timber is available from forests in certain regions only; and hydro-electricity can be produced in certain districts only. The consequences of the immobility of land are, indeed, endlessly ramified.

2   It is in fixed supply. The total quantity of natural resources in the world at any moment of time is fixed; there can be neither more nor less coal, oil, sunshine, rainfall, soil or anything else *naturally*. There may be *artificial* changes in supply (e.g., more rain through rain-making techniques), but then an element of labour (and/or capital) creeps in. A further point is that losses of ground caused by erosional processes are more or less balanced by gains accruing from depositional processes. However, an artificial control is exerted where possible: man protects his more valuable ground from erosion and encourages quickened deposition in areas likely to prove valuable; so—again—an element of labour or capital may creep in. Another point is that even though the *total* supply may be more or less fixed, the amount of land in actual use may vary considerably; which is, of course, a function partly of its immobility (and also partly of its quality and partly of the demand for its use).

3   It has no cost of production. Since—by definition—it exists irrespective of man, it clearly costs nothing to produce; it is called a 'gift of nature'. In a newly-settled land it is there free for those who wish to claim it; in an anciently-settled land it is not free to the individual citizen, but because the payment in exchange merely represents a transfer-claim from one person to another the land may be regarded as free to the society as a whole—it certainly cost the society nothing to produce the land in the first place.

4   It varies in quality. For example, iron ore may be high-grade or low-grade, soil may be fertile (e.g., river silt) or infertile (e.g., glacial outwash gravels), street-corner sites may be in the town centre or in the suburbs, and rainfall may be well- or ill-distributed throughout the year. Early economic theory tended to restrict its investigation of quality-variations to farmland, positing that land could be graded into that which it was profitable to use for some purpose or other and that which it was unprofitable to use for any purpose. The dividing line between profitable and unprofitable use was called the margin; its location varied with the demand for the use of the land—as demand increased, so unprofitable land became just profitable (i.e., sub-marginal land became marginal), and

as the demand decreased (perhaps through the application of more labour or capital to smaller quantities of land in existing use), so marginal land became unprofitable to use, and accordingly went out of use. An extension of this idea leads us to the concept of the **margin of transference**— if one use becomes more profitable than another then there may be a transfer of use from the less to the more profitable activity. The margin of transference is clearly higher than the margin itself, which merely separates some use from no use at all, and not one use from another.

5 There is a limit to the use to which land can be put. Common sense tells you that if a mine contains only 20 million tons of ore, then at most only 20 millions tons of ore can be extracted from it. Such a limit is called the *physical* limit to use. However, given a mine containing 20 million tons of ore, it is highly unlikely in practice that it would be worth making use of the resource to its physical limit. Sooner or later a point would be reached where it ceased to be worth making any further use of the mine, and it became more worthwhile to put the labour and capital which might continue to exploit the mine to some quite different use instead. The limit created by relative lack of profitability is called the *economic* limit to use. Such a limit represents the margin of production—the dividing line between production and non-production. Like all margins, its location is not fixed, but varies according to prices; in this context the relevant prices are the price (cost) of production and the price (revenue) earned by sale. Fluctuations in either or both of the prices *may* cause the margin of production to fall, thus putting the firm out of business. The firm can become sub-marginal if either the cost of production rises while revenue remains stable or the revenue falls while cost of production remains stable (or production costs rise faster or fall more slowly than revenue either rises or falls). Figure 5.6 is worth looking at again here. Apart from showing the effects of higher production costs on both output and profits, it also illustrates the tendency of average cost to rise once output is extended beyond the point where marginal cost equals average cost. Now, the term *rising average costs of production* is merely another way of saying that, on average, it costs relatively more to make additional units of a good (or produce additional units from, say, a mine). The sense is maintained if we invert the statement and say instead that fewer and fewer additional units of output are obtained in return for equal additions to cost; in other words, that the more additional units you put in the less in proportion you get out. For example, assume a mine is producing 300 tons of ore a month; by applying one extra unit of production (or input) factors, output can be increased by 50 tons to 350 tons a month, and then again, with a similar additional input, by 50 tons to 400 tons a month. However, a stage is eventually reached where the application of an additional unit of input brings a return of, say, only 40 tons, and the next time of perhaps only 30 tons. Total output continues to increase, but at a diminishing rate (increasing by 50 tons at first, then by 40 tons, and

subsequently by 30 tons). The reasons for the diminishing rate of increase in output may be that the extra miners get in one another's way, that the existing shafts cannot easily accommodate the increased traffic, or that the orebody becomes increasingly difficult to work as the less accessible parts replace the more accessible parts in the work schedule. Whatever the reasons, we have a clear tendency, *assuming techniques of use remain constant*, for output (returns) to increase at a diminishing rate while additional units of factor input remain constant. Since it is the additional, or marginal, unit of output which is smaller than the one immediately preceding it, the tendency is called the **law of diminishing marginal returns**. Nineteenth century economists related the law entirely to land, and in particular to farmland, and they foresaw mass starvation as population increased and land supply remained fixed; they did not foresee the immense improvements in techniques, which now permit vastly increased quantities of food to be produced from much the same area of land. That is why the law is qualified by saying *assuming techniques of use remain constant*. In fact, of course, techniques do not remain constant (especially in the long term); so we must accept deferment of the law during the times that techniques are obviously changing, and apply it only when techniques are relatively stable.

6D Characteristics of labour

Labour is any effort which satisfies an economic want; it is not the people who supply the effort, though it is a common contraction to use the word that way. Labour, strictly, may be regarded as the services of people employing physical and/or mental effort, whether pleasant or unpleasant, in the creation of goods and services which promise utility to consumers. That distinction noted, we shall continue, where appropriate, to use the word in its contracted sense.

The fundamental reason for labour is that people wish to stay alive; they have certain essential wants (necessities), such as for food and shelter, which must be satisfied in order to maintain life. However, the present highly-developed economies of the western world show plainly that—whenever something extra could be done—satisfaction of basic wants and mere existence were never enough for mankind. The improvement of standards of living is, indeed, a powerful motive to effort. People may also be driven to labour out of interest, or by a desire for fame or power, or from a sense of social duty, or through a search for status; or for any combination of the reasons.

The chief characteristics of labour are:

1   It is varied in type. The least that can be said about it is that some of it is specific and some of it is general. A great deal of labour is, indeed, highly specialised, being applicable to only a fairly narrow range of uses. We may regard professional people and those of high skill as being very specific labour; semi-skilled labour is fairly specific, and unskilled labour is general. However, that classification must be regarded as a very loose one; there is in fact an almost infinite variety of types of labour.

2 It is varied in quality. There are *innate* variations in physique, mental ability, aptitude and attitude. And there are *environmental* variations in physical fitness, education, opportunity and attitude. Attitude—you will notice—is in both groups. It is certainly influenced by innate character, and it is most likely also influenced by environmental conditions such as religion and the prevailing economic climate of the community.

3 It is perishable. It is so in the sense that it cannot live without a return (i.e., wages or food) and that it cannot be saved (i.e., one day's work cannot be saved and added to the next day's).

4 It competes with land and, especially, capital for employment. The possibilities of factor substitution were noted in section 3B, but we should now note additionally that labour competes on rather special terms. For one thing, labour is alive. If unused, therefore, it creates a number of special problems—chiefly of a social nature. For another thing, labour is capable of organising itself for bargaining purposes. Within limits, it can control its own supply (by strikes, for example). And, unlike land and capital, labour consumes whether it produces or not.

6E The division of labour

You probably don't bake your own bread; almost certainly, you don't make your own paper or mine your own oil or make your own nylon. Other people do these things for you. Your life would be poorer if they didn't, because you probably wouldn't be able to do them all yourself. It is the fact that people *specialise* in production that helps to create both the immense variety and the great volume of goods and services available to society. The division of labour, as this specialisation is called, is, in fact, the basis of the modern economic world.

No one knows when the process of division started; it was in existence even in remote prehistory—certain members of a tribe hunted game, others tilled fields, others built huts, others practised religious rites, others made pottery, and others made spears, axes and so on. Such division by trade is called simple division of labour. As time passed, experience gradually taught that even greater production could be gained if the actual processes within a trade were divided and performed by different people; so that within the trade of hunting, for example, the different processes of tracking, beating, trapping and slaughter came to be performed by different people. Such division by process is called complex division of labour. And it is that division which has been greatly extended in the modern world. So much so that even in the very early days of the Industrial Revolution, Adam Smith noted that there were as many as 18 different processes involved in the business of pin-making.

Any phenomenon which not only lasts for centuries but at the same time also grows in importance clearly offers a number of powerful advantages. The chief ones are:

1 An increase of skill in a more limited field. That is really what specialisation means—knowing more and more about less and less.

2   An increasing use of machinery. As jobs become more and more special-
    ised, and therefore more frequently repeated, so many of the purely
    repetitive tasks can be performed by machinery. For example, a machine
    cannot make a car, but different machines can perform many of the
    different tasks involved if the job is divided up—one machine can press
    wheels, another can cast engine blocks, another can make tyres, another
    can press body panels, and so on, provided the job of pressing wheels or
    casting engine blocks is done often enough to make it worth using
    machinery.

3   Duplication of machinery is avoided. For example, instead of everyone
    in a car factory having his own tyre-making machine, thus causing ex-
    pensive (and wasteful) duplication, such machines are centralised in the
    charge of specialised tyre makers.

4   A reduction in physical labour. Much of the drudgery has been removed
    from most types of work; and work in general takes a smaller portion of
    a person's life than it used to. Just think how combine-harvesters have
    eased the labour on grain farms, and how people in general have to work
    much less hard to obtain their necessary food supplies.

5   An increased likelihood of inventions. Familiarity with a single specialised
    job leads to a worker being more likely to be able to suggest improvements
    to the job, and also to the possibility that a worker may invent new
    machinery or techniques for the job.

6   A saving of scarce time. Workers need to learn only one task, and need
    not waste time moving from one job to another. The fact that only one
    task has to be learnt has an advantageous side-effect: low-ability labour
    which might otherwise be unemployable is enabled to gain at least some
    sort of employment.

7   An increased output per worker. Greater skill on the part of the indi-
    vidual worker, more machinery with which he can work, and the saving
    of time during his working-hours all help the worker to produce more.
    The result of this is inevitably to depress average costs of production;
    average costs may actually fall if factor costs remain constant while out-
    put per worker increases, though in real life what is more likely to happen
    is that average costs rise more slowly than factor costs do.

8   An increased total output for the community. If the workers produce
    more, and the number of workers remains constant (or decreases less
    than proportionately to the rise in output per worker), then the com-
    munity as a whole will benefit from an increased output. If the total
    population of the community remains stable (or increases less than
    proportionately to the rise in total output), then the community will have
    a higher standard of living (provided the extra output is desired and not
    destroyed). The number of conditional clauses merely illustrates the
    complexity of this particular topic; it is one of the worst problems which
    many countries face—if only the Indians, say, could hold their population
    stable or slow down its rapid rate of growth, then the increased output

from Indian farms might be able to feed the Indian population better. As it is, increases in total output are merely swallowed up by a faster increasing population.

9 An increased choice of work for the people in the community. Division of labour produces a manifold variety of jobs, enabling individual workers in the population to select the particular job that interests them most (and for which they are suited by ability, training and temperament). That does not *necessarily* mean that a person actually does the job he does best; for example, a man may be the best bricklayer in a community, and also better at bricklaying than at architecture, but if he is by far the best architect in the community (or if there is a relative scarcity of architects in the community) then he will probably be an architect.

10 An increase in trade. Specialisation inevitably brings about loss of self-sufficiency. If a person spends all his working time making boats then he must rely on other people making the other things he needs (and wants). People generally must trade their special products with the special products of other people in order to derive maximum utility from their consumption of goods and services; whole communities may also trade with each other for the same reason. If people and communities specialise, thereby increasing overall total output, then both sides of any trading partnership can gain a higher standard of living. You should relate this proposition to the concept of indifference noted in section 4I.

The advantages overwhelm the disadvantages. The most serious disadvantage is the fact that division creates dependence on other people; if bakers go on strike then there is inconvenience to the community, which is not equipped to produce enough bread from other sources. The degree of inconvenience varies with the job which has striking workers; the cessation of baking, for example, is probably less inconvenient than the cessation of electricity generation, but probably more inconveneint than the cessation of fortune-telling. But the fact that there can be any inconvenience at all rests on the existence of the division of labour.

Another possibly serious disadvantage—but one about which we know little yet—is the alleged monotony suffered by workers engaged in purely repetitive tasks. Allied to this is the problem of leisure (there actually are people who regard leisure as a problem!). Some regard increased leisure, resulting from greater output, as a reward for greater monotony during worktime; others regard increased leisure as a problem, since they anticipate that workers will be unable to fill their leisure time in interesting ways—in other words, they expect boredom at home to accompany boredom at work. We await the results of research—or perhaps experience—on this matter. Another disadvantage, about which there is no dispute, is the risk of special occupational diseases, such as silicosis. Other alleged disadvantages include loss of craftsmanship (but note that the new industries, such as electronics, often require craft skills of quite a new order), the risk of a narrow mental outlook on the part of the specialised workers (this is allied to the boredom and monotony problem, but note that new industries, such as motors and television, have often opened up entirely new horizons to many people), the development of different social classes (but note that they might have developed anyway), the restricted chances of employment in other jobs because of the narrow skills acquired in one (but, again, note that the simplicity of many specialised jobs makes them fairly easy to learn), and the rigorous inflexibility of the speed of assembly belts, making the worker work at the pace of the machine (which can, of course, be adjusted).

Quite apart from advantages and disadvantages there are also some neutral results. One is the development of the factory system; another is the standardisation of a great deal of production, like Henry Ford's Model T. However, the chief neutral result is certainly the creation of a money economy. When people are individually self-sufficient there is no need for trade, and therefore no need for money; when people are engaged in simple division of labour there is need only to barter—a pot for a coat, a pound of potatoes for a loaf—and there is still therefore no pressing need for money. But how can a person barter the fact that he pulls a lever on a machine all day? There is a need for money; but it is a huge topic, and we shall deal with it more fully later.

Despite the overwhelming nature of its advantages, division of labour cannot be carried out indefinitely. The operation of the law of diminishing marginal returns acts as a constant brake on the supply side (though note that supply quantities are actually determined by the *relationship* between market price and marginal cost). On the demand side, a major practical limit to the division of labour is imposed by the size of the market. Clearly, if the demand for a product is small, there is little advantage in a fine division of labour. The size of the market is affected by such factors as the adequacy of the transport system, the possibilities or otherwise of preserving the product for wider markets, the possible demand by the consumers for greater variety of produce, the general political and economic position both within and without the producing country, and the costs of transport in relation to the selling price of the product.

6F The mobility of labour

Mobility of labour is the term used to describe the ability of people to change either their place of work or the type of work they do. Geographical (or lateral) mobility refers to place-changes, and occupational (or vertical) mobility refers to work-changes. If people change either their place of work or the type of work they do fairly easily in response to changing economic conditions, then they are said to be **mobile**; if not, **immobile.**

In the long term, population is highly mobile. In the past, there have been vast migratory movements, from continent to continent (e.g., the peopling of North America in the 19th century), from place to place within a continent (e.g., the growth of population in California and Florida relative to the rest of North America), and from district to district within even quite small nations (e.g., from the Scottish Highlands to the Lowlands, from Wales to England, and from northern England to southern England). During this century alone, within Britain alone, there has been a change in the geographical distribution of population to the extent that the proportion of Britain's population living in London and the South East has increased from about 25% of the total to about 30% of the total, while that in Scotland has declined from about 12% to about 10%. During the same time, in England and Wales, the proportion of the labour force engaged in farming has decreased from about 7·5% to about 2·5%, while that in the service occupations has increased from about 35% to nearly 50%. These aspects of long term mobility are, however, not reflected in similar short term mobility; in any one year, the degree of movement is relatively small. For example, just over 250,000 people per year were emigrating from Britain in the mid-1960s, but 20 million people had emigrated over the preceding 100 years. It is the accumulation over a period of time which produces long term mobility; in the short term labour tends to be fairly immobile.

And it is immobile despite the fact that it might be better off elsewhere. Unemployment rates characteristically run higher in Northern Ireland, Scotland and Wales than they do in the South East and Midlands of England, and yet—despite some movement—the unemployed Irish, Scots and Welsh stay where they are. Why do they prolong this disequilibrium situation, where supply exceeds demand? What are the frictions which restrict the free movement of labour?

We may deal with the problem in two parts:

1 **Geographical mobility.** Many people think of moving to another place; relatively few actually move. There are, indeed, many strong ties between a man and 'his' place, chief among them being:

(a) Familiarity. The fact that on any level a worker and his family know an area, support its local teams, belong to its clubs, patronise its shops, and generally know their way about is a strong disincentive to a move elsewhere.

(b) Friendship. People are reluctant to leave an area if they have many friends there.

(c) Cost. Transporting a household costs a lot of money; establishing it elsewhere also costs a lot of money. Many people are not prepared to suffer these costs; so they stay were they are.

(d) Fear. A new area is unknown. Many people fear the unknown. More precisely, they fear things like higher costs of living, lower standards of living, lack of housing, harmful effects on their children's education, poorer promotion prospects, loss of pension rights; and—perhaps most of all—they fear failure.

(e) Age. Over 40, people tend to think of themselves as being too old to start a new life in a new place; others, though, maintain that life only begins at 40.

(f) Apathy. This is a very strong bond. It is often 'too much trouble' to move, or it is 'not worth moving'. In fact, with Unemployment Benefit in existence, much of the incentive to move has disappeared—and when people don't care to move then they are apathetic.

(g) Ignorance. People may be willing to move—but utterly ignorant of the opportunities elsewhere.

(h) Uncertainty about working conditions. This is an especial barrier to movement abroad, along with fear of language problems, different social customs, loss of welfare provision, the need for work permits and visas, the possible unacceptability of qualifications, the extra cost, and the loss of personal contact with relatives and friends.

If, for these reasons, a portion of the labour supply does not move from a region of unemployment to a region where employment is available, then it is quite likely that—in the long term—a 'distressed' area will develop. And it is not a pretty thing to have develop: small gangs of apathetic men standing about on street corners, houses unpainted, children in old clothes, dusty shops with a very limited choice of goods, bicycles (maybe) instead of cars, and a pervasive air of decay (plate 3a). That is the reason for mentioning earlier (sections 6B and 6D) that if labour is unused then there is a different order of problem from that produced by unused land or capital. It is at least as much a social as an economic problem, and has accordingly promoted considerable government activity. In Britain, Special Areas were first scheduled in 1934 for the receipt of government assistance, and the principle of assistance has now become an established part of government policy. The extent and intensity of assistance vary with the government in office; so there is little point in detailing the current situation. However, we should note some of the measures a government *may* take both to alleviate the effects of labour immobility (i.e., encouraging industry to move to the workers) and to increase mobility itself (i.e., encourage workers to move to the available industry):

(a) Measures to alleviate the effects of immobility.

(i) Governments may direct into the Development Areas (the new name for Special Areas) those parts of the economy which they control directly. For example, the Ministry of Social Security (Pensions) has been transferred to Newcastle, and part of the Income Tax service to Bootle.

(ii) Governments may entice new or expanding firms into establishing factories in the Development Areas. They may do this by creating New Towns and Industrial Estates in the Development Areas (see figures 6.1, 6.2 and plate 3b), and offering building grants, low-rent factories, loans and grants for fixed capital, and tax allowances for machinery and labour (tax allowances for machinery are called Investment Grants, and for labour, Regional Employment Premiums). In addition, governments may create a better general environment for new industries by building new roads and clearing away the unsightly debris of former industrial decay. They may also foster locally-sponsored advertising by Development Councils, aimed at attracting new firms to an area—for example, the advertising

1 BASILDON
2 BRACKNELL
3 CRAWLEY
4 HARLOW
5 HATFIELD
6 HEMEL HEMPSTEAD
7 STEVENAGE
8 WELWYN GARDEN CITY
9 MILTON KEYNES
10 NEWTON AYCLIFFE
11 WASHINGTON
12 PETERLEE
13 SKELMERSDALE
14 RUNCORN
15 REDDITCH
16 DAWLEY
17 CORBY
18 CWMBRAN
19 CUMBERNAULD
20 EAST KILBRIDE
21 GLENROTHES
22 LIVINGSTON
23 IRVINE

FIG. 6.1 Distribution of new towns (1968).

carried out by the Northern Ireland Development Council and by the North East Industrial Development Council (see figure 6.3).
(iii) Governments may ban fresh growth in existing growth regions. They use their powers of granting or withholding building certificates and licences to achieve this purpose. They may also use persuasion, such as

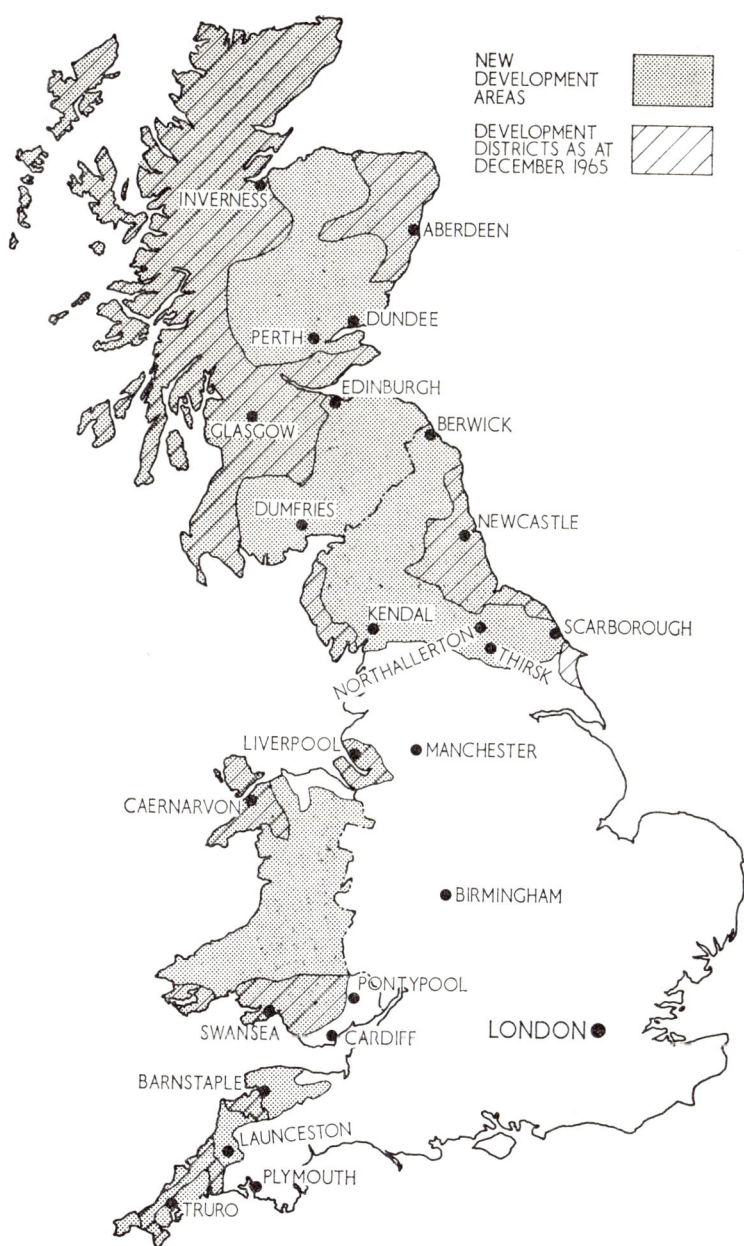

NEW DEVELOPMENT AREAS

DEVELOPMENT DISTRICTS AS AT DECEMBER 1965

INVERNESS

ABERDEEN

DUNDEE

PERTH

EDINBURGH

GLASGOW

BERWICK

DUMFRIES

NEWCASTLE

KENDAL

SCARBOROUGH

NORTHALLERTON

THIRSK

LIVERPOOL

MANCHESTER

CAERNARVON

BIRMINGHAM

PONTYPOOL

SWANSEA

CARDIFF

LONDON

BARNSTAPLE

LAUNCESTON

PLYMOUTH

TRURO

Fig 6.2 The Development Areas (1968).

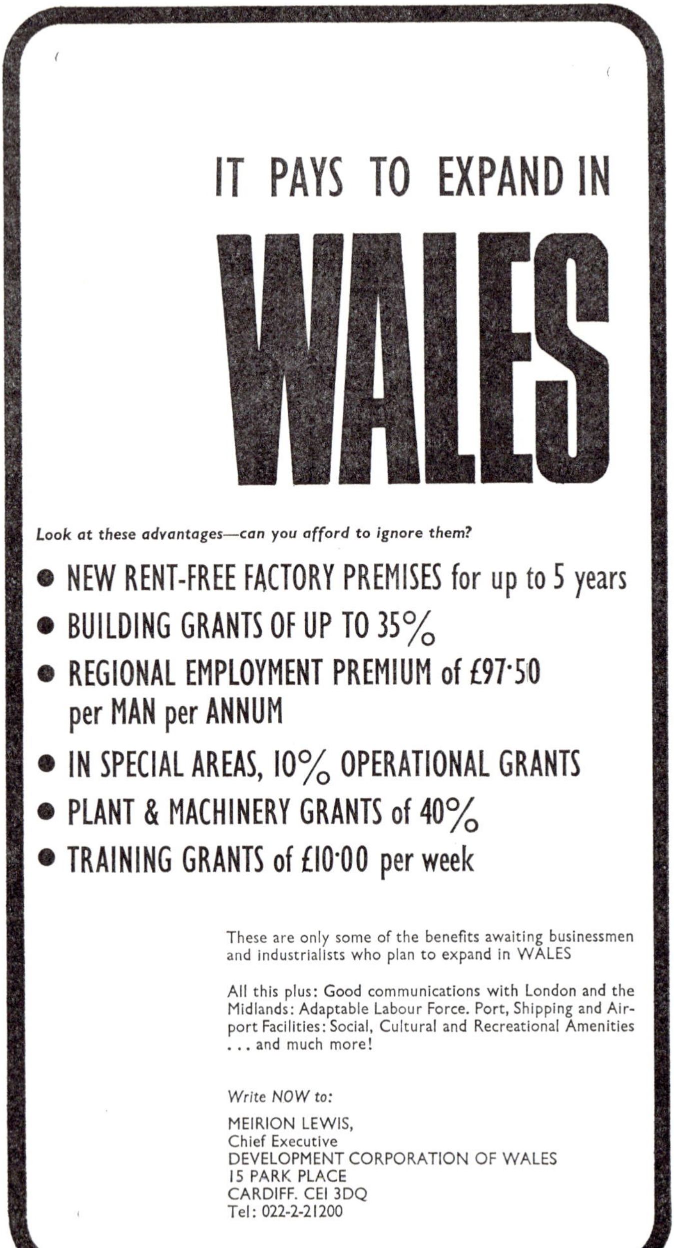

IT PAYS TO EXPAND IN

WALES

Look at these advantages—can you afford to ignore them?

- NEW RENT-FREE FACTORY PREMISES for up to 5 years
- BUILDING GRANTS OF UP TO 35%
- REGIONAL EMPLOYMENT PREMIUM of £97·50 per MAN per ANNUM
- IN SPECIAL AREAS, 10% OPERATIONAL GRANTS
- PLANT & MACHINERY GRANTS of 40%
- TRAINING GRANTS of £10·00 per week

These are only some of the benefits awaiting businessmen and industrialists who plan to expand in WALES

All this plus: Good communications with London and the Midlands: Adaptable Labour Force. Port, Shipping and Airport Facilities: Social, Cultural and Recreational Amenities . . . and much more!

Write NOW to:

MEIRION LEWIS,
Chief Executive
DEVELOPMENT CORPORATION OF WALES
15 PARK PLACE
CARDIFF. CEI 3DQ
Tel: 022-2-21200

FIG 6.3   Advertising by an Industrial Development Council (1971).

that attempted by the Location of Offices Bureau to get firms to move out of London.

(iv) Governments may pursue a policy of regional planning, aimed at allocating resources for the overall social as well as economic good of the nation. The individual measures of regional planning are not very different from those just noted, but they are used to serve a national strategy rather than to win a few local battles. A fairly new tactic which is being developed as an additional planning technique is the stimulation of local growth points, with the idea that they should act as counters to the primary attraction of an existing and natural growth point.

(b) Measures to reduce the tendency to immobility.

(i) Governments may direct labour from one place to another; but they are unlikely to do this in a democratic country except in war-time, when the population voluntarily surrenders some of its rights.

(ii) Governments may establish employment exchanges (there are about 1000 in England) where labour may be made aware of the opportunities in other parts of the country.

(iii) Governments may facilitate the movement of labour by the award of removal grants (e.g., the award of removal costs by many English Education Authorities, in order to attract teachers), by re-settlement grants, and by the increased provision of rental housing so that newly-moved workers may have somewhere to live with their families. Generally, such rental housing is Council housing, available at low rents; unfortunately, there is not enough of it in England—and most of what does exist is used for purposes other than housing migrant workers.

(iv) Governments may allow firms in existing growth areas freely to bid up the price of scarce labour, so that unemployed labour is more readily attracted in from regions of economic decline. Unfortunately, a great deal of Trade Union activity—by its insistence on nationally-agreed wage rates—prevents this from happening, or at least prevents it working with full effect. Governments, faced with this situation, could take measures to curb the power of the unions—if they wished to reduce labour immobility.

2   **Occupational mobility.** It is a fairly common thing for a person to wish that he had someone eles's job, but it is uncommon for him actually to go after it. Most people, indeed, are quite satisfied to 'stay in a rut'. The chief reasons are:

(a) The specialised nature of most labour. Through division of labour, people become expert in one or two limited fields, and then find that they cannot easily turn to any other sort of job.

(b) Cost. It takes both time and money to re-train for another job. If a person has spent, say, five years as an apprentice, then he is not readily going to throw that investment aside and spend perhaps a similar period learning a completely different sort of job. He may be forced to, of course, by cessation of demand for his particular skill; but it will be a difficult adjustment for him to make.

(c) Trade restrictions. Part of the purpose of any labour association, whether it be professional or industrial, is to secure relatively high wages for its members. It can do this by controlling the supply of labour from its members. If the supply is kept just slightly scarce relative to the demand for it, then relatively high wages can be gained. Partly—but *only* partly—for this reason, many labour associations impose barriers to entry; thus it is not always easy for a person wishing to take up a new job actually to gain entry to the job.

(d) Investment outlay. Many jobs require a sizeable initial expenditure on capital (e.g., establishing a dental practice, setting up a garage business), and it is accordingly not always possible for a person wishing to move into such a job actually to make the move.

(e) Status. A change of job could well require a change of social status. Not everyone willing to change his job is equally willing to change his social status, especially if the change is—embarrassingly—upwards.

If, for these reasons, a portion of the labour supply does not move from an occupation characterised by surplus supply to one characterised by unsatisfied demand, then inevitably a pool of unemployed labour will form. The results will be the same as if a 'distressed' area were to develop, though possibly less concentrated (the degree of concentration depending on the degree of areal specialisation achieved by the declining industries). Government measures to deal with the problem are based on two courses of action:

(a) The long term course. Schools form a useful instrument of policy in this matter. Specialisation of any sort can be delayed both by keeping children at school longer (i.e., raising the school-leaving age) and by preventing any particular subject specialisation while the children are at school (e.g., by insisting on more general courses or more general subject requirements for jobs and post-school education). Widened educational opportunity may also be provided by comprehensive schooling, so that children from socially restricted homes may at least have a chance of training for jobs which might otherwise have been considered by the children (or their parents) to be beyond their range of legitimate ambition. It is also a possibility that social barriers may be, if not broken, at least rendered a little less rigid by comprehensive schooling.

(b) The short term course. The immediate solution for occupational unemployment is to re-train the unemployed for other jobs. This is the problem of redundancy, the magnitude of which may be appreciated from the fact that the TUC estimates that in England in the 1970s as many as 600 000 people each year may have to change their jobs because of redundancy. Government-sponsored re-training centres, however, face two special problems: the disinclination of some labour unions to accept workers trained at the centres, and the disinclination of some workers to accept a lower income during their training at the centres.

6G The efficiency of labour

The efficiency—or **productivity**—of labour is reflected in the quantity of output achieved by a unit of labour (i.e., by a unit of effort) during a certain amount of time. It is often measured as the quantity of physical output per man per hour (or, sometimes, per man per year). For example, if it takes 20 men one hour to produce a ton of steel, then labour productivity could be stated as one ton of steel per 20 man-hours or as one-twentieth of a ton of steel per man-hour. Similarly, if it takes 20 men *half-an-hour* to produce one ton of steel, then their productivity is one ton of steel per 10 man-hours (i.e., 20 men × half-an-hour), or one-tenth of a ton of steel per man-hour. And if it takes them *two* hours to produce a ton of steel, then their productivity is one ton of steel per 40 man-hours (i.e., 20 men × two hours), or one-fortieth of a ton of steel per man-hour.

It is extremely difficult (if not impossible) to measure the productivity of some types of labour. How, for instance, do you measure the productivity of a doctor or a dentist—so many prescriptions issued per day or teeth filled per day, or what? The task is virtually impossible. Nevertheless, increases in labour productivity are the key to society's more efficient use of scarce resources, and therefore to a higher standard of real income; so we should have some idea of the factors that influence labour productivity. They are:

1 The character of the land resources. It is a point which hardly needs stressing that some countries are better endowed than others with natural wealth. Some countries, for example, have rich power, mineral, timber and soil resources, whereas other countries are poor by comparison; contrast the USA with, say, Thailand. There are also differences in the quality of similar resources in different countries; for example, most US coal is easy to mine because it occurs in thick and level seams, whereas most Belgian coal is extraordinarily difficult to mine because it occurs in thin and twisted seams. Other things being equal, therefore, the American coal-miner is likely to be very much more productive than his Belgian counterpart. Climate also plays a large part in determining the character of the land resources, not only directly either by creating barriers to human activity or by stimulating action, but also indirectly by promoting the occurrence of secondary barriers, such as disease. Climate, indeed, is a powerful agent of the physical environment, and should be regarded always as an important factor governing the efficiency of labour.

2 The quality of the individual worker. The quality of a worker varies with his physical fitness, mental ability and achievement, age, aptitude and attitude. The importance of the variation rests with the type of work done; a person may, for example, be physically crippled and yet produce work of great academic or artistic merit. Or he may be a numskull, and yet at the same time a superb window-cleaner. Nevertheless, most com-

munities find it expedient to produce via their health and educational services as physically fit and as fully educated a labour force as they can. Communities can also ensure that workers are employed only during their years of greatest efficiency, by preventing them gaining employment before a certain age (by raising the school leaving age) and by requiring retirement at the end of their (in general) most efficient working years.

3   The character of the general working and leisure environments. Workers are not likely to make their best efforts if they are cold, ill-clothed, under-fed, ill-housed, and insecure. Nor if their working conditions are grimy and dangerous and their leisure opportunities restricted. However, the creation of adequate warmth, clothing, food, housing, security, clean-ness, safety, and recreational opportunity is not easily measured in eco-nomic terms; it is merely something which—if done—we know to be effective in increasing the productivity of workers. The difficulties of assessing the cost of creating a productively congenial environment, and the kindred difficulties of relating such a necessarily imputed cost to a similarly imputed rise in productivity (i.e., the actual rise in productivity compared with the possible rise which might have occurred if the con-genial environment had not been created) have led to the development of a special perspective on economics by many 'social' economists in recent years; such a perspective being called **Welfare Economics**. It is con-cerned to investigate the allocation of scarce resources in the satisfaction of political, moral and social as well as of purely individual wants. But, however laudatory such a concern may be, however difficult the assess-ment of its cost-effectiveness (i.e., the degree to which its imputed cost is reflected in an ascribed increase in productivity), and however praise-worthy the creation of a welfare society, there is still a cost involved. That cost is both real, in that resources must be allocated to the creation of a welfare state, and nominal, in that taxes must be raised from society to pay for it. Here, indeed, is a counterbalancing factor: workers *may* de-rive such a disincentive effect from high taxation that the beneficent effects of general welfare provision are outweighed, and productivity actually suffers. Great care is needed to achieve an equilibrium situation.

4   The extent and nature of capital assets. It is self-evidently true that a worker with tools can, other things being equal, produce more than a worker without tools. Even palaeolithic man achieved an increase in his hunting productivity through his use of primitively-fashioned stone tools. At the present time, compare the wheat yields per acre of, say, Denmark with those of India; Denmark, with its strongly capitalised farmers, produces about 1·75 tons per acre, whereas India, with its weakly capital-ised farmers (see plate 4), produces only about 0·30 tons per acre. You will appreciate that it is rather rash to make such a straight comparison—other things, in fact, are not equal—but any *practical* comparison almost inevitably entails other things being unequal to some extent. Neverthe-less, it remains a fact that figures can be adduced in all spheres of eco-

nomic life to show that productivity per worker increases as the quantity and quality of capital assets increase.

5   The quality of management. Productivity can be increased by superior management. The increase is a reflection of better organisation and more refined division of labour. It is achieved by such techniques as time and motion study, organisation and methods control, critical path analysis, operational research and the use of computers.

6H The supply of labour

The supply of labour is, in general terms, the number of people in a community who are available for work; more specifically, it is the actual amount of work done by those people, and it may be assessed as so many hours of effort.

The total supply position in a community at any one moment of time is clearly governed by the size of the total population of that community. However, there are obvious limitations within that supply, imposed both by the community as a whole and by the individual members of the community separately. These limitations are only partly of an economic nature; the main ones are:

1   Age. Some countries, especially in the under-developed parts of the world, allow children to work from an early age, more or less until the age at which they die. Other countries, especially in the more advanced parts of the world, keep children off the labour market until they are at least about 15–17 years of age. Compulsory schooling, coupled with encouragement to higher education, not only keeps children off the labour market, of course, but it also helps to increase their overall efficiency and mobility when they do enter the market. At the other end of the age scale, advanced countries invariably make some provision for people to retire on pension at an age of about 60–65, thus, by age restrictions alone, keeping their labour supply to within, at most, a 15–65 age range.

2   Sex. Within the socially-permitted working age range, there is the further limitation of sex. Men can—and do—work at most jobs, but women are subject both to social pressures and to legal restrictions, affecting not only the number of jobs open to them but also the rate at which they take up the jobs available. For example, there are legal restrictions in England on the employment of women as coal-miners; there are social pressures against their employment in the Stock Exchange; and there are many personal and individual pressures against their employment in any sort of job at all. Nevertheless, women gain employment in England more easily than they do in many other countries; more than half the women between the ages of 15 and 65 are in some sort of employment, and they form about one-third of the total number employed. The highest level of female employment is among the 16 to 19 year-olds, with a secondary peak among the 45 to 49 year-olds; the lowest level, reflecting marriage and child-rearing, is among the 25 to 29 year-olds.

3   Health. Sickness and ill-health, whether chronic or acute, curtail the available labour supply still further. Some people, of course, are so chronically sick that they are incapable of work at any time; others are periodically removed from the available supply either by endemic illnesses such as the winter cold or by epidemic diseases such as Asian or Hong Kong flu.

4   Hours of work. An additional limitation to the total supply of labour is imposed—only partly voluntarily—by the individual workers themselves. They do not wish to work the whole day through. Some, indeed, do not wish to work at all, but they are the idle rich, the malingerers and the criminals; they are not normal economic men. The others, who wish to work, have to make some sort of decision about how many hours a day to work; in general, they have chosen to work for eight hours a day five days a week. However, there are numerous exceptions to the 40-hour working week—most professional workers and individual entrepreneurs, for example, are not tied to any particular number of hours of work, merely carrying on with their jobs until the work in hand is finished. Quite apart from the restrictions to hours in a normal working day, there are also limitations to the number of such days during a year; holidays, whether of the annual two- or three-weeks type or of the intermittent bank-holiday type, are acknowledged breaks in the working year, but strikes have a similar effect in curtailing the labour supply, and are much less socially acceptable.

5   Intensity of effort. Allowing for the fact that people actually do get to work, despite all the restrictions just noted, there is yet another limitation to the effective supply of labour. That is the intensity of effort which the workers make while they are at work. Most people are inclined to sit around and do nothing for at least some part of the day when they are supposed to be working (i.e., outside the normal lunch-hours and tea-breaks, which have an output-increasing effect). Such sitting around is, of course, tantamount to a reduction in the number of hours worked. Being late for work has a similar effect; so also have 'going slow' on the job and 'working to rule'.

The law of supply (that supply extends with a rise in price) is not fully applicable to the *total* supply of labour in the short term. As the price of labour—the wage—rises, the supply of it extends for a time because married women take up employment, the marginally ill return to work (or stay at work instead of going home), the regular workers perhaps work overtime, the malingerers take up at least some sort of work, and so on. However, there are limits to the amount of supply extension that either can occur or is likely to occur. For example, if wages rise sufficiently high some women might withdraw from the supply, preferring instead to rely on their husbands' greatly increased incomes. And there is a limit to the number of hours that workers are prepared to work; if wages rise sufficiently high, indeed, many workers might prefer to earn much the same sort of total income by working fewer hours. And, as an absolute limit, there are only so many people in the total population. Consequently, a supply curve illustrating a *total* supply schedule is likely to have a normal positive shape at the bottom, but to turn through an intermediate inelastic supply position to a negative slope at the top, as shown in figure 6.4. The upper negative part of the curve reflects the increasing desire of married women to stay at home and of regular workers to work fewer hours; under a high wage state, in fact, the total supply of labour could contract. In the long term, if wages remain high, the supply conditions could change—immigrants could be attracted to the area by the high wages offered, and, as more married women stay at home and the air of general economic well-being continues, the birth rate could increase. The changes are an instance of long term supply elasticity, as noted at the end of section 5B.

The supply position for *one* firm or *one* industry in a community is, however, very different from the total supply position. If we assume that one firm or one industry raises its offered wages, while all others continue to offer unchanged wages (i.e., other things remain equal), then, within the limitations imposed by the immobility of labour, there will tend to be drift of labour from the rest of the total supply to the firm or industry which is raising its offered

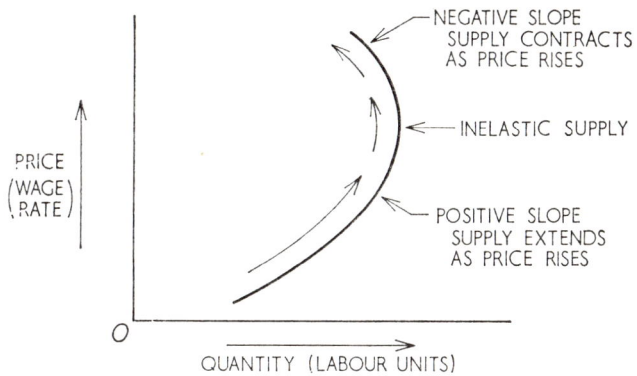

FIG 6.4   A possible total supply curve for labour.

FIG 6.5   A labour supply curve for a single firm.

wages. In such circumstances the labour supply curve for the single firm or industry will be of the normal positive shape throughout its whole extent, as shown in figure 6.5. You should consider its angle of slope. What will determine the elasticity of supply under these conditions? The answer is, of course, the mobility of labour. Mobility is greatest in the lower part of the curve; the supply extends, however, at a diminishing rate in proportion to wage increases, because the number of people remaining to be drawn on diminishes both absolutely (quantitatively) and in relevant skill-content (qualitatively). It should be clear from a comparison of figures 6.4 and 6.5 that what may be good for a single firm (obtaining more labour by offering higher wages) is not necessarily good for the community as a whole. Indeed, it is impossible except in the long term.

When we turn to the supply position of an individual worker (figure 6.6) we find that the curve behaves in much the same manner as for total supply; the reason is, of course, that in both cases we are dealing with the supply position of a full and complete unit, whereas for the single firm we are dealing

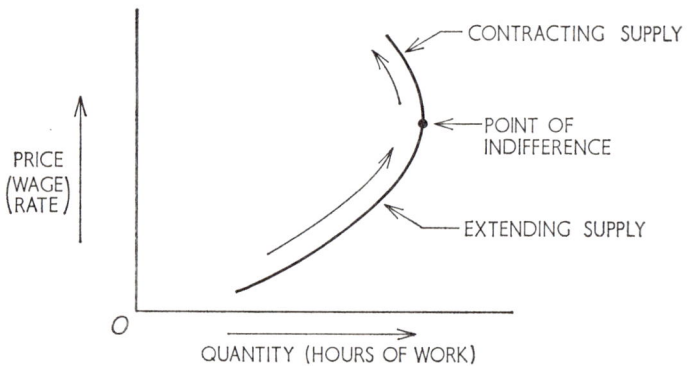

FIG 6.6   A labour supply curve for an individual worker.

with the supply of only *part* of a whole unit (i.e., only part of total supply). In the case of an individual worker the factor which produces a negative slope in the upper part of the supply curve is his likely increasing preference of leisure to work. Actually, an increasingly high wage rate has two opposite effects upon an individual worker. On the one hand, a higher wage rate is an incentive to greater work (i.e., it leads to a greater substitution of work for leisure); and on the other hand, it is an incentive to reduced work, since it allows the worker to gain a given income with less effort (i.e., it leads to a greater substitution of leisure for work). The net effect is usually one of increased effort up to a certain point, and then reduced effort beyond that point. The location of the point will vary from person to person, and may also be affected by the general economic climate prevailing in the community. For example, if there is a generally established and accepted standard of living in the community, then a higher wage rate will tend to reduce the amount of labour offered; but if the prevailing climate is one of 'keeping up with the Joneses' then a higher wage rate will tend to increase the amount of labour offered. The location of the point is also affected by taxation levels. If there is a high rate of taxation on the extra (marginal) earnings, then people tend to think that there is little reason to take on additional work or move to a higher-level job. In such a case, taxation has a disincentive effect on extra work.

The point where the individual worker's supply of labour ceases is also the point where the utility he derives from work is equal to the utility he derives from leisure, i.e., at the point of equi-marginal utility of leisure and work. It is also the point where neither work nor leisure is preferable to the other, i.e., at the point of indifference between work and leisure.

6I Labour and population

We have noted repeatedly the absolute limit to the supply of labour imposed by the size of the population. Any community has a population of a given absolute size, e.g., the population of Great Britain at the time of the 1961 census is given as 51 435 567. However, such an absolute figure gives us very little idea of the real character of the labour resource. We need to relate it not only to the overall quality of the population (i.e., skill, initiative, etc.) but also to both the area of land the population occupies and the standard of living the population has achieved. In other words, we need to consider the concept of **optimum population**, and the effects of increasing and decreasing population sizes.

Optimum population may be defined in two ways. First, the strict economic definition states that it is the population size which is capable of achieving maximum output of goods and services per person, given certain quantities of land, capital and enterprise. It also states that any population size larger or smaller than the optimum is either too many or too few to use the resources with maximum efficiency, and therefore yields an output per person lower than would be possible with either fewer or more people respectively. In other words, optimum population is that which, in combination with fixed quantities of the other production factors, yields optimum production. Second, the general economic definition states that optimum population is the size of population which, in combination with certain quantities of land, capital and enterprise, yields the highest standard of living per person. It also states that any population size smaller than the optimum is capable of yielding a rising average standard of living so long as additional units of population *produce more than they consume* (even if at a diminishing rate); and, conversely, that any population size larger than the optimum produces a falling average standard of living as additions to total population *consume more than they produce*. The chief difference between the two definitions is that in the first definition output per person is the sole test, whereas in the second definition output per person is related to the level of consumption per person.

Optimum population is not quantifiable; the age-composition of the population, its quality, and its social attitudes are all variables of too great a significance in production to allow precise quantification on the basis of mere numbers. Nor, even if it were quantifiable, would optimum population be a stable figure; techniques of production change in fact too rapidly, and conditions of enterprise and capital formation are too dynamic to permit of optimum population stability. The more one thinks about it, indeed, the more one might come to doubt the validity of the concept of optimum population; the fact that gross under- and over-population are easily recognisable does not mean equally that an optimum figure is distinguishable, nor even that there is one. Nevertheless, the concept, albeit imprecise (even vague), is a valuable bit of background theory to our consideration of optimum factor combination.

A population which is increasing in numbers and which is also below the conceptual optimum size offers a variety of economic advantages:

1   There is increasing scope for division of labour.
2   There is a growing market for goods and services; so production and employment are stimulated.
3   There is likely to be a greater proportion of young people in the community, thus tending to produce greater labour mobility and greater productivity.

Beyond the optimum size, however, an increasing population size produces increasing pressure upon available resources, and a reduced per capita distribution of wealth throughout the community; in other words, a falling standard of living. If prolonged, such a situation could theoretically reduce standards of living to a starvation level. However, there are many answers to the problem in practice: on the one hand, a larger population can be supported by the utilisation of new techniques of production, the use of virgin lands, the improvement of existing farmland, and the increased use of the sea as a source of food; on the other hand, population growth itself can be retarded by the use of various techniques of birth control.

The advantages of a decreasing population exist only when the original population exceeds the conceptual optimum; under such conditions, a decreasing size allows abandonment of use of the most marginal resources and concentration instead on the more profitable. A decrease in size below the optimum, however, produces a variety of disadvantages, chief among them being:

1   Narrowing scope for division of labour.
2   A declining market for goods and services.
3   The likelihood of an increasing average age for the population, and therefore of diminishing labour mobility and productivity.
4   A reduction in the average standard of living.

To some extent, the problem of a declining population can be offset by both (a) short term measures to increase the effective labour supply, e.g., by encouragement of married women to enter paid employment, by lowering the school leaving age, and by insistence on longer hours of work, and (b) long term measures to increase the population size, e.g., by encouragement of married people to a higher rate of reproduction through such measures as tax relief on children and the provision of 'free' baby foods, natal clinics and day nurseries.

6J   The unemployment of labour

As we noted in section 6B, the unemployment of labour poses problems of a different order from those created by the unemployment of land and capital. If land and capital are unemployed there is merely waste, and a tolerance by society of less-than-maximum production. If labour is unemployed, however, there are intolerable social evils as well. The evils arise from the fact that labour is provided by people and not by inanimate things; and that people are consumers all the time whether they are producers at any one time or not, and that they have to be supported in their consumption while they are unemployed by the efforts of those who are employed. The two sides of the evil of unemployment are, therefore, (a) the psychological distress suffered by the unemployed, who feel that they are being supported by charitable measures, and (b) the resentment of the unemployed by the employed, who feel that the unemployed should make more effort to find work instead of relying on charity.

The distress and resentment may be expressed in a variety of ways and on a variety of different levels. The unemployed individual worker loses not only his wages and his pride but also his savings and—possibly—his physical health; his wife and children suffer, too, and that may be sufficient to breed enough resentment of the 'system' to cause the worker to demonstrate, march, agitate, and in other ways cause general social unrest. Society, as a whole, of course, not only suffers the 'growth' of economically and socially depressed areas, but also the burdens of extra taxation to transfer at least some goods and services to the unemployed, the general social unrest created by the unemployed, and the possible development of extremist political parties.

Unemployment has never been readily avoidable, despite the social stigma attached to it, and the numerous problems it creates. In Britain, prior to 1914, it swung cyclically from about 2% of the labour force to about 10%; between 1918 and 1939 it ranged between about 5% and 15%; and since 1945, under official government policy of 'full employment', it has varied from about 1·5% to about 6%. At no time has it been less than about 1·5%. Moreover, even when the percentage has been small, there have been localised pockets of unemployment at a rate well above the average, often necessitating special government action such as the scheduling of Development Areas. The overall desirability of reducing concentrated unemployment stems from the basic fact that its evils can spread from region to region. A depressed area exerts a diminished demand for the products of the whole society, so depressing the earnings of the rest of society, and thereby increasing its chances of unemployment in turn. Such a diffusion of unemployment can also occur internationally, through the diminution of international trade; which is why any recession of economic activity in the USA is of such great concern to all countries which trade with the USA.

Much attention has been given to the matter of unemployment because of its evils and problems, and several causes have been identified:

1   Failure of the economic system to adapt smoothly to changing conditions. This happens either because of the operation of various economic frictions, such as the immobility of labour, or because of the 'faulty' combination of factors by entrepreneurs—'faulty', that is, in the social sense rather than in the purely economic sense (e.g., automation and the accompanying release of labour may be economic good-sense, but it is not necessarily social good-sense too). This is **frictional** unemployment.

2   The advent of substitute products and the accompanying loss or decline of markets for the original product. For example, the increasingly widespread use of synthetic fibres has caused the market for cotton to shrink, with resulting unemployment for cotton-workers in Lancashire; similarly, the development by overseas countries of their oil and hydro-electricity resources has caused a decline in Britain's foreign sales of coal, with consequent unemployment of miners in Britain's prime exporting coal-fields in South Wales and the North East of England. This is **structural** unemployment, which is really a sort of long term frictional unemployment.

3   Government action to combat excess demand for labour. When producers are short of labour, they bid up its price (i.e., offer higher wages) in order (a) to increase its total supply, and (b) to increase its supply to their particular firms. As we saw in section 6H, however, the total supply cannot extend indefinitely; so what happens is that individual producers vie with each other to attract what labour there is. The higher wages push production costs up, and there is no necessarily-accompanying rise in productivity. Under these conditions, governments may act to curtail the demand for labour. Unfortunately, the weapons of control are usually quite clumsy, and often more successful in their intention than is socially or economically desirable. **General** unemployment may therefore be caused.

4   Changes of the season. A certain amount of **seasonal** unemployment is inevitable. Hotel workers, for example, are not required in constant numbers throughout the year; nor are builders, farmhands, gardeners and ice-cream salesmen. Some people, of course, manage to obtain separate summer and winter jobs—but others fail, even if they try. Naturally, winter is the season of greatest seasonal unemployment.

5   Fluctuations in international trade and business activity. It has been a characteristic feature of trading economies to suffer from cyclical swings in activity. No one really knows why that should be so, but clearly any downswing of activity is accompanied by some release of labour. This is **cyclical** unemployment, and was the cause of the suggestion by the great English economist, Keynes, that during such times of downswing the government should endeavour to maintain the demand for labour by

initiating a programme of 'public works' (i.e., the creation of additional social capital).

It should be appreciated from a review of the causes of unemployment that a certain amount is normal in an economy. As labour moves from one job to another, people are—temporarily—registered as unemployed; as people leave a declining industry and train for an expanding one they are—temporarily—registered as unemployed; and as people seek or leave seasonal jobs they are—temporarily—unemployed. The official government policy of 'full employment', in fact, allows for such inevitable unemployment. It defines full employment not as an absence of unemployment but as an approximate equality of numbers unemployed and jobs vacant (i.e., a point where supply equals demand). Whenever there are more jobs vacant than there are unemployed people to fill them, the situation is called one of 'over-full employment'. The situation has occurred a few times since 1945 in Britain, and in each case has been remedied by government action—often to the extent of causing unemployment as noted under cause 3 above.

6K Characteristics of capital

The definition of capital is not an easy matter. We noted in section 2H that it 'constitutes the variety of things that help labour make the most economic use of land', but that is a wide denotement. For example, is *intelligence* capital?

Let us, therefore, try to be a little more definite. Assume, first, that a teacher, Black, wishes to produce a course leading to an elementary understanding of, say, history, and, second, that there are some people demanding such a course from him; the basic supply and demand positions are then established. Now, there are many ways in which actual production can occur. Black can meet a group of demanders in a field and simply talk to them, but that is a highly inconvenient thing to do unless the weather is reliably warm and sunny. To make it more convenient, Black can hire a hall (assuming there are sufficient demanders); as soon as he does that, however, he is using a man-made object (the hall) to assist him in production. Such artificial assistance, which cost someone time, effort and materials to make, is *capital*. It is simple capital, and helps Black's production only a little bit. He can go further with even more assistance; for example, if he writes out a set of notes for passing round, the additional capital employed (paper, typewriter, desk, etc.) helps him to produce a course reaching a greatly increased number of people. However, he is then starting to use complex capital, since the production of the paper, typewriter and desk require in turn the allocation to them of a variety of scarce resources; in other words, Black's increased production rests upon the prior production of a series of assistant goods, which in turn are made possible only by the initial production of wood-pulp, steel and timber (which themselves require the existence of pulp, steel and saw mills). To take the matter to its ultimate stage (under existing economic and technical conditions), Black's greatest production is possible through publishing; and there is then a greatly increased variety of assisting capital in operation—not merely the paper, typewriter and desk, but also the printing and binding machines hired by a publishing house, as well as all the apparatus essential for *their* production and marketing in turn. Black has now moved from the no-capital state in the field to the complex-capital state in the publishing house, and each successive stage in his progress has brought in train a whole new series of pre-established capital aids, as well as an increase in production. His course, indeed, is giving satisfaction to many thousands instead of to merely a few in a field, and it is enabled to do so through the application of capital in a **roundabout** sort of way, i.e., the manufacture of wood-pulp and paper, the establishment of steel mills and the production of machinery are all necessary—but *indirect*—aids to the printing of his course in book form. The more roundabout the chain of production is (i.e., the more indirect capital assistance there is employed), the greater is the amount of final production—and the longer the whole process takes.

But it takes a long time only if the start is from nothing. In practice, a community accumulates a stock of capital aids, so that they are already in existence for each fresh item of production. The paper mills and printing machines used in the production of a book are not created specially; they are part of a pre-existing stock.

Arising from the foregoing analysis, a more precise definition of the essential characteristics of capital can now be attempted:

1   Capital is anything which assists human labour in production. Tools and machinery are clearly covered by this statement, but what about intelligence? Bearing in mind what was said in section 6B about the arbitrary classification of production factors, it would seem best to relate intelligence to the *quality of labour* rather than to the *quantity of capital*, but, in practice, of course, there is often only a narrow dividing line between the two.

2   Capital is man-made. This statement gets us out of that difficulty just a bit; tools and machinery are obviously man-made, but intelligence is hereditary (or is it?—educationists, even when they feel able to define intelligence, debate its hereditary character).

3   Capital lengthens the productive process but increases productivity. A man may fashion a cup out of clay, and then another, but if he takes time to make a cup-making machine he may wait longer for his first cup; after that, however, his output of cups will increase rapidly. The creation of capital thus involves time, effort and material resources, and it necessitates deferring the satisfaction gained from final production; however, it yields greater satisfaction in the long run.

4   Capital is a stock of wealth intended for use in further production. Economists debate the extent of coverage of this statement. All agree that tools and machinery are covered, and there is also agreement about stocks of, say, coal, oil, cotton and rubber. But what about roads? And houses? And cars? And TV sets? Roads clearly assist production, though

they may be used for other things as well; houses also assist production by providing necessary shelter for workers, but their assistance is unusually indirect. Roads and houses are, in fact, both widely accepted as capital. Cars, however, may or may not be so accepted. Company cars are generally treated as mobile machines and are widely regarded as serving the productive process in much the same way as fixed machines; but privately-owned cars are not. The theoretical distinction is blurred by the fact that company cars are often used for non-productive business, while private cars may quite well assist production (because they increase the workers' co-operative attitudes as well as giving a focus to their work ambitions). TV sets can also assist production by creating more ambitious (or more contented?) workers. However, it is customary to omit private cars and TV sets from a consideration of capital, since their assistance in production is so indirect and so tenuous that it is impossible either to quantify the amount of assistance or to assess its cost. Theoretical analysis is therefore limited by purely practical considerations. However, it should be noted that the type of use of a good is a useful criterion of its being capital—a car is capital if it is used fairly directly in the productive process, but it is merely private property if it is of only very indirect benefit to production. Similarly, a sack of potatoes is capital if it is intended for sowing, since that will further production, but it is merely property if it is intended for eating. Curiously, a house is capital, not property.

The basic types of capital have already been noted, in section 2H and figure 2.1. It only remains to stress the distinction between real and nominal capital. The stock of wealth which both assists and increases production is physical in its nature; it can be seen and touched; it works; it is *real*. Nominal capital (money) is not real in the same sense. True, it can be seen and touched, and people talk of making money 'work', but its physical presence is intrinsically almost useless; just about the only thing you can do physically with a bundle of notes is make a fire. You cannot eat money, nor can you make it produce power or manufacture cars. The only way you can get money to 'work' for you is through the medium of real capital. If a community increases the amount of money in circulation while its real capital assets remain unchanged, then it is merely the *value* of money which will change; the additional money will not purchase any additional goods, because there are no additional goods. The only way to get additional goods is to make them, by applying either more land and labour or more *real* capital to the productive process. Applying more money on its own will not help at all.

Any community which employs a lot of real capital in its productive processes is said to be capital-intensive, as opposed to labour-intensive; if the community possesses its capital privately it is called a capitalist community, but if possession is communal then the society is a socialist or communist one. The full range of combinations is possible: thus, the USSR is a capital-intensive communist state, the USA is a capital-intensive capitalist state, China is a labour-intensive communist state, and Taiwan is a labour-intensive capitalist state. Whatever the political orientation of a community, however, the importance of capital in expediting its economic growth cannot be over-stressed.

6L Capital accumulation and investment

If capital is such an important factor of production, why don't all countries set about obtaining large quantities of it? And why haven't they all succeeded, as so many of the poorer countries so patently haven't? The wish, of course, is often far from the fulfilment, but some countries appear even to have had little wish to accumulate capital. India, for example, is a land whose people, despite almost perennial starvation, seem almost to reject capital accumulation. No doubt the caste system had much to do with this attitude, and even though now officially abolished the system still lives on in people's minds. Perhaps, also, the fatalistic religions of the country have helped to prevent the development of much of a dynamic attitude on the part of the bulk of the population. Other reasons could be the devastatingly widespread peasant indebtedness, the ignorance and conservatism of a scattered rural population, and the political legacy of wealth-concentration into a few exacting hands. Whatever the reasons of the past, and their surviving traces, however, the situation is now slowly changing.

Assuming, then, that countries wish to accumulate capital, what stops some of them from doing so? The reasons lie in the methods of capital accumulation. Since the creation of real capital involves the allocation of real resources to that end, then, in opportunity cost terms (see section 1A), the creation of real capital necessarily involves the non-creation of some other (alternative) goods. If the goods which are *not* created are not immediately essential to life, then the country can afford to allocate some of its resources to the formation of real capital; in other words, it is capable of surplus production—surplus, that is, to immediately essential needs. However, not all countries are in this fortunate situation. Some would find, if they allocated resources to capital formation, that the alternative goods which were *not* made were vital to existence. Such countries are not in a position to allocate any resources to capital formation, otherwise some of their people would starve. And yet they are faced by the vicious alternative that if they don't initiate a programme of capital formation then their people will continue to go hungry. The countries which have no surplus production to set aside for capital are called the Developing Nations, a euphemism for economically-backward countries. Their salvation rests either in aid from more advanced nations or in a tyrannical government which enforces capital formation at the cost of great starvation and perhaps death to part of the population. There are examples of both methods of salvation in 20th-century history.

Those countries which have successfully accumulated capital have done so by means of **investment**. It should be understood that the *real product* of a community is the same as the *real income* of that community. The quantity of goods and services produced is the same as the quantity available for consumption, provided either that there is no trade with other communities

PLATE I   Men, money and markets.

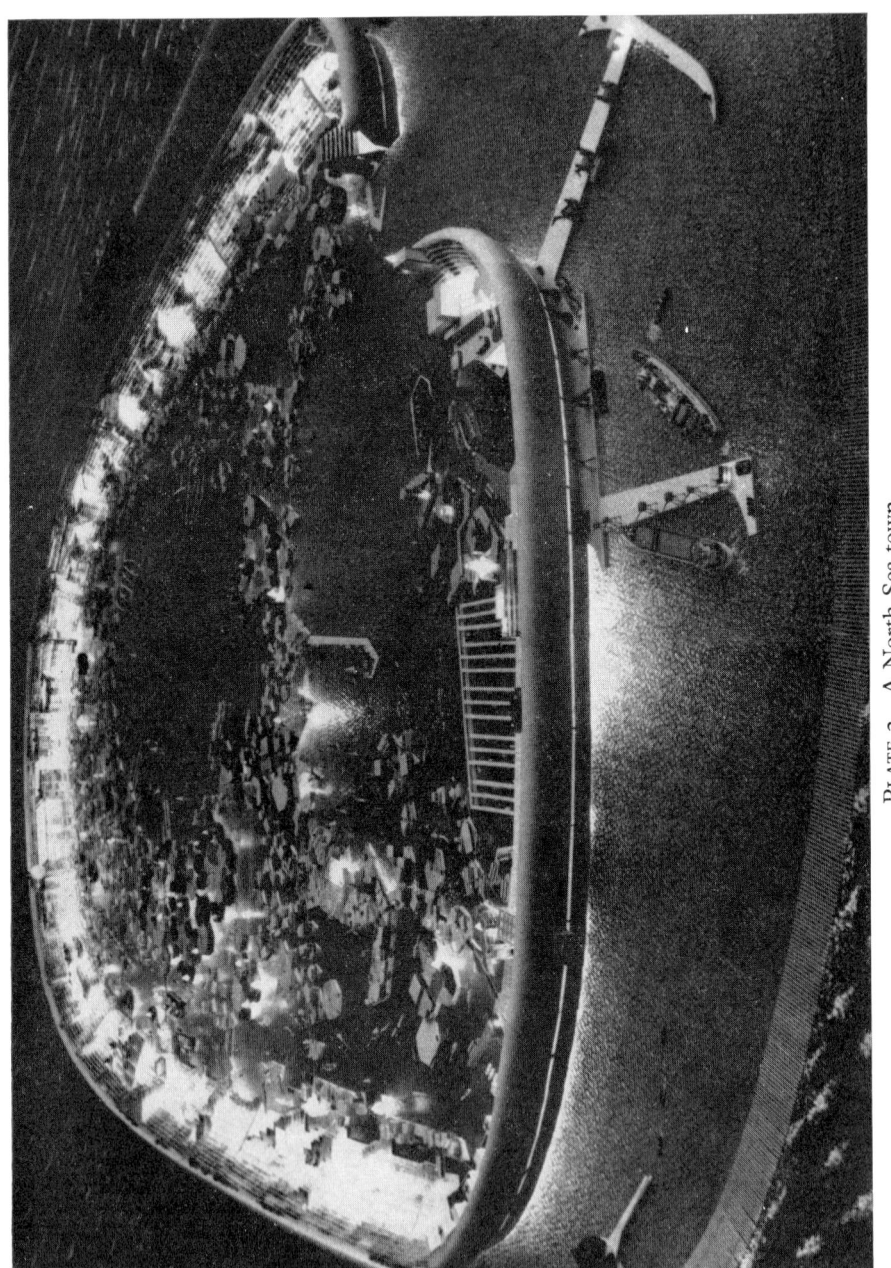

Plate 2 A North Sea town.

or that there is a net balance of exports and imports; real product, in other words, equals real income. If a certain amount of real product is set aside as capital, then of necessity so also is a similar amount of real income. Indeed, it is one single quantity only which is set aside, and it is taken from one single total quantity of goods and services. Looked at from the production (supply) side, the total quantity is called *product* and the quantity set aside is called *capital*; and looked at from the consumption (demand) side, the total quantity is called *income* and the quantity set aside *investment*.

Just as a certain amount of product has to be surplus to immediate requirements before capital can be formed, so—equally—a certain amount of income has to be surplus to immediate requirements before investment can occur. In nominal terms, surplus income set aside for preferred future use is called **savings**, and we can now turn to an expansion of the concept of saving already noted in sections 4A and 4B.

The first thing to note is that saving is not *exactly* identical with investment; saving is of money and investment is of real product. The difference is important because money, being liquid (see section 2H), can leak out of the economic system; it does that whenever a person who is setting aside some of his unspent income (saving) stuffs it into a suitcase under the bed (or into some other 'safe' place).* The money is then taken out of general circulation; no one—not even a bank—has hold of it; it is hidden away and no one can make use of it. If the monetary savings are to be of any use at all to the whole community, then they must be channelled into some form of real productive investment. Saving, therefore, provides merely the *possibility* of capital investment; and it is one of the functions of banks to attract the savings, and thus— collecting many small and relatively useless sums into a few large and more useful sums—permit the realisation of that possibility.

The second thing to note is that saving is not necessarily *automatic,* i.e., people in general do not automatically set aside some of their limited income. Some—the rich—might do so, simply because all their immediate needs are capable of satisfaction through only partial use of their large incomes; others, however, have to be given some incentive to save—some incentive, in other words, to postpone their spending ability. The desire to spend current income in the present rather than in the future is called **time preference,** and the incentive to save must therefore be sufficient to overcome the time preference. It used commonly to be thought by economists that the rate of interest on savings was a sufficient incentive, but nowadays several other factors are acknowledged to be influential.

The chief factors influencing saving are:

1   Prudence. The desire to have a 'bit put by' in case of emergency and the idea of saving 'for a rainy day' are widespread reasons for saving on a

---

* A Central Statistical Office report in January 1970 noted that about 150 million coins, with a face value of £2.8m, are lost or otherwise unaccounted for every year in Britain.

small scale; on a larger scale, saving for old age is very common, through either superannuation and insurance schemes or bank savings-plans. Clearly, superannuation funds, insurance companies and banks are all major channels through which small savings are directed to capital investment.

2 Special purposes. People may save specially for such things as a holiday, a car, a house, and a boat. Whatever the special purpose, it represents the expectation of conferment of future utility greater than that available in the present.

3 Personal nature. Thrift is not a universal habit, even though it is considered by many people to be a good habit; others, however, are spendthrifts by nature, and accordingly save little—even though there may be strong practical reasons for saving.

4 Expectation of future income. People are more likely to save some of their current income if they fear that their future income may be smaller. Partly, of course, that is the reason for saving through insurance schemes, the benefits of which are intended to be added to pensions which are lower in amount than pre-pension earnings. On the other hand, people are less likely to save if they expect larger future earnings.

5 Desire to leave wealth to descendants. This is a common, though often unvoiced, reason for saving. Plain life insurance is the chief method.

6 Expectation of future enjoyment of savings. People are more likely to save, other things being equal, if they feel that they will be able to enjoy the fruits of such saving; in other words, impending disasters such as war, death and collapse of currency values are likely to induce people to spend current income rather than save some of it. It is only when people are generally optimistic about the future that they are likely to save.

7 Provision of facilities for saving. It is pretty obvious that people are less likely to save (as distinct from *hoard*) if they have to walk five miles to put their savings into a bank than they are if they can get to a bank easily. A widespread network of bank branches is therefore conducive to saving; so also is the wide provision of savings facilities by (a) the state, through the agency of the Post Office Savings Bank and the National Savings Movement, and by (b) voluntary trustees, through the Trustee Savings Banks.

8 The size of undistributed profits. Commercial firms which are owned by shareholders regularly share out (or distribute) some of the yearly profit to the shareholders in the form of **dividends**. If the firms do not distribute all the profit but set some aside instead, as **reserve**, then they are saving just as private individuals save. Firms' reserves account for almost a half of all savings. They are very important—not only because of their amount, but also because they are in the hands of the people who actually make the capital investment decisions.

9 The rate of interest. There is no direct relationship between the rate of

interest on savings and the amount of saving which takes place, though savers may switch their existing savings from one 'investment' to another in search of the highest rate. The previously common idea that the rate of interest was the equilibrium price balancing the demand for money capital and its supply has now been severely modified by the existence of the other listed factors. It is highly uncertain just how far in practice a change in interest rates affects the level of total savings; however, a higher rate of interest is likely, other things being equal, to produce a greater amount of saving, since sub-marginal savers (i.e., potential rather than actual savers) may start saving, and regular savers may save more. It is worth noting, though, that in certain cases a higher interest rate may actually reduce the quantity of money saved, since the higher interest rate makes possible the realisation of a certain total sum (savings + interest) with smaller savings. Another point to note is that a higher interest rate confers a greater amount of consumer surplus (or *windfall gain*) to those savers who would save even at a low rate of interest (or for no interest at all), and that is clearly something which the people who pay interest (the borrowers) prefer to minimise rather than augment.

10   The amount of personal disposable income. Every consumer's income is limited, in the sense that it is a finite quantity, and every consumer's expenditure contains a number of absolutely essential payments. Income must exceed essential expenditure if there is to be any disposable income, which is, therefore, the sum available to the consumer to dispose of as he wishes. Savings come most commonly from disposable income (only in a few cases can savings be regarded as essential expenditure), and therefore the larger the disposable income, the greater the amount of possible saving.

In any country, the total amount of real product obtained during a year is called **Gross Domestic Product (GDP)**. If a country is able to accumulate capital by any of the means already noted, then the amount of real product set aside is called **Gross Investment**, and the deduction of such an amount from Gross Domestic Product leaves the quantity of real product available for immediate consumption. However, capital itself gets consumed, though much more slowly than goods for immediate consumption. Machines wear out, factories become derelict, roads crumble, and so on, and in each case the capital item needs to be replaced or repaired in order merely to 'maintain the capital intact'. The rate of decrease of value of a capital item over a period of years is called its *depreciation rate*, and the setting aside of a certain amount of product each year so as to be able eventually to replace the worn-out capital is called the *amortisation* of capital. However, if all a country does is merely replace worn-out capital, then that country is not going to get much richer very quickly. In order to sustain a rapid growth rate, a country must not only replace capital as it wears out but also add to it. Accordingly, the sum of gross investment must include a portion for **net investment** (i.e., adding to the capital stock) as well as a portion for **reinvestment** (i.e., replacing worn-out capital). One of the chief troubles of the British economy since 1945 has been its low rate of net investment.

Another point: we should note that investment, whether net or replacement, may be made inside the country (domestic investment) or abroad (foreign investment). The choice depends partly on the relative expected quantities of product per unit of investment, and also partly on other considerations, such as political stability, relative currency values, government regulations, and so on.

Figure 6.7 gives a simplified idea of how the types and directions of investment fit into a product-income flow.

6M The entrepreneur

Land and labour are the two absolutely essential factors of production. The addition of capital allows greater efficiency to labour in its application to land, but *maximum* efficiency is obtainable only through proper organisation. The development in time of a rather specialised form of labour, whose purpose is the organisation of land, labour and capital, led increasingly to greater factor productivity, and to more rapid overall economic growth. The person who co-ordinates the land, labour and capital resources available to him, and in consequence increases both factor productivity and overall production, is the entrepreneur. It is important to note (well) that the co-ordinating process takes place in advance of actual production; you cannot, for example, produce a West End play without first acquiring a theatre, a script, actors, a director, and suitable costumes—and you have to undertake to pay these factors of land, labour and capital long before you ever actually see the play performed before an audience. And then you may possibly find that the audience doesn't like the play, and that the demand from future audiences dwindles rapidly as word of a poor play gets around; and that you are therefore out-of-pocket on the enterprise. On the other hand, the play may be a 'hit', and you may find yourself very rich as a result. Nevertheless, the need to acquire and pay production factors in advance of actual production inevitably entails a degree of *uncertainty* in the enterprise. It is an essential characteristic of the entrepreneur that he bears the uncertainty inherent in an enterprise.

The chief functions of the entrepreneur are:

1 Planning new enterprises. This includes the decisions relating to type, quality and quantity of goods and/or services to be produced, as well as those relating to factor hiring, marketing, and plant location.

As far as the hiring of production factors is concerned, the entrepreneur seeks to achieve that combination of factors which yields maximum efficiency. This may mean either of two things: first, a combination yielding the lowest average cost of production, and, second, a combination yielding maximum profit on sales. The difference between these two possible combinations was examined in section 5A, and you will remember that the point of combination yielding maximum profit on sales differs from the point of lowest average cost (optimum) combination only if the

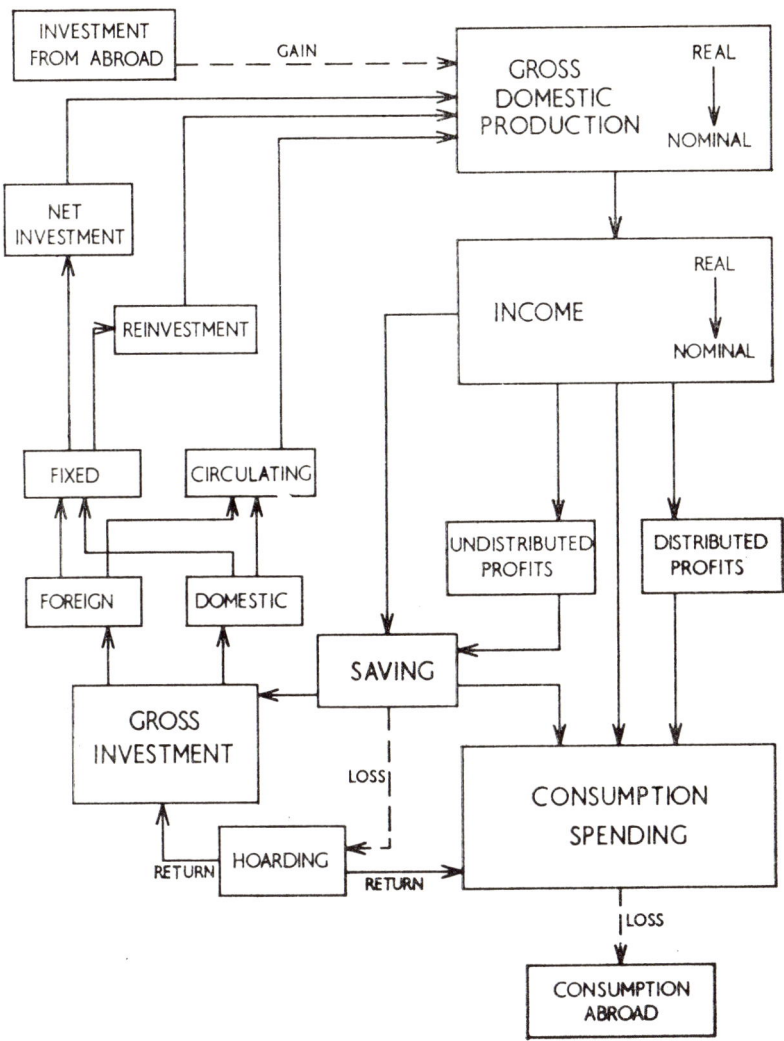

FIG 6.7 A simplified product-income flow.

selling price of the good is higher than the lowest average cost level. Figure 5.2 shows that optimum production occurs at point J (the point of lowest average cost), with a product quantity of OV, and that if the selling price of the good is OQ then point J will be the point of actual production. The figure also shows that if the selling price rises above OQ, then production can be *more profitably* expanded first to point K (price OR, quantity OY) and then to point L (price OS, quantity OZ). To a certain extent, therefore, the entrepreneur's decision regarding the quantity of production, and hence the quantity of production factors required, is determined by the *prevailing* market selling price for an established type of good, and by the *expected* price for a new type of good. The point of production is clearly more easily assessed for an established type of good than for a new good, since the price is less of an unknown quantity. Having decided the point of production by reference to the prevailing or expected price, and having established the total quantity of production factors required, the entrepreneur must then decide the quantities of the individual factors which must be brought together in combination. In actual practice, of course, the complex decisions are made interconnectedly.

The decisions of the entrepreneur regarding the quantities of the individual factors which he hires are influenced by the relative prices of the different factors and their degree of substitutability for one another. In general, cheaper factors will be substituted for more expensive factors, provided—assuming a level of output has been selected—the total quantity of product does not diminish. The substitution of one factor for another will, in theory, continue until no further reduction in cost is possible for a given quantity of product. At such a point, by implication, the production of product per factor is in direct relationship with the factor cost as a proportion of total cost; thus, if the contributory factor proportions to total product are land 20%, labour 15%, capital 50%, and enterprise 15%, then the factor proportions of total cost are also land 20%, labour 15%, capital 50% and enterprise 15%. Under these conditions, it would not matter if an additional unit of factor investment were made in one factor rather than in another, for the returns in proportion to cost are equal for all factors. There are, however, practical limitations to the process of cost-minimising through factor substitution. The first limitation is imposed by the necessity to have, say, at least *some* land and *some* labour. On a farm, for example, a given output may be gained by employing either more land and less labour or more labour and less land, but at each end of the scale *some* land and *some* labour are required. Factors are therefore not perfectly substitutable for one another. Indeed, because of the need to have at least *some* quantity of a factor, there is, towards each end of the scale of possible combinations or any two factors, a diminishing rate of substitution. For example, it may be possible at the start, for a maintained quantity of output, to substitute one extra man for an acre of farmland, but the next time it may be worth sacrificing only a half-acre for one extra man, and the time after that perhaps only a quarter-acre for one extra man. Since it is always the *additional* factor units which are concerned in this process, the tendency is to a **diminishing marginal rate of factor substitution**. The second limitation is imposed by the fact that the production factors are not infinitely divisible; they are, indeed, 'lumpy' in character, and cannot always be employed in the exact proportions which theoretical considerations demand. An entrepreneur could not easily employ, for instance, a combination of factors consisting of one-quarter of a coal mine, ninety-one and seven-eighths workers, five and one-half units of machinery, and two-thirds of a delivery truck, even though in theory that combination might be the most profitable for a chosen level of output. It is, however, worth remembering that production is a *process*, and takes place over a certain amount of time, thus making it possible for an entrepreneur to achieve a position closer to the ideal combination than might at first sight seem likely; the entrepreneur can do this by employing his factors for different amounts of time—though obviously within limits.

2   Bearing the uncertainty of the business. Uncertainty arises because the entrepreneur operates in the real (imperfect) world, and cannot know in advance the results of his decisions. Many things can happen to upset the expected outcome: demand can change, for any of the reasons noted in section 4F; the availability of factors can change; government taxation policies can alter; international political and economic events can cause either supply or demand conditions to change; and so on. Some of the uncertainties are coverable by insurance (for example, the risks of fire, flood and theft), but others are not coverable in any way, and must be borne by the entrepreneur.

Now that the functions of the entrepreneur have been identified, it should be possible for us to identify the entrepreneur himself. However, that is not such an easy task. In the case of the one-man business, the answer to the question 'who is the entrepreneur?' is easy, but in the case of almost every other type of business organisation the answer is less easy, and sometimes it is impossible. For example, large companies are owned by hundreds of shareholders, but run by managers according to decisions taken by a board of directors—so who is the entrepreneur? The shareholders take the financial risk—if their company does well they take their share of the profit (dividend), but if it does ill they lose their money; the managers take care of the organisation of production, the hiring of the factors and the marketing of the product; and the directors take the decisions regarding the type and quantity of goods to be produced, as well as bearing some of the uncertainty of the enterprise. The functions of the entrepreneur are, in fact, divided. Many economists assert that the key test of entrepreneurial identity is 'who bears the financial uncertainty?', but this is probably too limited a test. Even in a large company, the salaried managers (who may not bear the final financial risk) still have a high degree of indirect responsibility for the outcome of the enterprise, and, of even greater—but unassignable—importance, they also have their business reputations (and therefore future livelihood) at stake. But, more than that even, growing numbers of enterprises are being established and operated by governments—and who takes the risk of failure then? The taxpayers, of course. Under these conditions, the test 'who bears the financial uncertainty?' has become so widely passed that it would seem that the test is no longer an entirely valid one. It is difficult to replace it satisfactorily, but perhaps 'whose business reputation is at stake?' would be a more appropriate test, especially in its concentration of attention on the 'activity' aspect of enterprise.

Under perfect economic conditions the supply of entrepreneurs is related to the expectation of profits. Expectations of increasing profits in an industry attract more entrepreneurs to that industry, while fears of falling profits drive some entrepreneurs out of the industry. If we regard profit as the equilibrium price of enterprise, i.e., the price which is just sufficient to draw forth the exact quantity of supply to satisfy the demand, then—under perfect conditions—the supply of entrepreneurs conforms to the ordinary law of supply. However, economic conditions are not perfect: profit is determined by factors other than the equilibrium factor supply mechanism, and the supply of entrepreneurs is determined by factors other than profit alone. Apart from the expectation of profit, which is clearly an important factor, we should also note the attractive status of an employer or manager, the psychological desire for power, the attraction of economic independence (not a realisable attraction, of course, but often voiced—'being one's own boss'), the pull of family ties and other environmental factors (e.g., So and So & *Son*), the instinct to gamble, the drive to personal fame, the ambition to found a commercial empire, and the existence of a sense of social obligation. In conclusion, it is worth noting that an inefficient entrepreneur may well put up with low profits for the sake of the benefits conferred by one of the other factors; on the other hand, an economically efficient entrepreneur will be guided primarily by profit.

Section 7
The costs of production

7A The nature of production costs

The goods and services produced to yield satisfaction to consumers are not free. They have a cost of production. The cost may be analysed either on the basis of whatever monetary inducements are needed to cause the *individual* production factors—land, labour, capital and enterprise—to enter into supply, or on the basis of the total monetary inducement to the factors *collectively*. The money paid to the factors individually as an inducement to enter production is, of course, income to those factors, and we shall accordingly defer analysis of individual factor costs until we deal with income as a topic. For the moment, we shall concern ourselves solely with factor costs in combination. The term *costs of production* refers, therefore, to factor costs in combination, and not to factor costs individually.

The ultimate drive to production comes, as we have already noted, from the existence of unsatisfied demand, but the initial motive is the expectation of at least normal profit on the part of entrepreneurs. An entrepreneur, in fact, seeks to organise the 'passive' factors (land, labour and capital) into a productive channel at a level yielding maximum profit. Such profit can be gained only if costs of production (i.e., factor costs in combination) are kept as low as possible, and—as we have noted—such low costs are possible only through the substitution of cheaper for dearer factors where feasible. It is worth remembering here that there is a diminishing marginal rate of factor substitution (section 6M), but that the possibilities of substitution increase as the supply term extends (section 5B). In the short term, therefore, we should regard the existence of some production factors as fixed and incapable of either substitution of variation in quantity, while other factors may be more readily variable in quantity. In the long term, on the other hand, the increasing elasticity of factor supply means that we need not regard any factor as either fixed in quantity or incapable of substitution. Production costs may, therefore, be analysed for two periods: first, the short term, when there are both fixed and variable quantities of factors in the total factor combination, and, second, the long term, when all factors are variable in quantity. However, before we make an analysis of short term and long term costs, let us review the various types of cost we have so far come across throughout the book.

7B Types of production cost

So far we have mentioned:

opportunity cost
real cost
nominal cost
factor cost
total cost
fixed cost
variable cost
average cost
marginal cost

And we can now add:

average fixed cost
average variable cost

It will be useful revision to run briefly through the definitions:

1 Opportunity cost. This represents the production or consumption of a less-desired and foregone alternative. If, for example, for a given set of production factors, the choice of production lies between a school and a hospital, and the school is chosen, then the opportunity cost of the school is the hospital, since that is the alternative foregone. In practice, the choice is usually between one thing and a nearly infinite number of possible alternatives, any one of which could be called the opportunity cost of the thing chosen. And similarly with consumption: the opportunity cost of, say, a visit to a theatre is one of the great variety of things which could have been consumed instead.

2 Real cost. This is the cost of an item expressed in goods and services. It could mean the same as opportunity cost, or it could mean the quantity of real production factors actually employed in the production of the preferred goods and services (and not the alternative forgone.) In the latter sense, real cost is so much land, so much labour, etc. For example, the real cost of a school may (in the first sense) be a hospital, or it may (in the second sense) be so much land, so much labour, so much capital and so much enterprise.

3 Nominal cost. This is the cost expressed in money terms; for example, say, land worth £500, labour worth £2000, capital worth £10 000 and enterprise worth £100 complete a total cost of £12 600.

4 Factor cost. This means the cost of an individual factor. It is usually expressed nominally, but it may at times be expressed in real terms. You could say, for example, that the cost of land for a particular project is either £500 (nominal cost) or 10 acres (real cost). Usage, in fact, often distinguishes between the two meanings by referring to the real factor cost as the cost *in*, say, land.

5   Total cost. This is the sum cost of all factors employed in the production of a particular item; it is expressed nominally. It includes *all* the expenditure on land, labour and capital, but only the *normal* profit element of expenditure on enterprise. If you are not sure what is meant by normal profit, read section 5A again; and bear in mind that excess profit is a pure surplus, and that it does not form any part of total production costs.

6   Fixed cost. This is the cost incurred by the employment of fixed production factors in the short term (remember: in the long term, no production factors are fixed). Fixed cost usually refers to the cost of such production factors as machines, a factory, and transport equipment (which are commonly and collectively called 'plant'), as well as the necessary cost of such items as rent, rates, interest on borrowed money, and salaries of essential staff. Generally, production cannot commence until fixed costs have been contracted, and such fixed costs then remain constant over a range of output. There is a close similarity between fixed cost and what is called **supplementary cost**; fixed cost is the cost incurred in starting a business, even though production may be zero, whereas supplementary cost is the cost incurred in maintaining a business, even though production ceases. The similarity is obvious—both are essential minimum costs under conditions of zero production; the difference is slight—fixed costs are slightly higher because of the different definition of 'essential staff'. If production is just starting, the 'essential staff' is going to be at least more than a couple of night-watchmen.

7   Variable cost. This is the cost incurred by the employment of variable production factors. In the long term, all production factors are variable; so in the long term all production costs are variable costs. In the short term, however, only some production factors are variable, chiefly raw materials, power supplies and general labour. The *quantity* of variable factors employed depends directly upon the quantity of real production; so also, therefore, does the *cost* of the variable factors. If production expands, variable costs rise, and if production contracts, variable costs fall; and if production is zero, variable costs are nil. There is a close similarity between variable cost and what is called **prime cost**; variable cost is the cost incurred by actual output, whereas prime cost is the cost incurred in keeping a plant working. The similarity is, again, obvious—both are essential additional costs, under conditions of more than zero production; the difference is, again, slight—prime costs are slightly higher because they include, in addition to variable cost, that part of fixed cost which might be avoided by closing down the plant under the care of a couple of night-watchmen. For all practical purposes, however, we may regard prime cost as synonymous with variable cost, just as we may regard supplementary cost as synonymous with fixed cost. Variable cost and fixed cost together make up total cost.

8   Average cost. This is the nominal cost per unit of real product. It may be obtained by dividing total cost by the number of units of real product.

The point of lowest average cost is also the point of optimum—or most efficient—production, but, as we have seen, it is not necessarily the point of maximum profit (see section 5A).

9 Marginal cost. This is the cost of producing either the last or the next unit in a series. It can only be estimated, since the only *known* cost is that for actual production (see section 2C). Because maginal cost is concerned with the actual volume of production (at the margin) it is clearly part of the variable cost structure.

10 Average fixed cost (often called oncost). This is the fixed portion of total cost divided by the number of units of real product. For example, if the fixed portion of total cost is £500 (in the short term, of course) and the number of units of real product is 10, then average fixed cost is £50. If output in the short term expands to, say, 20 units, while fixed costs remain constant (as, by definition, they do in the short term), then average fixed cost declines to £25. In fact, as output expands throughout the short term, average fixed costs *invariably* diminish. In the long term, on the other hand, fixed costs may rise (or fall); but in the short term which follows that rise (or fall), the rule about diminishing average fixed costs is still observed.

11 Average variable cost. This is the variable portion of total cost divided by the number of units of real product. For example, if variable cost for an output of 100 units of product is £1000, then average variable cost is £10. If, as output rises to 200 units, variable cost rises to only £1800, then average variable cost declines to £9. And if, further, output rises to 300 units while variable cost rises to £3300, then average variable cost rises to £11. You can see from these figures that variable cost—as an element of total cost—invariably rises as output expands, but that *average* variable cost may fall *or* rise from its initial level.

7C Production costs in the short term

The short term is that period during which some, *but not all*, production factors may be varied in quantity. We therefore have some fixed factors, with fixed costs, and some variable factors, with variable costs; a production situation, in fact, involving the application of different quantities of variable factors to a given quantity of fixed factors. In such a situation there is an initial tendency for output—or product—to increase at a faster rate than the increase in the application of the variable factors. For example, a factory (fixed factor) may produce 100 units of product if 10 men (variable factor) work in it, but it may raise production to 300 units if 20 men work in it; in other words, output has trebled while application of the variable factor has only doubled. The reason for this over-proportionate increase in output is that a great deal of fixed capital is capable of efficient operation only if a minimum number of variable workers (and power and raw materials) are also employed; any quantity of variable factors less than the minimum necessary for efficient use of the fixed factors inevitably causes inefficiency, and thereby permits increasing efficiency and relatively greater output as the quantity of variable factors is raised.

Note carefully, in the above figures, that it is the addition of 10 men that produces the greater additional output; in other words, it is the *marginal* increase in the quantity of variable factors employed that causes the relatively greater *marginal* product. So long as the marginal product (i.e., the additional output) is relatively greater than the marginal increase in the quantity of variable factors employed (i.e., the additional men, power, etc.), production is said to be characterised by **increasing returns**.

Looked at from the cost (rather than the product) standpoint, the figures reveal that it costs (in real terms):

a factory and 10 men to produce 100 units, and
a factory and 20 men to produce 300 units.

Clearly, the cost per unit of output is lower in the second case than in the first. If we now express the figures in nominal terms (£s), we can see that the costs are, say:

fixed cost (factory)	variable cost (workers, etc)	total cost	output (units)	average fixed cost	average variable cost	average cost
6000	300	6300	100	60	3	63
6000	600	6600	300	20	2	22

Falling average fixed costs (an invariable rule in the short term) and falling average variable costs (because of the operation of increasing returns) combine to produce falling average costs.

Eventually, as the variable factors combine with the fixed factors to achieve optimum efficiency, a point is reached in the process of production where marginal increases in the quantity of variable factors employed yield exactly proportional increases in the marginal product. At this stage, production is said to be characterised by **constant returns**. For example, using the above figures as a base, an additional 10 men yielding an additional product of 200 units represents a situation no different from that of the preceding stage. The duration of the phase of constant returns depends upon the nature of the fixed and variable factors employed in the production process. If the fixed factor is a large number of machines capable of operation by individual units of variable factors, then marginal product is likely to be more or less constant over a substantial range of output, since additional variable factor units can be used to operate previously idle machines. But if the fixed factor is a large indivisible unit, requiring a certain quantity only of variable factors for operation at optimum efficiency, then marginal product will tend to rise rapidly at first and then fall with equal rapidity after the quantity of variable factors required for optimum efficiency has been obtained. The additional variable factors may either get in each other's way or be forced to stand idle, thus cutting average variable product and raising average variable costs. For example, if a train is to run between two points, one driver is sufficient; the marginal product of a second driver is virtually zero, the average variable product is halved and the average variable cost is doubled.

Sooner or later, therefore, the phase of constant returns comes to an end, and the production process becomes characterised by **diminishing returns**. Using the figures already noted as a base, the onset of diminishing returns would be shown by the similar addition of 10 men (marginal variable factors) and a less than proportionate increase in output by, say, 150 units (marginal product). Under these conditions, total product continues to increase, but at a diminishing rate, since each successive addition is smaller than the preceding one, despite the fact that equal quantities of additional variable factors are being applied successively to the fixed factors. Marginal product, therefore, forms a diminishing proportion of marginal variable factor input.

Average cost continues to fall during the phase of constant returns, partly because average fixed cost (oncost) falls anyway as total product increases, and partly because average variable cost also falls, as shown by lines 2 and 3 in table 7.1. Even after average variable cost has begun to rise during the phase of diminishing returns, average cost itself continues to fall so long as any increase in average variable cost is more than offset by the continuing fall in average fixed cost. As output increases, however, there is a declining rate of diminution of average fixed cost, for purely arithmetic reasons.

fixed cost	variable cost	total cost	output (units)	average fixed cost	average variable cost	average cost
6000	300	6300	100	60	3	63
6000	600	6600	300	20	2	22
6000	900	6900	500	12	1·8	13·8
6000	1200	7200	650	9·2	1·85	11·05
6000	1500	7500	750	8	2	10
6000	1800	7800	800	7·5	2·25	9·75
6000	2100	8100	810	7·4	2·6	10
6000	2400	8400	810	7·4	2·97	10·37

TABLE 7.1 Schedule to illustrate cost composition (£) for a producer.

Eventually, therefore, a point is reached where the diminution of average fixed cost fails to offset the rising average variable cost, and average cost itself accordingly begins to rise too. In table 7.1 average cost falls to its lowest point t £9·75 for an output of 800 units, but thereafter it rises, even though average variable cost started to rise after an output of only 500 units.

The last line in table 7.1 illustrates a position of **zero returns**; despite the same marginal addition to variable cost, total output does not increase at all—the additional input, in other words, has produced no output. In such a case, average fixed cost remains constant (since the same output is divided into the same fixed cost), but average variable cost continues to rise (since the same output is divided into an increased total variable cost), thus pushing up the average cost. Obviously, production would cease before the stage of zero returns was reached.

Where, then, is the exact point of production? It is, indeed, impossible to say on the basis of the analysis presented so far, simply because production is not governed solely by cost considerations. Levels of production are, in fact, determined chiefly by the ambitions of entrepreneurs to maximise profits; and profits are a function of production costs *and* market selling prices. As a rule, profits are maximised when an entrepreneur establishes a production level at a point where marginal revenue equals marginal cost; at this point an entrepreneur derives as much revenue from the sale of an additional good as he expends in making it. At any production level before the point where marginal revenue equals marginal cost, an entrepreneur is not maximising profits, since the additional goods are costing less to make than they would earn by sale; and at any level beyond the point where marginal revenue equals marginal cost, an entrepreneur spends more on making additional goods than he receives by selling them, and so he is again not maximising his profits. The only point of production for maximum profit is where marginal revenue equals marginal cost. The answer to the question at the start of this paragraph, therefore, is that the exact point of production occurs wherever *marginal revenue (price) equals marginal cost*. There are three possible places for this:

1   At a point where marginal cost equals average cost. You will remember from section 5A that this point (see figure 7.1) is also the point of optimum production, where average cost is at its lowest. An entrepreneur, operating under this condition, has only one level of output, since both a smaller output and a larger output would raise average cost above the prevailing price level, rendering the output unsaleable.

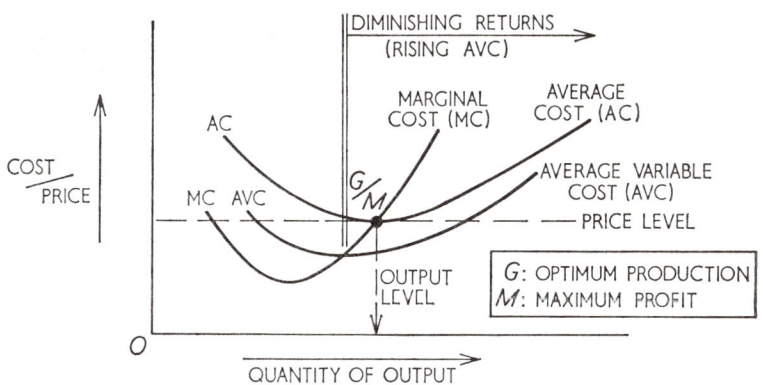

FIG 7.1   Output level when marginal cost/price equals average cost.

2   At a point where marginal cost exceeds average cost. Unlike the first position, where revenue only just covers lowest average cost, thus yielding only a normal profit to the entrepreneur, the second position is capable of yielding excess profit to the entrepreneur. Excess profit is gained accord-

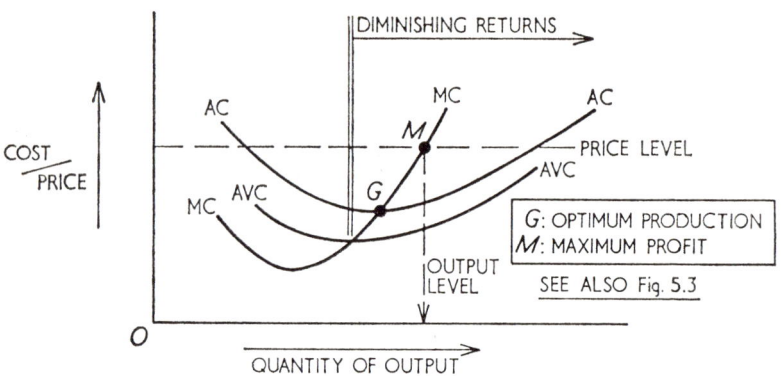

FIG 7.2 Output level when marginal cost/price exceeds average cost.

ing to the amount by which revenue (price) exceeds the average cost line at the maximum-profit output level (see figure 7.2). Don't forget that average cost includes normal profit, and that any revenue in excess of average cost is classified as excess profit.

3 At a point where marginal cost is lower than average cost. Under this condition, revenue (price) is lower than average cost. New firms will clearly be discouraged from entering into production, but established firms—faced by the fall in prices—may maintain production, *so long as they at least cover their variable costs.* They will do this, of course, for only a very short time, and then only in the hope of a future price rise. Pessimistic firms will cease production as soon as the price level falls below their average cost line, since they will be unwilling to meet all (fixed and variable) commitments; optimistic firms, however, will defer payment of the fixed factors and concentrate instead on paying the variable factors—

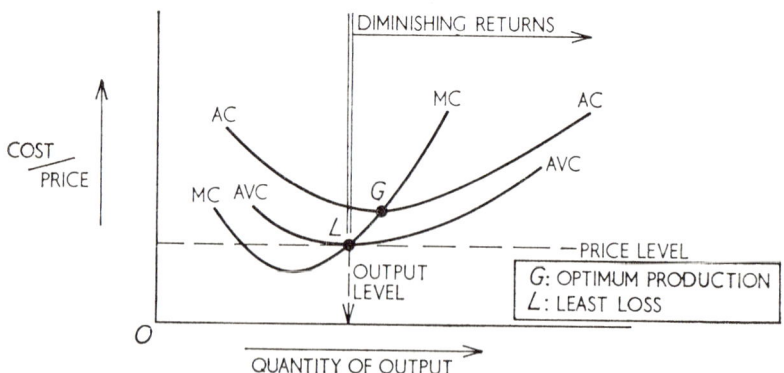

FIG 7.3 Output level when marginal cost/price is below average cost.

without which there can be no production (because there will be no workers, no power, no raw materials, etc.). The lowest possible output level for even an optimistic firm is at the point of lowest average variable cost; below this point, revenue fails to cover even variable costs, and the firm must cease production. The point of lowest average variable cost is determined by its intersection with the marginal cost line; remember— marginal cost represents additions to variable cost, and once the additions become larger than the average then the average itself begins to rise too. In the very short term, therefore, production can contract down the marginal cost curve as far as its intersection with the average variable cost curve—but no further. Figure 7.3 illustrates such a minimum production level.

You will notice from an examination of figures 7.1–3 that the minimum output level coincides with the onset of diminishing returns, and that at that level an entrepeneur gains little or no profit (since his average costs are not covered). Any output level greater than the minimum, including all levels of profitable production, is therefore achieved under conditions of diminishing returns. This inescapable—and perhaps surprising—conclusion is brought about, of course, by the downward pull exerted on average cost by the continuing diminution of oncost even after marginal cost and, subsequently, average variable cost have begun to rise.

7D Production costs in the long term

The long term is that period during which *all* production factors may be varied in quantity. All costs are therefore variable costs. In such a situation one would expect that if the inputs of all production factors were doubled then so also would the output of units of product. That may happen, but it is by no means a universal truth. In fact, as a firm increases the input of all factors it is likely that its output will rise initially at a faster rate, and then eventually at a slower rate—the two phases possibly being separated by another phase wherein both input and output increase at an equal rate.

Such varying returns to additional input quantities (of all factors) in the long term are called increasing, constant and decreasing **returns to scale**. They should be carefully distinguished from increasing, constant and diminishing **returns**, which apply in the short term to situations where different quantities of variable factors are combined with a given quantity of fixed factors. Since those factors which are variable in the short term are also variable in the long term, the chief difference between the two notations lies in the variability in the long term of those factors which are fixed in the short term; in other words, the plant. The word *scale* relates therefore to plant size.

Increasing returns to scale, in which output rises at a faster rate than total input, can be attributed to two factors: first, the indivisibility of certain factors, and second, specialisation. The indivisibility of factors means that factors cannot be divided into smaller units without either partial loss of efficiency or complete loss of usefulness. An engine, for example, cannot be divided into two without becoming useless; admittedly, small engines can be made instead, but a one horse-power engine costs a lot more than 1% of a 100 horse-power engine to make (because of the more intricate engineering required). Larger sizes of individual factors and larger quantities of multiple factors are, indeed, often not only relatively less costly but also absolutely more efficient than small sizes and small quantities. Larger quantities of labour, for example, permit the benefits of greater productivity which accompany the division of labour (see section 6E). As productivity increases, then, by definition, so do returns. Increasing returns to scale are therefore possible when (a) larger units of indivisible factors, and (b) larger quantities of divisible labour are employed.

Constant returns to scale, in which output rises at the same rate as total input, occur as a firm produces under conditions where it has already acquired the most suitable types of capital equipment available and where it is already gaining the complete benefits of division of labour. Under these conditions, a doubling of the inputs (i.e., all factors, including capital equipment) causes a doubling of output. It is as if there is *one* fully-working production unit, and then *two*.

Decreasing returns to scale, in which output rises at a slower rate than total input, are caused chiefly by the increased problems of larger-scale management. Beyond a certain scale of production, the red tape of decision-making, the lack of co-ordination of general business policy, and the difficulties of correlating production lines all help to create a situation in which returns to scale may start to decrease.

It should be stressed that, like other economic principles or laws, the principle of varying returns to scale is valid only if other things remain equal. This means, for one thing, that production techniques should remain constant. However, that immediately raises a problem: production techniques in practice may remain constant over the short term (or for a particular scale of production), thus giving validity to the practical application of the concept of variable returns in the short term, but in the long term (or for a variety of different scales of production) they are likely to change, and the change may deny practical application of the concept of variable returns to scale in the long term. Nevertheless, as a theoretical concept—with perhaps occasional practical validity whenever techniques remain constant—it is of value in indicating a tendency. Another problem in practice is that additional units of factor input may be of an inferior quality to those already employed, there being a natural tendency to employ the superior factors first. If (in proportion to their diminishing inherent abilities) the additional poorer factors cost less, there is no problem. However, especially in the case of labour, additional units usually cost the same as previous units, even though the additional units may be (and often are) of inferior quality; and that clearly produces a more rapid onset of decreasing returns to scale than would normally be the case with factors of uniform quality.

Production costs in nominal terms are impossible to assess in the future, because of changing factor prices and money values. A long term cost curve, therefore, does not show what future costs are *expected* to be; instead, it shows what present costs *are* at a variety of different possible scales of production. A long term cost schedule, therefore, relates paradoxically **to** one moment of time only—and not to a long term extension into the future. In that sense, it is like a single demand schedule or a single supply schedule; it illustrates a variety of alternative possibilities, only one of which can be chosen at a time. Thus, a long term cost schedule shows the variety of cheapest production possibilities throughout a range of alternative scales of production. At each scale level, the cheapest production possibilities are determined according to short term cost analysis (note: the long term is composed of a series of short terms). Figure 7.4 shows a series of short term average cost curves; the spacing of the curves depends upon the divisibility of the factor units—so that inset (a) illustrates closely spaced curves arising from a high degree of factor divisibility, which permits a number of different, but closely spaced, scales of operation to exist, and inset (b) shows widely spaced curves based on a low degree of factor divisibility, the 'lumpiness' of the factors creating a wide separation of the alternative production scales.

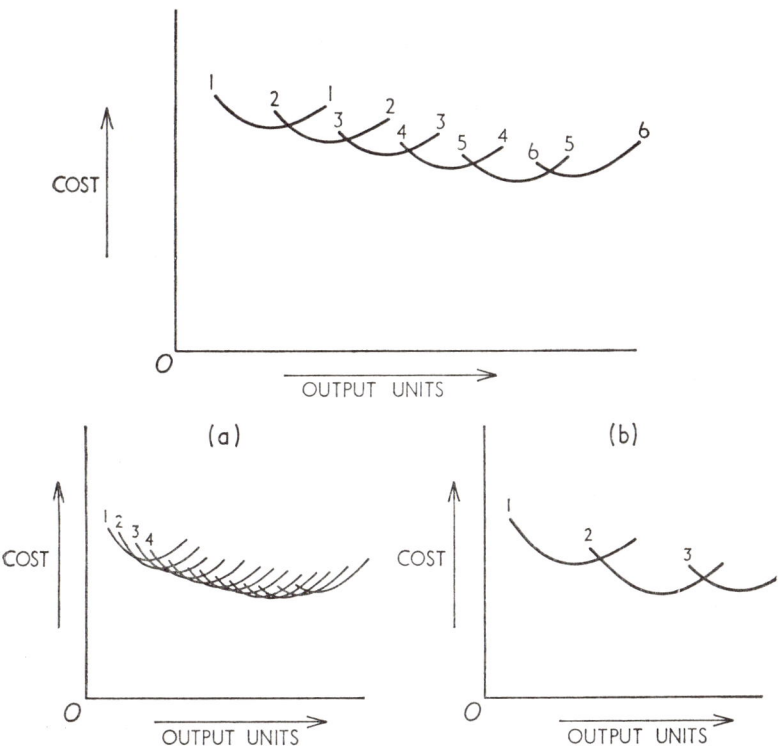

FIG 7.4 A series of short-term average cost curves.

Long term average cost, for each scale of production, is shown by those parts of the short term average cost curves between each set of intersections, as illustrated in figure 7.5. In the case of closely spaced alternative scales of production (inset (a) of figure 7.2), the intersections occur frequently, and the enveloping long term average cost line is accordingly almost smooth; in the case of widely spaced alternatives, however, the long term line is highly indented.

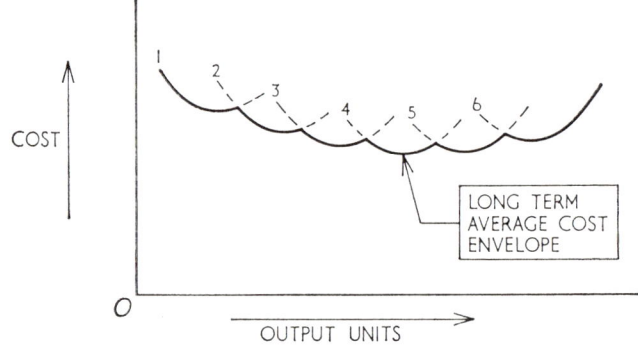

FIG 7.5   The relationship between a series of short-term average cost curves and a long-term average cost curve.

The long term average cost curve is sometimes called the **planning curve,** since it illustrates the cost data for alternative scales of production and is therefore useful to a firm when it is considering at what level of output to produce. A new firm is able to assess the lowest cost and the necessary quantity of its forthcoming output, and an established firm is able to decide if any changes of scale are likely to prove more profitable than the existing scale. Having decided at what scale to produce, a firm is then bound by short term cost considerations; and its actual production at that scale is governed by the behaviour of marginal cost in relation to the particular short term average cost curve relevant to the chosen scale of output.

Our analysis so far has proceeded on the basis of a *single* firm determining its cost position while other things remain equal. However, we should note that if *all* firms simultaneously expand their output in the expectation of achieving lowest average cost positions, then inevitably there will be an accompanying rise in the demand for employable production factors. In practice, the short term supply of production factors is fairly inelastic; and a positive shift in demand along a fairly inelastic supply curve will, as you will appreciate, produce quite a large rise in price. The price which rises is that of the employable production factors, and such a rise is bound to offset (or negate) the expected lower average costs caused by those economies in production which accrue from extensions of scale throughout the zone of increasing returns to scale. Thus, while a *single* firm can legitimately plan its output level to conform to a position of lowest average cost, *all* firms cannot. The totality of change would cause incalculable changes in factor prices; the only certainty being that prices would rise—provided techniques of production remained constant. But—if we start taking that into account too—we are then introducing too many variables for satisfactory analysis at this stage.

The scale of production

8A Determinants of the scale of production

The trouble with long term average cost curves in general is that they show the stages of increasing and decreasing returns to scale only in relation to unspecified output units. They do not indicate whether the units are measured in tens or in thousands; in other words, they do not indicate whether the *range* of scales is for a series of fairly small or fairly large outputs. What factors, then, determine the range of scales? We may list them as follows:

1   The size of the market. This was noted in section 6E as a limit to the division of labour; it is equally a limit to large scale production. There is clearly no point in making goods on a large scale unless the goods can also be sold on a large scale. Consequently, those factories and firms which either produce goods to satisfy small-scale local needs or produce goods which are restricted by their perishability to local markets are forced into a small scale of production, whereas those factories and firms either producing for a wide market or producing durable goods can operate on a larger scale. You should note, however, that a large *local* market can support a large scale of production; a bakery in London, for example, can operate on a larger scale than a bakery in a small village. The size of the market is also affected by the type of product; for instance, a factory producing imperishable glass eyes for the whole nation is likely to be smaller than one producing highly perishable daily newspapers for a large town.

2   The ease of obtaining the factors of production. The supply of all factors is fixed in the market term, but becomes more and more variable as the term extends. However, the different factors have different rates of increase of variability. It is difficult to be exact in this matter, because of the internal diversity of the factors, but generally land is less variable in supply than either labour or capital. Accordingly, the primary industries (such as mining), which are direct users of land, tend to find it difficult to escape from the operation of the law of diminishing returns, and the production units (not necessarily the firms themselves; but the actual units—the mines, the farms and so on) therefore tend to operate on a fairly small scale. Secondary and tertiary industries, on the other hand, rely more on labour and capital than they do on land, and—because of the greater variability in supply of labour and capital—can therefore escape more readily from the short term operation of the law of diminishing returns. Further, the even greater long-term variability in the supply of labour and capital permits very wide differences indeed in the scale of operations of

secondary and tertiary productive units. Secondary production may range, for example, from the motor engineering of General Motors to that of the Morgan Company; and tertiary production from the large scale of, say, Pickford's to the small scale of the local one-truck haulier. Because of the greater variability in the supply of the factors important to secondary and tertiary industries, such industries are better able than primary ones to adapt their scale to meet different sizes of market; in other words, whereas primary production has to be carried on within a certain range of scales if it is to be at all economic, secondary and tertiary production can more easily be large or small in scale as the market warrants.

3   The ambition and skill of the entrepreneur. Firms may fail to expand their scale to the point of lowest long term average cost simply because the entrepreneur lacks either the ambition or the skill necessary. The reason may be that the entrepreneur is satisfied with a small scale of production, since it enables him to supervise everything personally; it may also be that the entrepreneur is motivated by either pride of ownership or the desire for economic 'independence' rather than the desire for maximum profits. Whatever the actual reason, many entrepreneurs remain in a small scale of operation even though they could benefit economically by extending that scale.

The long term average costs of a firm or factory may be affected by what are called external and internal factors. External factors are those which apply to a whole industry, irrespective of the size of the firms or factories in the industry; they include such things as individual factor costs and the development of subsidiary trades. For example, if the price of labour or power rises, then *all* firms within the industry, regardless of size, will have to pay more for their supplies of those factors (or contract their demand, and attempt to maintain the same output through increased efficiency). The development of subsidiary trades, such as secure cash-transfer or independent research, means that *all* firms, regardless of size, can share in the benefits. Internal factors are those which exist within the firm or factory alone; they are related directly to the scale of production. Any advantages of diminishing average cost which accrue to a firm or factory because of its increasing size of operation are called **economies of scale**; equally, any disadvantages resulting from rising average cost caused by the increasing size of operation of a firm or factory are called **diseconomies of scale**.

What factors, then, cause economies and diseconomies of scale to develop, with their collateral increasing and decreasing returns to scale?

8B The economies of scale

You should be aware at the outset of the distinction between the firm (the unit of control and ownership) and the factory (the unit of production). You should also be aware of the fact that a large firm (i.e., large in relation to others in its industry) may operate either one or more large factories or a number of small ones, and that a small firm may operate only one or more small factories.

For example, Cadbury's is a large firm, operating only one large factory, while British Leyland Motors is a large firm operating several large factories; on the other hand, Woolworth's is a large firm operating many small 'factories'. If you were given an example of a small firm, operating just one or two small factories, the chances are that you would not have heard of it; so select a local example yourself.

Economies of scale accrue to either a firm or a factory as its size increases. However, it is important to note that a large firm will not extend its factory size indefinitely; if a single factory starts to reach the point of diminishing returns in its output, then the *firm* is likely to open another *factory*. In other words, the firm's scale of production may change, as well as the individual factory's.

The chief economies which accrue from extended scale are:

1 Technical economies. These occur mostly within the factory unit, and comprise:

(a) Increased possibilities for the division of labour.

(b) The use of assembly belt techniques.

(c) The use of specialised machinery, which may either be too expensive for a small firm to buy or require too great a minimum use for a small firm to be able to employ it economically. For example, a computer is beyond the reach of most small firms, unless either they band together into some sort of co-operative undertaking or a computer firm establishes a time-sharing function as an external economy.

(d) The possibility of internal research facilities, whereby a large firm can both more readily improve its existing production techniques and also evolve better products for the market.

(e) The development of by-product industries to make economic use of what would—on a small scale—be waste materials.

(f) The full use of machines of different capacities. Let us assume that a productive process requires the use for separate purposes of four different machines, in order W, X, Y and Z, and that their respective capacities are 10, 20, 30 and 40 units of output per hour. If only one machine of each type is employed, then maximum output per hour from all machines can be only 10 units, since that is the capacity of the slowest machine (W). Two W machines will raise maximum capacity to 20 units per hour, since machine X (but not machines Y and Z) will also be working to capacity. Three W machines will produce too much for machine X to handle, and maximum output will remain at 20 units per hour, since machine X is now the bottleneck. In order to get each of the four machines operating at its own maximum capacity it is necessary to find the lowest common multiple of the different capacities; in this case, 120 units per hour. The production of 120 units per hour involves the use of 12 W machines, 6 X machines, 4 Y machines and 3 Z machines; and these are the *mini-*

mum quantities necessary to ensure full use of each machine. Any production in excess of 120 units per hour must be in multiples of 120 (i.e., 120, 240, 360, 480, etc.), and the quantities of the different machines must also be multiplied by an exactly equivalent number, otherwise bottlenecks will recur. Obviously, the greater the scale of production, the easier it becomes to maximise use of machines of different capacities.

2   Commercial economies. These occur mostly within the unit of the firm rather than in the individual factory, and comprise:

(a) The ability to buy cheaply in bulk. Discounts may be allowed for quantity; and it may be worth employing specialised buying staff. It is a major economy in practice.

(b) The ability to employ bulk transport modes for both finished products and raw materials. Large oil users, for example, can afford (i.e., find it more profitable) to charter (or own) giant supertankers, which carry oil at roughly half the cost per ton-mile of the ordinary 70 000–80 000-ton tankers.

(c) The ability to employ specialised selling staff and use market research techniques. If a firm is large, the costs of selling, though high, can be spread over a very great volume of output—and the average selling cost per unit of output may therefore fall to insignificance. The same considerations apply to the use of large-scale advertising, which—if it successfully causes a positive shift in demand—induces greater output and thereby further cuts selling costs per unit of output.

(d) The ready ability of a large firm to sell its product in many different markets, thus reducing the risk of high demand elasticity in any single market.

(e) The ability of a large firm to attract high-grade and more productive labour, by means of the reputation it has and the fringe benefits it offers (such as a training scheme, canteen, sports club and pension fund). A large firm can also easily attract able and ambitious management personnel, the best of which may be under-utilised in a small firm.

3   Financial economies. These also accrue to the firm rather than the factory, and comprise:

(a) The great ease with which a large firm of established reputation may borrow money from banks.

(b) The great attraction which a large firm has to investors. It is quite possible that a large firm may find that the public wants to lend it more money than it wants to borrow, as ICI found in 1965–66.

4   Structural economies. These accrue to either factories or firms, and are related to the existence of a large business organisation to which factories and firms belong. For example, given two factories or firms of equal size, one independent and the other belonging to a large parent organisation, it is the one belonging to a large organisation which gains the structural economies of scale. The economies may be either commercial or financial

in character; for example, the sharing of bulk-bought materials, the use of common marketing and advertising programmes, the benefits of skilled joint management, and the ease of borrowing money.

Generally, an ever-increasing scale of production has been characteristic of the industrialised countries of the world. The reasons are varied, but among them we should note:

1. Growing markets, which have permitted greater sales and thereby stimulated a search for the economies of increased production scales. The markets themselves have grown for a combination of reasons, not least being the rise of living standards through greater productivity, the development of widespread rapid-transport networks, and the use of mass media for advertising.

2. Technical progress, which has permitted larger (but more efficient) capital equipment. Thermal power stations, for example, are much larger now than formerly, but also disproportionately more efficient.

3. The growth of large companies, made possible through the shared ownership of a business concern by many different people. This was not legally possible until 1862, but after that time shared ownership allowed the development of many large firms. No single person could own, say, ICI or Unilever; but many people sharing ownership facilitate the development of such large firms.

4. Government action, which may directly create large scale enterprises either by nationalisation (National Coal Board, British Rail) or by parliamentary licence (BBC, BOAC), or which may indirectly stimulate the formation of large scale enterprises by ordinary commercial methods (e.g., the activities of the IRC—see section 3C).

As scale extends beyond a certain level of production, a time is eventually reached when diseconomies of scale start to become apparent. The chief diseconomy is almost certainly the incapacity of senior management to regulate and co-ordinate all the different aspects of a growing business. It is interesting to note that in 1966 Sir Paul Chambers (then of ICI) said in his inaugural address as president of the Confederation of British Industry that ICI—then Britain's largest company—had grown too big for efficient management. Inefficiency at managerial level is reflected in inefficiency at lower levels, too: supervision is less efficiently carried out, economic waste may occur, and workers begin to feel more and more like uncared-for cogs in a mindless machine. An added diseconomy stems from the minute division of labour which extended scale can cause: the psychological stress of monotonous repetition at work, and the corresponding decline in productivity. The Ford Motor Company in the USA some years ago tried an experiment in which it at first stopped the morning break for the workers; output initially rose, and then subsequently fell. Two breaks were then instituted, and again output at first rose and then later fell. One break was then tried, with similar results. Ford drew the conclusion that anything breaking the monotony led to improvements in output. Another diseconomy resulting from extended scale is the decline in output caused by deteriorating management-labour relations, with the ultimate reduction to zero output during a strike.

A larger scale of production may be sought not only for the sake of its economies, but also to achieve monopoly and to satisfy personal ambition. If monopoly and/or personal ambition are the chief motives to larger scale, there is a strong probability that the onset of diseconomies of scale (decreasing returns to scale) may be ignored by the entrepreneur. Large size alone, therefore, is not a guarantee of economic efficiency.

8C Small-scale production

Small firms, employing 10 persons or fewer each, collectively employ only about 5% of the labour force in Britain; yet they outnumber the large firms, employing 1000 or more persons each, by over 100 to one. The reasons for the existence of such a multitude of small firms are:

1 The limitations of the market. Dry-cleaners and motor repair garages, for example, are forced to operate on a fairly small scale by the general disinclination of their patrons to walk very far; so they must be scattered thickly over the ground, each serving a small local market. Even a firm producing a good for a national market may be forced to operate on a small scale if the total demand for the product is small, as may be the case with, say, the glass eye manufacturer noted in section 8A.

2 Difficulties of expansion. A small firm, wishing to extend its scale of production, may be restricted by the difficulty of attracting additional investment capital; it may not get loans easily from banks, and it may also have difficulty in mounting large scale advertising campaigns to make its product known in a wider market.

3 Unwillingness to expand. Many entrepreneurs, even though able to expand, may prefer to remain small, because their chief motives are either pride of ownership, care in craft-quality production or the desire for close involvement in (and supervision of) production. Other entrepreneurs, of course, merely lack the ability to expand their scale of production.

4 Personal initiative. Small firms provide a good opportunity for the expression of small-scale ambitions and the exercise of individual judgment. Their existence also provides a strong incentive to personal achievement.

5 Flexibility. Small firms are better able than large firms to cater for individual orders; their flexibility also allows them to adjust to changing demand conditions with relative ease (as shown by the firms in the 'rag trade').

As the number of large firms increases, governments become more mindful of the advantages accruing from the existence of a multitude of small firms; they see the advantages chiefly in the social 'buffer' nature of small firms in relation to unemployment. If small firms cease to reward the entrepreneur satisfactorily, the people thrown into unemployment are relatively few in number. It is not a disaster to society if, say, Fox's of Dunchester cease operation; but the effects of a failure by, say, ICI would be immense. Indeed, governments in some countries—notably Japan, West Germany and the USA—have established agencies to cater for the needs of small firms, chiefly in finance, management techniques and marketing (especially export marketing). The encouragment is given partly for economic reasons (flexibility, personal initiative and inventiveness) and partly for social reasons (buffer against *large-scale* unemployment, service to local markets); which is probably how it should be.

Section 9
Types of business organisation

9A The one-man business

The most common type of business organisation is that owned and controlled by one man, who is responsible for all the decisions, rewarded by all the profits, and liable for all the debts. Its strength lies in the freedom it allows for individual achievement; it is a vehicle for both personal pride in ownership and initiative in the development of new ideas. It permits great flexibility in supply, since decisions can be made by the entrepreneur without recourse to any other persons, and it encourages economic efficiency, since all profits accrue directly to the owner, who is the man in charge and on the spot. The chief disadvantage of the one-man business is the unlimited liability of the entrepreneur for all debts incurred by the business; bankruptcies, indeed, are common. Other disadvantages are the limited ability to acquire investment capital, the possible lack of equal ability in all parts of the business on the part of the entrepreneur, and the impermanence of the enterprise (not all entrepreneurs have sons with either the capacity or the willingness to carry on the enterprise; and not all entrepreneurs have sons).

The one-man business is common in farming, and in the retail and service trades.

9B The partnership

Individual entrepreneurs may wish to expand their scales of production, but lack either the necessary capital or the managerial ability. The oldest device for expansion is the partnership, which is defined as a combination of at least two and not more than 20 persons engaged in 'business with a view to profit'. Some or all of the partners may be *active*; on the other hand, some of the partners may be *sleeping*, in that they take no part in the running of the enterprise apart from providing money. The partnership of at least two active partners permits—and in practice is commonly characterised by—some division of labour; and this is one of its chief advantages. Other advantages are the possibility of acquiring more money or new skills by the admission of new partners, and the greater permanence of an organisation with overlapping ownerships. The main disadvantages are the possibility of clashes over policy decisions, the possibility of mutual mistrust among the partners, the possible restrictions to individual initiative, and the unlimited liability of the partners individually for the collective debts of the partnership. It *is* possible to concentrate the disadvantage of unlimited liability for debt on to one partner, provided he has management control, by establishing what is called a *limited partnership*. In such a case, the debt incurred by the partners is payable only by the General Partner (the one with control); the other partners are liable for any debts only to the extent of their original capital investment in the partnership—*their* liability for debt is said to be *limited*.

Partnerships are fairly common in retail and service trades, and exceedingly common in the professional field. Sometimes they are quite specific in name (e.g., Burrard & Gander); at other times they are somewhat vague (e.g., Weyburn & Co.).

9C The limited company

One-man businesses and partnerships were the chief types of business organisation until the 19th century. During that time, the factors which operated to keep business organisations small were:

1 Limited markets, caused by inefficient transport modes, lack of purchasing power on the part of the bulk of the population, and the scattered and rural distribution of the population.

2 Primitive technology, characterised by largely labour-intensive production, little use of machinery, and low productivity.

3 The difficulty of raising investment capital, caused by the disinclination of entrepreneurs to incur debts larger than their own personal wealth could redeem, because of the unlimited liability of the entrepreneurs for all debts incurred.

However, the process of industrial revolution, which began in the 18th century, gradually brought about a widening of markets through improved transport techniques, and a strengthening of markets through the concentration of a wage-earning sector of the population into the rapidly growing towns. Mechanical techniques of production improved dramatically, and led to a growing need for large-scale investment in plant. The increasing demands by entrepreneurs for additional investment capital to finance constantly increasing scales of production inevitably put great pressure on, initially, the owners of fortunes gained from commerce and landholding, and, subsequently, the multitude of tiny local banks (many of which lent too much too rashly, and accordingly went bankrupt) and the entrepreneurs themselves (to plough back profits to sustain growth). Eventually, during the mid-19th century, such sources of investment capital were seen to be inadequate to finance continued expansion, and the small savings of individual citizens came to be widely regarded as an additional source of capital. However, the twin disinclinations of entrepreneurs to borrow more than they could repay and of savers to become part-owners of a risky undertaking for whose debts they would be liable without limit posed a problem which was not solved until the Companies Consolidation Act of 1862 accorded to the owners of companies the privilege of limited liability. The Act provided that the owners of a limited company were liable for the debts incurred only to the extent of their original investment in that company. The result of the Act was to permit entrepreneurs to gain investment capital by selling shares in the ownership of the company to the general public. Equally, the many small savers in the community were allowed to become part owners of a large enterprise without any fear of being bankrupted if the enterprise failed, since each saver was liable for debt only to the extent of his initial investment in the company; he might lose all that, but nothing more.

The capital sum which an entrepreneur is permitted by the Board of Trade to solicit from the general public by the sale of shares of ownership in the company is called *authorised capital*. The capital sum which an entrepreneur actually seeks to obtain—the *issued capital*—is often less than the authorised capital, since he may keep some of his permission in reserve, as it were, hoping to use a subsequent sale of shares to finance a later expansion. The amount of issued capital actually bought ('subscribed for') by the general public is called *paid-up capital*. The shares of ownership held by the general public are called *shares*, and are certified by *share certificates*.

Shares themselves are of two basic types: preference and ordinary. **Preference shares** take preference in the distribution to the shareholders (owners) of any profits made by the company. Normally, however, the amount of profit allocated to preference shareholders is small and fixed. If the company does badly, the preference shareholders are the first to be paid out of any small profits the firm makes; but if the firm does well, the preference shareholders still receive only a small and fixed share of the profits. If the company makes no profits at all, then preference shareholders get nothing. Some firms issue what are called *cumulative preference shares*, which give the owners the right to have any shortfall in profit distribution during a bad year made up in a year when the company makes bigger profits. There is generally little risk attached to preference share ownership, and accordingly the shares do not usually carry voting rights. **Ordinary shareholders,** on the other hand, carry the main burden of company ownership; they receive nothing if the company makes profits at most sufficient to cover distribution only to preference shareholders, and yet they may receive large sums if the company makes large profits. The proportion of profit distributed for each ordinary share is called the **dividend**. Ordinary shares are, therefore, characterised by a variable dividend rate; because of the risk, they usually carry voting rights. Since they represent a potential claim against the assets (or equity) of a company, they are often called **equities**.

Limited companies may also raise capital by borrowing it—as distinct from selling shares of ownership. Apart from straight loans from banks (a common method of borrowing), companies also issue loan certificates, called **debentures**, in return for money borrowed from the general public. The regular interest which a company has to pay on these borrowings is one of the fixed costs of production, and you must not regard payments to debenture holders as being in any way made out of the company's profits. On a strict definition of profit, of course (see section 5A on normal profit), you should only regard as profit that part of a company's revenue which it has to distribute as dividend in order to maintain a sufficient supply of shareholders (i.e., to maintain a sufficient amount of paid-up capital from entrepreneurs). However, usage and the companies themselves have sanctioned the reference of *profit* to all money either distributed as dividend or set aside as reserve. And, as we noted in section 6M, it is not readily apparent in a limited company just who are the entrepreneurs anyway.

Limited companies, of shared ownership, are occasionally called **joint-stock companies**, since the capital stock is owned jointly by several shareholders. They are of two main types: private and public. Private limited companies have from two to 50 owners; they cannot appeal to the general public for capital, and their shares of ownership must be sold privately. Up to 1966 they used not to have to publish an annual balance sheet, but the Companies Act of that year destroyed the privilege of privacy. Nonetheless, private limited company status offers the valuable privilege to all shareholders of limited liability for all debts, and it thereby has a distinct advantage over the partnership.* Public limited companies must have at least seven owners and publish an annual balance sheet; their shares, however, can be sold publicly, and they can appeal to the general public for investment capital.

The public limited company has played a vital role in the growth of industry since the late 19th century. Its advantages are:

1 Economies of scale. The large sizes permitted by shared ownership with limited liability for debts favour the pursuit of economies of scale.

2 Permanence. The ready transferability of share ownership to new owners, coupled with the frequent absence of any personal or family name in the title of the company, gives the company a degree of independence and permanence not attributable to one-man businesses and partnerships. This fact is recognised by law, which treats the company as a separate legal entity distinct from its owners.

3 Risk spreading. Shared ownership, by an unlimited number of persons enables the risks of a giant enterprise to be shared, so that no single person is daunted by the enormity of the risk.

4 Capital liquidity. Individual owners can pull out of an enterprise and transfer their investment capital elsewhere merely by selling their shares of ownership to other potential owners.

5 Effective use of small savings. The possibility of shared ownership of limited liability companies has undoubtedly tapped a major source of additional investment capital, whether individual small savings are attracted to investment *directly* through capital issue offers to the general public or *indirectly* through institutional investment by insurance companies.

6 Portfolio creation. Before the advent of limited liability and shared ownership in 1862, wealthy people often tied up large sums of investment capital in just one or two enterprises. The possibilities of shared owner-

---

* It is interesting to note in this context that the Dutch-owned English department store chain of C & A Ltd changed back to a partnership form in order to preserve the secrecy of its accounts, rather than be forced to publish a balance sheet as a private limited company.

PLATE 3 (a) A distressed area.

PLATE 3 (b) A new industrial estate.

PLATE 4 (a)   In India, manpower is used to make up for lack of machinery.

PLATE 4 (b)   In Canada, machinery is employed widely.

ship permit wealthy people to spread their investment over a large number of companies, thereby lessening the risks of capital loss arising from the failure of any single company. A list of the companies in which partial share-holding is maintained is called an investment portfolio.

The disadvantages of the limited company are few in number, but it is worth noting the danger of take-overs as competing firms attempt to buy enough shares of ownership to give control. There is also the risk of speculation in share ownership, leading to a firm's never knowing who owns it. And, of course, if the company grows too large, there are the general disadvantages accruing to an over-large scale of production.

9D The co-operative

A co-operative enterprise may be established for either production or consumption purposes. The motive for each purpose is the gaining of economies of scale by a large number of separate small-scale units. Producers may gain economies through the shared use of expensive capital equipment and the bulk-buying of raw materials; consumers may gain economies through bulk purchase accompanied by subsequent division of the purchase among the members of the co-operative. Generally, while consumer co-operatives have enjoyed great success in Britain, producer co-operatives have languished. Probably the most notable successes in producer co-operatives are to be found in the field of Danish agriculture, where production is organised almost entirely on a co-operative basis. Collective farming on Russian *kolkhozes* is based on the same principle; the peasants own the land, farm it co-operatively (i.e., they purchase in bulk and share capital equipment), and are remunerated according to their individual productivity.

9E The public corporation

Governments may assume the running of industries either in whole or in part, for any one or more of the reasons noted in section 3C (which you should now read again). The most common type of organisation used for the purpose is the public corporation, which is established by Act of Parliament, and which is ultimately responsible to parliament through a government minister. The Central Electricity Generating Board, for example, is responsible to parliament through the Minister for Trade and Industry. There are no shareholders in a public corporation; ownership is by the whole community.

The chief aim of a public corporation is to provide an efficient public service at a price *low* enough to avoid the creation of profit and *high* enough to cover the often very high capital investment costs of the enterprise. Remember, in this context, that gross capital investment (reinvestment and net investment together) should count as one of the fixed costs of production, i.e., a certain amount of nominal product is set aside each year on the principle of amortisation, such an amount ranking as one of the essential overhead costs of production. It should not be regarded as something paid for out of profits, even though it is often described in that way. Further, since the expectation of profit is not a factor in inducing production, the element of normal profit, which is a necessary factor cost in privately owned industry, should be eliminated from the cost structure of a public corporation. In practice, of course, it is difficult for a huge public corporation to pursue a pricing policy which brings in exactly sufficient revenue to cover all essential costs. More usually, revenue exceeds or falls short of that exactly sufficient sum. Excess revenue is generally treated as an offsetting sum to general taxation requirements, rather than as a means of reducing prices, whereas shortfall revenue is usually met not only from general taxation but also from raised prices. Pricing policy for public corporations is, however, an extremely difficult matter, since, transcending the problem of getting an 'exact' price there is the question whether prices should be subsidised from general taxation to keep down the cost of living or allowed to achieve an equilibrium point balancing demand and supply (including gross investment needs). The tendency throughout the 1960s was to the achievement of an equilibrium price; witness the work of Beeching with the railways, Robens with the coal industry, and Jones with North Sea gas.

9F Take-overs

If a firm (a) makes very large excess profits and sets considerable sums to reserve, (b) acquires a large borrowing capability because of the strength of its assets, or (c) has a large number of authorised but unissued shares, it then becomes able either to further its own expansion or to obtain shares in another firm. The process of obtaining shares in another firm in order to gain control of that firm is called a take-over. Usually, when a firm is attempting a take-over, it buys the shares of the victim company as secretly as possible on the open share market (the Stock Exchange); when it has acquired *enough*, it then makes a bid for the remaining shares. The bid may take the form either of a straight cash offer or of an offer of shares in the bidding company (most commonly the latter). There is no rule about how many shares are *enough*; that is always a matter for the bidding firm alone to decide. However, it will inevitably be less than half the number of ordinary voting shares, since anything over half would give control without the need to bid for the remaining shares. From being a rather 'shady' sort of deal in the first half of the 20th century, take-overs and bids have gradually gained a large measure of respectability, though not without an accompanying increase in the amount of supervision by the financial authorities in the City of London. The *City Working Party* published its 'Queensberry Rules' of conduct in take-overs in 1959; these were revised in 1963 and strengthened in 1968, by the publication of the *City Code on Take-Overs and Mergers* and the creation of an overseeing panel. In mid-1968, for the first time, a government agency actually took part in a commercial take-over bid, when the IRC used public money to buy shares in the Cambridge Instrument Company in order to help the George Kent Company achieve a successful take-over against the competing bid by the Rank Company. In early 1969, the IRC went even further, by actually launching a bid for the Brown Bayley Organisation.

There are many reasons for making a take-over bid:

1 To gain economies of scale, by widening operations in the same line of business. This is called **horizontal integration**; the grouping of several shipyards on the Clyde to form the Upper Clyde Shipbuilding Group and the take-over of AEI by GEC (in late 1967) are examples.

2 To gain control of the productive chain. If a firm wishes to ensure supplies of essential raw materials, then it may take over a firm supplying those materials; it may similarly take over a marketing firm in order to achieve control of the distributive part of the productive chain. This is called **vertical integration**; the major oil companies, which control the whole productive chain from exploration and drilling to final sale, are excellent examples. Throughout the late 1960s, the giant textile firm of Courtauld's ran into fairly persistent trouble with the Monopolies Commission because of its attempts to achieve a high degree of vertical integration by means of take-overs.

3 To diversify production, by acquiring firms with different types of production. Occasionally, a firm operating at the level of maximum profit in its own industry may seek to enter other industries characterised by increasing returns in the hope of gaining a greater return on its investment in firms in those industries than it could obtain by additional investment in its own industry. This is called **conglomerate integration**; the Rank Organisation is an example, with interests in film-making, photographic wholesaling, office copying-equipment manufacture (Xerox), high-fidelity electronics, optical and scientific instrument manufacture, motorway service centres, tenpin bowling, ballrooms, and hotels. The original cause of the Rank Organisation's diversification was a gradual decrease in the demand for its staple product—cinema entertainment. It was therefore induced by the desire for higher returns on investment into a series of take-overs of firms in other industries.

4 To eliminate competition, by taking over competitors and either closing them down or taking their profits (as the House of Frazer did with Harrods department store). The end result of this process is the achievement of monopoly power. Occasionally, as when ICI attempted to take over Courtauld's in the early 1960s, the bid fails.

5 To obtain control of a site. Firms in the service trades, especially those owning hotels, restaurants and shops, may try to buy control of other firms occupying important street-corner sites, because of the greater frontage and display-possibilities which those sites confer. This was one reason for the take-over of Woollands by Harvey Nicholls in Knightsbridge in 1966.

6 To rationalise an industry, by eliminating wasteful duplication of productive processes and permitting a smaller number of firms to gain increased economies of scale. The Lancashire cotton industry experienced this type of rationalisation in the late 1950s, and the brewing industry

throughout the 1960s. Aircraft manufacture, shipbuilding, and motor engineering have all been similarly rationalised, yielding such giant companies as the British Aircraft Corporation and British Leyland Motors. The British governments of the 1950s and 1960s favoured take-overs and mergers for purposes of rationalisation, since they hoped constantly to be able to improve Britain's international competitiveness, and rationalisation was seen as a useful device to that end. It is in this field of take-overs that the IRC was such a particularly active instrument of government policy, successfully supporting, either prestigiously or financially, such take-overs as those of AEI by GEC, of Elliott Automation by English Electric, of BMC by Leyland, and of Edwards High Vacuum by British Oxygen.

7 To create a commercial empire. Pride of ownership, or of entrepreneurial achievement on a grand scale, has led to the creation of vast 'personal' empires, such as Thomson Newspapers Ltd and Sears Holdings Ltd.

8 To gain control of part of a foreign economy. Much of Britain's motor industry (Ford, Rootes group, and Vauxhall, for example) is controlled by parent companies in the United States. Indeed, multinational companies of this type now control the bulk of private-sector industry throughout the economies of the western world. Which of the following, for example, are primarily British-owned companies: Esso, Mobil, Regent, Shell, BP, Goodyear, Firestone, Procter & Gamble, Kodak, Philips, Pirelli, Nestlé, Electrolux ? In fact, only BP is primarily British-owned (and 49% of that ownership is held by the British government). Shell is half Dutch, Philips is wholly Dutch, Pirelli Italian, Nestlé Swiss, and Electrolux Swedish; the rest are American. The importance of multinational companies in the world is indicated by their vast output: at the start of 1970 it was widely accepted by most economists that the combined production of the world's multinational companies was worth at least twice as much as the total value of world trade.

9G The holding company

Control of a joint-stock company is exerted by unitary ownership of just over 50% of the ordinary voting shares, which may be only a small part of the total issued capital (the rest being non-voting preference shares). Company A, for example, with an issued capital of 500 ordinary voting shares and 2000 non-voting preference shares, can be effectively controlled by a unitary ownership of 251 ordinary voting shares. If we assume that companies B, C and D have the same issued capital composition as company A, then clearly each can be controlled by possession of 251 of its ordinary voting shares. Indeed, all four companies, with a total issued capital of 10 000 shares, can be controlled by possession of only 1004 (251 × 4) ordinary voting shares. It is the function of a purposely-established holding company to possess those shares. The principle of 'holding' may be extended both upwards and downwards. For example, if the holding company itself has an issued capital of 100 voting shares, then

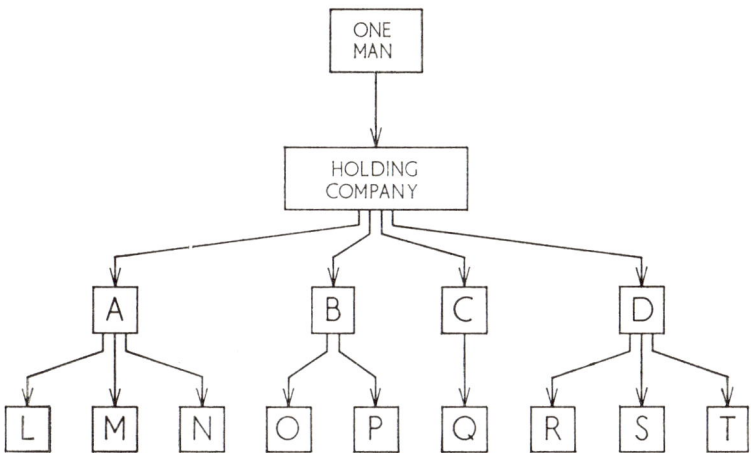

FIG 9.1   The pyramid of control in a holding company.
NOTE:
Control is exerted in the direction of the arrows by ownership of just over 50% of the controlled firm's ordinary
voting shares.

one man, with a holding of 51 shares, controls the whole organisation; and—
the other way—companies A, B, C, and D may in similar manner control
companies L, M, N, O, P, Q, R, S, and T. Figure 9.1 illustrates how this so-
called *pyramiding* of control is built up.

Section 10
The location of industry

10A Localising factors

Industrial activity is not evenly spread over the occupied face of the globe; even though most parts might be said to have at least some sort of industry, there exist nevertheless several well-defined climax regions, where industrial activity is highly concentrated. On a global scale, western Europe is such a climax region; but within western Europe, closer examination reveals a number of separate climactic zones, such as south Lancashire, the Rotterdam district, the Ruhr valley and the lower Thames valley. Within any one of these zones, there is a tendency—sometimes strongly, sometimes weakly, marked—for industrial specialisation to occur. For example, there is a tendency in the Ruhr valley for a specialisation on steel and heavy engineering industries, and in the Rotterdam district on shipbuilding and oil refining. Such locational specialisation is the geographical equivalent of the division of labour, and it is the result of the fact that it is more profitable to operate a particular industry in one area rather than in another.

In a competitive, or free enterprise, economy (as distinct from a planned economy), the chief motive to economic action on the part of entrepreneurs is the drive to obtain maximum profits. They therefore seek to achieve not only the lowest average *output* costs at the chosen scale of production (consistent with equating marginal cost and marginal revenue at the chosen scale) but also the cheapest *access to market*. The aims of lowest cost output (at the factory gate, as it were) and of lowest cost marketing may, and, indeed often, do, conflict. The actual location of an industry, then, may be a compromise between conflicting factors, yielding a site which offers the *maximum net advantage* in cost. The determining factor in the choice of a compromise site is the cost of transport—not only for the factors required for output but also for the marketing of the finished commodity. In general, the complex of output factors weighs more as a determinant of location for the primary industries, while the market is the stronger determinant of location for the tertiary industries. Secondary industries, however, are affected in varying degrees, according to the relative values per unit of bulk of both resources and product. If the values per unit of bulk of raw materials are low relative to product, then transport costs tend to form a large proportion of factor assemblage costs, and the industry tends accordingly to be located near its factor supplies (especially power and raw materials). If, on the other hand, the factor resources have a relatively high value per unit of bulk, they will be better able to stand high transport costs, and the industry can accordingly be located to take advantages of economies in marketing. Brick-making is an example of an industry whose location is influenced primarily by the geographical distribution of supply factors; the manufacture of fashion clothing, on the other hand, is essentially market-oriented in its location. More usually, however, a secondary industry may be sited almost anywhere within the range of possibilities between factor-orientation and market-orientation. A clear-cut decision is, in practice, only rarely possible.

The chief localising factors on the **output** side are:

1   Land. The different land factors have an important localising effect on industry. Cheap access to coal was vital in the early days of mechanical industrialisation, and many of the industries which were then located on or near coalfields are still on the same sites; the North Staffordshire pottery firms, for example. Today, coal is less important as a source of direct power, being more frequently converted into cheaply-transportable electricity; and even in those industries which are direct users of coal, such as the steel industry, more advanced and efficient techniques of coal burning have lessened the need for a coalfield location. Oil and gas are fairly easily transportable, and, like electricity, permit industries using them to move closer to a market location.

Minerals, supporting extractive industries, are fixed in location, and —apart from the choice of which deposit to work—the mining industries are located entirely in response to factor availability. Sometimes, therefore, mining operations are carried on in areas devoid of all other locational attractions; witness the production of North Sea gas, Saharan oil, high-Andean copper, Australian-desert iron and north-Canadian uranium.

Vegetable and animal raw materials, such as cotton and wool, are generally limited in their production by climatic and soil factors, though new seed strains and cross-bred animals, combined with irrigation, soil control, pesticides and so on, are currently stimulating an extension of those limits.

Climate also exerts a localising effect on production through its influence on water supplies: all types of farming and most types of manufacturing industry (especially the manufacture of power) are tremendously large users of water, and the availability of sufficient quantities of water is often a critical factor in the choice of an industrial site. And quite apart from using water directly, many industries use it indirectly, such as for transport and effluent disposal, and as a coolant and source of hydroelectricity. You can probably list numerous examples of industries located in response to water availability: think of the canal- or tidewater-based industries relying on cheap water transport for bulk materials (e.g., steel production at Port Talbot on the Bristol Channel and oil refining on the shores of Milford Haven); of the riverside or coastal locations required by chemical companies for effluent disposal (e.g., the chemical industries of the lower Mersey, where cheap transport is also a factor); of the coastal sites of most nuclear power stations where sea water provides a cheap coolant (e.g., Hunterston, Wylfa and Sizewell); and of the electrometallurgical industries in Norway and western Scotland (e.g., aluminium production at Kinlochleven).

Simple position, as an aspect of the land factor, can also produce particular industrialisation. Swindon and Crewe, as railway towns, for example, owe much of their growth to the splitting of lines necessitated by marine division of the land—Crewe, for instance, occupies a site where the main west-coast rail routes are split by the Mersey/Dee/Irish Sea waters into a North Wales branch and a Lancashire/West Scotland branch.

The cost of land for industrial use is a final aspect to mention. Some industries—especially those characterised by a horizontal assembly-belt lay-out—are extensive users of land, and consistent with the needs to obtain other factor supplies cheaply and get the product to market cheaply, land costs can be critical in the choise of an actual site. The Ford Motor Company, for example, selected Dagenham because it offered a low cost site (reclaimed urban rubbish dumps) within easy access of markets (London and south east England in particular and the world via London docks in general), and with easy raw material assembly possibilities (cheap water transport via the lower Thames)—virtually an ideal location.

2 Labour. Both the quantity and the quality of the labour supply available in an area may be deciding factors in the location of a particular industry. There are numerous instances where *scarcity* of labour has been made up by importation of labour from elsewhere, either forcibly (e.g., Russian east Siberian industry, West Indies sugar plantations, old American cotton plantations) or by the offer of high financial inducements (e.g., American oil-men for North Sea gas exploration, British academics to American universities, Pakistani doctors to Britain). More usually, however, lack of labour has a general disincentive effect on the growth of industry, provided the necessary production is possible elsewhere; the disincentive effect can be seen in the low rate of industrial growth in many of the countries of tropical Africa and South America. On the side of labour *availability* rather than scarcity, the existence of an unused reservoir of skilled labour is one of the attractions offered to industry by the Development Areas in Britain. There may still be a need to import management personnel and technically-skilled labour, as there was in the case of Rootes at Linwood, but the attraction of a (usually) engineering-trained labour force is a powerful incentive. Even if the skilled labour is fully employed, its existence in an area is still an attraction to new industries, which hope to 'poach' it rather than start labour training from scratch. Moreover, in an area with skilled labour, there is also likely to be an educational system (trade schools) and technical colleges geared to supplying additional skills. In an established area, too, there is likely to be a variety of existing subsidiary trades (security, by-product use, waste disposal), and these pose a further attraction to new industries.

3 Capital. The availability of physical capital for purchase by new firms is greatest in an established industrial area, and there is therefore a tendency for new firms to locate themselves near their capital suppliers in an existing industrial area. Nominal capital is much more mobile, and may be sought far afield without reference to the site of the potential industry; for example, nominal capital for new British electricity generating stations may be sought in Europe.

4 Enterprise. Entrepreneurs, seeking to maximise profits, usually locate their enterprises wherever the total costs of production and marketing are lowest; occasionally, however, they may act slightly less than rationally, and locate their enterprises according to other considerations. Examples of other considerations are personal wish, place of birth, and the amenity attractions of a town; thus Rowntree at York, Morris at Oxford and Beecham at St. Helens. The only qualification for success is that the chosen site should be within a generally favourable area.

The chief localising factors on the **marketing** side are:

1 The nature of the industry. Manufacturing industries producing fashionable or more generally perishable goods tend to be located near their markets; 'rag-trade' clothing and local baking are examples of such industries. Highly perishable daily newspaper production is an exception, since there is a great dependence on highly centralised production facilities (supported by rapid transport to market) in order to gain maximum economies of scale. Tertiary service industries (e.g., education, health, banking) are closely attached to their local markets; the chief localising criterion, apart from a sufficiently large market to warrant operations, being the principle of centrality. For example, the essential minimum of service industries (perhaps a doctor's surgery and a bank agency) may be located in a village which is either larger than its neighbours or more centrally placed within a small region. A greater provision of services may be made in a small country market town; and above that perhaps the county town will offer a range of more specialised services. The hierarchy of service provision continues upwards through major regional 'capitals' (such as Bristol in the West Country) to the national capital. The attachment of tertiary industries to their markets is reflected in the common jargon of *catchment areas* and *service areas*.

2 Proximity to existing routeways. The prior existence of major trade arteries has frequently proved to be an attraction to firms seeking a production site. The growth of industry along river and canal banks—partly for ease of obtaining factor supplies and partly for ease of access to market—has been a historical phenomenon of considerable significance in this context; witness the industrial concentrations along the Manchester Ship Canal, the lower Thames, the lower Tyne, the Rhine, the Great Lakes and the lower Yangtze. In all cases, markets are available either locally (because the bulk of the world's population is distributed in close proximity to rivers, lakes and seas) or abroad (via relatively cheap

water transport). Inevitably, for all the reasons noted, the major estuarine sites in Britain are among the most rapidly growing industrial areas in Europe (see figure 10.1). On a smaller scale, note the attraction of a trunk road site: the North Circular Road of London and its equivalent in Dundee are well-known examples of the recent past. Look now for any new industrial groupings which are emerging in response to the construction of motorways. In general, as technological advances weaken the locational grip of the production factors, rapid access to market assumes an increasingly large degree of locational importance.

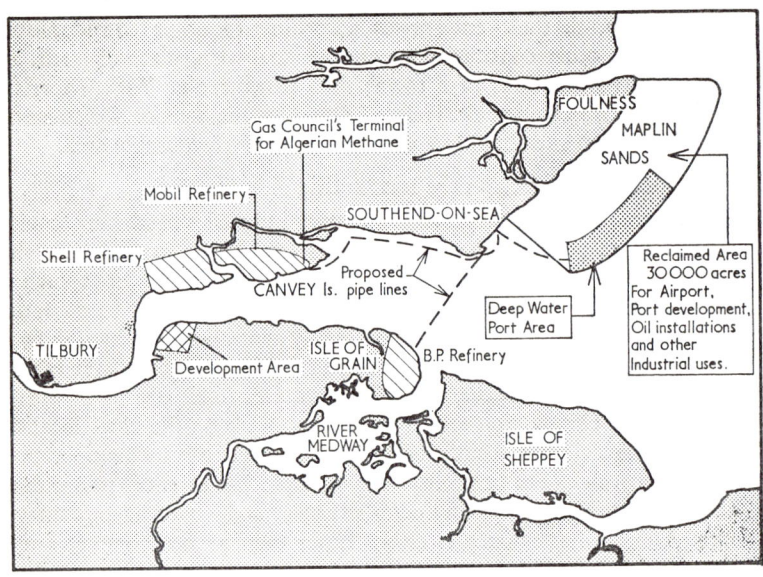

FIG 10.1 New industrial development proposals for the Thames estuary.

However, while private entrepreneurs seek to obtain maximum profits through lowest-cost production, they also impose rising cost burdens on the rest of society. Any growing industrial area necessarily faces increasing pressure of use on its publicly-provided roads, schools and hospitals; and the cost of such provision (social cost) is neither assessed by an individual firm nor even readily assessable by society. The cost of pollution is even more difficult to assess. These are all costs, which, unless rather arbitrarily expressed in the form of local rates, are ignored by a firm in its computation of profits. Governments, however, assume that a cost is involved, and, despite a lack of quantification, they act to restrict the rising social cost by some insistence on planning. Limitations to office building in London (after 1964) and the persuasions of the Location of Offices Bureau to an out-of-London site are attempts by governments to restrict the over-growth of tertiary industry in London. And not without success; several companies have moved out of London, including even one of the hallowed City merchant banks (N. M. Rothschild, which moved to Croydon in early 1969).

Governments also act to influence the location of industry more positively—instead of saying 'don't build here', they say as well 'go and build there'. The 'there' places are the Development Areas, and as we noted in section 6F (the paragraphs dealing with 'measures to alleviate the effects of immobility') governments have developed a wide range of incentives to attract industries into these areas. Proponents of free enterprise assert that firms persuaded to open factories in Development Areas in order to offset local unemployment are not in a proper position to maximise their profits, since there must be some element of unnecessary high cost in the selection of a Development Area site (such as unnecessary costs of marketing). However, you should bear in mind as a counter-argument the existence of social cost, which, even though unquantified (and probably unquantifiable), certainly exists. It becomes, then, something of a matter of belief whether gross domestic product increases or decreases as a result of the 'contrived' dispersal of industry to the Development Areas.

10B Geographical inertia

Once a firm has established itself in a certain locality, there is a tendency for it to stay there. Even though *individual* factors may be mobile (e.g., the 'Drift South' of labour in England during the 1950s), it is rare for a *whole* production plant to change its location. Apart from the Head Office locational changes inspired by the Location of Offices Bureau, probably the best examples of 'works' transfers in the recent past are the moves of the entire Lotus motor engineering stable from Cheshunt to Norwich and of the Celotex building suppliers from Wembley to Hadleigh in Suffolk.

If an established firm prospers in its chosen location, there is no incentive for it to move. If, for any reason, however, average costs start to rise in relation to average revenue, and profits correspondingly begin to diminish (perhaps even disappear), then there are strong economic reasons for a transfer to another site offering improved profit opportunities. A move is an expensive business, however, and not likely to be undertaken unless the future in the established location appears hopeless. What is more likely to happen in practice is a gradual run-down of the decreasingly profitable established site and a concurrent build-up of production in a more profitable alternative location, until eventually the low-profit site can be closed and all output concentrated in the new location. The year-long run-down and eventual closure in 1968 of the AEI plant in Woolwich is an example; during the run-down period, workers were offered employment elsewhere within the GEC-AEI organisation, but—because of labour immobility—there was strong public pressure in the final stages against any closure.

There are, in fact, many powerful reasons for a firm to remain in its original location, i.e., to be **geographically inert** (or to have **industrial momentum**, which is merely a way of saying that when an industry has started it has a tendency to keep going). The chief reasons are:

1   Cost. The cost of moving is both high and difficult to assess. It comprises not only the establishment of a replacement plant but also the complete amortisation of the immovable existing plant.

2   Public pressure. Any community is unwilling to suffer unemployment caused by the closure of a factory; and that unwillingness is strengthened by labour immobility, which makes people prefer work in their own community to unemployment in their own community, but unemployment in their own community to employment in another community. A degree of public pressure against factory closure may also be applied by reason of the pride which a community takes in supporting a prestigious firm, even if the firm is experiencing falling profits, e.g. Rolls-Royce in 1971.

3   The reputation of the place-name. Goods on the market acquire a reputation based on the prior success of either the producing firms or the place where the firms are located. Chocolate produced by Cadbury's, for example, has a reputation based on the prior success of the *firm* of Cadbury's, regardless of the place of manufacture; on the other hand, many small firms rely on the reputation of the *place*, rather than on their own names. Cutlery 'Made in Sheffield' has a reputation based on the prior collective success of many small firms in Sheffield, regardless of the identity of the actual manufacturer. Swiss watches, German cameras and Japanese transistor radios are other examples of goods with a place-based reputation. There is a clear marketing advantage to a firm if it remains in an area with an established place-name reputation, even though profits may (only may; there is a risk attached to movement) be higher elsewhere.

4   The existence of a trained labour supply. Even though the entrepreneur may be willing to move the plant to another location, it is highly unlikely that labour will be equally willing to transfer itself. Section 6F contains an examination of the reasons for labour immobility, which is a powerful 'drag' on industrial mobility, especially if a firm requires labour with high technical skills which might not be readily available elsewhere.

5   The existence of subsidiary trades. Few firms can operate in an industrial vacuum; they require a variety of supporting industries, such as security provision, use of by-products, industrial consultancy and advertising. The mesh of interlocking industrial dependencies is usually very tight, and binds a firm with considerable force to an established production area.

6   The existence of infrastructural services. Infrastructure is the term used to denote supporting services such as the provision of power, transport, banking, education, health, and Board of Trade advice. Mostly, these services take the concrete form of social capital—power stations, roads, canals, bridges, schools, hospitals, and so on. In any established industrial region there is a fairly full development of infrastructural services, helping to produce industrial immobility.

7   Government policy. In order to restrict regional unemployment, prevent the over-crowding of growth areas, and obtain the maximum use of exist-

ing social capital, governments may try to persuade firms to remain in an area suffering relatively decreased industrial profitability. The measures employable by governments are similar to those listed in section 6F under the heading 'measures to alleviate the effects of immobility'. The net effect of government help to a region of potential unemployment is a partial transfer of profits (via taxes and state aid) from a growth area to a region in decline. The true cost of the transfer is impossible to assess accurately, even in purely economic terms (i.e., without counting the social costs), since the comparison is between what is and what might be. Justification remains a matter of faith.

Any inertial area will remain economically viable only (discounting infinite state aid) so long as it does not compete directly with areas characterised by lower (and perhaps diminishing) average costs. Avoidance of direct competition can be accomplished in three ways:

1 Specialisation. Instead of producing a variety of goods, a firm can concentrate its productive energies on one type of good only, attempting thereby to gain maximum economies of scale. The concentration of production on blankets undoubtedly helped Witney to survive the devastating competition of cheaper Yorkshire woollens during the early years of the Industrial Revolution.

2 Improved quality. A firm can avoid direct competition by raising the quality of its product and seeking marketing outlets at a level above those of competing firms. Sheffield has successfully 'made it' in this way.

3 Tariff protection. Several British industries have come to face intensive competition in their established markets from newer and cheaper producing regions. The Lancashire cotton industry, for example, has survived competition from India, Portugal, Hong Kong and Japan largely by the device of tariff protection. Cheaper cotton goods entering Britain have been forced to pay duty, thus raising the selling price in the British market. There have also been several agreements whereby, say, Portuguese exporters of cotton have accepted a limitation on the quantity exported to Britain. Naturally, tariff protection does not enable a firm to compete in other markets (provided it is a *higher cost* firm which is enjoying protection); tariffs, in fact, protect a firm's *national* market, but no more than that. Inevitably, tariffs are attacked as a means of avoiding direct competition more than specialisation and improved quality are, since—alone of the three methods—they permit the continued operation of relatively inefficient firms. Aside from reasons of national defence and social distress, there are therefore strong arguments for trade to be as free as possible. It is, indeed, one of the prime purposes of the General Agreement on Tariffs and Trade (GATT) to achieve a reduction of tariff barriers as quickly as is practicable.

11A The final stage of production

In the last section we saw how marketing costs are a considerable factor in the entrepreneruial decisions regarding industrial location; we also noted again that the process of production is not complete until the goods and services are available for purchase by consumers. Producers, then, are intimately concerned with marketing as the final stage of their economic activity. While market*ing* is a phase of production, the market itself is the means whereby suppliers on the one hand and demanders on the other are brought into mutual business contact. It is the link between producers and consumers; it enables and facilitates exchange.

The market may be a place, such as Billingsgate fish market or the 'market place' of a country town, or it may be a network of separate but linked functions serving the essential purpose of a market (i.e., *exchange*), such as the property market, which is handled chiefly by estate agents and newspaper advertising. In general, though there are many exceptions, a market provides not only contact between buyers and sellers, but also rules of behaviour and a record of dealings and prices. Whether it occupies a particular place or not, the market in economics is invariably of the second type; in other words it is a network of linked functions and its definition is by purpose rather than by place.

11B Types of market

A rigid classification of markets is impossible, because of the immense variety of goods and services on offer. Nevertheless, it is possible to construct an indicative classification:

1 **Markets according to the degree of competition.** Competition is unlimited in perfect economics, and there is an unlimited number of buyers and sellers. However, in real life, or imperfect economics, competition is not unlimited; it may be limited both on the selling side and on the buying side. The degrees of limitation on the selling side are through what are called imperfect competition, oligopoly and monopoly, and on the buying side, monopsony. Consideration will be given to these in the next section. For the moment we shall confine our attention to perfect markets.

2 **Markets according to time-span.** At the end of section 5B we noted the existence of three time-categories in relation to supply positions; the same three are also relevant in relation to markets. The shortest supply

position—market term—is characterised by highly, even perfectly, inelastic supply; the corresponding *immediate market* is characterised by the exchange of perishable goods and daily necessities. Since the supply in an immediate market is inelastic, price is determined almost entirely by demand. The Christmas Eve turkey market is an example.

The middle supply position—short term—is characterised by the adjustment of supply within the limits imposed by the existence of fixed equipment; the corresponding *short-term market* is characterised by the hopes of both sellers and buyers for price movements in their favour. Any good with a fashion content (clothing, cars, and furniture, for example) has the quality of in-built obsolescence, and is likely to be traded in short-term markets; sellers hope that the new fashion will 'catch on' and permit higher prices and excess profits, while buyers hope that they can get the product at a 'bargain' low price before it becomes obsolete.

The longest supply position—the long term—is characterised by elastic supply as fixed factors are adjusted; the corresponding *long-term market* is characterised by contractual exchange. Supply does not take place (i.e., the cost of fixed factor adjustment is not incurred) unless there exists a contractual guarantee to cover the marginal supply price. The guarantee may be given by the demander directly, so that the supplier is 'under contract' to supply a particular good or service at a stated time in return for a guaranteed price. Much shipbuilding is done in this way for the long-term market, though some is also done speculatively for the short-term market (i.e., ships are built in the hope that they can be sold at a profit, even though no one has ordered them). On the other hand, the guarantee of a minimum price sufficient to cover supply costs may be given by a government, even though the government is not the demander. Governments give such guarantees on behalf of the population (the ultimate demanders) in order that essential production may take place. Guaranteed prices for farm produce are an example.

Where governments do not guarantee prices over the long term, production for market may still take place with the aid of the technique of 'hedging on futures'. **Hedging** is the term used for the making of two self-cancelling contracts, like betting on both finalists to win the cup. **Futures** are contracts for the future delivery of a commodity. The technique works in the following manner. Suppose a merchant pays £35 a ton for sugar, with the intention of storing it for release to market some time before the next sugar harvest. He reckons that it will cost him £1 a ton (including his normal profit) to store it until then; so he looks for someone who will buy the right to obtain delivery of the sugar before the next harvest for anything over £36 a ton (£35 cost + £1 storage). Whoever buys the future will be something of a gambler; he will hope, with the support of his 'expert' opinions, to sell the contracted right (the right, not the sugar; almost the last thing the gambler will want is a delivery of sugar) for anything over £36 a ton—but, being a gambler, or *speculator*, he will be prepared to accept a loss on the deal if a loss is inevitable. If the price rises to £40 a ton before the next sugar harvest, the original storer will be able to sell his store (the speculator doesn't want sugar, remember) for £40 a ton; but in order to do that he will also have to buy back the future, because the future contains the rights of ownership, and that redemption will cost him £40 a ton too. The speculator has made a profit of a little under £4 a ton (i.e., £4 minus the interest which the speculator could have obtained by putting his original £36 units into a bank deposit account, say), or as he will regard it, a return of just under £4 for each £36-worth of investment; so he is happy. Meanwhile, the merchant has made his desired £1 a ton return to cover storage costs and normal profit; he bought initially at £35 a ton and sold at £40 a ton, making £5 a ton on the actual physical purchase and sale of sugar, but at the same time he lost £4 a ton on the futures contract because he sold it initially at £36 a ton and redeemed it at £40 a ton. The device of hedging has guaranteed his normal trading profit. If the merchant had also been a gambler there would have been no need for hedging; but in practice merchants seem seldom to be gamblers.

If the price of sugar falls, on the other hand, to, say, £30 a ton just before the next harvest, the merchant's trading profit is still guaranteed, while the speculator takes the loss. The merchant has to sell his sugar at £30 a ton, even though he originally paid £35 a ton; so he loses £5 a ton. More even: it has cost him £1 a ton to store the sugar; so his real loss is £6 a ton. However, whereas he received £36 a ton on his futures contract, he has to expend only £30 a ton on its redemption; so he gains £6 a ton on the paper transaction. That gain covers his £5 a ton loss on the sugar as well as his £1 a ton storage and trading costs. The speculator, meanwhile, has lost £6 on each £36-worth of investment in futures, together with the interest he might have earned on that money if it had been invested elsewhere without risk. Just so long, therefore, as there are people prepared to risk money for a chance of gain (i.e., speculators), the device of hedging remains a possible means whereby long-term markets are guaranteed a supply of commodities.

3 **Markets according to area served.** Narrow markets are concerned with dealings in small areas only, e.g., the markets for local newspapers and bakery products. Wide markets, however, may be world-wide in extent, such as those for the supply and purchase of Leyland buses and Kodak film. Wider markets may be gained by a good if it is:

(a) Easily graded, sampled, described or labelled. Demanders at a distance then know precisely what they are buying. The value of easy grading, etc. is shown by the wide markets achieved by, say, Californian fruit growers, Canadian wheat farmers, Indian tea planters, and Malayan rubber producers.

(b) Durable. Increased marketing distances necessarily involve increased journey times; and the commodity must not deteriorate. Wool, grain, oil, and cotton, for example, do not normally deteriorate rapidly, and so readily achieve wide markets; other goods, however, e.g., butter, meat, bananas, and flowers, have achieved wide markets only with the help of preservation (refrigeration, canning and drying) and/or rapid air transport.

(c) Readily transportable. Some goods, such as oil and grain, are easily bulk-handled by means of compression or suction pipelines, and therefore—other factors being favourable—readily achieve wide markets; other goods have to rely on a high value per unit of bulk, so that transport costs form only a small proportion of final selling price (for example, Swiss watches). Still other goods satisfy neither requirement, and they are therefore restricted to narrow markets. You should note here the experiments to widen coal markets by turning the coal into a slurry and using pipeline transport.

(d) From an area of established reputation. A great many second-rate Japanese cameras, for example, have gained wide markets because of the high reputations achieved in the field by such makers as Nikon, Asahi and Canon.

4 **Markets according to function.** The process of production is intimately concerned with markets at all stages. Factors have to be obtained from their suppliers to start the process, and goods have to be sold to consumers to end the process. It is the function of different markets to facilitate the whole process:

(a) Factor markets

(i) Land may be exchanged in either estate markets or commodity markets (remember: land includes raw materials). Estate markets are extraordinarily widespread, consisting as they do of estate agents, auctioneers, and newspaper advertisement columns. Commodity markets are usually more place-located, such as the market for cotton at the Cotton Exchange in Liverpool and the market for wheat at the Baltic Exchange in London. Nevertheless, many deals are made through the widespread medium of the telephone, and actual place-location is gradually becoming less important in commodity dealings.

(ii) Labour supply and demand find their markets in labour exchanges and newspaper advertisements. Look, especially, at the newspaper job-adverts in the *Daily Telegraph* and the *Sunday Times* in order to see how important that market is. For the satisfaction of supply and demand in teaching, for example, *The Times* publishes a special weekly Educational Supplement. Do not underestimate the importance of newspapers in the labour market.

(iii) Markets for capital are rather different, and, because of the variations in the types of capital (see figure 2.1), very varied. Fixed capital is usually bought and sold either at its place of production (by its nature, fixed capital is not very easily transportable) or indirectly by mailed catalogues and specification-details. Circulating capital is usually traded on the commodity exchanges; and nominal capital on the capital and money markets (more about these later—section 13—but note now that banks form a prominent part of the capital and money markets).

(iv) Enterprise does not really have a market; indeed it is the entrepreneurs who buy and sell in the other factor markets.

(b) Distributional markets. In the later stages of production, wholesale and retail markets (often called *outlets* by suppliers) are designed to ease the flow of goods to consumers. They are operated by what are called *middlemen*, whose essential function is to *break bulk* for the convenience of traders and consumers on the buying side of the market, as shown in figure 11.1.

Other functions of middlemen include:

(i) Carrying stocks of goods. This is an important function, since it permits greater elasticity of supply (see section 5B), thereby enabling suppliers to hold goods off the market during times of glut (thus preventing the price falling drastically) and to release goods to the market in times of shortage (thus preventing the price rising drastically). Stock-carrying therefore tends to promote a measure of price stability, thus allowing consumers to optimise their expenditure schedules, and producers to minimise one of the risks of enterprise.

(ii) 'Giving' trade credit. When wholesalers receive shipments of goods from manufacturers it is rare for there to be a simultaneous balancing payment; more usually, wholesalers settle their bills after several weeks. The payment delay is repeated by the retailer, who may not settle his bill with the wholesaler for several weeks; and also by many consumers, who may not settle their retail bills for several weeks. The practice of delaying payment to the immediate supplier is a common one; it is so widely accepted indeed that were it to be abandoned the whole distributive process would come under the severest strain, since the goods-payment relationship would be reversed (i.e., retailers would have to have sufficient money to pay for the goods *before* ordering them from wholesalers, and wholesalers would have to get that money *before* ordering goods from manufacturers), and the entire burden of financing the supply would be borne by the retailer—the smallest link in the distributive chain, and the one least likely to be able to bear the burden.

(iii) Having specialised knowledge of local markets. By virtue of their bulk-buying function, wholesalers and retailers tend to operate in relatively narrow markets. The concentration of their operations into narrow markets encourages middlemen to have specialised knowledge of those markets, thereby facilitating the flow of appropriate goods to different consumers.

(iv) Presenting new lines. Wholesalers and retailers have two tremendous advantages over mass-media advertising: they offer the opportunities to the retailer and consumer respectively of both physical sampling and immediate purchase.

The services of middlemen have been attacked frequently on the

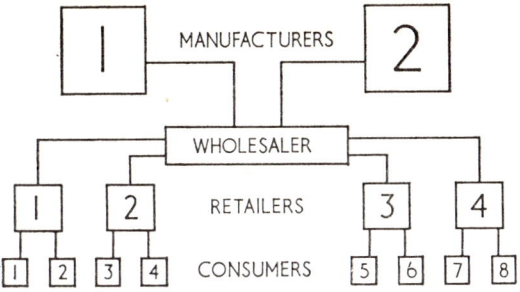

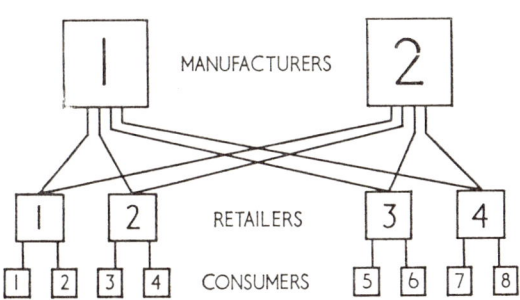

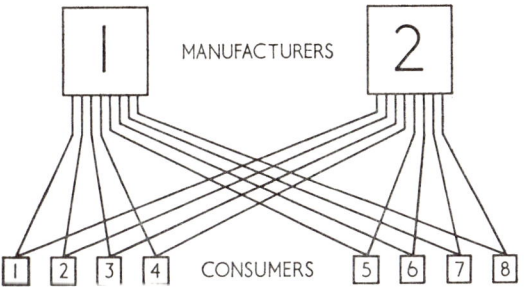

FIG 11.1　The bulk-breaking function of middlemen.
(a) The most common pattern. Note how the wholesaler breaks 2 shipments into 4, and how the retailers each break 1 into 2.
(b) The absence of the wholesaler means that manufacturers must break bulk themselves, making 4 shipments instead of 1, thereby losing an important economy of scale.
(c) The absence of all middlemen means a major scale-economy loss to the manufacturers, who now have to break bulk into 8 shipments.

grounds that they produce allegedly higher supply prices, but if you examine the functions of middlemen you will appreciate that they are of great economic value (i.e., they encourage efficiency): the yielding of scale economies in handling to manufacturers *helps* to keep prices down, the carrying of stocks *helps* to keep prices stable, the 'giving' of credit *helps* to facilitate the distribution of goods, the understanding of local market conditions *helps* to give consumers the chance of deriving maximum utility from their consumption of goods, and the presenting of new lines *helps* both to stimulate enterprise and to produce a more varied way of life. In fact, if middlemen were eliminated, and the pattern of retail distribution was as shown in section (c) of figure 11.1, it is highly likely that supply prices would increase—or, perhaps, that, at the prevailing market price, many manufacturers would become sub-marginal, so cutting supply and forcing market prices up (assuming demand remained constant). Nevertheless, there are many examples of ways in which the services of middlemen have been rendered superfluous:

(i) Those attempted by manufacturers.

Direct selling. Manufacturers sell direct from the factory, either over a counter or by mail (e.g., Ripolin Paint Co., Southall, and Brentford Nylon Co., London). Both wholesalers and retailers are eliminated.

Manufacturers' shops. The services of specialised wholesalers are dispensed with when manufacturers open their own retail shops, as Charles Clore (Dolcis shoes) has done.

(ii) Those attempted by middlemen, to eliminate other middlemen.

Mail order. A mail order company, such as Freeman & Co. of Clapham, is really a giant wholesaler, selling direct to the consumer by catalogue and postal delivery. The retailer is eliminated. Mail order shopping, because of its elimination of trudging round shops (there being no shops) and its guarantees of free consumer credit and 'sale or return' facilities on goods ordered, has become the major growth point in the distributive trades sector. From 1961 to 1966, for example, mail order sales increased by 84% against an average shopping growth of 25% and a growth by the independent retailers of only 19%.

Large retailers and department stores. Giant stores attempt—often—to dispense with the services of wholesalers by making orders direct to manufacturers. Some of the largest retailers and department stores virtually act even as their own manufacturers, by contracting supplies to be sold under the 'house' brand name, as is the case with both the *Jonelle* brand of the John Lewis Partnership and the *St. Michael* brand of Marks & Spencer.

(iii) That attempted by consumers.

Co-operative buying. The principle of co-operation was noted in section 9D, but even though consumer co-operatives figure prominently in the British retail trade (having about 10 million members and handling about 10% of all retail trade), their growth has been markedly uneven and—on average—the slowest for all types of distributive organisation. An interesting new development in the field of co-operation in Britain is the growth of co-operative bulk-buying from manufacturers on the part of numerous independent 'small' grocers, such as those in the *Spar* group. It is their attempt to remain economically viable in the face of competition from supermarkets, department stores, and mail order companies, all of which sell 'grocery' goods.

11C Advertising

Advertising—one of the most commonly maligned aspects of business activity —is not in fact so simple as to permit of its wholesale condemnation. Much advertising indeed aims at satisfying basic social needs, and its ambitions are entirely non-economic in character (though not necessarily its effects, since scarce economic resources have to be adapted to these non-economic ends). Examples of social advertising include the numerous governmental appeals to *post early for Christmas, keep death off the roads, be a blood donor* and so on. The vast bulk of advertising, however, is commercial in character, some of it being what is called simple competitive advertising, where a particular type of commodity or service is 'promoted' without reference to the actual supplier (such as *join the tea set, drink more milk,* and *go to work on an egg*), but most of it being complex competitive advertising, designed to attract consumers to a particular 'brand' of good or service, which is available only from a particular supplier.

The chief aim of all commercial advertising, whether simple or complex, is to shift the demand curve for the advertised commodity farther to the right; a secondary aim is to produce greater demand inelasticity, so that if prices rise an element of 'brand loyalty' will result in only a slight fall in the quantity demanded, and therefore an increase in total revenue to the supplier.

On the assumption that the total market for the satisfaction of any single want is limited (not necessarily a valid assumption as living standards rise), criticism of commercial advertising is levelled at the 'fact' that demand for one commodity can be shifted positively only if there is a balancing negative shift in the demand for substitute commodities. It is probably impossible to verify this in the case of simple competitive advertising (for example, if people drank more milk, would they thereby drink less coffee, tea, or beer?), and accordingly the main burden of criticism is borne by complex competitive advertising. It is much more likely that within, say, the total detergent market the demand for one branded good can be shifted positively only if there is an equivalent negative shift in the demand for substitute branded goods. Thus, if the Unilever products enjoy a positive shift in demand, then the Procter & Gamble products are likely to suffer an equivalent negative shift in demand. Since the total detergent market in England is worth about £90 million a year, neither company dare let the other enjoy a positive demand shift for its products without attempting 'retaliatory' advertising of its own products; so the companies spend about £5 million a year each on advertising, merely to maintain their positions in the market (and in the hope, too, of course, of claiming part of the share held by the other company). This type of complex competitive advertising is naturally largely self-cancelling unless the total market expands, and yet it still has to be paid for (both in real terms—labour and resources directed to advertising instead of to some more socially beneficial activity—and in nominal terms—the consumer ultimately having to pay a perhaps unnecessarily high price).

You should remember, however, that complex competitive advertising is only one type of advertising, and that, despite the self-cancelling disadvantages, there are several advantages claimed for it:

1 It enables a manufacturer to gain economies of scale, since it increases the demand for his product. This in turn enables the manufacturer either to lower his supply price or to take excess profits. If he lowers his prices, less successful competitors will be driven out of business and he will gradually come to occupy a monopoly position—provided he keeps his prices low. If, however, he takes excess profits, then other firms will be drawn into competition by the expectation of similar high profits; if the other firms compete successfully, the manufacturer will be forced either to contract his production scale and forgo the accrued economies or to maintain his production scale and forgo the excess profits (by lowering his supply price). In either case, the consumer tends to benefit—first, by lower prices at the possible expense of monopoly, and second, by the lower prices resulting from increased competition. However, it should be borne in mind that economies of scale may be achieved without the help of advertising; though advertising might expedite the process.

2 It brings new products to the attention of consumers. This is patently true, but you should remember that not all products are socially acceptable. Mass-media advertising in particular tends to be indiscriminate in its incidence, and certain goods are therefore never advertised in those media; others, such as cigarettes, have suffered partial withdrawal in their advertising promotion.

3 It is a guarantee of quality. In the case of a 'household' name advertiser, it is undoubtedly true that advertising guarantees quality, since the manufacturer has a considerable reputation to maintain. However, it has always seemed particularly strange that many new commodities should be advertised in shops with the tag *as advertised on television*, as though mere advertisement in that medium should in any way be a guarantee of quality.

4 It permits the sale of newspapers and the provision of television programmes to the consumer at a price much lower than would be the case if those media did not carry advertising material. Certainly, newspapers would cost more than 2p–5p if they failed to receive additional revenue from advertisers, and commercial TV could not operate at all without revenues from advertisers. Whether you regard this state of affairs as socially good or bad depends entirely upon your own convictions.

5 It acts as an incentive to increased productivity. By opening new consumer vistas, advertising helps to make labour more hard-working. It is

possible, of course, that it merely switches demand from established patterns to new patterns; but it is also possible that workers will work harder in order to get a colour TV or a holiday in Spain.

The effects of advertising are immensely difficult to assess, and part of any decision you might make about the matter will rest on your own attitude of mind. As the chairman of Unilever once joked, 'Half of our advertising is wasted, but we don't know which half'.

Section 12
Prices under competition and monopoly

12A Characteristics of perfect competition

Real-life economic activity is so complex that it is virtually impossible to analyse it successfully without first constructing theoretical frames of reference against which the real activity can be assessed. The first theoretical frame of reference—or *model*—used for this purpose is called perfect competition. You must not regard the word *perfect* as implying any moral goodness; it merely means complete.

Perfect—or complete—competition, then, does not exist in fact; it is a concept which is useful as an analytical tool, and its chief characteristics are:

1 Large numbers. There must be large enough numbers of both sellers and buyers for no single one to be able to influence the market (equilibrium) price on his own.

2 Perfect knowledge. Each producer must be aware at all times of the costs and profits of other producers, and each consumer must be similarly aware of the prices charged in all parts of the market.

3 Perfect mobility. There must be no limits imposed on entry to production, and all producers must have unrestricted access to an infinitely variable supply of production factors. All consumers must be able to move freely from one part of the market to another.

4 Homogeneity of goods and services. All goods of a particular type must be identical; so that there are no consumer preferences for the goods of one supplier over those of another.

5 Competition. There must be unrestricted competition among sellers competing to sell identical goods, buyers competing to buy identical goods, factors of production competing for employment at the highest rate of return, and human wants competing for satisfaction.

12B Characteristics of pure monopoly

Pure—or complete—monopoly is the theoretical antithesis of perfect competition. It is characterised by the monopolist's being able to influence price through his complete control of supply (the term for the ability to influence price through complete control of demand is *monopsony*). The four main types of monopoly are:

1 Legal. The holding of patents and copyrights confers monopoly powers upon the holder. Competition is legally barred, though it may exist illegally—for example, French *Champagne* producers have faced competition from other 'Champagne' producers around the world, and in most

cases have had their rights to the name *Champagne* upheld by local courts.

2 Natural (or Social). In those cases where—as in the provision of gas and water supplies—competition would merely produce wasteful duplication of fixed capital resources, a single supplier (monopolist) may be accepted by the community. Such 'natural' monopolies are most common in the sphere of public utilities (postal services, telephones, gas, water, electricity), and are often subject to a considerable degree of government supervision, if not outright ownership.

3 Industrial (or Commercial). Take-overs and mergers are the devices by which entrepreneurs may seek a monopoly position, provided the incentives are sufficiently strong, e.g., greater profits through the economies of increased scale, less expense on complex competitive advertising, and personal aggrandisement through extended ownership.

4 Geographical. Sole control of an element of land (for example, a shopping site or a raw material source) confers a geographical monopoly upon the owner.

12C Limitations to perfection

It is conceivable that in real life some of the conditions of either perfect competition or pure monopoly may be satisfied all the time, and that all the conditions may be satisfied (or nearly satisfied) for part of the time. For example, there are several cases where the competitive condition of large numbers is easily satisfied in practice—the markets for, say, nails, newspapers and shares are sufficient witness; and there are also examples of complete, but temporary, satisfaction of the pure monopoly conditions—such as the monopoly of television broadcasting in Britain held by the BBC until the independent companies started broadcasting in 1955.

In practice, however, there are many factors hindering the widespread satisfaction of the conditions of both complete competition and complete monopoly. The chief limitations to the achievement of perfection are:

1 Those relating to competition (see list in section 12A).

(a) Large numbers. Increased profits and/or lower prices can often be achieved if producers aim at obtaining the economies of extended scale; but within a given market this often results in a small number of fairly large producers. Consumers may also contract their numbers by forming co-operative buying associations.

(b) Perfect knowledge. Most consumers are ignorant not only of the relative qualities of the goods they actually buy, but also of the relative and absolute qualities (and prices) of the competing goods which they don't buy. Even where advertising presents factual information, most consumers don't know what the technical language means (and still less are they aware of its significance). Hexachlorophene, iridium, SR, gardol and stannous fluoride are ingredients in various makes of toothpaste—but what do they all mean? And, more to the point, what do they all do? And how effective, for instance, is the Ignition Control Additive (ICA) in Shell petrol compared with the alcohol additive in Cleveland petrol? Many consumers, in an effort to increase their knowledge of goods and services available on the market, have subscribed readily to *Which?*, the magazine of the Consumers' Association, founded in 1957 by a small group of individual consumers. The range of goods and services tested, reported on, recommended and not recommended has been wide, including such items as detergents, bank charges, motor cars, insurance, methods of saving, washing machines, cameras, and rejuvenation aids.

(c) Perfect mobility. Production factors are not infinitely variable in real life, nor do producers have unrestricted access to them. The factors are 'lumpy', and producers often have to make do with what they can get.

(d) Homogeneity of goods and services. Most producers usually attempt to give their product a degree of individual identity by 'branding' it. The multiplicity of brands and the promotional advertising of such product differences as occur counter any possibility of achieving homogeneity. Even in the field of unadvertised professional services (where a minimum standard of product is supposed to apply), word still gets around that *A* is a better dentist than *B*, and that *X* is a better solicitor than *Y*.

(e) Competition. In practice, competition is frequently limited by some form of *combination*, whereby two or more demanders or suppliers pool their individual purchasing or productive powers in order to gain a measure of control over price.

2 Those relating to monopoly.

(a) Government action. The unhindered operation of take-overs, mergers, and other forms of combination can readily result in the creation of a firm in monopoly position. Most governments in the world act to curtail such monopoly growth, especially when they regard the monopoly as being against the public interest (which is always a very difficult thing to define). The British government has as its disposal the powers granted to it by the Monopoly and Restrictive Practices Act of 1948 and the Restrictive Trade Practices Act of 1956. The Board of Trade is empowered to refer actual or potential combinations to the Monopolies Commission, if the combinations are thought to act against the public interest by controlling either at least one-third or a 'substantial part' of the total output of their particular industry. The proposed merger in 1968 of Barclays Bank, Lloyds Bank, and Martins Bank was thus referred to the Monopolies Commission, and the ensuing unfavourable report (by a vote of six to four against) was sufficient to prevent the merger taking place. 1968 also saw the first criminal prosecution under the Restrictive Trade Practices Act, when two firms in the traffic light supply business were accused of jointly fixing prices. British governments also have the threat of nationalisation as an added weapon. Even the 'free' economy of the United States is held in check by numerous anti-trust laws, which go back in time to the Sherman Act of 1890. The Federal Trade Commission (established in 1914) has powers to investigate monopolies on its own initiative, and also to issue enforceable orders against monopolies.

(b) Foreign competition. A monopolistic producer in one country is still open to competition in his domestic market from foreign producers, unless tariff barriers to competing imports are erected by a complaisant government. On world markets, though, he is subject to open competition (but there may be international production and marketing agreements in force). When the British steel industry was nationalised in 1967 under its assumed name of the British Steel Corporation, it acquired a monopoly position inside Britain—but spent much of its early advertising effort on assuring readers that it occupied a strictly competitive position because of the importance to it of world markets.

(c) Collateral competition. Wants are normally general, while goods are normally specific. A want may therefore usually be satisfied by any one of a great variety of different specific goods, such goods being substitutable for one another. The products of a monopolist may therefore be subject to competition from substitute goods; the safest monopolies are clearly those which control essential supplies (preferably in inelastic demand), such as of salt and water.

(d) Potential competition. If a monopolist takes excessively high profits, other firms may be drawn into competition. They may even have to 'fight' their way in. The danger of such effective competition may prevent a monopolist exploiting his monopoly powers to the full—for example, 'token' competitors may be allowed to remain in business, and the prices charged may not be exorbitant.

12D Imperfect competition

Between the limiting theoretical abstractions of perfect competition and pure monopoly there is a range of real possibilities characterised by the blanket term *imperfect competition*. For ease of analysis, the range may be broken into two parts: monopolistic competition and oligopoly.

1 Monopolistic competition. If the number of producers is large (thus satisfying a requirement of competition), but each is the sole supplier of a branded good (thus satisfying the requirement of monopoly), the conditions are established for what is called monopolistic competition. Even though the branded goods may be closely cross-substitutable, there is usually a certain amount of consumer loyalty to a particular brand, and this is generally sufficient to permit slightly different pricing policies on the part of the different producers.

2 Oligopoly. Oligopoly occurs whenever there is a small number of interdependent producers, the actions of one being based on the expected or agreed reactions of the others. If the reactions of the other producers are expected rather than agreed upon, the oligopoly is *spontaneous*, but if the reactions are agreed upon beforehand then the oligopoly is *collusive*. If

the oligopolists produce a homogeneous product (such as imported bananas), the oligopoly is *pure*; a *differentiated* oligopoly, however, produces separately branded—and slightly different—goods (such as petrol). A *complete* oligopoly exists when there is a high degree of interdependence, whether collusive or not; a *partial* oligopoly when the interdependence is weak (and spontaneous). In most actual oligopoly situations there is a great deal of uncertainty about the reactions of competitors; actions tend to be based more on expected reactions than upon agreed policy. The existence of a complete and collusive oligopoly is, like monopoly, subject to reference by the Department of Trade and Industry to the Monopolies Commission (as happened in 1968 to the electric lamp manufacturers in Britain).

12E Types of combination

Separate firms may combine in various ways in order to achieve a near-monopoly or oligopoly position. The chief methods of combination (not all of them legal) are:

1   Area agreements. These exist whenever two or more competitors in the same market agree to divide the market into a number of separate regional monopolies, as two major London dairies (Express and United) have done with their door-to-door deliveries to the bulk of the London market.

2   Cartels. These are joint selling agencies established by a number of firms which would otherwise compete with each other on price. The cartels act as channels for all output, and they are usually given the powers to fix a selling price and set production quotas for the member firms. Germany was the original home of the cartel; in the 1930s there were about 3000 cartels in Germany, the largest being the Rhenish-Westphalian Coal Syndicate and the I. G. Farbenindustrie. Cartels are less important now than formerly, but you should be aware that the marketing boards for agricultural produce in England (e.g., the Milk Marketing Board) serve a very similar purpose.*

3   Corners. Suppliers may try to corner the market in a particular commodity by buying up available supplies of the good for subsequent resale at an artificially high price. Ideally, the good should be in fairly inelastic demand (so that higher prices do not produce smaller total revenue) and also have no close substitutes (i.e., yielding a low cross-elasticity of demand).

4   Holding companies. These were outlined in section 9G, and it should be clear from a re-reading that unitary control can be exerted over a large number of firms by the holding company technique. The many 'separate' companies give the appearance of competition without the reality.

---

* In a booklet published in February 1970 by the Institute of Economic Affairs, it was asserted that the price of milk to the consumer would be 20% lower if the Milk Marketing Board was abolished. The National Farmers' Union replied that the proposals 'could throw the industry into chaos'.

5   Interlocking directorates. A number of apparently separate firms may have several directors in common. This state of affairs clearly favours (even if it does not cause) a measure of common production policy. It certainly favours the development of collusive oligopoly.

6   Mergers. When two firms amalgamate their shareholding (and also their separate identities) for the purpose of achieving one or more of the advantages of larger size (e.g., economies of scale, oligopoly or monopoly power, industrial rationalisation), then a merger takes place. In distinction to a take-over, a merger is usually peaceful—and entered voluntarily by the weaker firm. The formation of International Computers Limited in 1968 was a government (IRC)-sponsored merger for the purpose of more effectively combating foreign competition.

7   Price rings. These exist when separate firms (preferably in an oligopoly situation where the small number involved makes collusion easier) agree on a common price for their similar products. SGE Road Signals and Automatic & Telephone Electric were prosecuted in early 1968 at the Old Bailey for a price-fixing agreement; and in late 1968 the Monopolies Commission reported that there had been 'no appreciable increase in price competition' among the British electric light-bulb manufacturers, even though collusive price fixing was supposed to have been ended in 1956 after the passing of the Restrictive Trade Practices Act.

8   Pools. Arrangements (usually voluntary) are made to pool profits and then divide the sum out in proportion to the quantities of product of the different members of the pool. British petrol supplies were so 'pooled during World War II; and the Canadian Wheat Board currently has a similar purpose.

9   Quotas. Agreements may be made by separate producers to set themselves production limits. Price fluctuations caused by over- or undersupply (and damaging to the weaker producers) are thereby lessened. The device is fairly commonly used at the international level to protect the economies of relatively weak countries, e.g., the International Tin Council, the European Coal and Steel Community, the International Air Traffic Association (which oversees the supply of flight routes), and the International Coffee Organisation.

10 Share exchange agreements. These are the shareholders' equivalent to interlocking directorates. Naturally, because of the problem of communication, they are most easily used to give a measure of common control by shareholders of small local or family firms.

11 Take-overs. See section 9F.

12 Trusts. These were of American origin, and were outlawed by the Sherman Act of 1890. The idea behind them was that—in return for trust certificates—shareholders of separate firms vested their holdings in a trust, which then had effective common control over several different firms. The idea has been greatly refined in Britain, and now forms the basis for the numerous (and popular) unit-trust companies.

12F Price under perfect competition

Under perfect competition no individual supplier or demander can influence price, and suppliers and demanders react to each other solely through the price mechanism. The situation was described in sections 3A and 5D, and nothing more need now be said about the workings of the actual mechanism.

The advantages claimed for the perfect equilibrium mechanism are that:

1 It provides scope for the development of personal initiative.
2 It protects society against the taking of excess profits by entrepreneurs.
3 It produces the most economic (efficient) allocation of resources.
4 It produces optimum consumer satisfaction, since the system is geared to the satisfaction of consumer wants as the main motive power.

The disadvantages ascribed to perfect competition are that:

1 It permits phases of boom and slump as demand and supply conditions alter.
2 It does not necessarily produce prices as low as possible because producers may be too small to gain economies of scale.
3 It produces waste of resources because of duplication of research and plant by competing firms.
4 It allows consumers to be exploited because of their lack of perfect knowledge.
5 It causes great differences in personal wealth because of the great differences in human ability and luck.
6 It causes a lack of socially and strategically essential goods and services (roads, schools, armed forces, etc.) because the perfectly competitive system caters for the satisfaction of *individual* wants (even in aggregate), and not for the satisfaction of *common* wants. As J. K. Galbraith wrote, 'private affluence amid public squalor'.

12G Monopoly prices

Any firm, whether under perfect competition or pure monopoly, aims to maximise profits, and, as we noted in section 5A, that can be achieved only when *marginal cost equals marginal revenue.*

The essential difference between a firm in perfect competition and one in pure monopoly is that in perfect competition a firm is merely one of many and in pure monopoly it is the only one. In perfect competition, therefore, an individual firm has to accept a *market-established* selling price for its product, and since, by definition, an individual firm cannot influence that price then it must also accept that its marginal revenue equals its average revenue, i.e., if a firm sells one more good then it will do so at the same price as that obtained for each of all the previous goods. For a firm under perfectly competitive conditions, then, marginal revenue and average revenue are identical, at a level established by the market, as illustrated in figure 12.1 (cf. figure 5.1).

The great number of competitors ensures that surplus (excess) profits are not taken, and figure 12.1 therefore shows the *only* possible production position for a firm in perfect competition.

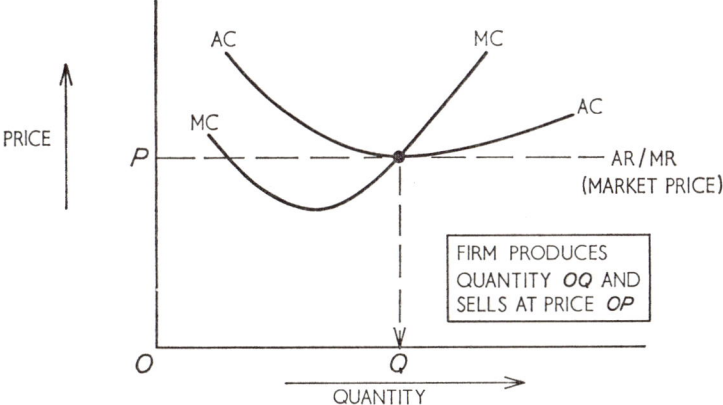

FIG 12.1   The production position of a firm in perfect competition.

In monopoly, however, the firm *is* the industry, and it is faced by the *total* demand from the market for the product of that industry. The nature of total market demand is that it extends only upon a fall in price; the monopolist can sell additional goods, therefore, only if the price is lowered. This is a key difference: the firm in perfect competition has to sell additional goods at the same price; the monopolist can sell additional goods only at a lower price. For the monopolist, therefore, marginal revenue is *less* than average revenue. Since profit maximisation occurs (*always*) at the point where marginal revenue equals marginal cost, then the fact that for the monopolist marginal revenue is less than average revenue means always that the monopolist is in a position to take excessive profits (provided, of course, that average revenue equals or exceeds average cost, otherwise there are no profits at all—and probably no production either). Figure 12.2 illustrates the possible production positions of a monopolist. Notice how the average revenue line falls steeply to the right (a reflection of the necessarily inelastic market demand), and how the marginal revenue line falls even more steeply to the right (*less* than average must be added each time in order to pull the average itself down). Notice also how the point of production is established by the intersection of the marginal cost and marginal revenue lines, and how the selling price is determined by the extent of demand above that intersection. The average revenue line reflects the market demand, and projection upwards from the point of maximum-profit production to the average revenue line yields the selling price (i.e., the maximum price that can be charged—for maximum profit—at the established level of output).

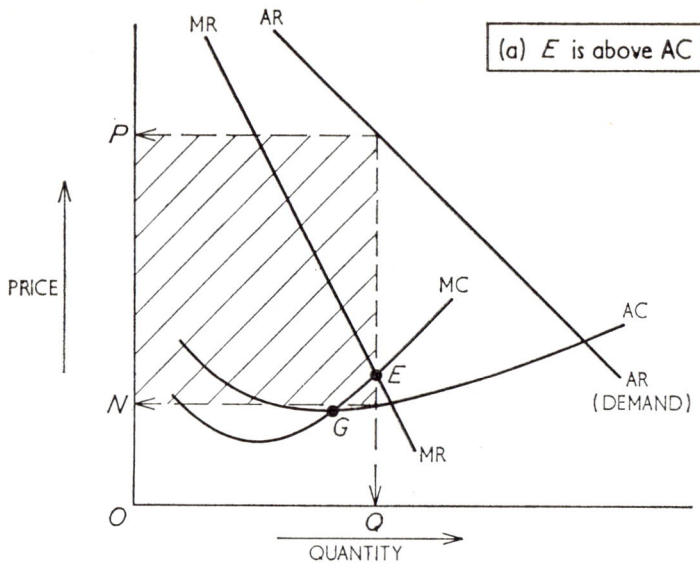

G : Point of optimum production (MC = AC)
E : Point of maximum profit (MC = MR)
OQ : Output for maximum profit
OP : Monopoly price for output OQ
ON : Minimum price needed to cover the average cost (AC) of producing OQ
▧ : Zone of excess profit (monopoly profit)

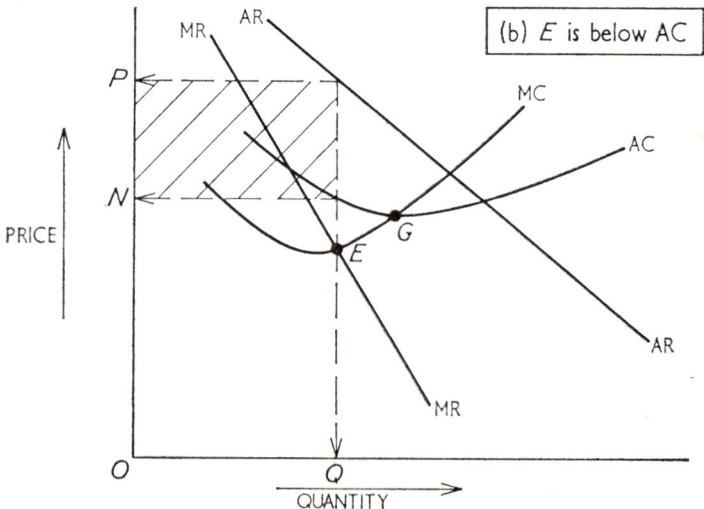

FIG 12.2   Possible production positions for a monopolist.

Graphical analysis of monopoly pricing can be supplemented by analysis of demand schedules. Let us assume that a market demand schedule is:

Price	Quantity demanded
17p	400
16p	700
15p	1100
14p	1600
13p	2200
12p	2900
11p	3700
10p	4600

The monopolist has to accept this schedule—remember, he controls only the supply side of the market (though he may attempt to shift demand in his favour by means of advertising). His production position can now be analysed according to whether his average costs of production are stable, falling or rising.

1   Monopoly prices under stable average costs of production. Let us assume that the monopolist's costs, *excluding profit of any sort*, are 12p per unit. If he is to make any profit at all he must sell for at least 13p per unit, at which price market demand is 2200 goods and the monopolist's profit therefore 2200p. A selling price of 14p yields a total sale of only 1600 goods, but a total profit of 3200p (1600 goods × 2p profit per good), while a selling price of 15p contracts demand to 1100 goods but raises total profit to 3300p (1100 × 3p). A selling price of 16p, however, contracts not only sales (to 700 goods) but also total profit (to 2800p), while a selling price of 17p still further reduces both sales (to 400 goods) and total profit (to 2000p). In order to maximise profits under these conditions the monopolist will clearly fix output at 1100 goods and sell at 15p per good.

2   Monopoly prices under falling average costs of production. If the monopolist's average costs of production, *excluding any profit at all*, fall to 11p then his minimum selling price falls to 12p. The table summarises the profit position at this and other levels of possible selling prices:

Selling price	Goods sold	Total profit
17p	400	2400p (400 × 6p)
16p	700	3500p (700 × 5p)
15p	1100	4400p (1100 × 4p)
14p	1600	4800p (1600 × 3p)
13p	2200	4400p (2200 × 2p)
12p	2900	2900p (2900 × 1p)

Maximum profit is achieved at a selling price of 14p and an output of 1600 goods. If average costs of production fall still farther to 10p, the position is then:

Selling price	Goods sold	Total profit
17p	400	2800p (400 × 7p)
16p	700	4200p (700 × 6p)
15p	1100	5500p (1100 × 5p)
14p	1600	6400p (1600 × 4p)
13p	2200	6600p (2200 × 3p)
12p	2900	5800p (2900 × 2p)
11p	3700	3700p (3700 × 1p)

Maximum profit is here achieved at an output of 2200 goods and a selling price of 13p. Clearly, a monopolist has a strong incentive in the face of the given market demand to reduce average production costs in order to achieve the greatest maximum profit.

3   Monopoly prices under rising average costs of production. The table shows what the price and output situation is like when the costs of production, *excluding profits*, rise to 14p per unit.

Selling price	Goods sold	Total profit
17p	400	1200p (400 × 3p)
16p	700	1400p (100 × 2p)
15p	1100	1100p (1100 × 1p)

12H Price discrimination

Under perfect competition one price only will be charged in the market for the same good at one moment of time. The monopolist may also charge only one price, but he has—if he wishes to use it—the power to charge different prices. He can pursue a policy of price discrimination. However, he can do that only if he can divide his total market into separate and exclusive sections, so that buyers in the high-price market cannot buy the product in the low-price market. The different markets must therefore be separated by such things as tariff barriers, geographical distance, inconvenience, time, social custom, and individual personal use.

1   Tariff barriers. Goods sold more cheaply abroad than at home may be prohibited re-entry to the domestic market by government-applied tariffs.

2   Geographical distance. If distances are to be overcome, then transport costs must be incurred. So long as the transport costs equal or exceed the difference between the prices in two separate markets there is no incentive for buyers in the high-price market to seek supplies in the low-price market. This is the reason for the National Coal Board's ability to sell coal at a higher price in London than in the Yorkshire coalfield.

3   Inconvenience. A good may be on sale at the other side of town at a price which more than allows for getting there and back; but it might be too much trouble for you to go there and get it. Similar feelings on the part of a number of consumers permit a monopolist to charge different prices in different places.

4   Time. Those industries which are characterised by high fixed costs (such as railways and electric power generation) often find that any revenue is better than no revenue (provided immediate variable costs are covered) during the times when there would normally be no sales. Railways may therefore run excursion trains or sell cheap day return tickets, provided the revenue at least covers the variable costs of providing the service; even a small surplus above that level goes some way to meeting the inevitable fixed costs, which occur whether the service is provided or not. For a similar reason, electricity boards provide off-peak electricity at a price substantially lower than that normally charged.

5   Social custom. Consumer 'snobbishness' or habit and ignorance often permit a manufacturer to sell the same good at different prices in different markets. The difference in beer prices between the public bar and the saloon bar is a good example; often, just a wooden partition separates the two markets.

6   Individual personal use. Personal services are impossible to transfer, and accordingly permit a great deal of price discrimination. Doctors may charge one price to a wealthy patient and a vastly lower one (if any) to a poor patient—for the same service. Manufacturers occasionally obtain a similar facility; for example, electricity is sold at different prices to different classes of consumer (domestic consumers paying more than industrial consumers, for instance).

A monopolist has the ability to be discriminatory in his pricing policy because of the existence of different demand elasticities in different markets. If he charged the same price throughout all markets, he would almost certainly be forfeiting the higher revenues he could gain from those consumers prepared to pay a high price (the inelastic demanders) as well as the additional sales he could make to those consumers prepared to pay only a low price (the elastic demanders). By means of price discrimination he is able to tap both ends of the market, and thus appropriate the consumer surplus which would normally accrue to the inelastic buyers. The inelastic buyers would be prepared to pay more than a 'medium' price for their purchases; so the discriminating monopolist charges them more, and their surplus accordingly disappears. Moreover, by supplying the low-price market the monopolist may achieve economies of scale because of the greater volume of production, and accordingly bring down his long-term average costs of production.

12I Dumping

Dumping is an international form of price discrimination, practised when possible by a monopolist whose production is characterised by decreasing average costs. A monopolist is in a better position to dump than a firm in competition because he can more easily restrict supply and keep prices up on the home market.

The act of dumping involves selling goods abroad at a price lower than that in the home market, and necessitates a higher-cost or tariff prohibition on re-entry. The enabling characteristic is a decreasing average cost of production on the part of the monopolist. Two cases will illustrate the principle:

1   Different scales of production.

Home demand Price	Quantity	Average cost	Total cost	Total revenue	Net revenue
68p	250	34p	8 500p	17 000p	8 500p
62p	300	32p	9 600p	18 600p	9 000p
56p	350	30p	10 500p	19 600p	9 100p
46p	400	26p	10 400p	18 400p	8 000p
36p	450	22p	9 900p	16 200p	6 300p

We have here a fairly common case, illustrating three *different* possible scales of production (as illustrated in figure 7.4): the smallest scale is represented by outputs of 250, 300 and 350 goods and characterised by *de*creasing average costs and *in*creasing total cost; the middle scale is marked by an output of 400 goods and characterised by both a lower average cost than the first scale and also a lower total cost (economies of scale); the largest scale has an output of 450 goods, and still lower average and total costs. Under these conditions a producer can bring down both his total and average costs by extending his scale of production. However, at the larger output the low selling price (say 36p) reduces net revenue (profit) well below the maximum possible at a smaller scale of production. Maximum net revenue is achieved, indeed, at an output of 350 goods, when total costs are 10 500p and net revenue is 9100p. Costs at this level, though, are higher than at the larger production scales. If only the producer could produce at the larger scale of output and sell at the lower level! In fact, he can. Provided he keeps the extra goods resulting from the larger scale of output *off the market* then he can gain both advantages: lower total costs and higher net revenue. He can, for example, make 450 goods at a total cost of 9900p, keep 100 off the market, sell 350 at 56p each, and take a net revenue of 9700p (i.e., 9100p + 600p, the 600p being the difference between the total costs of producing 350 goods and of producing 450 goods). The goods can be kept off the market by either physical destruction (burning or ploughing-in crops, for example) or dumping in another market. Any sales in another (preferably foreign) market yield additional revenue once the costs of transport have been met. In consequence, the selling price abroad can be extremely low.

2   A single scale of production

Home demand Price	Quantity	Average cost	Total cost	Total revenue	Net revenue
74p	220	38p	8 360p	16 280p	7 920p
68p	280	37p	10 360p	19 040p	8 680p
62p	340	36p	12 240p	21 080p	8 840p
56p	400	35p	14 000p	22 400p	8 400p
48p	460	34p	15 640p	22 080p	6 440p
40p	520	33p	17 160p	20 800p	3 640p

The conditions illustrated here are those of a *single* scale of production characterised by decreasing average cost. Maximum net revenue of 8840p is achieved at an output of 340 goods and an average production cost of 36p. Dumping abroad at any selling price over $27\frac{1}{2}$p plus transport costs yields even more revenue to the producer, provided he extends output to 520 goods. The minimum selling price abroad is computed by dividing the *number of additional goods* (180) into the *additional total cost* (raising output from 340 to 520 requires raising total cost from 12240p to 17160p, i.e., an *additional* 4920p). It is possible in this way to sell abroad not only for less than in the home market but also for less than the average cost of producing the goods ($27\frac{1}{2}$p abroad compared with a domestic selling price of 62p—for the 340 goods sold there—and an average production cost of 33p—for the 520 goods produced in total).

The advantages of dumping accrue to a domestic monopolist for two main reasons. First, he can more easily restrict supply and keep prices up on the home market than can a firm in competition; and second, he is more likely, other things being equal, to be able to benefit from the economies of extended scale than is a firm in competition, since, supplying the whole domestic market, his level of output is likely to be larger. Even though dumping may benefit a domestic monopolist, it may yet be harmful to competing firms in foreign countries. Accordingly, the General Agreement on Tariffs and Trade (GATT) permits countries suffering from dumping to levy counterbalancing import duties. It is, however, worth a thought that the consumers in the suffering country are thereby being deprived of goods imported cheaply; it is also worth a thought that if the suffering country's home firms become sub-marginal through competition from dumping then the monopolist dumper has effectively widened his monopoly market, and he may then raise prices in it without competition.

12J Prices under monopolistic competition

Monopolistic competition exists when there is a large number of firms producing similar but not identical goods. The goods may be more or less physically identical, and differentiated merely by style, packaging and name, or they may be slightly different physically; they all, however, satisfy the same particular want. Each firm has a monopoly in the supply of its own brand; but, being closely substitutable, the different brands compete with one another. The competition is imperfect because of the operation of frictions: successful advertising, goodwill, habit, ignorance, social and personal relationships, the provision of delivery and after-sales services, and other frictional phenomena all serve to some extent to tie consumers to particular brands. It is possible therefore for a supplier to raise the price of his product and perhaps lose some—but not all—of his customers; it is equally possible for him to lower the price and perhaps gain some—but not all—of the customers of his competitors. Where the competing brands are close substitutes the cross-elasticity of demand (see section 4F) is likely to be high, and a firm therefore has only small powers to vary its prices from the general market level. On the other hand, a low cross-elasticity of demand (i.e., a low possibility of substitution, or a position of more monopoly and less competition) allows a firm greater latitude in its pricing policy.

Only in perfect competition, by definition, is an individual firm incapable of influencing market price; in all other forms of production—monopoly, monopolistic competition, and oligopoly—the firm has at least some influence on the price of its product. However, that influence is subject to the overall requirement of demand—that demand only extends on a fall in price. Whereas, therefore, the sales line for an individual firm in perfect competition is perfectly elastic (i.e., the price remains constant whatever the level of the individual firm's output), under all other conditions—monopoly, monopolistic competition, and oligopoly—the sales line is negative (i.e., it slopes down to the right, indicating that additional sales can be made only if the price falls). In monopoly, where the firm is the sole supplier and there are no close substitutes for the product (otherwise there is no monopoly), the sales line is likely to be inelastic, as we saw in section 12G. In monopolistic competition, however, where the firm is only one of many and there are several close substitutes for the product, the sales line of an individual firm is likely to be highly elastic, as shown in figure 12.3.

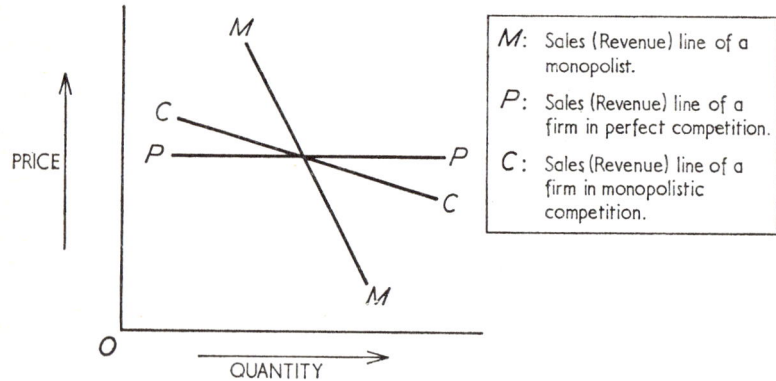

FIG 12.3 Sales (revenue) lines.

In relation to the individual firm, the price is constant over the entire range of possible output only in perfect competition; in *all* other cases the individual firm has to lower its prices in order to extend the demand for its product. Only in perfect competition, therefore, is an individual firm's marginal revenue equal to its average revenue; in all other cases marginal revenue is less than average revenue, and average revenue itself falls as the quantity sold increases.

As always in elementary theory, the pricing policy of a supplier is assumed to be guided primarily by the desire to maximise profits (it may also be guided by such considerations as government legislation, a sense of social duty, the desire to establish goodwill, and fear of Investigations or Enquiries). And, as always, profit maximisation occurs at the point where marginal

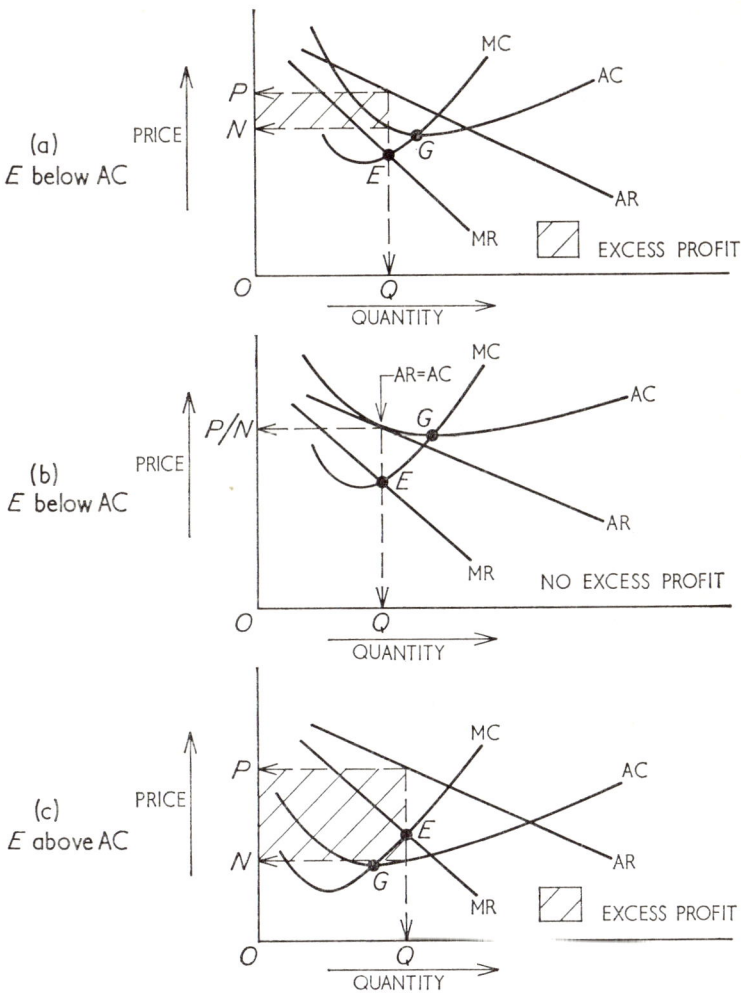

G: Point of optimum production (MC = AC)
E: Point of maximum profit (MC = MR)
OQ: Output at maximum profit
OP: Maximum (monopoly) price for output OQ
ON: Minimum price needed to cover average cost (AC) at output OQ

FIG 12.4 Possibilities of price and output determination for firms in monopolistic competition.

cost equals marginal revenue—where, in other words, an additional good costs as much to produce as it earns by sale. Beyond that point, an additional good costs more to produce than it earns by sale, thereby decreasing total profits.

The determination of both output level and price so as to yield maximum profit is done graphically in the same way as that employed in section 12G for monopoly. It does not matter whether the intersection of marginal cost and marginal revenue is above or below the average cost line; it only matters (in the long run) that the projection upwards from that intersection meets the average revenue line *at or above* the average cost line, otherwise average costs are not covered and the firm may cease production after a short time. The amount by which the intersection of the upward projection and the average revenue line lies above the average cost line indicates the excess profit which the firm can make. Average cost, you will remember, includes the normal profit needed to draw enterprise into production; any revenue above that is therefore excess profit. Figure 12.4 illustrates some possibilities. If the excess profits are high, more firms will be drawn into competition, and it is likely that—depending on the strength of the frictions tying consumers to a particular brand—the excess profits will be competed away.

Figure 12.4 also shows that it is unlikely that a firm in monopolistic competition will be operating at the point of optimum production (lowest possible average cost). Optimum production occurs at the point where marginal cost equals average cost, and that is only one of many possible points of production under monopolistic competition. Further, even if optimum production is achieved, figure 12.5 shows that the firm will still gain excess profits. Note that maximum profit occurs where MC = MR, and that optimum production occurs where MC = AC; maximum profit at

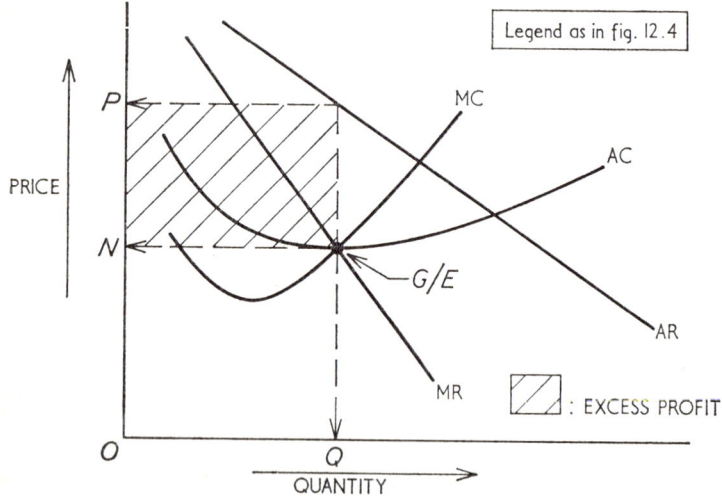

FIG 12.5 Excess profit at optimum production for a firm in monopolistic competition.

optimum production therefore entails that MC = MR = AC. Under monopolistic competition, however, AR is greater than MR, and the firm inevitably
takes the difference in the form of excess profits. If, by competition, the excess
profits are eliminated, so that average revenue equals average cost (the middle
diagram in figure 12.4), it is clear that production is taking place at a level
somewhat below the optimum point. In practice, therefore, monopolistic
competition may be criticised in that it yields either excess profits to the firm
or less than optimum production to society. Conversely, it may be defended
on the grounds that it provides product identification for those consumers (the
majority, by observation) who want it, and that it enables at least some economies of scale to be gained, since there are fewer, but larger, firms supplying
the total market (thus permitting lower prices, despite the existence of excess
profits).

12K Prices under oligopoly

Oligopoly is characterised by a small number of interdependent sellers in the
market. It is of great importance in real-life situations. As noted in section
12D, there are many different grades of oligopoly, and therefore many com-
plexities in analysis. At this stage, however, it is possible to generalise. The
assumption is accordingly made that firms in oligopoly have a demand elasticity for their products somewhere between those for firms in monopolistic
competition and firms in pure monopoly (this assumption is consistent with the
place of oligopoly in the perfect competition—pure monopoly series). The
sales line, and therefore the average revenue line, for a firm in oligopoly is
consequently as shown in figure 12.6. Generally, the more collusive the
oligopoly the closer will its sales line approach the steepness of the monopoly
line.

Based on the above assumption regarding demand elasticity and also on
the standard assumption that oligopolists—like firms in other conditions—
will attempt to maximise profits, the graphical analysis of pricing and output
policy for an oligopolist follows the patterns already established for monopoly

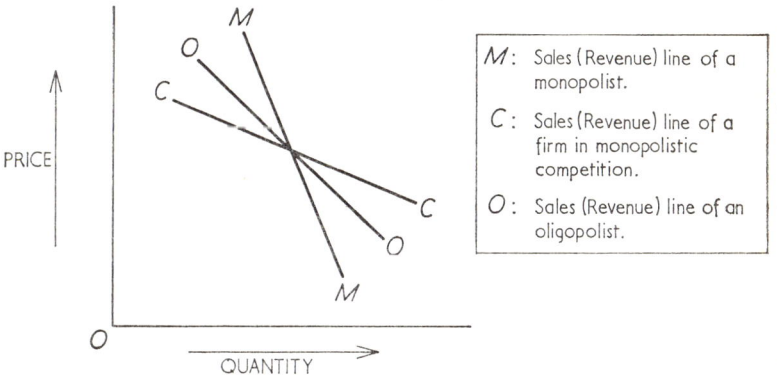

M: Sales (Revenue) line of a
monopolist.

C: Sales (Revenue) line of a
firm in monopolistic
competition.

O: Sales (Revenue) line of an
oligopolist.

FIG 12.6   Sales (revenue) lines. See also fig. 12.3.

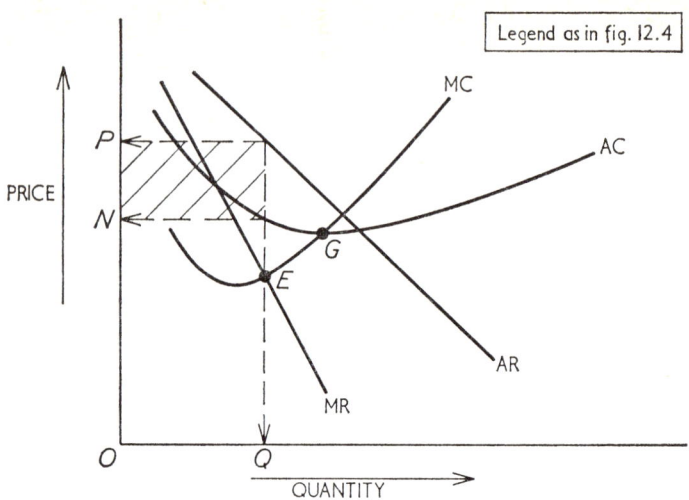

FIG 12.7 Price and output determination for an oligopolist.

and monopolistic competition (see figure 12.7). The difference is merely in the degree of elasticity accorded to the average revenue line.

A special feature of *spontaneous* oligopoly, requiring a little more elaboration, is that a rise in price has a different sort of effect from a fall in price, as far as an individual firm is concerned. If only one of the oligopolists raises his prices (i.e., there is no collusion), the others will be unwilling to follow his lead, hoping instead to attract some of the trade from the firm which has raised its prices. On the other hand, if a single oligopolist lowers his prices, the others are likely to follow rapidly, for fear of losing trade themselves. As a result, a single oligopolist has to assume that if he raises prices he will probably lose quite a large part of his sales, but that if he lowers prices he will probably not gain many extra sales. A single oligopolist in spontaneous oligopoly may therefore regard the demand for his product (and hence the average revenue line) as being 'kinked', showing great price elasticity at prices higher than the kink point and great price inelasticity at prices below the kink point (see figure 12.8). In order to extend demand beyond the kink point the oligopolist must accept a sharp cut in his marginal revenue; indeed, most economists assert that he must take a sudden cut. The marginal revenue line is therefore usually shown as dipping vertically at the kink point, resuming its fall to the right (but more steeply because of greater inelasticity) only after it has fallen vertically for some distance. The vertical fall is called the **region of indeterminacy**, and it is almost certain that the intersection of the marginal revenue and marginal cost lines occurs somewhere in this zone. Since selling price is determined by the location on the average revenue line of the point directly above the marginal revenue-marginal cost intersection, the existence of a vertical region of indeterminacy on the marginal revenue line permits cost

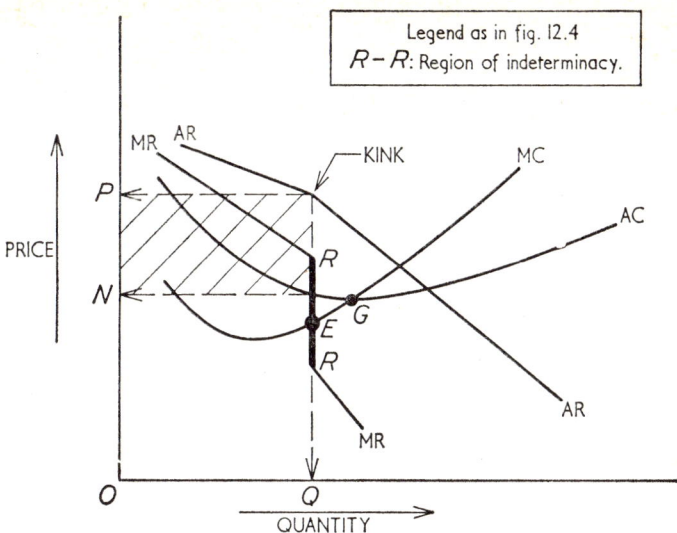

FIG 12.8   Price and output determination with kinked demand.

levels to vary without affecting price. Cost levels can move up or down within the limits of the region of indeterminacy and still produce the same selling price. What this means in practice is that a number of oligopolists can have slightly different cost conditions and yet still sell profitably at the same price as each other. There is a tendency in fact for a degree of price rigidity—the suppliers absorbing higher costs or taking additional profits without changing the selling price.

Section 13
Money, banking, and public finance

13A The importance of money

No one really needs to be told how important money is. Countless millions of people the world over spend hours thinking of ways to get more of it; more millions spend sleepless nights trying to think of ways to make what they have got go further than they fear it will; there are suicides and murders because of it, marriages and divorces because of it, misery and happiness because of it, and hope and despair because of it. Why?

Simply because money is the most easily exchanged form of wealth. If a person has money he can get almost anything else (not all the best things in life are, in fact, free). If he has a field full of wheat or a factory full of machines there is very little he will be able to get *directly* for them; but if he has money he can get almost anything. The term in economics denoting the ease with which wealth may be exchanged is **liquidity**. Money is highly (indeed, perfectly) liquid, whereas real wealth is often highly illiquid. However, it is the real wealth which ultimately matters, and money is therefore a claim on real wealth; in other words, money is an exchange-claim on goods and services.

The prime function of money, then, is to act as a *medium of exchange.* Money separates the business of exchange into two distinct parts: not only does it enable the seller to sell where and when it is most convenient but it also permits the buyer to buy where and when it is most convenient. In other words, it confers freedom of choice on both sellers and buyers. This is the essence of liquidity. Money also acts as a *measure of exchange value*, which means that since all economic goods and services are priced in terms of money then comparisons of value are readily possible. In addition, money can be saved; and so it also acts as a *store of wealth* and a *standard for deferred payments* (as in hire purchase deals). Finally, money acts as a *unit of account*, enabling accurate records of all transactions to be kept.

The desire to hold money instead of spending it is called the demand for money. This is a rather more specialised use of the word *demand* than that noted earlier, and it is used here to indicate a preference for liquidity over the holding of real wealth. Keynes suggested three distinct reasons for a person's **liquidity preference:**

1 The transactions motive. It is possibly only millionaires and royalty who can manage their daily affairs without cash; others, however, need cash for meals, taxis, cinema visits, shopping, football matches, etc.

2 The precautionary motive. Most people keep some liquid assets as a contingency against accidents and ill-health; in other words, liquidity for a rainy day.

3 The speculative motive. Betting on football pools and on horses and dog racing is a widespread reason for having cash to hand. Surplus liquidity may also be retained for speculation in share prices—anticipated favourable price movements may cause a potential purchaser to reserve liquidity so as to permit purchase at a time gauged to be the most opportune.

Instead of a preference for liquidity, there may be a preference for illiquidity, i.e., people may prefer to spend their money on goods or services rather than keep it ready to hand. A great deal of commercial advertising is aimed at inducing people to prefer illiquidity, and it may be extremely successful when people anticipate future price rises—as they did in early 1968 before the expectedly severe March budget. The demand for money is, indeed, the product of two conflicting forces: on the one side the desire for liquidity, and on the other the desire for goods and services. It is yet another example of the core problem in economics—how to achieve an equilibrium position from the interaction of competing factors; in other words, how to allocate a resource which has alternative uses.

13B The development of money and banking

Money has become necessary as society has developed. Indeed, it is becoming increasingly impossible for the world to manage without money, even though its form may not remain the same as most of us now know it.

Primitive societies had no money; people used to barter their real wealth instead. If one person had surplus pottery and wanted more clothes he would look round until he found someone who had surplus clothes and wanted pottery. Such a *coincidence of wants* was unlikely, and production along specialised lines was therefore hampered. Other disadvantages of barter were that storage of some surplus products (e.g., food) was difficult, and so saving was hindered; service trades could not thrive, since it was difficult to barter, say, a look-out function for clothing; and there was difficulty in obtaining any sort of measure of value, since no one could readily determine, say, how many pots were worth one cow.

People gradually 'invented' money in order to overcome the problems of barter. Goods came to be exchanged not directly for other wanted goods but for some third commodity which could itself be exchanged directly for other goods whenever they were required. This third commodity acted as a medium of exchange, thus satisfying the prime purpose of money. Its ideal qualities were (and are) that it was:

> easily recognisable
> portable
> uniform in quality
> durable
> divisible into smaller units
> scarce
> acceptable

Of these, the chief quality was (and is) acceptability, since if people refused to accept it then it could not act as a medium of exchange.

Early money, such as coral, sharks' teeth, stones, iron bars, and so on, did not satisfy all these conditions easily. The chief problem was acceptability. Who, in his right mind, would exchange a sack of wheat for, say, a bag of sharks' teeth, unless he knew that someone else would accept the teeth in return for some other goods later on? In consequence, early money was often a commodity which could at least be used for the direct satisfaction of some want or other if the worst happened and other people refused to accept it in payment. Commonly, cattle have been thus used as money. A recent example of a third commodity with an alternative 'standby' use being employed as money was the use of cigarettes as a medium of exchange in Germany in 1945. Apart from the problem of acceptability in the use of goods as a third commodity, there are also problems of storage, divisibility and quality variation.

In order to circumvent some of the problems associated with the use of goods as money, people gradually began to employ metals as money. Gold eventually emerged as the most acceptable. Other metals could perhaps have been used instead—and, indeed, sometimes were—but they suffered variously from a number of disadvantages. They rusted, they were variable in quality, they were less easily recognisable than gold (gold has both a distinctive colour and a distinctive density), and they were less easily portable than gold because, being more common, they had a lower value per unit of bulk in terms of commodities for which they could be exchanged. And so they were generally less acceptable than gold. Compared with gold, diamonds have the big disadvantage that they cannot be divided into smaller units without serious loss of value; nor are they so readily identifiable as gold.

The use of metals promoted the development of coins. Instead of certain bar-sizes or certain weights (e.g., a pound), metals came to be accepted (and therefore produced) in readily-identifiable sizes and shapes, with their exchange values impressed upon their face. Today, for example, a 10p piece is identified by both its size and its face value, and it is recognisably different from a 5p piece (but note that when the 50p piece was introduced in 1969 there was a considerable outcry from the public because the coin was not easy to distinguish from the 10p piece—indeed, even the canteen in the Royal Mint at first refused to accept it). Coinage, nevertheless, satisfies the essential requirements of money: it is recognisable, portable (except in large sums), uniform in quality, durable, divisible into smaller units (change), scarce (in so far as a person cannot obtain anywhere near enough of it to satisfy his varied wants), and acceptable. Those coins which contain their face value in their metal are called *standard coins*, and those which have a face value in excess of their metal value are called *token coins*. Until 1968 the Swiss franc was an example of a standard coin, but during that year the price of silver rose sufficiently for the owners of Swiss francs to find it worth their while melting the coins down and selling the silver. The Swiss government accordingly stopped issuing silver francs, and began replacing them with token coins.

The widespread acceptance of gold bars (bullion) and standard coins (mostly gold and silver) naturally—human nature being what it is—entailed fear of theft on the part of their owners. In consequence, a specialised safe-keeping function developed, and from this we can trace the growth of banking.

In England, the original safe-keeping function was performed by the Jews, and—after the expulsion of the Jews from England in 1290—by Italians from Lombardy. The Lombards (n.b. Lombard Street in the City of London) traded on benches, and from this we derive the name 'bank' (bench = It. *banco*). Gradually, the early safe-keepers came to be called goldsmiths, and their functions widened concurrently. The goldsmiths realised through experience that not all the gold deposited with them was being reclaimed at once, and that frequently the receipts which they had issued for deposits of gold were being exchanged for payments to third parties (and fourth and fifth parties, etc.) without being presented for redemption at all. The owners of the gold (the depositors or receipt-holders) seemed, in fact, quite content to use the receipts as money instead of drawing out the gold on each occasion. The goldsmiths at first, therefore, found it safe to lend out some of the gold on deposit and make profitable interest charges on the loans. However, with the growing realisation that receipts were just as useful as money as the gold itself was, the goldsmiths found that they could make their business even more profitable. They started lending more money than they had gold on deposit; and they could do this provided they could persuade the borrowers to take the loans in the form of exchangeable paper receipts (which they could easily print) rather than in gold (which they did not have). Eventually, the gold-smiths found that it was more convenient (because of greater acceptability) to print the receipts in certain values, so that instead of issuing a single receipt for, say, £97, a goldsmith would issue nine receipts for £10 each, one for £5 and two for £1 each. By this means, the requirement of divisibility was satisfied, and the money system became more flexible.

The acceptability of goldsmiths' receipts rested on confidence—on the part of the goldsmiths that not all receipts would be presented for redemption in gold at once; and on the part of the receipt-holders that if they did present a receipt it would be redeemed. Not unnaturally, many goldsmiths took advantage of the system by issuing far more receipts (notes) than they should have done, thus earning a great deal of interest from loans but at the same time undermining confidence in themselves. A goldsmith, therefore, could safely issue receipts in excess of his actual gold holdings only so long as the depositors and borrowers were ignorant of his doing so. As soon as it became obvious that there were more receipts in circulation than could possibly be backed by a particular goldsmith's holdings of gold (which he clearly tried to keep as secret as possible), then the receipt-holders dashed to the goldsmith to redeem their receipts for gold. There was a run on the bank: first come, first served (with gold). There were innumerable bank failures, and only slowly did the bankers (the functional heirs of the goldsmiths) learn by experience that they had to maintain a liquid reserve sufficiently large to justify public confidence in the system; and as that confidence has developed so the size of the liquid reserve has dwindled. For the most part the confidence of today is based on ignorance: many people fondly imagine that there is gold equivalent to the note issue, and that the relict phrase 'I promise to pay the bearer on demand the sum of . . .' actually means what it says.

By the 17th century in England, the governments, which were large borrowers, had established a very poor reputation for repaying loans made to them, and goldsmiths were accordingly wary of lending to a government. However, the abuses of the early banking system by many of the goldsmiths produced a climate favourable to government intervention, and the strength of the government will both to borrow and to intervene was exercised in 1694 to create the Bank of England. A small group of goldsmiths adopted the idea of Thomas Paterson to lend the government a sum of £1 200 000 in return for the privileges of limited liability and joint-stock operation and the right to issue notes over and above their normal issue to the extent of the sum lent to the government. For the first time in England, therefore, confidence in a government's ability (and intentions) to repay became the basis of note issue. It is now the sole basis. Though, as we have noted, the government of today has neither the ability (gold) nor the intention (lack of ability precludes intention) to repay, and the phrase 'I promise to pay the bearer on demand . . . is valueless. However, the confidence exists, and that is all that matters—just so long as the notes are accepted everyone is content, whether the gold exists or not.

The privileges granted to the new Bank of England were consolidated by an Act of 1708, whereby the Bank was accorded the monopoly of joint-stock banking in London and the sole right of note issue in England and Wales for joint-stock banks with seven or more stock-holders. In the main, the result of the Act was that other banking in England and Wales was restricted to small private local banks, operating only in the areas where the proprietors and stock-holders were known and trusted. Even so, many of the hundreds of small 'country banks' over-issued notes and consequently failed. Towards the end of the Napoleonic wars alone there were over 500 local bank failures, yet in 1821 there were still 843 private banks in business.

Meanwhile, as trade grew during the 'take-off' period of the Industrial Revolution during the early 19th century, the demand for larger and larger loans to finance expansion put serious pressures on the small local banks, which found themselves increasingly incapable of supplying safely the larger sums demanded. Many small banks succumbed to the pressures, and issued loans for which they had inadequate liquid reserves. There were many bank failures. The clear and growing need for bigger banks caused a partial removal in 1826 of the Bank of England's monopoly of large joint-stock bank note issue—but only if the big new note-issuing banks operated more than 65 miles from Charing Cross in London. In 1833 the Bank of England's monopoly of joint-stock operation in London itself was removed, but the new joint-stock banks in London were not allowed to issue notes. Many banks remained small and private in order to retain their power to issue notes, and even in mid-century there were still over 400 private banks in existence.

However, in 1844 the government took measures to effect a gradual concentration of the country's note issue in the Bank of England. The Bank Charter Act of 1844 prohibited the right of note issue to any new banks and caused any bank which amalgamated with another or which opened a new office within 65 miles of Charing Cross to surrender its power of note issue, such lapsed note issue to be taken over by the Bank of England. The Bank of England itself was empowered to issue notes to a sum comprising the value of gold currently held by the Bank as well as the value of the loans made by the Bank to the government (at that time, £14 000 000).

By the mid-19th century the banks were fully prepared to accept this new legislation. The amalgamation of banks was increasingly essential to finance expanding businesses, and the existence of a London office more and more desirable as trade grew (note that London was—and still is—Britain's chief port). Gradually, therefore, as banks amalgamated and opened London offices, the Bank of England assumed the monopoly of note issue in England and Wales (not Scotland), achieving it completely in 1921 when the last re-maining private note-issuing bank (Fox, Fowler & Co.) was amalgamated with the Midland Bank.

During the 19th century the enormous expansion of world production and trade was financed largely by gold. Even the notes issued by the banks (especially the Bank of England) were fully convertible into gold on demand; and this was the basis of their acceptance. However, production and trade were expanding at a faster rate than new supplies of gold were being dis-covered. If trade was to continue growing, some third commodity other than gold had also to be used as a medium of exchange. Gradually, then, wide-spread acceptance of notes on their own was achieved. People had become accustomed to trading pieces of paper, and when, after 1914, the British government withdrew the gold backing, rendering the notes inconvertible (i.e., not exchangeable for gold), people continued to accept notes in payment just as they had done before 1914. The acceptance of the inconvertible notes was based on the faith people had in the issuing authority, and for this reason the incovertible notes are often called **fiduciary** issue. The acceptance of inconvertible notes offers a number of positive advantages to the community. First, they are cheap to produce, and—provided a strict check is kept against counterfeiting—few real resources need to be employed in creating them; resources may accordingly be employed in the production of real wealth in-stead (for example, the increasing use of gold in the electronics and aerospace industries). Second, the supply of notes can be expanded or contracted more or less at will in order to meet the varying needs of trade; the Bank of England, for example, usually ensures that there is more paper money circulating in England and Wales during the summer holiday season and before Christmas than there is during the rest of the year.

The disadvantages of paper notes are, first, the dangers of counterfeiting, and, second, the temptations to over-issue by governments. Most govern-ments, including the British, are periodically tempted to issue notes in quanti-ties greater than those needed to finance existing trade. It is often easier, for example, to print additional notes than it is to raise taxes. Whenever this happens, and the supply of real wealth remains constant, then all that happens is that prices rise (i.e., more money units are needed in exchange for a given amount of real wealth). The classic case of prices rising for this reason was 'The Great Inflation' in Germany in 1922-23, when the note-printing presses were used with pride by the government. During the worst excesses of this period, prices were adjusted upwards twice daily, and a meal was often dearer by the time it had been eaten than it was when ordered. From 1920 to 1923 the German mark fell in value from 250 to a £ to 20 000 000 000 000 to a £, and prices in Germany were approximately 1 250 000 000 000 times higher in 1923 than they had been in 1914.

The concentration of note issue in the Bank of England during the 19th century was accepted by the banks because they foresaw the possibilities as a medium of exchange of still another type of paper—the cheque. The chief advantage of the cheque over notes is that it can be made out for any sum at all; the principle of divisibility is realised absolutely. The chief problem, however, as with all money, is that of acceptability. People will accept a cheque in payment only if they have faith in the issuing authority; in other words, in the person making out (drawing) the cheque. The use of cheques depends directly upon the existence of bank deposits, the cheques themselves being merely written instructions by the depositors (drawers) to the bankers to transfer part of their deposits to the person(s) named as recipients (payees). The bank deposits are therefore money; they act as a medium of exchange—through the agency of cheques.

Bank deposits in England amount to about £12 000 000 000. There is, however, only about £3 000 000 000 in cash (notes and coin) in England, and only about one-third of *that* is held by the banks; so bank deposits obviously consist of more than cash. In fact, experience over the years has shown the bankers that only about 8% of all the cash deposited with them is ever likely to be withdrawn at any one time, and this knowledge has given the bankers the ability to 'make' money by means of the **credit mechanism**. When £100 is deposited in cash at a bank, the bank knows that it needs to keep only £8 as a liquid reserve; it therefore lends the other £92 and charges interest on the loan. If we assume a closed system, then the £92 will be deposited complete in—probably—another bank. The second bank knows that it needs to keep only 8% of that £92 deposit (i.e., £7·36) as liquid reserve, and so it lends out the remaining £84·64. On receipt of a deposit of £84·64, a third bank will keep 8% (i.e., £6·77) and lend £77·87. A fourth bank, receiving £77·87, will keep £6·23 and lend £71·64; and a fifth bank will keep £5·73 and lend £65·91 of the £71·64 it receives as a deposit. After just five moves, the original £100 has grown to £392·96 (i.e., £92·00 + £84·64 + £77·87 + £71·64 + £65·91). The startling fact is that, simply by following the process of credit creation through, a total value of bank deposits *some 12–12½ times greater than the original cash deposit* is produced. The difference between the £12 000 000 000 or so of total bank deposits and the £1 000 000 000 in cash held by the banks is, therefore, entirely of the banks' own creation. It is **bank money** or **bank credit,** and is transferable from one person to another by means of cheques.

It is now the most important type of money by value of transactions. The mechanism is allowed to work by virtue of the fact that people are prepared to accept cheques instead of cash in the settlement of debts, so that relatively little cash (8%) is required.

The quantity of cheques passing through the banking system has now become so great that the banks are finding the sheer volume of paper difficult to deal with. There are two measures in train to alleviate the problem: first, computer processing of magnetically-encoded cheques, and second, the introduction of credit cards. The only bank with a paper-diminishing credit card is Barclays—the Barclaycard permitting card holders to settle their monthly trade bills by means of a single cheque. The cards of the other banks merely guarantee the worth of a cheque, thereby increasing the likelihood of acceptance but doing nothing to reduce the quantity of paper. In time there is every prospect of a completely integrated inter-bank computerised accounting system, thus cutting the flow of paper; indeed, a start has already been made. There is also a (remoter) possibility that more and more transactions will be made using 'personalised' credit cards (voice or finger printed, for example), which need merely to be pushed into a machine, which is itself linked to a central computer for immediate adjustment of account balances.

The 19th century bank amalgamations, which were accompanied by loss of note-issuing rights and the corresponding development of cheque payments, came to a halt around 1920. The Treasury Committee on Bank Amalgamations (the Colwyn Committee) indicated in 1918 that further mergers between major banks might be against the public interest, though at the same time it accepted that small regional mergers could be beneficial. The later stages of amalgamation which produced the Westminster Bank (so named in 1923) illustrate the progress which was being made at around the time of the Colwyn Committee. Following the amalgamation in 1909 of the London & Westminster Bank and the London & County Bank, the bank grew by the additions of the Ulster Bank in 1917, Parr's Bank in 1918, the Nottingham and Nottinghamshire Bank in 1919, Beckett & Co. in 1920, Stilwell & Sons in 1923, and the Guernsey Commercial Banking Corporation in 1924. Banking in England then settled into an oligopoly situation, consisting of the 'Big 5' (Barclays, Lloyds, Midland, National Provincial, Westminster) with about 80% of the banking business, and the 'Little 6' (Coutts, District, Glyn Mills, Martins, National, Williams Deacon) with about 15% of the banking business.

However, world trade and production did not stand still. The immense international growth of American-based businesses (including banks) and the creation of the European Common Market produced not only very great competition but also very great opportunities for British industrialists. A round of industrial amalgamations and take-overs of great magnitude began to characterise British industry in the 1960s, thus greatly increasing the demand for very large loans from the banks, and the government accordingly began to look favourably upon the idea of renewed bank amalgamations. In May 1967 the report of the National Board for Prices and Incomes on bank charges (an investigation into oligopoly prices) said that 'the Bank of England and the Treasury have made it plain . . . that they would not obstruct some further amalgamation if the banks were willing to contemplate such a development . . .' The banks reacted quickly. A spate of mergers and merger attempts was started by the proposal on January 26th 1968 of the biggest merger in the history of British banking between the National Provincial and the Westminster banks. It was followed on February 7th by the announcement of the intentions of the Three Banks Group (Glyn Mills, Williams Deacon, and the Royal Bank of Scotland) and the National Commercial Bank of Scotland (which operated the National Bank) to merge their banking interests. Meanwhile, Martins Bank had decided that its best interests would be served by a merger with one of the Big 5, and it had accordingly indicated that it would welcome merger or take-over proposals. Only Barclays and Lloyds had submitted bids, and these were under consideration when the other merger proposals were announced. The effect of the other proposals was to push Barclays, Lloyds and Martins into an attempt at a triple merger. However, while the National Westminster and Williams & Glyn's mergers were eventually successfully completed, the Barclays-Lloyds-Martins proposals were referred sharply by the Board of Trade to the Monopolies Commission, and subsequently rejected. Upon rejection of the triple merger, Barclays acted on its own to take over Martins.

The money used to finance world trade is not quite the same as that used to finance domestic exchange. People are generally more prepared to trust their fellow-countrymen, and to accept incovertible paper money and cheques from them in payment for goods and services, than they are to trust foreigners. Moreover, there is no generally accepted world money authority in whom all countries place trust. For these reasons, gold is still widely used as a medium of international exchange; it is still the only truly universal money. However, the supply of international gold has failed to keep pace with the growth of world trade, and the countries of the world have thus come of necessity to rely increasingly on the use of trusted and available paper currencies in order to finance their international trade. Any widely trusted and available paper currencies may be used (for example, Sino-Japanese trade is financed with Swiss francs), but the most-widely accepted currencies are sterling and US dollars. This means, for instance, that Argentina and France may trade with each other, and finance that trade with payments to each other in sterling and US dollars as well as in gold. Trading countries try to build up their holdings of sterling, dollars and gold so that they can afford to pay for their imports in any year during which their exports fail to earn enough money. Sterling, dollars and gold are therefore a sort of international liquidity (money) kept for transactions and precautionary motives. The holdings are called **gold and foreign currency reserves**. Sterling and dollars are the chief currencies held in this manner, and they are accordingly termed **reserve currencies**. The increasing importance to world trade of the reserve currencies (especially the dollar) and the diminishing relative importance of gold are illustrated in the following table:

	1937	*1949*	*1966*
Gold	91·3	77·0	60·8
US dollars	1·5	6·6	21·3
Sterling	6·1	14·1	10·6
Others	1·1	2·3	7·3

TABLE 13.1   Percentage changes in the composition of world gross monetary reserves, 1937–66.

If countries wish to obtain reserve currencies they have to earn them: the USA and Britain do not scatter dollars and pounds about the world simply so that other countries can use them for trade. In order to earn dollars and pounds, other countries must sell more goods and services to the USA and Britain than they buy back; in other words, they must make a profit on their transactions with the USA and Britain. Unfortunately, this inevitably means that the USA and Britain must make a loss, and a prolonged trading loss is not conducive to international confidence. Since confidence is essential to acceptability, the USA and Britain have been forced periodically (out of a sense of international obligation as well as to protect their own trade) into taking measures to reduce or eliminate their trading deficits, with resulting contractions of available international liquidity. The measures were, however, frequently unavailing, and the persistence of the deficits has caused a series of crises of confidence since 1945. Both the dollar and the pound (especially the pound) have been subject to speculative international monetary pressures, and as a result both the USA and Britain would willingly see their currencies lose their reserve status—provided that the alternative was not gold, which is not only bulky to transport but also in inadequate supply.

Regrettably, the complete demonetisation of gold (i.e., gold no longer being used even for international trade, which is its last monetary use) and the discontinuance of dollars and sterling as reserve currencies can happen only if some other third commodity comes to be acceptable as a medium of international exchange. And not merely acceptable; preferable. Until that time comes, it is likely that gold, dollars and sterling will continue to be used to finance international trade. The first major proposals for a separate third commodity were put forward by Keynes at the international monetary conference at Bretton Woods in 1944. The proposals for a partly gold-backed international currency called 'Bancor' were, however, rejected by the USA, which then had the world's largest reserves of gold and whose dollars were not so widely used interntionally as they were later to become. The increasingly widespread international use of dollars, accompanied by persistent US trade deficits, had begun, by the early 1960s, to produce serious speculative pressures, and there was, therefore, a growing awareness on the part of the US authorities that another third commodity really was needed. The International Monetary Fund (IMF) therefore sponsored a major investigation throughout the 1960s into the creation of a new form of international liquidity. A measure of agreement to activate in 1970 a special form of international liquidity called Special Drawing Rights (SDR) was reached among the chief trading nations (France excepted) at meetings in London (August 1967), Rio de Janeiro (September 1967) and Stockholm (March 1968). Apart from possible problems of acceptance, the chief disadvantage of the new money is its cumbersome name.

Table 13.2 shows, in conclusion, the sources of supply of the main types of money currently in use in the economically advanced parts of the world.

National	International
coins—governments (mints)	gold—gold mines
notes—governments	(chiefly South Africa)
(and some banks)	dollars—US trade deficits
bank deposits—banks (subject to	sterling—UK trade deficits
government	SDR—International
influence)	Monetary Fund

TABLE 13.2   The chief sources of supply of money.

13C The money market

The money market is the organisation of institutions where short-term liquidity is bought and sold. Unlike other markets, the money market does not sell what its name implies; what it does sell is the *use* of money for short periods of time—perhaps hours only, or maybe a year or two at most. Money is therefore being lent and borrowed over the short term.

The price for the short-term use of money is called **interest** or **discount**, depending upon the method of payment. Interest is an addition to the total sum borrowed; for example, if £100 is borrowed, then £100 is taken away by the borrower and—after a specified time—£100 plus interest is returned to the lender. The sum of interest charges depends upon what is called the interest rate; thus, if the interest rate is 5% per annum, and the £100 is borrowed for exactly one year, then the return sum is £105 (i.e., £100 + £5). If the £100 is borrowed for six months only, the return sum is then £102·50, since for half a year exactly half the annual rate is charged. If no time period is specified for the interest rate, you should assume that it is a year; so that a quoted rate of 8% means £8 for each £100 for a year. Discount is rather different in that it is deducted from the total sum borrowed at the time the loan is taken out; for example, if £100 is borrowed, then a deduction of, say, £5 is made at the time of the loan, and the borrower takes away only £95, returning the full £100 at the end of the loan period. The amount deducted in this way depends upon what is called the discount rate, which is obviously very close to interest rate in amount.

The institutions which sell liquidity are naturally those which have most of it, i.e., the banks. The buyers, on the other hand, are immensely varied in type; and they also buy for a variety of different purposes. In general, the buyers of liquidity to finance production seek the use of money for long periods, and their needs are more commonly met in what is called the capital market, which we shall deal with in sections 13L–N. The buyers who wish to finance consumption (e.g., buy a car on hire purchase) generally seek their funds from specialised finance houses on the edge of the money market proper. The money market itself is more concerned with the financing of exchange, or trade, where the chief need is for relatively short-term funds. Various types of banks engage in money market activities, but, because the trading of money in London is so great and has reached such a high peak of development, it is worth having separate specialised banks to deal with the trading of certain short-term funds. Such banks are either (a) discount houses, e.g., Alexanders Discount House, or (b) acceptance houses, which are often also called merchant banks, e.g., Hill, Samuel & Co. Ltd. There is usually a risk attached to lending money, and it is possible that at times the discount houses and merchant banks may consider the risk too great for them to bear. In such cases, the more risky business may be taken to bill-brokers for financing.

Discount houses and merchant banks prefer to handle the more reliable business, but even where the business is completely risk-free they insist on written *security* for the loans. The insistence is often more to help the accounting process—to keep track of the money—than because of any lack of trust. The written securities are of two main types:

1   Bills of exchange. A bill is a form. A bill of exchange is a form which facilitates the process of exchange. It is therefore a specialised medium of exchange; it is specialised money. Since it is based, like a cheque, on the existence of bank deposits, it is also a form of credit instrument. Its purpose is to help finance foreign trade by providing a means whereby the exporter in England can obtain immediate funds, more or less equivalent to the value of his exports, without having to wait until the foreign importer either receives the goods or sells them. The exporter's first step is to make out (draw) a bill showing the nature and price of the goods to be exported and then send the bill to the importer. The importer then 'accepts' it by signing his name on it, thus indicating his willingness to trade; he then returns the bill to the exporter, who in turn immediately arranges both to ship the goods and to obtain money on the security of the bill. Shipping the goods is usually a simple matter, but obtaining money on the bill is rather more complex. Part of the complexity arises from the risks of eventual non-payment by the importer: he may become insolvent or go out of business, his country may impose currency controls and trade restrictions, or there may be a war. Usually, these risks can be covered by an Export Credits Guarantee Department insurance policy (the ECGD is a branch of the Board of Trade). Armed with his accepted (by the importer) bill of exchange, his ECGD insurance and documents offering evidence of shipping (e.g., a bill of lading), the exporter then approaches a bank for funds. The bank may be either a commercial one or a discount one; it does not matter.

On the security of the documents (chiefly the bill of exchange) the bank may make a direct loan to the exporter, repayable when the foreign importer eventually pays. Or it may arrange to discount the bill. Often the bank will discount the bill for the exporter before the bill has been accepted by the importer, particularly if the importer is a reputable one in a politically stable country. Once the bill has been discounted, it is sent by the bank to the correspondent bank in the importer's country; that bank then in due course obtains the importer's payment for remission to Britain. Meanwhile the exporter has got his funds more or less immediately (less the discount he has paid); and so everyone is happy. The only snag that could occur is if the importer fails to pay—and then the discounting bank has a claim against the exporter for return of the money (unless the ECGD insurance was absolutely unconditional, in which case the ECGD pays).

The acceptance credit is a specialised refinement of the ordinary bill of exchange. The exporter obtains all his usual documents (bills of exchange and lading, and ECGD insurance) and goes to a merchant bank for funds. The merchant bank takes the documents and sends the bill of exchange out to its correspondent bank in the importer's country for collection in the manner outlined above. However, the merchant bank does not give the exporter any money in return for the documents; what it does do is to permit the exporter to make out a draft drawn on the merchant bank itself (i.e., the exporter makes out a form which promises that the merchant bank will pay the bearer the sum mentioned on the date specified). When the merchant bank has 'accepted' this draft—in other words, when the 'acceptance house' has agreed to honour the draft on its presentation—the exporter takes it for discounting to a commercial bank or discount house, neither of which has any hesitation in discounting the draft, since it is issued on the reputation of the merchant bank. The draft is dated to mature (i.e., become payable) shortly after the foreign importer will have paid the bill of exchange to the merchant bank's correspondent bank; so that the merchant bank is at no time out of funds. If the foreign importer fails to pay, the merchant bank can reclaim its money from the exporter (unless the ECGD guarantee is unconditional).

2 Treasury bills. Introduced in 1877, treasury bills are a somewhat similar device for borrowing short-term funds in the money market, and—like bills of exchange and cheques—are also sometimes called credit instruments. The purpose of treasury bills is to smooth out the flow of government revenue: taxation revenue usually comes in very irregularly, and yet there are numerous regular commitments for which money must be found. Governments, via the Treasury, accordingly borrow regularly in the money market. They do so on the strength of paper promises to repay the loans at the end of—usually—a three month period. Since the promises are made by the government, which is the ultimate monetary authority in the country, there is naturally absolute trust on the part of the money market suppliers. There is no risk of non-payment, and no need for the acceptance house procedure. The discount rate, compared with that for bills of exchange, is therefore . . . higher or lower?

Because of the great safety of treasury bills they are often used by all banks as part of the fairly liquid reserve which they keep. A treasury bill is, of course, a highly acceptable credit instrument; after all, it is a government promise to repay a loan in a specified time, and is therefore not essentially dissimilar from ordinary inconvertible paper money (which, remember, carries a promise 'to pay the bearer on demand the sum of . . .'). Banks treat treasury bills therefore much as cash, and use them to settle inter-bank indebtedness; the initial loaning bank may in consequence be different from the bank which is eventually repaid.

The different sort of bills may be ranked according to their degree of acceptability (and, accordingly, of liquidity):

1   Treasury bills, which are backed by the promise of the currency authority, and are therefore completely acceptable in the money market.
2   Bank bills, i.e., drafts which have been accepted by a merchant bank, and which—because of the very high regard given to those banks—therefore have a very high degree of general acceptability.
3   Fine trade bills, i.e., bills of exchange which are discounted in the normal way because of the excellent reputations of the merchants on whom they are drawn.
4   Trade bills, i.e., those bills of exchange which carry even a slight risk of non-payment, and which are discounted by bill-brokers.

The greater the acceptability and liquidity of a bill, based on a low redemption risk, the lower the discount rate will be. There will always be at least some discount, because of the trouble involved in mobilising liquidity as well as sacrificing it temporarily to a third party. Higher discount rates will be charged for more illiquid or risky loans, as illustrated by the rates quoted in certain newspapers; for example, *The Times* of May 7th 1969 quoted:

Treasury bills (91 day)	$7\frac{13}{16}$	$(= 7 \cdot 825\%)$
Bank bills (91 day)	$8\frac{3}{8} - 8\frac{7}{16}$	$(= 8 \cdot 375 - 8 \cdot 4375\%)$
Fine trade bills (91 day)	$9\frac{1}{2} - 9\frac{3}{4}$	$(= 9 \cdot 5 - 9 \cdot 75\%)$

Trade bills are not quoted, because of the variations in risk which attach to them; discount rates for them are given individually—there is no general figure.

13D Types and functions of banks

The financial specialisation in London is reflected in the existence of a great variety of different types of banks. Some banks specialise in one thing, some in another, and yet others specialise in providing a range of general services. The chief types of bank are:

1   Central banks. These act as agents for government monetary policy, and are usually responsible for the country to the IMF. There is one in each country, e.g., the Bank of England.
2   Banks of issue. These banks are responsible for the issue of cash; they are often the central banks also, but note that Scotland has several banks of issue quite separate from the Bank of Scotland.

3　Commercial joint-stock banks. These carry on the bulk of the country's normal banking business, and provide a full range of services for their millions of customers. Barclays and Lloyds are examples.

4　Merchant banks. These accept and discount bills as well as arranging the issue of new shares and generally advising firms in mergers and take-overs. They also operate in the foreign exchange market, manage investment trusts, and provide a range of general services for their customers. Morgan Grenfell and Rothschild's are examples.

5　Discount houses. These discount bills. They are grouped into the London Discount Market Association, which has 12 members.

6　Investment banks. The prime purpose of these banks is to channel savings into capital investment projects. Lombard Banking is an important example.

7　Savings banks. The chief purpose is to attract small savings from the general public. The money from both the Post Office Savings Bank and the many separate Trustee Savings Banks is invested under the supervision of the National Debt Commissioners. In addition, the Trustee Savings Banks provide a limited range of general services for their customers.

8　Finance banks. The main concern of these banks is to organise the availability of liquidity for industrial and commercial use, including that for capital investment projects as well as for consumption purposes (e.g., hire purchase). United Dominions Trust is an example.

9　Mortgage banks. These have the very special purpose of mobilising loan capital for private house purchase. The largest in England is the Halifax Building Society, but there are dozens of others—some large and national (e.g., Abbey National) and others small and local (e.g., Coventry Provident Mutual Building Society).

10　Overseas banks. These are concerned primarily to ease the difficulties of international trade, both by arranging international monetary movements and by providing information about particular parts of the world. There are nine British-owned overseas banks, with head offices in London and as many as 4,500 branches scattered over 70 different countries. The Standard Bank and the Hong Kong & Shanghai Banking Corporation are examples. In addition, there are also branches in London of foreign-owned banks serving the same general purposes, e.g., the Bank of Montreal and the Chase Manhattan Bank. Indeed, the growth in London of American-owned banks has been one of the most phenomenally spectacular events in the recent development of the City.

13E The commercial joint-stock banks

These are the banks whose task is the provision of a full range of services for their customers. What are those services? Before you read the following list, try to make up one of your own—and then check it against:

1   Accepting deposits on:
(a) Current account, whereon the bank pays no interest to the customer but instead charges him for handling all the cheques which are drawn on the account (these are *bank charges*). Cash is withdrawable on demand, by cheque.
(b) Deposit account, whereon the bank pays interest to the depositor at what is called banker's deposit rate. Cash withdrawals may be made at seven days' notice, or immediately with the loss of seven days' interest in lieu of notice, but not by cheque. The old home-safe and savings accounts are now incorporated into the deposit account structure.

2   Making loans (creating credit) in the form of:
(a) Personal loans, whereby the bank lends an agreed sum of money at a predetermined rate of interest and requires repayment of the loan, together with interest, in a fixed number of equal monthly instalments. Because the interest is charged on the full amount of the loan at the outset and yet the loan itself is repaid in instalments, thus constantly diminishing the amount still outstanding, the *effective* rate of interest is almost double the nominal rate. Personal loans are the most expensive way of borrowing from a bank.
(b) Bank loans, whereby the bank lends an agreed sum of money and requires repayment in a fixed number of equal monthly instalments, but treats the interest charge as a separate transaction. The interest on the loan is charged—usually each Quarter—only on the outstanding sum, at whatever rate of interest happens to prevail at the time of charging.
(c) Short-term loans to the discount houses and bill-brokers, at what is termed call and seven-day rate. Money lent at call must be repaid immediately it is recalled.
(d) Discounting bills, as outlined in section 13C.
(e) Overdrafts, whereby instead of adding (crediting) loan money to a customer's account the bank allows the customer to go 'into the red'. Naturally, the bank and the customer agree beforehand on the maximum amount by which the customer can overdraw his account; if the customer just tries to go overdrawn without prior agreement he is likely to find that his cheques are returned to him as unacceptable. Since the customer will probably receive occasional credits to his account from other sources it is highly unlikely that his account will be frequently overdrawn up to the agreed maximum, and since the bank charges interest only on the daily amounts by which the customer is actually overdrawn overdrafts are clearly a relatively cheap method of borrowing money from banks.
(f) Personal budget accounts, whereby the annual total of a customer's likely bills is estimated and divided by 12; the customer then pays 12 equal monthly instalment to the bank, which in turn undertakes to meet all the estimated expenditure on bills as and when the bills become payable. The service is of considerable importance to many customers, because it smooths out the flow of their expenditure, which would otherwise tend to be highly irregular.

3   Money transfer. Cash can be sent through the post from one town to another, but the only safe way is by expensive registered mail. The Post Office also provides postal and money orders, as well as a Giro service, for money transfer, but these all require the sender to go to the local post office. Cheques are much more suitable for postal transmission, since they can be made out at any time and in any place—but even they have the disadvantage that a separate one needs to be made out for each transaction. The banks have therefore further refined the procedures of money transfer by introducing:

(a) Standing order payments, whereby the bank makes regular payments on behalf of a customer. Mortgage payments, insurance premiums, and society-membership subscriptions are commonly paid by banks in this way.

(b) Credit transfers, whereby several bills can be paid by means of a single cheque, provided that the bank is informed of the bank accounts of the several recipients.

(c) Direct debiting, introduced in October 1967, whereby a customer who expects to receive periodic payments from a third party can, by agreement with the third party, instruct the bank to collect the payments as they fall due.

(d) The bank Giro, introduced in November 1967 in response to potential competition from the Post Office Giro, whereby the British commercial banks have agreed to use centralised computer facilities (at the Inter-Bank Computer Bureau in London) for the recording of electronic money-transfers between any two places in Britain. The Giro system is rapidly absorbing the payments of bills by standing order, credit transfer, and direct debiting.

(e) Cables and foreign drafts for transmission of money to other countries.

4   Night-safe facilities. In order to get their book-keeping finished at a reasonable hour each day, banks close before shops do. Accordingly, shopkeeper-customers are provided with a key to open a special wicket in the bank wall, through which they can deposit their cash takings for the day instead of having to keep them overnight.

5   Stimulating saving by the offer of interest on deposit accounts, and mobilising capital by the creation of loans based on such savings. Many small savers can do little—individually—with their savings, but banks, by attracting the savings, can channel the small sums into a worthwhile flow of liquidity.

6   Safe custody, whereby a bank will take care of a customer's valuables, storing them in its vaults. Anything can be so stored, e.g., deeds of property, insurance policies, jewellery, objets d'art.

7   Drawing arrangements. If a traveller is likely to need cash at a particular place on his travels, or if a customer works or lives a long way from his usual banking office, then the bank will make drawing (cashing) arrangements at any office which the traveller or customer thinks suitable.

8 Credit cards. Most bank credit cards merely guarantee a customer's cheque to a third party (e.g., a shop) up to a certain sum. The real purpose of credit cards, however, is to dispense with the multitude of separate cheques for individual transactions, and replace them with an equal multitude of signed bills which are collectively payable by a single cheque once a month. Only the Barclaycard fulfils this requirement in England, though the National Westminster Bank is sufficiently closely associated with the international Diners Club not to need to have a separate real card of its own. Shops and other establishments which accept Barclay-cards and Diners Club cards are provided with window-stickers, and card-holders are given a list of such establishments.

9 Cash dispensing services. A number of branches of most banks are equipped with special machines set into the outer bank wall which will issue set sums of money in response to a special customer code—at any hour of the day or night.

10 Foreign exchange. All banks will obtain, on commission, any foreign currency that may be needed for business transactions or holidays—provided the government of the day permits the exchange of sterling for other currencies.

11 Gift cheques. Banks will sell specially decorated cheques for use on such occasions as birthdays and weddings.

12 Travellers' services. Quite apart from obtaining foreign currencies, banks will also supply travellers' cheques, which may be cashed abroad provided an acceptable means of identification (e.g., a passport) is produced. Banks will also obtain passports and visas, and forward mail.

13 Insurance. Banks have brokerage departments which will advise customers on the relative merits of different policies for such things as life, car, house, and travel insurance. The brokerage departments will also arrange the selected insurance with the companies concerned.

14 Advice in financial matters. For a fee, banks will take care of a customer's income tax returns and claims; they will advise him how to invest his savings; they will buy National Savings Certificates for him; and they will arrange the purchase and sale of stocks and shares (each bank has a stock-broker through whom it operates). Many banks even operate their own investment schemes on behalf of customers; for example, the Westminster Hambro Growth Investment Units scheme.

15 Intelligence services. All banks regularly publish commentary journals, with information concerning the state of the economy; they also supply special information regarding particular problems faced by customers, e.g., the marketing prospects in a Development Area, the ways of overcoming trade difficulties with a foreign country, the growth potential of particular industries, and so on.

16 Referee in business deals. Banks will supply trade references for their customers; for example, in supporting a customer's monetary standing in his application for, say, a house mortgage.

17 Executor services. People die—often without friends capable of handling the details of a will. Even if friends are capable enough, the testator may prefer not to trouble them—putting the handling of a will into the skilled and permanent capability of a bank.

18 Issuing shares. Until the mid-1960s this was a specialised field left to the merchant banks. In November 1967, however, Glyn Mills broke with tradition by being the first commercial bank to promote a new share issue (Beatson, Clark—a firm of bottle makers). The Westminster followed in April 1968 by offering shares for sale in a plant-hire firm (H. Cox & Sons).

19 Anything else? Banks are always happy to discuss any arrangements they can make to help any customer over any financial difficulty he may have. If a solution is not listed above, that does not mean that it does not (or need not) exist. If you have a problem, go—as the banks say—and talk it over with your bank manager.

In fulfilling their first function—accepting deposits—the banks automatically create *liabilities* for themselves; any money which customers deposit in the banks belongs to the customers and not to the banks, so the banks owe that money to the customers. However, in fulfilling their second function—making loans—the banks create credit by the means noted in section 13B, and therefore also produce *assets* for themselves, since the customers now owe money to the banks. In total, therefore, the accounts of customers comprise two basic components:

1 Sums paid in by customers (i.e., bank liabilities).
2 Sums credited by the bank as loans (i.e., bank assets).

Even so, it is obvious that the loans (assets) are made possible only by the prior existence of sums paid in (liabilities); so it is paradoxically possible to regard the existing liabilities as assets, since they make possible the superstructure of credit by which the banks earn profitable income. Furthermore, by making loans the banks give the right of immediate money withdrawal to the borrowers, so that the assets can also be regarded as liabilities (the banks, having made the loans, must pay the money to the borrowers on demand).

The situation is further complicated by the practice of the banks of calling all money in customers accounts *bank deposits*, whether they comprise cash paid in (liabilities) or loans credited (assets), and whether they are in current or deposit accounts. Some economists would exclude money in deposit accounts when referring to **money supply**, because money in those accounts is not transferable by cheque. The banks, however, do not make such a distinction, since a transfer from one type of account to another is a very simple matter indeed.

You can check the actual deposit figures for the different banks in a newspaper such as *The Times*, which publishes the monthly returns sometime around the 25th of each month. The figures vary considerably from time to time because of the actions of governments in restricting or encouraging the formation of credit, but as an indication of their size the following figures for

May 1969 (during a period of severe credit restriction) provide a basis for comparison:

	£ millions
Barclays Group (Barclays and Martins)—excluding Barclays DCO	3052·9
National Westminster Group (National Westminster/ District/Coutts)	2998·6
Midland Bank	2177·9
Lloyds Bank	1959·1
Three Banks/National Group—excluding Royal Bank of Scotland	300·6

The largest banks in the world are all American. For comparison, the 1969 deposits of the three largest were:

	£ millions
Bank of America (not the central bank)	9300
Chase Manhattan Bank	8000
First National City Bank	8000

The British commercial banks are owned by share-holders, and in addition to the services which the banks provide for customers it is one of their fundamental concerns to make a profit for their shareholders. They do this, as we have noted, by making loans. The most profitable loans are generally the long-term ones, called advances, but these are also the least liquid in so far as they cannot readily be called in. The banks cannot sink too many of their funds into such illiquid loans, otherwise they may find themselves lacking short-term lending ability. The principle of profitability must therefore be tempered with the principle of liquidity. On the other hand, the short-term loans may be liquid in so far as they can be readily recalled, but they are not so profitable. There is therefore a conflict of interests in banking practice: whether to aim for high profits or for safe liquidity. Experience has shown—and the government has insisted—that at least about 8% cash must be retained as the **prime liquidity reserve**; but that does not mean that all the other money can be lent for long periods. There must still be a component of short-term fairly liquid loans, and experience—and the government—has shown that these should form about another 20% of total deposits, thus giving a **total (or secondary) liquidity ratio** of about 28–30%. Throughout the 1960s there was a tendency to aim for profitability—and, within the general limits imposed by necessary liquidity ratios, there has been quite a considerable change in the composition of bank deposits, as shown in table 13.3.

	April 1959 %	April 1969 %
Cash (*prime liquidity ratio*)	8·3	8·8
Call money	7·2	13·3
Treasury bills discounted	14·0	3·5
Bank and trade bills discounted	2·0	5·1
Total liquidity ratio	31·5	30·7
Advances	37·3	51·2
Investments	28·2	11·7

Table 13.3   The changing structure of bank deposits, 1959–69.

The significance of the figures rests in:

1   The decline in treasury bill purchase, thereby giving the banks a measure of independence from the policy wishes of the government (the government being able—through the Treasury—to regulate bank liquidity and lending by sale and redemption of treasury bills, which the banks customarily discount).

2   The growth of loans at call (to discount houses and bill-brokers) and the increase in the discounting of bank and trade bills. These loans are only slightly less liquid than those to the government, but are correspondingly more profitable (see the end of section 13C).

3   The growth of fairly illiquid advances, which are very profitable.

13F Cheque clearing

Cheques have both advantages and disadvantages. The chief advantage is that they make possible the creation of credit; the chief disadvantage is that there are increasingly too many of them. In order to get round the problem of the near-overwhelming number of cheques, the banks are likely in time to have to resort to some sort of electronic funds-transfer system (EFTS), whereby computer-maintained accounts are electronically adjusted in response to account-identifying coded plastic cards. Meanwhile, a start has been made (attempted?) in diminishing the volume of cheques: Barclays has a credit card system in operation. The quantity of cheques continues to rise overall, however, and there are now about 1 000 000 000 cheques drawn each year. Established—but certainly doomed—methods of dealing with cheques are outlined below:

1   Same bank branch. In the simplest form of cheque clearing the drawer and the payee are the same person. The drawer makes out a cheque payable to himself in his capacity as payee, and presents it at the bank counter for cash. The bank branch keeps the cheque with others the drawer has drawn, until such a time as a statement of account is sent out to the drawer. Next simplest, the drawer and the payee are different persons, but having accounts at the same bank branch. The drawer gives the cheque to the payee, who pays it in over the counter for the credit of his account. The bank merely alters the respective accounts, debiting the drawer and crediting the payee, and then sorts away the cheque with the others drawn by the drawer.

2   Same country town (local clearing). Provided that there is some convenient centrally-located meeting place (and there *is* likely to be, since banks in country towns often figure prominently in the town centres), then cheques which are paid into banks different from those of the drawers may readily be sorted into appropriate bank-piles and exchanged by hand. As banks face an ever-mounting number of cheques, it is possible, but unlikely, that the idea of local clearing may be extended to the newly evolving bank 'regions'—provided all the different banks have the same regional outlines; on the other hand, sorting procedures would be

aggravated, and it is therefore more likely that the banks might move more quickly instead to EFTS.

3 Head Office clearing. This occurs whenever the bank-branches of both drawer and payee are parts of the same bank, but located in different parts of the country. It is not worth the payee's branch posting the cheque back directly to the drawer's bank, since it would have to do the same for a multitude of other cheques paid in—and all the big banks in Britain have over 2000 branches each. What happens, therefore, is that the payee's branch collects all the cheques drawn on other branches of the same bank, and posts them off in a single pile to the Head Office of the bank. It is then up to Head Office to sort them all out, together with all the other piles it has received from the other branches; after sorting, the cheques are then remitted by Head office to the branches on which they were drawn.

4 Clearing House clearing. A bank-branch receives cheques drawn not only on other branches of the same bank but also on a variety of branches belonging to other banks. The cheques which are drawn on the branches of other banks are sent along with the Head office clearing to Head Office, which in turn passes them on to the appropriate Head Offices of the different banks. Meanwhile, in order to determine the extent of inter-bank indebtedness, the listings of all cheques drawn on branches of other banks are passed by each Head Office to the London Clearing House. After the listings have been tallied and sorted, the extent of indebtedness can be seen:

		cheques paid into banks (£ million)		
		A	B	C
cheques drawn on banks	A	—	120	110
(£ million)	B	115	—	120
	C	125	105	—

The figures show, for example, that cheques worth £115 million and £120 million have been drawn on B and paid into A and C respectively. The indication is that B owes these sums of money to A and C; however, the claims can be simplified:

	to collect (£m)	to pay (£m)	balance (£m)
A	240	230	collect 10
B	225	235	pay 10
C	230	230	—

It can be now be seen that equity is maintained if B transfers merely £10 million to A. And even at this stage there need not be any movement of cash, because the *clearing banks* each keep an account at the Bank of England; and paper adjustments are made there instead of having bullion vans dashing around the City (those bullion vans that do dash around are simply delivering 'till money' to the branches for issue as cash to those customers who request it).

13G The Bank of England

Founded in 1694 with the privilege of joint-stock operation, the Bank was nationalised in 1946. Its chief functions are:

1 To act as England's central bank in the nation's dealings with other central banks, the World Bank (formally called the International Bank for Reconstruction and Development) and the International Monetary Fund (IMF).

2 To act as the sole note-issuing authority in England and Wales.

3 To act as the agent of the Mint in the purchase of bullion and the issue of coin.

4 To keep the nation's gold and foreign currency reserves.

5 To act as banker to the government by opening and operating accounts for government departments.

6 To act as banker to the commercial banks.

7 To carry on normal banking business for staff and privileged customers. Until 1967 such customers were chiefly old-established London trading houses, and the Bank was not seeking new accounts. In 1967, however, the Abbey National Building Society was accepted as a new customer.

8 To act as lender of the last resort to the money market by discounting bills at Bank Rate when the money market is temporarily short of funds. Whenever money-market houses are forced to borrow from the Bank (at Bank Rate or slightly under) they are said to be *in the bank*.

9 To advise on government-sponsored investment through both the Industrial and Commercial Finance Corporation (ICFC) and the Finance Corporation for Industry (FCI).

10 To regulate borrowing in the money market according to the wishes of the government. It can do this by using any one or more of five different techniques which are known collectively as *monetary measures*, i.e., Bank Rate changes, Open Market operations, Special Deposits, Request Letters, and Control of Liquidity.

Bank Rate is the rate at which the Bank discounts treasury, bank, or fine trade bills if it has to. It prefers to leave the process of discounting to the specialised money market, doing so itself only in the last resort (function 8), when the market has temporarily exhausted its own supplies of liquidity. When Bank Rate is changed, the other discount rates (and also the closely-allied interest rates) move in sympathy. If Bank Rate is raised, then:

1 Other discount and interest rates throughout the market are also raised.

2 Borrowing becomes more expensive, thereby tending to diminish the demand for loans.

3 Saving becomes more gainful, thereby tending to increase the amount of saving and decrease the amount of spending out of current income; in other words, the community's liquidity preference is increased.

When people find that loans are more expensive to obtain and that savings are more profitable to accumulate they tend to spend less, thereby cutting demand for goods and services. When demand decreases against existing supply the inevitable tendency is for prices to fall, thereby cutting profits and possibly forcing marginal firms to cease production; so causing a measure of unemployment (or maybe easing the pressure of over-full employment). If Bank Rate is lowered the opposite effects are encouraged.

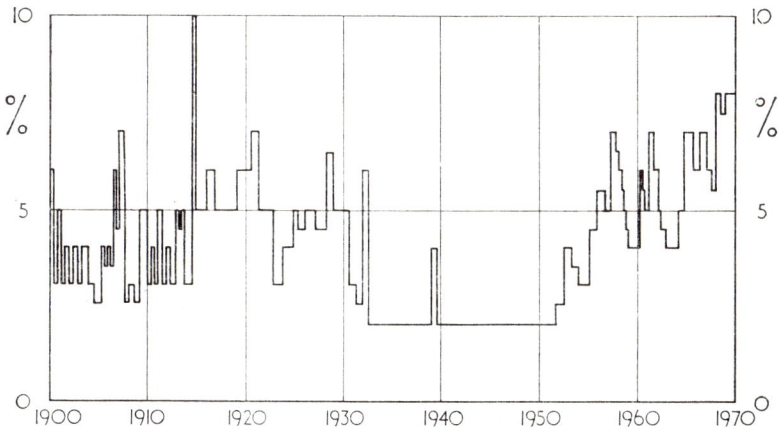

FIG 13.1   Bank rate changes, 1900–1970.

Figure 13.1 illustrates the changes in Bank Rate during this century. The first 30 years of the century continued the extremely vigorous use of the Rate which had characterised the 19th century; in 1873, for example, the Rate changed 24 times, and it had been as high as 10% in both 1857 and 1866. After the Great Depression of the early 1930s, and throughout the war and post-war years, however, Bank Rate was pegged at a stable level of 2%. It was only during the 1950s that changes in the Rate began to be used again as a weapon of monetary policy. The re-developing use of Bank Rate changes was encouraged by the Report of the Committee on the Working of the Monetary System, August 1959 (the *Radcliffe Report*), which suggested a much more flexible approach in the use of monetary measures to regulate the economy. Not all the recent changes in the Rate, however, have had the prime purpose of regulating borrowing in the money market; some, as in 1967, have been designed to reduce the out-flow of foreign-held money from the country. As a result of the new frequency of change of Bank Rate, the changes have lost much of their 1950s' psychological impact, and are now merely regarded as technical adjustments to part of the monetary machine. As the monetary aspect waxes, so the monitory aspect wanes.

Open Market operations occur whenever the Bank of England, acting via the government broker, buys or sells treasury bills in the open money market. The theory behind the operations is based on the credit mechanism employed by the commercial banks. If the policy of the government is to *expand* credit, and therefore increase the supply of money, then the Bank *buys* treasury bills from the commercial banks, paying for them by increasing the cash assets of the commercial banks in their accounts at the Bank of England. The commercial banks can then in turn create additional credit in the proportion $12\frac{1}{2}:1$ on the strength of their increased cash assets. Conversely, if the government policy is to *contract* credit (as in a credit squeeze), the Bank *sells* treasury bills to the commercial banks, thereby taking cash assets from them and so cutting their credit-creating ability. The commercial banks, in order to pay for the treasury bills, may even have to call in some of their short-term loans, thus forcing producers who want bills discounted to turn to the Bank for discount at Bank Rate.

In practice, the effects are slightly more complex. The commercial banks, as we have noted, treat cash as their primary liquid reserve, holding it to about 8% (i.e., $1:12\frac{1}{2}$) of their total deposits; they also treat treasury bills as part of their liquid reserve, but only in a secondary way. Nevertheless, loans are made on the strength of treasury bill holdings—though only in the proportion of about $3:1$. Consequently, when treasury bills are bought by the Bank of England in order to expand credit the commercial banks find that some of their $3:1$ lending ability is replaced by a more liberal $12\frac{1}{2}:1$ lending ability; and when treasury bills are sold by the Bank of England in order to contract credit the commercial banks find that some of their $12\frac{1}{2}:1$ lending ability is reduced to a tighter $3:1$ lending ability. The commercial banks co-operate in the contraction of their lending ability (and profitability) in this way simply because stronger measures might be used against them if they did not. There is no law making the commercial banks buy treasury bills surplus to their wants; merely the fear of a possible law.

Special Deposits were first required in April 1960. The money which the commercial banks keep in accounts at the Bank of England is largely for the convenience of settling inter-bank indebtedness; it is still treated by the banks as part of their prime liquidity reserve, and credit is based on it in the proportion $12\frac{1}{2}:1$. Special deposits are those in addition to the normal accounts; they are made only at the request of the Bank of England, and are not allowed by law to form any part of the liquidity reserve of the commercial banks. The aim is a direct reduction in the cash assets of the banks, thereby cutting their lending ability by the prime ratio of $12\frac{1}{2}:1$ to the extent of the cash assets involved in the Special Deposits. The device not only cuts credit but also withdraws cash from circulation; it is a double-edged weapon. The release of Special Deposits, as in 1962, has the opposite effect.

Request Letters are sent from the Bank of England to the various houses and banks in the money market with the express purpose of telling the market precisely what is wanted by the government. They have the considerable advantage over Bank Rate, Open Market operations, and Special Deposits, therefore, in that they are specific. It is worth quoting from the first letter to be made public. It was sent out in November 1967 immediately after the devaluation of sterling, at a time when there was an urgent need for Britain to reduce imports and increase exports.

'. . . this notice describes the task the banks are now being asked to undertake.

Severe but very selective restrictions will need to be placed on bank lending. . . . It is essential that credit for the finance and production of exports should be free of all restriction. . . . Lending for most (other) purposes must be held down in aggregate to the current level. . . . Within the ceiling and subject to normal banking criteria, priority should be given to finance for production and investment necessary to sustain or increase exports, for the promotion of invisible earnings, or, as in the case of agriculture, for securing a saving of imports. . . .

The recent upward trend in lending to persons should be halted without delay. . . .

Lending for other non-priority purposes in the United Kingdom must be severely restricted, in particular credit that is associated with imports of manufactured goods. . . .

The authorities recognize the difficulties that the banks may encounter in seeking to give effect to the guidance now given. The Bank of England will therefore be inviting all the main banking groups to regular and frequent discussions with the Bank, so that progress may be better examined and difficulties more easily surmounted.

Bank of England, 19th November 1967.'

The final paragraph of the letter clearly indicates the increasingly close contact which the Bank of England wishes to have with the money market. The days of coarse control are going; now is the time for fine adjustment.

Control of liquidity is the fifth measure of monetary policy available to the Bank of England. The commercial banks have arrived by experience at prime and secondary liquidity ratios of about 8% and 30% respectively. It is on these ratios that they base their lending ability. If the absolute quantity of cash (prime) or cash and short-term loans together (secondary) rises or falls then the lending ability of the banks moves in sympathy. The government insists on maintenance of the 8% prime ratio, thereby lending weight to the Special Deposits technique, but it has also taken powers (via the Bank of England) to vary the secondary ratio. Since the commercial banks have in practice kept their cash assets at usually slightly more than 8%, it is perfectly possible for the 30% ratio to be depressed without actually forcing the prime ratio below 8%. As a means of encouraging lending in 1963, the Bank announced that it would accept a reduction of the secondary ratio to 28%. The figure can, of course, be raised or lowered at any time to suit the wishes of the government.

There is a further possibility in the development of this particular technique: the removal of bills of exchange from the conventional secondary liquid asset structure of the banks. The commercial banks have been reducing significantly the proportion of treasury bills which they hold as part of their secondary reserve (see table 13.3); the difference being made up by increased holdings of bills of exchange as well as by increased lending at call, neither situation being so readily controlled by the Bank of England as the quantity of treasury bills. The changing pattern of assets seriously weakens the Bank's ability to control the market through Open Market operations, because the possible leverage is so much reduced. This new and growing weakness could mean the removal of either the technique or the weakness. Because the general desire of governments is for finer control, it is more likely that the weakness will be eliminated than the technique abandoned.

13H The Value of money

We noted in section 2F that the value of any commodity is what it can be exchanged for. The value of money is similarly what it can be exchanged for, i.e., its purchasing power. This is indicated in inverse ratio by price levels, so that as *prices rise* then a given sum of money *buys less*—and its value (i.e., purchasing power) correspondingly *falls*.

One of the earliest ideas concerning the value of money was that the value varied inversely with the amount of money available; so that if the supply of money increased, prices would rise and the value of a given sum of money would fall. This **simple quantity theory** was developed during the Age of Discovery, when huge quantities of gold were brought to Europe from the New World and there were the most disastrous price rises throughout the 16th century.

Irving Fisher, an American economist, gave definition to the growing dissatisfaction with the simple quantity theory early this century by putting forward his famous equation of exchange:

$$MV = PT$$

where M = the money supply, including coin, notes and (later) credit,
$\quad V$ = the velocity of circulation (i.e., the number of times a year a particular piece of money is used),
$\quad P$ = the general level of prices, and
$\quad T$ = the number of money transactions in a year.

This **refined quantity theory** (or Fisher theory) was based essentially on the concept that the real quantity of money is not merely the sum of coin, notes and credit, but also the number of occasions it is used over a period of time. For example, a £1 note changing hands 50 times during a year does as much work as 50 £1 notes changing hands once only; its velocity of circulation is 50, and an increase or decrease in that velocity is equivalent to an increase or decrease in the quantity of money. According to Fisher, therefore, the real quantity of money is the product of both the actual sum of money and its velocity of circulation. Velocity is influenced by a number of factors, chief among them being the spending/saving habits of the population, the distribution of the population (if geographically scattered, velocity will tend to be low), the rate of technical progress (new products will tend to stimulate demand and increase the velocity), the prevailing economic climate (if optimistic, velocity will tend to be high), and the frequency of payment to the population (people paid weekly will tend to cause money to circulate faster than will those paid monthly). The equation of exchange is axiomatic: the sum of money (M) times the frequency of use (V) *must* equal prices (P) times the number of transactions (T), i.e., $MV = PT$. The worth of the equation lies in its drawing of attention to the possible factors determining the value of money.

The new factors introduced by Fisher, namely V and T, represented a great conceptual advance over the simple quantity theory; they showed that the quantity of money was more than the sum of coin, notes and credit, and that prices were coupled to the existing amount of goods and services available for money transactions. Unfortunately, the concepts were incapable of precise quantification.

Further refinement of the Fisher theory eventually resulted in the production of the **Cambridge theory**, which states:

$$p = \frac{M}{kR}$$

where $p =$ the prices of ultimate consumer goods,
$\quad M =$ the money supply in coin, notes and credit,
$\quad k =$ the liquidity preference of the community (see section 13A), and
$\quad R =$ the real income of the community, i.e., the quantity of goods and services available for purchase. Money income, of course, does not on its own matter very much: it is what you can get for it (i.e., its purchasing power) that really counts.

Let us see how the Cambridge formula may be applied. Suppose a community has £1000 in money units, a real income of 1000 bicycles, and a desire to keep one-tenth of its income in the form of money. The formula could then be written:

$$p = \frac{£1000}{1/10 \times 1000} = \frac{£1000}{100} = £10 \ (\textit{the price of a bicycle})$$

Now calculate the price of a bicycle when the liquidity preference is reduced to one-twentieth. You will see that when people wish to retain a smaller proportion of their income as money, preferring instead to *spend more* on goods and services, *the price rises*, provided other things (M and R) remain constant. In practice, M and R are likely to remain constant for only very short periods; and in the short term k itself is not likely to change very much either. In the long term all three factors are liable to change considerably; and herein lies a weakness of the Cambridge formula. Economists, in fact, have been prone to lay greater stress on the importance of the k factor than on that of the money supply, simply because it was both novel and associated with Keynes. In recent years there has been something of a reaction against the relegation of importance of the money supply in the determination of price levels and money values.

The **Chicago School**, with Milton Friedman as its leader, and with growing influence in the IMF, has pioneered the re-establishment of the im-

portance of the money supply in influencing the value of money. The fundamental notion is that M is the most volatile (and therefore most significant)
constituent in either the Fisher or the Cambridge formula. It is suggested
that both real income and either velocity of circulation or liquidity preference
are fairly stable and predictable variables, and that price changes are therefore
more a result of variations in the money supply. A sizeable body of statistical
support has been built up, but the idea is by no means universally accepted
yet. Nevertheless, the British government in early 1970 more or less com-
mitted itself to a policy of controlling the value of money primarily through
control of the money supply. The policy was one of controlled Domestic
Credit Expansion, allowing for an approximate 5% annual increase in the
money supply.

13I Price stability

Is rare.

Stable money values have been sought by many governments throughout
the ages, but only occasionally—as in late 19th century England—with any
success. Stability is pursued because it offers a number of advantages:

1   It eliminates one of the risks of production. The risk entailed by un-
    expected changes in factor prices is excluded from the cloud of uncer-
    tainties hanging over a productive enterprise.

2   It promotes voluntary saving. People are more prepared to save if they
    know that the money set aside will be worth the same in the future as it is
    in the present. And saving is desirable, of course, because it means a flow
    of funds for capital investment—and hence a higher real income (R) in
    the future.

3   It maintains equity between:
    (a) Debtors and creditors, for if the value of money falls a debtor repays
    less in real terms than he initially borrowed (note that the potential loss
    of real income to a lender may be offset by unusually high interest and
    discount rates during a time of rapidly falling money values).
    (b) Those on fixed incomes (such as pensioners) and those on variable
    incomes (such as engineering workers), for those on fixed incomes cannot
    so readily gain additional income if prices rise.

13J Changes in the value of money

Are common.

Nearly always downwards.

In England there have been several periods during which the value of
money has fallen drastically. One of the most serious was the 16th and early-
17th centuries, when vast quantities of gold and silver were brought from the
New World. Another was World War I, which imposed severe strains on the
English economy. The most infamous example of falling money values in
recent history is the Great Inflation of 1920–23 in Germany; during that time
prices rose to 80 000 000 000 times their original level. All countries, indeed,

tend to experience falling money values over any prolonged period of time; figure 13.2 illustrates the falling value of the British £ during this century.

Even though the persistent long-term trend of change is downwards, there have been short-term periods when the value of the £ has risen, notably in the early 1920s when the government was attempting to re-establish the money values of the pre-war era.

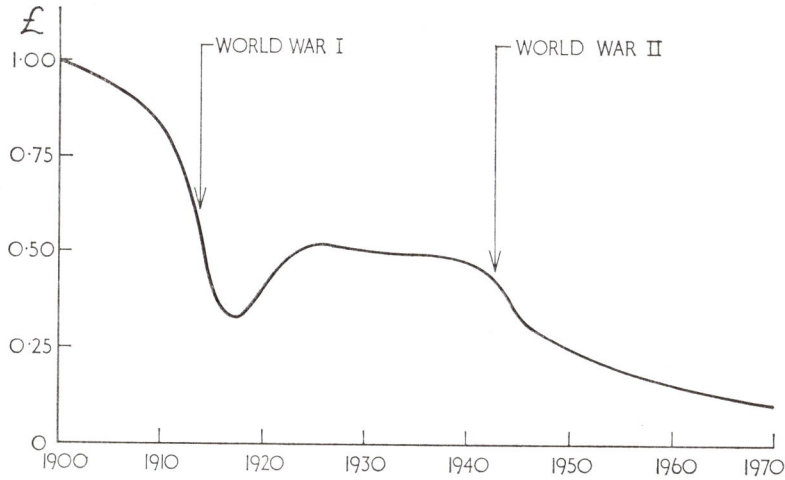

FIG 13.2   The declining purchasing power of the £, 1900–1970.

The different types of change in the value of money are called inflation, deflation, reflation and disinflation. The most common is inflation.

Inflation occurs whenever the amount of money spent on goods and services is in increasing proportion to the quantity of goods and services available. This means any one or more of three things:

1   That the money supply increases in relation to the availability of goods and services.

2   That the community's liquidity preference diminishes in relation to the goods and services available (i.e., people spend more and save less out of an unchanged total money supply).

3   That the quantity of goods and services declines either absolutely or in relation to money supply and spending desires.

If the Cambridge formula is applied, you will appreciate that the price level of consumer goods (p) will rise—or, put another way, the value (purchasing power) of money will fall—whenever either/both M increases and/or k decreases at the same time as R rises less rapidly, remains fairly constant, or actually declines. The fundamental point is that inflation occurs whenever an *increasingly* wide gap opens up between the amount of money being spent and the quantity of goods and services available. It does not really matter (for a definition) whether the extra money being spent comes from a rise in the money supply—stressed by the new Chicago School—or from a decline in saving—stressed by the old Cambridge School; but it does matter for a solution. The causes of 'too much money chasing too few goods' are varied:

1   An increase in money supply (M), produced by governments issuing coin and notes at a rate faster than any increase in R (this is called *monetary inflation*) and/or banks issuing credit at a rate faster than any increase in R (this is called *credit inflation*).

     The demand for currency and credit additional to that required to finance trade at existing price levels comes from four main sources:

(a) Governments, which may resort in ignorance to the printing presses in order to pay for any of the things governments normally pay for (war-damage, reparations, social welfare, armed forces, civil service, etc.). Even governments with the best of intentions may run into trouble by trying to do too much in a short space of time. Such reforming governments may be tempted to borrow more than they should or to print more notes than the increase in wealth warrants—and, note particularly here, a reforming government will tend to produce more social wealth than other governments will, and social wealth is not exchangeable. In consequence, the extra money generated to pay for the increase in social wealth will be concentrated for exchange on the private sector of the economy, thereby disproportionately putting up prices in that sector. The higher prices will then tend to cause bids for higher wages, which will in time therefore put up the cost of labour and also the cost of producing social wealth, thus inevitably inclining a reforming government to even further inflation. There is, under these conditions, an in-built *inflationary potential*.

(b) Organised labour, which may threaten to strike unless higher wages are paid—irrespective of any increases in output.

(c) Employers of labour, who may offer higher wages in a time of labour scarcity in order to obtain for themselves what labour there is. This is called *wage drift*, and, together with the higher wages gained by means of actual or threatened strike action, is responsible for what is generally called *wage* or *push inflation*, since the higher wages are usually passed on to the consumer in the form of higher prices.

(d) Entrepreneurs, who may seize the opportunity to make excess profits when the demand for goods and services (supported by more money in most consumers' pockets) exceeds the supply. This type of inflation is usually called *price* or *pull inflation*. The whole wage-price complex is called the *inflational spiral*: a rise in wages puts up prices, which in turn are used as a reason for claiming even more wage increases; or a desire for greater profits puts up prices, which are then used as a basis for wage-claims. In practice it is virtually impossible to disentangle the separate motives.

2   A decrease in liquidity preference (k), caused by people generally saving

less and spending more—such as when the future is either uncertain (as in a war) or certainly worse than the present (as before the expectedly severe budget tax-increases of 1968, when the government of the day was silly enough to announce—months ahead of time—that large increases of tax were coming).

3 A decrease in real income (R) without an equivalent reduction in the money supply (assuming k to be stable). Destruction of real wealth is likely to be avoided whenever possible; so we should look to natural disasters (earthquakes, floods, etc.) as a prime cause. However, the man-made disaster of war is also a major cause of destruction—and not only of destruction, but also of the diversion of real productive resources to destructive ends. In addition, wars promote a vast increase in government borrowing and spending, as well as a general decrease in the community's liquidity preference; so that money supply is increased (through both monetary and credit inflation) at the same time as saving is decreased. In total, therefore, a war provides all the ingredients for devastating inflation: M rises and both k and R fall. During the first World War inflation was allowed to run more or less unchecked, and only the wealthy were able to maintain their standard of living. During World War II, however, the government took measures to control prices, and the allocation of goods to the public was done by means of rationing.

Just as the causes of inflation are complex, so are the results. More or less in order of occurrence, as the severity of inflation increases, the chief results are:

1 Increased consumer spending, partly because of an increase in M and a decrease in k and partly because of anticipation of further price rises in the future (the so-called *inflationary psychology*). The effects of increased spending are: first, to raise prices by causing a positive shift in demand (see figure 5.8); second, to extend supply as a response to higher prices, thereby leading to full or even over-full employment; and third, to cause higher wages as a result both of wage drift and of claims based on higher prices.

2 Social discontent, caused by any or all of: persistently rising prices; loss of value of accumulated savings; declining standards of living of those on fixed incomes (e.g., pensioners, and landlords of controlled tenancies).

3 Decelerating rate of economic growth, caused by a reduction of saving and a consequent slow-down in the rate of capital formation and replacement.

4 Declining or less rapidly growing exports, since not only are domestic costs of production increasing because of higher factor prices, so making exports uncompetitive in overseas markets, but also domestic profit opportunities are being increased by the rising prices in the home market. There is therefore not only less ability but also less incentive to export. In time, it is possible for there to be unemployment in the export in-

dustries; and that unemployment may then spread (via diminished demand) to the rest of the community (see section 6J).

5 Depreciation of the currency, meaning that the domestic currency loses value in relation to foreign currencies. This happens because foreigners gradually lose faith (which is essential to acceptance) in an inflated currency; they therefore require more of it in exchange for units of their own currencies. The domestic government may officially acknowledge the depreciation by the act of devaluation—Britain, for instance, devalued its currency in both 1949 and 1967 as a result of strong and persistent inflation. Unfortunately for Britain, imports then cost more—and led inexorably to demands for higher wages based on the existence of higher prices; so inflation continued.

6 Overthrow of government, either democratically or by revolution, since the majority of the people blame the government for the continuing inflation. They may well be right; but a new government may be no better.

Any government attempting to combat inflation must be strong. Upon investigation, it would certainly find itself to be responsible for a large part of the inflation: over-ambitious reforming, over-issuing currency, and over-borrowing from banks (thus also permitting them to increase their credit to the private sector). It would also find the private sector to be culpable too: entrepreneurs seeking excess profits, workers demanding higher wages, consumers spending rather than saving, and banks making easy loans. In these circumstances there is clearly no single—or simple—solution: the causes are complex and the results are complex; the solutions must also be complex.

The situation whereby money is losing value through inflation may be likened to a bath-tub losing water through many different holes. Individual holes may be plugged, but the water keeps on draining out of others. The solution is either to plug all the holes or to get a new bath-tub. Britain has spent years plugging holes; other countries have from time to time got themselves a new bath-tub (i.e., a new currency). Since World War II, for example, both France and Belgium have re-equipped themselves with new currencies, but this is a very drastic solution—and on its own, of course, will work only if the sole cause of inflation in the first place was over-use of the government note-printing presses. It does nothing to eliminate the other causes, except, perhaps, to give people a little more confidence to save (and it might have quite the opposite effect).

The most unrealistically optimistic solution is to attempt to hold prices steady. Not only does this impose a distorting rigidity on a dynamic economy, but it also does little to solve the fundamental problems, i.e., an increase of M and decreases of k and (possibly) R. It is rather like trying to hold the level of water in the bath-tub steady merely by commanding it to stay where it is. However, *in conjunction* with measures to attack the basic causes of inflation, the holding of prices at a steady level may have point, since it at least eliminates the spiralling sympton of wage-price inflation; but on its own it is of little value.

Any successful attack by a strong government must, indeed, aim to deal with the root causes of inflation. The measures may accordingly be listed under appropriate causes:

1   Money supply. Since governments are directly responsible for the issue of coin and notes there should be no excuse for any failure to curtail that issue if the supply exceeds the needs of trade at current prices. Bank credit can be restricted by means of one or other, or all, of the monetary measures outlined in section 13G. However, because inflation has been so persistent in Britain, and the monetary measures used so frequently, there is now a certain amount of ill-feeling developing between the clearing banks and the government. In 1969, for example, in response to a Bank of England letter insisting that the clearing banks should 'sharply . . . increase their pressure for repayments' of loans, the clearing banks stated that 'we can give you no positive assurance that we shall succeed, the more so because successive "squeezes" can hardly be equally productive.' It is essential for greater co-operation, of course, that governments themselves do not continue to borrow freely while asking for restrictions to private sector borrowing; it is also vital as a direct attack on inflation that governments do not borrow so much anyway.

2   Liquidity preference. Since a rising liquidity preference means that people spend less and save more out of their income, the aim of a government must be to raise the liquidity preference. This can be achieved in four different ways:
(a) Enforcing saving. The only example of this in Britain has been post-war credits, which represent sums exacted out of income during World War II and repaid on the retirement of the individual creditors after the war. Some creditors will not retire until the late 1970s, of course.
(b) Encouraging saving. This can be done by means of higher interest rates (e.g., Bank Rate). the provision of an extensive network of Trustee and Post Office Savings Banks, the offer of bonds and certificates which can be purchased easily (e.g., Premium Bonds, British Savings Bonds, National Savings Certificates), and the provision of facilities for contractual savings schemes, whereby a savings deduction from salary is made in the manner of a tax deduction (e.g., Save As You Earn).
(c) Controlling spending. The only occasion on which this has been done in Britain was the period of rationing throughout the 1940s, when purchases of many goods could be made only against the production of government-issued coupons.
(d) Discouraging spending. This can be achieved by any, or all, of: leaving people with less of their income to spend, by raising income tax; making goods and services more expensive for people to buy, by raising purchase tax or introducing some other sort of sales tax; and by tightening the controls on hire purchase schemes. The advantages of higher income and purchase taxes are not only that a disincentive to spending is created but also that the government's need to raise money by borrowing is reduced.

3 Real income. This is the sum of goods and services produced for purchase. If inflation is to be countered, real income must rise at a rate commensurate with the growing spending power of the community. And here lies the difficulty: spending power is a function of M and k, and can be fairly readily controlled (in theory, at least) by limitations to money supply and spending. Notes can be destroyed, credit curtailed and taxes raised almost by the stroke of a pen, but *real* resources have to be mobilised in order to obtain *real* income. As most of the world knows only too well, this is a difficult enough task at the best of times; it is virtually impossible as a solution to inflation. Clearly, an increase in R must constantly be sought, not solely as a palliative to inflation but also as an end in itself, for it is only by increasing R that the countries of the world can enjoy a rise in real living standards. As a solution to inflation, therefore, an increase in real income can rank only as a palliative measure: the main burden of attack rests on the measures to control money supply and liquidity preference.

Inflation persists—and probably always will, even if only in a 'creeping' form—despite all its disadvantages and the existence of a battery of measures to attack it. Why?

There are many answers, some inclining towards condemnation of lazy and inefficient governments, and others towards criticism of active and interfering governments. There is probably some truth in both groups of answers: inefficient governments take measures too late, take the wrong measures, or take no measures at all; interfering governments may create a strong inflationary potential. Heaven help a country if it has a government which is both inefficient and interfering! Nevertheless, there will be a tendency for inflation even in the best-run country: the existence of a credit mechanism means inevitably that the money supply is increased before the equivalent goods and services are available; the government payments (out of borrowed money) to private-sector factors for the production of non-exchangeable social capital necessarily concentrate the available money supply on the exchange of private sector goods and services; and—while individual human wants may be satiable—total human wants are not, so people will always tend to want higher wages, higher profits, higher returns on investment, and so on, without always wanting to make the equivalent economic effort.

Deflation is the opposite of inflation; it occurs whenever there is a reduced amount of spending in relation to the quantity of goods and services available for purchase. Unlike inflation, it does not usually happen spontaneously, but is instead the result of deliberate government action. If the government thinks that inflation is getting out of hand (runaway or galloping inflation), then it will apply the measures of control already outlined. The art of prediction is not yet an exact science, however, and it is quite possible that the application of the measures may produce an actual down-turn in the economy. People will certainly spend less; so demand will fall, thereby cutting prices, contracting supply and reducing entrepreneurial profits. Margina firms will cease production and other firms will produce less; either way there will be a reduced demand for labour, and either wages will fall or some labour will become unemployed (see figure 3.4 and the end of section 3B). People on fixed incomes, on the other hand, will find that their real standard of living rises as their money income becomes worth more in terms of goods and services (whose prices fall). The last time severe deflationary measures were applied in Britain was the early 1920s, when the government was attempting to return to the money values of the pre-World War I era. More recent doses of mild deflation have characterised the periods of *squeeze* in 1961–62 and *freeze* in 1966–67, when it was thought that the economy was getting 'overheated'. The repeated application of deflationary measures throughout the post-war period, interspersed with phases of permitted (or uncontrolled) inflation, has come to be known as *stop-go* policy.

Reflation happens when a government thinks that the measures of deflation have done their work (perhaps too well, if there is much unemployment), and when it feels the temptations of inflation again. It may wish to borrow more, for example, to finance some pet schemes that were promised to the electorate. At such a time as the government thinks fit, therefore, it begins to ease the measures of control: credit is made easier to obtain; interest rates are lowered; taxation is reduced; and government spending of borrowed money is increased. The chief problem with a policy of reflation is that of getting the extra money available translated into a greater demand for goods and services, for otherwise there will be no incentive for producers to start producing more and so mop up the pool of unemployment. After a period of rising money values (deflation) people tend to hold on to money, spending it only with reluctance, i.e., they have a high liquidity preference. There is a psychological barrier against spending which has to be broken down. The government can help, of course, by a policy of public works (adding to social capital)—paying its workers directly in order to get more money into immediate circulation, as the US government did in its New Deal programme of the 1930s.

Disinflation is a mild form of control which can be applied if it looks as though reflation is turning into inflation. The measures of disinflation are similar to those of deflation, but are different in purpose: whereas deflation is a policy designed to turn the economy positively downwards, disinflation is a policy designed merely to stop the economy getting any further overheated. The mythical pendulum is not so much swung the other way as prevented from swinging any further in the direction it was already travelling.

13K Measuring changes in the value of money

Any government faced by the problems of rising or falling money values and the consequent need to take corrective measures is then automatically faced by a second problem: with what intensity should the measures be applied?

A guide can be obtained by measuring the amount of change which is known to have occurred, and—on the basis of such a recorded change—

estimating the general trend and then taking measures of the appropriate intensity. It is, however, a difficult task to carry through, even though the start is fairly simple. The first step is to obtain a record of the purchasing power of the currency; a task which can be done merely by taking a list of common consumer goods and assessing their cost in the local shops. The amount of change over a period of time can be ascertained by comparing two such similar lists from different dates. If many such similar lists are used from many different dates then it is possible to compute a trend; and once a trend is established it becomes possible (but difficult) to project it into the future. The difficulty arises because the trend may change in the future, rendering any measures that may be taken on its basis either too severe or too lenient in practice.

The task remains an essential one, however, and a degree of initial precision can be introduced by the use of index numbers, which are percentage figures based on the averages of selected prices. The use of percentages permits international comparisons to have some (but only some) validity, and it also allows fairly valid internal comparisons over periods of time. There are two fundamental prerequisites for a successful price-index:

1   The selection of a *normal* base year. It is plainly useless to base comparisons and actions on the prices of an abnormal year.

2   The selection of *common* consumer goods. There is not much point yet in tracing the price changes of, say, yachts and colour TV sets, since these are not in general and representative use.

The first of these prerequisites can be obtained only by the exercise of common sense; the second by ascertaining what goods and services people in general actually buy.

Before examining some actual price indexes, however, let us first look at the two chief principles which govern the construction of an index:

1   The principle of standardised units. The separate commodities to be included in the index will almost certainly vary in their units of measurement; for example, coal per ton, cloth per yard, petrol per gallon, etc. The solution to this problem is to standardise all the individual prices in the base year to an index value of 100, e.g.,

coal	£10	per ton	index value = 100
milk	4p	per pint	index value = 100
potatoes	3p	per lb	index value = 100
cloth	50p	per yard	index value = 100
			total index value = 400
	average index number in base year (400 ÷ 4) = 100		

If, after one year, the prices of the individual items have changed, then the amount of change is expressed as a percentage of each individual index value of 100, and a new average calculated on the new values, e.g.,

coal	£11	per ton	new index value = 110
milk		4p per pint	new index value = 100
potatoes		4p per lb	new index value = 133·3
cloth		60p per yard	new index value = 120
			total index value = 463·3

average index number after one year (463·3 ÷ 4) = 115·8

2   The principle of weighting. Even if a wide range of goods is selected—and the wider the better, so long as it is representative—it is still possible for a relatively large change in the price of one commodity to influence the average index number more than could be warranted by the actual amount of money involved. A device called weighting is used to overcome this disadvantage; if we decide, arbitrarily, that—in relation to cloth—coal is twice, potatoes five times, and milk ten times as important, then we can apply this weighting as follows:

coal	£10	per ton	index value 100 × 2 = 200
milk		4p per pint	index value 100 × 10 = 1000
potatoes		3p per lb	index value 100 × 5 = 500
cloth		50p per yard	index value 100 × 1 = 100
			total weighting = 18
			total index value = 1800

average index number in base year (1800 ÷ 18) = 100

After one year, with the same price changes as in the unweighted index, the weighted index shows:

coal	£11	per ton	new index value 110 × 2 = 220
milk		4p per pint	new index value 100 × 10 = 1000
potatoes		4p per lb	new index value 133·3 × 5 = 666·5
cloth		60p per yard	new index value 120 × 1 = 120
			total weighting = 18
			total index value = 2006·5

average index number after one year (2006·5 ÷ 18) = 111·4

The unweighted and weighted average index numbers are dissimilar, despite being produced from the same price changes. Indeed, different methods of weighting can produce a very varied series of average index numbers, and—clearly—very great care needs to be exercised in the choice of weighting figures. It is partly for this reason that index numbers lack the exactness required for precise economic forecasting.

The general defects of index numbers are:

1   The impossibility of assessing accurately the relative importance of a wide range of different commodities.

2   The fact that contrary price movements may be hidden, simply because the final figure is an average.

3   The possible variations in the quality of the commodities over a period of time, irrespective of price changes.

4   The variations in consumer tastes over a period of time, causing some goods to lose, and others to gain, importance, thereby necessitating

deletions from, and additions to, the representative list and adjustments to the relative weighting factors. Comparisons over any long period of time are therefore made difficult; even invalid.

5   The differences from place to place in consumer habits and tastes, making regional comparisons very difficult (even invalid); and the differences from country to country in consumer tastes, government farm-price support policies, product-marketing subsidies, and so on, making international comparisons certainly invalid (except possibly for comparisons of rates of change over a period of time).

Despite their several disadvantages, index numbers remain about the best guide available for estimating changes in the value of money through the means of price changes.

The first **cost of living index** was introduced in 1914, based on a door-to-door investigation of the expenditure patterns of 'working-class' families actually carried out in 1904. The itemised figures are shown in table 13.4. On the basis of this recorded distribution of expenditure, weightings of 60 were given to food commonly bought by working-class families, 24 to housing, fuel and light, 12 to clothing, and so on. A new index was introduced in 1947—based on a necessary revision of the 1914 index carried out in 1937—and subsequently modified in 1952. The modification in 1952 was the result of a recommendation of the Cost of Living Advisory Committee, which was set up in 1951 to act as a permanent watchdog to the index. The Committee published its first full index—**the index of retail prices**—in 1956, and since 1962 has been publishing annually the result of its continual reviews. The reviews are based on data supplied by the labour exchanges, one of whose tasks is to ascertain the prices of certain index goods in the local shops. The data are assembled into a three-year moving average index, whose weighting is changed annually to reflect changing expenditure patterns. In 1968, for example, there were slight changes in weighting even from 1962: food had

	1914	1947	1952	1956	1962
Food	60·0	34·8	39·9	35·0	31·9
Alcohol	{ 0·8	21·7	16·8	7·1	6·4
Tobacco				8·0	7·9
Housing	{ 24·0 }	8·8	7·2	8·7	10·2
Fuel and light		6·5	6·6	5·5	6·2
Durable household goods	0·5	7·1	6·2	6·6	6·4
Clothing and footwear	12·0	9·7	9·8	10·6	9·8
Transport and vehicles	—	—	—	6·8	9·2
Services	1·2	7·9	9·1	5·8	5·6
Miscellaneous	1·5	3·5	4·4	5·9	6·4

TABLE 13.4   The expenditure patterns used in cost of living indexes.

dropped from 31·9 to 26·3, tobacco from 7·9 to 6·6, and clothing from 9·8 to 8·9, while housing had risen from 10·2 to 12·1 and transport and vehicles from 9·2 to 12·0. In 1968, also, a new class of expenditure was introduced, i.e., meals outside the home, which accounted for 4·1% of total 1968 spending.

In addition to forming the basis of numerous wage claims, the index reflects in its expenditure patterns the growing affluence of the British people—the steadily declining proportion of income which has to be spent on food, the growing amounts which are spent on housing and cars, and the introduction of meals outside the home as a separate class.

Interesting and useful though it is, the index is by no means a completely efficient econometric tool (econometric means the application of statistical methods of analysis to economic phenomena). The defects listed earlier, for example, are not eliminated merely by annual changes in the weighting. And there is still the fundamental problem of uncertainty when considering projection into the future. We should regard the index (and the index system as a whole) as at best providing us with nothing more than an imperfect indicator for economic forecasting.

13L The capital market

Capital, remember (section 2H), is what helps labour make the most efficient use of resources. It is really machinery, factories, roads, bridges, ports, power stations and so on; and such things are highly illiquid—even though London Bridge was in fact sold to Lake Havasu City in the USA in 1968. Generally speaking, resources which are used for the production of capital are said to be *invested*; and the investment has, of course, to be paid for, since the resources are scarce and therefore have an exchange value. The money which is sunk into paying for capital investment projects is therefore highly illiquid too.

The market for these long-term illiquid funds is called the capital market, in distinction to the short-term money market. This division of the market is yet another example of the high degree of specialisation which characterises British monetary matters; in many other countries there is no similar division. And within the specialised English capital market there is even a further division:

1   The New Issues market, wherein completely new capital investment is raised.

2   The Stock Exchange, where existing long-term capital investments are rendered less illiquid than they would otherwise be.

13M The New Issues market

Any firm wishing to expand its capital investment (e.g., build a factory extension, open a new plant, modernise its machinery) needs additional supplies of money. The firm may, of course, have saved the money itself, out of profits put to reserve, but more usually it will wish to borrow. If it either cannot or does not wish to borrow, then it may decide to invite the public at large to buy shares of ownership. Whether by borrowing or by selling shares of ownership, the firm will be in a position to raise additional finance; which is its chief purpose.

The public at large will either lend to the firm or buy shares in it only if the firm can show itself to be reputable and of good prospect. The firm has therefore to issue a prospectus showing the nature of the business, the aims and plans, the trading record, and various other details. You should be able to find a prospectus in one of the recent copies of *The Times*; if you can't, Qualitex Yarns Ltd published one on November 27th 1967, offering a million shares at a minimum price each of 17/- (85p). The prospectus took a full page, and gave details of: the history, achievements, and aims of the firm; the background to the textile trade; a profit record; the current balance sheet; a list of directors; the articles of association; details of bankers, brokers, solicitors, and auditors; and a cut-out space for the public to send in its requirements.

As well as making arrangements for the publication of a prospectus, the firm also has to make arrangements for the disposal of the shares or debentures (see section 9C). This is most commonly done through one of the merchant banks, in their capacity as issuing houses, but it may be done instead through one of the commercial banks. The chief issuing houses in London are:

> Baring Bros
> Hambros
> Hill, Samuel & Co
> Kleinwort Benson
> Lazard Bros
> Morgan Grenfell
> Rothschild
> Schroder Wagg
> Warburg

Once the firm has been accepted as a client, an issuing house will do its best to dispose of the shares or debentures most advantageously. The sources of investment capital available for approach are:

1 Private investors, approached through newspaper advertising.
2 Firms with large reserves, approached through newspaper advertising, word-of-mouth, and direct letter. Remember that many firms which have reached the stage of maximum profit in their own industry may be actively seeking investment opportunities in some other industry.
3 Institutional investors, comprising:
   (a) Insurance companies, which invest the premiums they receive from policy holders.
   (b) Investment and Trust companies, which offer shares in themselves to the public and then use that money for investment in other companies.
   (c) The Church of England and the Roman Catholic Church (chiefly), which receive bequests and offerings and then invest them.
   (d) Trade Unions and Friendly Societies, which invest the subscriptions they receive from their members.
   All the institutional investors serve the prime purpose of channelling small and otherwise relatively useless savings into larger and more useful capital investment sums.

It is quite possible that the issuing house responsible for disposal of the shares or debentures may fear that not all of them will be taken up; in such a case an arrangement is made with a firm of underwriters to guarantee that the required amount of investment capital will be raised. The underwriters undertake to buy from their own funds any shares or debentures that might not be taken up by the usual sources of investment capital, hoping that if the firm does well they will be able to sell the shares or debentures to investors at a later date. If the firm does not do well, the underwriters may lose on the deal; so they usually cover themselves by charging commission for their services. With some firms, of course, there is virtually no chance of failure, and there may indeed be a scramble by investors to obtain the offered 'blue chip' shares. A person who tries to obtain such new issues in the hope of being able to sell them almost immediately at a considerable profit to himself (because demand greatly exceeds supply) is called a **stag**; a 'blue chip' issue almost always produces a stag market.

Some firms—chiefly those too small to attract public confidence for long-term finance—are unable to tap the supplies of investment capital available through the new issues market. One of the first established alternatives for these firms was the Bankers' Industrial Development Company, which did much to help the small firms in the cotton industry during the 1930s. In 1945 it was replaced, under government encouragement, by the Industrial and Commercial Finance Corporation (ICFC) and the Finance Corporation for Industry (FCI). The purpose of the ICFC is to help very small firms with supplies of loan capital, the original source of which is for the most part the London clearing banks, with a nominal participation by the Bank of England. The FCI is concerned more with those firms which require capital additions of about £250,000, the money coming from insurance companies (40%), investment trusts (30%) and the Bank of England (30%). In addition to the ICFC and the FCI there are also other sources of long-term capital finance—in general by way of renewable bank loans or overdrafts and in particular by way of specialised sources such as the Agricultural Mortgage Corporation and the Ship Mortgage Finance Company.

13N The Stock Exchange

The most useful function of the Stock Exchange is—by acting as a market for shares—to increase the liquidity of capital investment. Few investors would wish to put their money into a firm if they felt that the only way they could get their money back was for the firm to go into liquidation, i.e., sell its capital assets for money (liquidity). The Stock Exchange exists to allow an investor to sell his shares of ownership in a firm to someone else, thereby bestowing the benefit of liquidity to the original investor's money and yet not depriving the firm of the original investment. The firm itself benefits from this transaction only by virtue of the fact that if the transaction were impossible then the firm would almost certainly have trouble raising capital in the first place.

It is not only firms which raise capital, but also governments. As we have noted already, tax revenue is erratic, thus forcing governments to borrow regularly in the money market. Tax revenue is also usually inadequate in any single year to finance the undertaking of various government capital schemes, such as road building and power station construction. Governments therefore borrow for capital investment as well as for routine current expenditure. Whereas firms give debentures or shares in return for liquid capital, governments give bonds. Debentures, shares, and bonds are all just pieces of paper, i.e., they are representative wealth (see section 2F), and are collectively called *securities*.

The Stock Exchange, then, is primarily a market for the exchange of securities. The different forms marketed are:

1   Interest-bearing securities. These represent loans. The three main types are:
    (a) Bonds, which are issued in return for a loan to the government (usually the national government, but, increasingly, the various local governments). Examples of bonds are: 4% Consols, which have no date of redemption set by the government (i.e., the government will repay the loan whenever it thinks fit; in other words, probably never); and 5% Treasury Bonds 1986–89, which the government will redeem in 1986–89. In the meantime, interest is paid at 4% and 5% respectively on each £100 ·bond, regardless of the market price of the bond.
    (b) Debentures, which are issued in return for a loan to a firm (see section 9C). If they are not paid, the debenture-holders can force the firm into liquidation.
    (c) Unsecured loan stock, which is broadly similar to a debenture loan but without the right of the holders to enforce liquidation upon failure of the firm to pay the agreed interest. In order to borrow funds on these safe terms, a firm has to be of excellent reputation; it may also offer a higher rate of interest than that given on debentures.

2   Dividend-bearing securities. These represent shares in the ownership of firms. There are two main types (see also section 9C):
    (a) ordinary shares, which carry a variable dividend rate paid out of profits. They are often called equities.
    (b) Preference shares, which carry a low fixed dividend paid out of profits. They rank as an investment risk somewhere between debentures and ordinary shares, but because of their low yield are now of decreasing importance as a means of investment.

The marketing of securities to increase liquidity in capital investment developed into a paramount need during the early growth of factory industry in the 18th century, because of the growing quantities of fixed capital investment at that time. The first permanent Stock Exchange opened in London in 1773, and others followed in a number of important provincial cities. The London Exchange is now one of the most important in the world, with about 10,000 different securities quoted to a nominal value of some £50,000,000,000,000.

In its operations the Exchange forms an almost perfect market. Anyone can buy or sell shares—even, as we shall see shortly, if he has neither the money nor the shares. All that a person has to do is instruct a stockbroker; there are hundreds to choose from, and each charges a small commission on each transaction. Remember, any bank can arrange this for you. It is then the broker's task to contact one of the stockjobbers at the Exchange. The stockjobbers usually specialise in particular groups of securities, such as oils, insurance, banks, and mines. They buy and sell on their own account; so that when a broker sells securities the jobber pays for them out of his own money, and when a broker buys securities it is the jobber's own shares that he buys. The prices are different for each type of transaction: the jobber clearly tries to make an income out of his work (providing liquidity for invested capital) and he accordingly sells (or *offers*) the securities for a higher price than that which he is prepared to pay (or *bid*). If the broker is satisfied with the prices quoted by the jobber the two men shake hands and register the deal on paper; no money changes hands, except for deals in bonds. The registrations are allowed to accumulate for periods of two to three weeks, each such period being called an *account*. After each account, there is a settlement of the net transactions which have occurred. It is quite possible, of course, for the securities bought by a jobber near the beginning of an account to have been sold by him to another broker during the same account, so that on settlement day the person who first sold the securities passes them via his broker to the final buyer and receives the money for them in return. If the final buyer wishes to postpone payment until the next settlement day then he must pay a special form of interest—called *contango*—on the outstanding sum due.

While most buying and selling in this way is done for purposes of private or institutional investment—to obtain a regular income from the holding of securities—the existence of the account can lead to abuse by speculation; in other words, attempts to make a quick capital gain by rapid buying and selling at opportune times. It is partly (only partly) as a disincentive to such speculation that there is now a capital gains tax. A watchful eye on speculative abuse is also kept by the Stock Exchange Council, which has powers in emergency to suspend dealings completely in any particular security.

The chief forms of speculative abuse can happen under conditions of either rising prices (a bull market) or falling prices (a bear market):

1 A bull market. Knowing that he will not have to pay any money until settlement day and guessing that prices will keep on rising, a bull buys shares at the start of the account and sells them at a profit (provided he has guessed correctly) before the end of the account. On settlement day the bull is in credit on the net transaction; so he can manage the whole deal without any money to start with. Indeed, he finishes up with a profit, without even having handled the shares.

2 A bear market. Guessing that prices will keep on falling, a bear sells shares which he has not got at the start of the account, hoping to buy them at a lower price before the end of the account; so that when settle-

ment day comes he has the shares (or at least the right to them) for delivery. The price he gets from the sale will be greater than his outlay on the eventual purchase (provided he has guessed correctly); so a profit is made on the net transaction. Again, no money is needed to start with.

What factors determine share prices? The prices quoted by a jobber are entirely his own, and are influenced by what he—as an expert—thinks of the economic situation in general and the individual securities in particular. Among the factors affecting his decision we should note:

1 Inflation. The characteristic decline of the k factor is expressed in a general desire by the public to put its income into real wealth. The sale of goods therefore increases, and firms accordingly take higher profits. Dividends consequently increase, and investors therefore bid up the price of equities in order to gain a share of those increased dividends. Further, as prices rise under inflation, the capital assets of a firm appreciate in money value; and since equities represent shares of ownership of (or claims on) those capital assets there is pressure from investors to own the equities. Owning equities during a period of inflation—that is, owning paper claims to real wealth during a time of falling money values—is called a *hedge against inflation.*

2 World political and economic events. Any event that is likely to lead to rising or falling profit levels will influence share prices. For example, the possibility (not, in fact, realised) of an increase in the price of gold in early 1968 led to a great increase in the demand for—and price of—gold-mining company shares. Gold prices had been fixed at $35 an ounce since the 1930s, and mining companies were finding it increasingly difficult to make profits when selling at this price. The possibility of a price rise for gold opened up the possibility of higher profits for the mining companies—and so investors began to buy their shares and bid up the price. For another example, metals were in great demand for armaments during the 1950–53 Korean war; so mining companies made higher profits, with the effect of raising their share prices. Fear of foreign appropriation of overseas holdings has the opposite effect—that of reducing the expected profitability of a firm—and so brings share prices down, as happened with the oil firms at the time of the nationalisation of the Suez canal (1956) and of the Arab-Israeli war (1967).

3 Expectation of shortages and surpluses. Whenever shortages are expected (as—perhaps—during a time of rapid technical progress or of bad harvests), investors realise that firms supplying goods in the fields of shortage will be able to charge higher prices than usual—and take higher profits as a result. Investors therefore bid up the price of the available shares. In this context it is useful to note that a firm can—and sometimes should—argue backwards from rising equity prices: rising prices are the result of an increased demand for shares, based on the expectation of higher profits, which may themselves be anticipated because of the possi-

bility of higher shop prices caused by the probability that the firm will be operating in a seller's market (i.e., goods in short supply). There is an indication under these conditions that there is insufficient productive capacity available. The converse is an equally valid indication: falling share prices could show that investors fear reduced profits because of either overproduction (excess supply) or shrinking markets (reduced demand). Firms which see their share prices falling should at least consider the possibility that there might already be enough—even more than enough—investment in their particular industry.

4   Government monetary policy. By means of its influence on commercial interest rates, government policy has a marked effect on the price of shares. If interest rates are high, and people can obtain a superior return by putting their money into bank deposit accounts or the like rather than by investing in shares, then the demand for shares contracts and their price falls. This is the reason for the declines in Stock Exchange prices which accompany credit squeezes.

130 The expenditure and sources of state revenue

At the start of section 3C we noted that the government in Britain is responsible for organising about 50% of the nation's production and consumption of goods and services; and at various other stages throughout the book we have noted how the government is responsible also for a variety of other aspects of the economy—such as money supply, location of industry, and certain types of business organisation. The government has charge of what is called the public sector of the economy; it employs directly over 30% of the nation's manpower and over 60% of those with a higher education, it owns over 50% of the nation's capital assets, it accounts for over 50% of the nation's fixed capital investment, and it pays for about 65% of the nation's technical research and development.

Out of each £ spent by the government, the chief destinations—in rounded figures—are:

defence	17p
pensions	17p
education	12p
debt interest	11p
health services	10p
capital formation by the nationalised industries	10p
housing	4p
roads	4p
others	15p

The miscellaneous costs—accounting for 15% of the total—are on such things as foreign aid, the maintenance of the administration (civil service, etc.), the provision of embassies abroad, the organisation of the judiciary, and the upkeep of the royal family.

In order to meet this expenditure, the government must raise revenue The chief sources of revenue are:

$$
\begin{array}{rl}
\text{borrowing} & 10\% \\
\text{taxation} & 80\% \\
\text{public sector trading profits} & 10\% \\
\text{note-printing presses} & \text{—}
\end{array}
$$

As we noted in section 9E, public sector profits are usually used as a means of offsetting higher taxation requirements; but it is useful to note also that many public sector enterprises (see section 3C) will not be operating at a profit at all —for the simple reason that they were taken into public ownership solely to keep them operative, even at a loss. It is also worth noting—again, that any government which resorts to the printing presses as a means of raising revenue is merely priming the inflationary pump. The two chief methods of raising revenue are therefore borrowing and taxation.

13P Borrowing and the National Debt

The National Debt is the name given to that sum of money—currently about £35/40,000,000,000—owed by the government both to its own citizens and to foreign governments. The bulk of the debt is internal, i.e., owed to the citizens of the country. The people to whom the money is owed are the holders of government bonds, treasury bills, national savings certificates, tax reserve certificates, premium savings bonds, and so on. The debts were incurred by governments for a variety of purposes, chiefly to finance the wars during this century, but also to pay for a number of capital projects (housing, roads, schools, etc.) undertaken since World War II. The total debt is divided into two parts: funded debt and unfunded debt.

Funded debt is that part which the government—despite paying regular interest—has no intention of repaying by any particular date. The most common example of bonds representing funded debt is Consols; the name being short for Consolidated Funds. There are $2\frac{1}{2}\%$ and 4% Consols, both of which are sold in nominal £100 units. If you look in the financial columns of a newspaper, however, you will notice that the Consols are not traded on the Stock Exchange at anything like £100. The trading price of Consols depends, in fact, on their *yield*, which is the amount of interest payment received by a bond-holder in relation to his original outlay in buying the bonds. The yield is expressed as a percentage figure; so that if a person paid £100 for a £100 unit of 4% Consols and received his annual interest payment of £4 the yield would be £4 on a £100 investment, i.e., 4%. If the investor could obtain a higher yield elsewhere, say 8% from a finance company, he would be unwilling to pay £100 for the 4% Consols. He might be prepared to pay £50 for the 4% Consols, however, since he could then obtain an equivalent 8% yield (remember that £4 annual interest is paid on the nominal value of 4% Consols, and that if the Consols are traded at £50 the buyer still gets £4 interest, giving him a yield of £4 on a £50 investment, i.e., 8%). The trading price of Consols is therefore geared to prevailing interest rates in the market; as interest rates rise so the price of Consols falls in order to maintain a competitive yield. If 4% Consols are ever to trade at £100, then clearly the alternative prevailing interest rates must fall from their present level to about 4%; and in practice that is very unlikely to happen, because of the immense and growing worldwide demand for borrowed money.

Borrowing of a funded nature has one important advantage for governments: it relieves them of the necessity of repaying large sums at specified times. A disadvantage—common to all forms of borrowing—is that interest payments have to be made. They are made out of revenue received from taxation, and you should take note of the amount of taxation which is spent in this way. Servicing debt interest, in fact, takes about 11% of taxation revenue.

Unfunded debt is that part of the National Debt which the government —as well as paying regular interest or discount—has every intention of repaying by a particular date. The unfunded debt falls into three main groups:

1 Medium to long term debt, represented by dated bonds such as $5\frac{1}{2}$ Treasury Bonds 2008–12, which pay annually the stated interest per £100 unit and are redeemable at par at the stated dates.

2 Floating debt, which is composed of short-term loans, represented by treasury bills as well as what are called Ways and Means Advances, which are really overdrafts on government accounts at the Bank of England.

3 Foreign debt, which is money owed to foreign governments, to the IMF, and to any other international financial agency. It is mostly short to medium in term.

Borrowing of an unfunded nature often allows a government to overcome temporary and periodic difficulties, but it also has the disadvantage that repayments may fall due at awkward times as well.

13Q Taxation

The total annual tax collection in Britain amounts to about £12,500,000,000. On average, each person employed in the tax collection service has a 'product' of some £175,000–£200,000; and it costs the tax service something like £1 for every £125 collected. The chief sources of this vast collection are:

income tax	38%
corporation tax	11%
tobacco tax	10%
petrol tax	8%
alcohol tax	7%
purchase tax	6%
selective employment tax	4%
motor tax	3%
others	13%

The purposes of taxation are varied:

1 To raise money for the functions of government listed in the second paragraph of section 13O.

2 To take purchasing power out of the hands of the community in order to combat inflation (see section 13J).

3 To equalise the distribution of wealth by taxing the rich and transferring some of the money to the poor by means of 'free' welfare services (see section 2G).

4 To protect the home market by tariff barriers against foreign competition (see the end of section 10B).

5 To encourage the location of industry in certain districts and to discourage it in others (see sections 6F and 10A).

6 To improve the health (and morality?) of the population—for example, by taxing tobacco and alcohol.

7 To switch the employment of labour from one sector of the economy to another, as the Selective Employment Tax (SET) attempted to switch labour from tertiary to secondary industry after its introduction in 1966.

The principles of taxation are—in general—that it should be productive of revenue and interfere as little as possible with normal economic life. To meet these general principles, a number of detailed requirements (or canons) have been suggested:

1 Certainty, i.e., that people know exactly how much they are being required to pay in tax. This particular canon is not regarded these days as one to be stressed, since it is a possible source of intense dissatisfaction.

2 Consistency, i.e., that a fairly regular revenue is produced in order to reduce the need for government borrowing.

3 Convenience, i.e., that taxes should be levied at times and by methods as convenient as possible to the taxpayer. This is the principle behind the device of Pay As You Earn (PAYE).

4 Difficulty of evasion, i.e., that people cannot readily escape the payment of taxes. You should distinguish here between tax *avoidance*, which is the perfectly legal arrangement of one's financial affairs so as to minimise one's tax liabilities, and tax *evasion*, which is an illegal attempt to escape a tax altogether (or to pay less than necessary).

5 Economy, i.e., that collection costs should be as low as possible in relation to the total tax yield.

6 Elasticity, i.e., that it should be possible to vary the tax revenue as required. This is best achieved by taxing goods in *in*elastic demand, since the existence of a tax will not change the demand for such goods by very much and it is therefore fairly easy to estimate the variations in revenue which can be achieved by different levels of tax.

7   Equity, i.e., that there should be a measure of fairness among individual taxpayers. This is not especially easy to obtain. Equal contributions are unfair because the poor then pay a greater proportion of their income as tax than do the rich; equal-contribution taxes are called *regressive*. Even *proportional* taxes (such as 25% of all earnings) are unfair, since larger incomes can endure greater reductions from taxation than can small incomes. The current solution to the problem is based on the concept of equality of sacrifice, whereby larger incomes pay tax at an increasing rate, e.g., 10% on the first £200 of taxable income, 15% on the next £200, 20% on the next £200, and so on. This is called *progressive* taxation, and results in some people in Britain paying as much as 90% tax on their marginal income above certain high levels. The rate of tax levied on the marginal income is called the marginal rate of tax; it is the rate which is levied on the last (or next possible) units of income. Under a system of progressive taxation, taxes are levied at low rates on early (or low) units of income; it is only the additional income which suffers the higher tax rates.

The seven canons of taxation are often contradictory in their application; for example, convenience may clash with consistency, and equity may be secured at the expense of economy. Accordingly, although any single tax is open to criticism, any criticism which ignores the total tax *system* is invalid.

The classification of taxes is not simple. We can, indeed, distinguish four main systems of classification:

1   Progressive and regressive taxes. Progressive taxes are characterised by a gradually increasing marginal rate, whereas regressive taxes are ungraded in character.

2   Income and outlay taxes. Income taxes are levied on earnings; examples are income tax, capital gains tax, corporation tax and property tax. Outlay taxes are levied on expenditure; purchase tax, petrol tax and tobacco tax are examples.

3   National and local taxes. National taxes are levied by the central government; for the most part they are uniform throughout the country, though the Selective Employment Tax (SET) is a variable one. Local taxes are levied by local governments (usually on property) and are called *rates*.

4   Direct and indirect taxes. Direct taxes are those in which the impact and incidence of the tax fall on the same person. The impact of a tax is felt by the person on whom the tax first falls; the incidence of a tax by the person who finally pays it. Income tax is an example of a direct tax, since the person on whom the tax impact falls is also the person who finally pays it. Indirect taxes are those in which the impact and incidence fall on different persons; the person who feels the impact being able to shift the tax on to someone else for payment. Purchase tax is an indirect tax, since the person who feels the impact (the supplier) is able to shift the tax on to the

customer, who therefore feels the incidence of the tax. Note that the supplier's ability to do this is governed by the nature of demand elasticity for his product; some suppliers can shift the whole tax, others a part of it only, and others no part of it at all. Indirect taxes are of two main types: *customs duties*, charged on imported goods, and *excise duties*, charged on home produced goods. Both customs duties and excise duties may be either (i) *specific*, meaning that the tax is levied on a particular quantity—weight or bulk—of a good, or (ii) *ad valorem*, meaning that the tax is levied on the monetary value of a good.

The arguments relating to direct taxation are:

For: that it is economical to collect; that it can be made progressive; that its incidence is fairly clear; that it is convenient to collect through PAYE; that the taxpayer is certain how much he is paying; that excess spending can readily be checked by reducing the disposal income; and that estimates of yield are fairly accurate.

Against: that it is difficult to assess on irregular incomes; that it is inconvenient to collect if there is no PAYE system; and that the certainty may be too great, leading to discontent, lack of effort at the margin, and perhaps to avoidance (legal) and evasion (illegal).

The arguments relating to indirect taxation are:

For: that the tax is usually paid in small and convenient amounts at the time of purchase, when the consumer is predisposed to pay; that the choice of payment is left to the consumer, since he does not have to buy the goods carrying the tax (necessities are often free of tax); that the tax burden is often not felt—or even known about—therefore there is generally little hostility in collection; that the taxes reach nearly everyone in the community, thus preventing tax concentration; and that the taxes can be used selectively to encourage or discourage the consumption of certain goods.

Against: that they work well only on goods in inelastic demand; that they are usually regressive; that they are often expensive to collect; that their incidence is not clear; and that the person upon whom the incidence probably falls (the customer) may pay more than the actual tax because of the fairly common practice among suppliers of 'rounding up'—i.e., a production cost of 8p plus tax of $1\frac{1}{2}$p may be rounded up to a selling price of 10p, thereby yielding the supplier a measure of excess profit.

In addition to the arguments for and against indirect taxes, there are also certain side-effects which need to be borne in mind. If there is a tax on necessities, for example, then the consumer will pay the tax, since its incidence can safely be passed on to him by the suppliers because of the inelasticity of his demand. This payment will then cut down the amount of money the consumer has left to spend on other commodities, and the suppliers of these other commodities will therefore suffer part of the burden of the initial tax because of the reduced demand for their own products. If the consumer spends just as much on the other goods, then it is likely that the quantity of his saving will diminish; so capital investment suffers instead. On the other hand, if the tax is imposed on luxuries, for which there is a highly elastic demand, then the suppliers will probably bear a large part—or even all—of the tax themselves rather than suffer a great reduction in demand. On those goods being produced under increasing returns (decreasing costs), any price rise caused by a tax increase will—by increasing demand—cause smaller sales and therefore higher average costs of production; so the price of the goods will tend to rise by even more than the amount of tax. Conversely, for those goods being produced under decreasing returns (increasing costs), any price rise occasioned by a tax will tend to decrease demand and cause lower average costs of production, thereby raising the price of the good by less than the amount of tax. If there is no change in demand at all, then the price of the goods will rise by an amount equivalent to the tax, and other producers, as first noted, will bear part of the burden of the tax through reduced sales of their own products.

Arguments rage about the topic of **tax disincentives** to production: people with high incomes generally take the view that surtax (a progressive addition to income tax) is the major disincentive to extra effort; people with low incomes assert that the onset of the standard tax rate is the chief disincentive to extra work; and other people point out that the whole British tax system is monumentally complicated and inefficient. In May 1967, *The Times* published a selection of charts illustrating the rising marginal tax rates in a number of different countries: Britain came markedly the worst out of the comparison, in that at incomes of £20,000 a year (or equivalent in other countries) the marginal tax rates were (figures rounded)—U.K. 90%, Netherlands 70%, Australia, New Zealand and South Africa 65%, Germany and USA 50%, and France 35%. The paper also noted that 'Once a man is earning £6000 per annum, for example, his enthusiasm and ambition will be tempered with the knowledge that, of every additional £ he earns, more than 10/- (50p) would go in taxation.' In October 1967, *The Economist* ran a 'Business Brief' on *Incentives and Taxation*, and came firmly to the conclusion that the whole structure of the tax system needed overhauling. Of particular interest is *The Economist*'s view that 'if incentives are deficient it is not so much at the top as round the £1000 a year mark and a little above. The average weekly wage is in fact £20.10.0 (£20·50), or £1060 a year. It is people around this level who are often expected to make the biggest adjustments in the name of productivity. Yet it is at just this point that people begin to encounter the cliffs of the standard rate. . . . Equally at this level a man or woman often has little chance to shine. Getting more money is therefore even more important. . . . A tax system which is tough at this level may have very serious consequences in discouraging initiative and thwarting a sense of personal progress.' In January 1969, Political and Economic Planning published a broadsheet entitled *Personal Taxation and Incentives*, and noted in it that 'It is inequitable that the only way to become rich is to have income which is not earned.' The reason for this, the authors said, was because the very high marginal rates of tax on the highest levels of earned income made it almost impossible to become very rich through hard work and initiative rather than inheritance. A few days later, the Industrial Policy Group (a group of Britain's top industrialists aiming to solve the problems of the British economy) put out its pamphlet *Taxation*, which contained the statement that 'the general burden of taxation is much too heavy for the health of the economy and it must be reduced.' The industrialists reported in the pamphlet that 'our experience as employers leads us to the view that in the case of wage earners the net balance of the effect of income tax is a deterrent to work', and they also noted that 'high marginal rates of tax undoubtedly dull the urge among many executives to find the line of activity where their work would be most rewarding and most effective.'

One of the troubles with the problem of tax disincentives is that there is a serious lack of detailed studies; too much is guesswork. On the basis of research done in the USA, Political and Economic Planning came to the very tentative conclusion that the disincentive effects of the British tax system compared with a possible alternative system might be a loss of effort of 1%. Most people would probably put the figure much higher, but they would do so on a basis of ignorance. The figure, however, may well be much higher; there is just not enough known about the problem.

13R The Budget

The purposes of the budget are to raise revenue for government needs and to regulate the national economy. Budgetary measures of regulation are called *fiscal* to distinguish them from the *monetary* techniques available to a government and outlined in section 13G.

The Budget is usually presented to Parliament in April. It contains not only a review of the previous year's achievements (matched against the previous year's estimates) but also the estimated expenditure for the coming year and the proposed sources of revenue. The details are then incorporated in the Finance Bill, which—after discussion in the House—usually receives the Royal Assent in July.

The Budget statement consists—broadly—of two parts: first, that dealing with the *Consolidated Fund*, called 'above the line' expenditure and revenue; and second, that dealing with the *National Loans Fund*, called 'below the line' expenditure and revenue. Table 13.5 shows the division.

The Consolidated Fund is concerned to show current expenditure on both supply services and Consolidated Fund standing services as well as current revenue out of taxation. Supply services account for the vast bulk of expenditure; most of this is on the provision of regular services such as defence, health, education, agricultural subsidies, and overseas aid. Consolidated Fund standing services are the permanent commitments of the government, e.g., interest payments on the National Debt, and transfer payments to the government of Northern Ireland. Taxation receipts include all the taxes collected by both the Inland Revenue (income taxes) and the Customs & Excise Office (outlay taxes). There are also a few minor receipts from such things as government trading, the sale of government property, and the issue of wireless licences.

The National Loans Fund is concerned with government borrowing.

Consolidated Fund

Revenue:	(£m)
Taxation	10 819
Miscellaneous receipts	413
Total	11 232
Expenditure:	
Supply services	9 976
Consolidated Fund standing services	893
Total	10 869
Surplus	*363*	The

Line

National Loans Fund

To nationalised industries	1 199
To local and harbour authorities	356
Other	185
Total	1 740
less: Consolidated Fund surplus	363
Net borrowing of National Loans Fund	1 377

TABLE 13.5 Summary of the 'outturn' statement of the 1968 Budget.

Governments borrow in order to lend: they borrow from the capital and money markets and lend to the nationalised industries and local authorities. Any surplus achieved 'above the line' by an excess of taxation revenue over, largely, supply service expenditure is paid into the National Loans Fund, where it is used to diminish the government borrowing requirement. If there is a deficit 'above the line' the National Loans Fund merely enlarges its borrowing requirement and transfers money to the Consolidated Fund to make up the deficit.

The Budget has assumed over the years a most important place in the government's range of measures to control the economy. It gives the government the power to redistribute the country's wealth, the ability to select goods and industries for encouragement or discouragement, and the capacity to regulate general price levels.

General price levels—together with all the production and market phenomena related to price levels—may be regulated by the techniques of budgeting for either a surplus or a deficit. A surplus in the Consolidated Fund, when paid into the National Loans Fund, does nothing on its own to prevent the government from running up such large borrowing debts that the whole Budget statement shows a deficit overall. Budgeting for a surplus does not mean merely a surplus 'above the line', for that is of little economic significance in relation to general price levels. It is the overall balance that matters. If there is an overall surplus, the effect is to take out of the economy more money by taxation than is put back by credit creation through government borrowing. The net effect of an overall *surplus* is therefore *deflationary*. Be careful here, because you will often hear politicians talking about an 'above the line' surplus being deflationary, when it is nothing of the sort unless accompanied by an overall surplus. All Budgets in the late 1950s and early 1960s, for example, supported 'above the line' surpluses, and were often hailed as deflationary; but every single one carried an overall deficit. Budgeting for a deficit (**deficit financing**) has the result of adding to the money supply by creating more money through credit (based on government borrowing) than is collected from the community by taxation. The effect of an overall Budget *deficit* is therefore *reflationary* at best and *inflationary* at worst.

International trade

14A The law of comparative costs

Division of labour within a firm permits the gain of both internal economies and greater total production; but it necessitates the exchange of goods and services among the specialists. Similarly, division of production among the nations of the world permits the gain of both internal economies and greater total output; and it necessitates the exchange of goods and services among the specialising nations.

International trade is, indeed, the larger scale of exchange brought about by the international division of production. There is little doubt that—among the technically advanced countries, at least—most parts of the physical environment could be made to yield most types of product (except minerals) in current demand; but for most parts the returns would not repay the economic effort. Tomatoes, for example, can be produced inside the Arctic Circle; but the cost of that production (in real as well as in nominal terms) renders them unsaleable. The output is a technical curiosity, not an economic possibility.

Trade, then, develops in response to specialisation. What determines the specialisation? Obviously, some countries just lack completely one or more necessary commodities (necessary, that is, to their current economic development); Britain, for example, virtually lacks oil, and must import it for its industries. Other countries may not be able to produce enough of whatever it is they want; China, for instance, cannot yet produce enough wheat for itself. And still other countries may be perfectly able to produce certain goods, and yet still import them; the USA, for example, is capable of producing enough cameras and transistor radios for itself, but it still imports many. The reason is that the USA is able to put the bulk of its productive effort *more profitably* into something else.

Apart from those few cases of trade caused by the importing country being unable to produce a commodity either at all or in sufficient quantity, the main reason for trade arising out of specialised production is that some countries find it more profitable to concentrate their efforts on certain goods than on other goods. The reason for this is given in the explanation of the **law of comparative costs**, which states that countries will benefit from trade if there is some difference in the relative efficiency of the production of certain goods. Two examples should help to clarify the law:

Example one. Let us assume that two countries, Vinland and Roseland, can both produce motor cars and yachts, and that—*per equal unit of production factors (land, labour, etc.)*—

Vinland can produce either 100 motor cars or 40 yachts
Roseland can produce either 80 motor cars or 50 yachts.

Vinland is more efficient at producing motor cars, Roseland at producing yachts. Using *two* production units each, in order to be able to produce both motor cars *and* yachts, both countries together are capable of producing a total of 180 motor cars and 90 yachts. However, if each country were to specialise on the product in which it had the greatest relative efficiency, then Vinland—using two production units—could make 200 cars and 0 yachts, while Roseland could make 0 cars and 100 yachts. Total production from both countries under specialisation is now 200 motor cars and 100 yachts, compared with a total production without specialisation of only 180 motor cars and 90 yachts. There are 20 more motor cars and 10 more yachts, and they have been produced from the same production units; no extra land or labour has been employed. The difference is merely specialisation instead of non-specialisation. Trade is, of course, necessary, since Vinland will want some of the yachts made by Roseland and Roseland will want some of the cars made by Vinland; and there are now 20 extra cars and 10 extra yachts to enter into trade. There is clearly greater satisfaction all round.

Example two. Let us assume that two countries, Upland and Downland, can both produce oranges and lemons, and that—per equal production unit—

    Upland can produce either 100 oranges or 40 lemons
    Downland can produce either 50 oranges or 32 lemons.

Upland is more efficient at producing *both* commodities, and would at first sight appear to gain no advantage from specialisation and trade. However, notice Upland's *relative* superiority: in the production of oranges its superiority is of the order 100:50, or 2:1, while in the production of lemons its superiority is merely 40:32, or 1·25:1. Its superiority is greater in the production of oranges than of lemons. The law of comparative costs states that *both* countries will benefit if specialisation occurs—in oranges for Upland, where its *superiority is greatest*, and in lemons for Downland, where its *inferiority is least*. If both countries use two production units each, in order to produce both oranges and lemons, then total production from the two countries together is 150 oranges (100 from Upland and 50 from Downland) and 72 lemons (40 from Upland and 32 from Downland). If each country specialises on the product where its superiority is greatest or its inferiority least, then total output from both countries together is 200 oranges (all from Upland) and 64 lemons (all from Downland). There are therefore 50 more organges and 8 fewer lemons than the combined totals without any specialisation.

	Without specialisation		*With specialisation*	
	oranges	lemons	oranges	lemons
Upland	100	40	200	0
Downland	50	32	0	64
Total	150	72	200	64

Let us assume now that each country exchanges goods to restore itself to at least the output position prior to any specialisation. Upland will exchange 100 of its oranges for 40 of Downland's lemons—such a trade giving Upland 100 oranges (left out of 200 produced) and 40 lemons (gained by trade), and leaving Downland with 100 oranges (gained by trade) and 24 lemons (left out of 64 produced). Upland is now in the same position as it would have been without specialisation and trade, but Downland has 50 more oranges (100 instead of 50) and 8 fewer lemons (24 instead of 32). Upland is clearly neither worse nor better off; but what about Downland? The extra 50 oranges represent a full production unit to Downland; so it is better off there. The 8 fewer lemons, however, represent a loss; but a loss of only 25% of a production unit (a full Downland production unit is capable of producing 32 lemons; so 8 lemons represent 25% of a full unit). Clearly, Downland has gained the equivalent of 75% of a production unit (100% gain minus 25% loss). If the exchange is carried out the other way, Downland—to restore itself to a pre-specialisation output level—will exchange 32 of its 64 lemons for 50 of Upland's 200 oranges, leaving Downland no worse off with 50 oranges and 32 lemons, but giving Upland the advantage of having 150 of its 200 oranges left as well as an additional 32 lemons gained by trade. Upland therefore has 50 more oranges (150 instead of 100) and 8 fewer lemons (32 instead of 40). The extra 50 oranges represent 50% of a production unit to Upland; and that is entire gain. The 8 fewer lemons, however, represent only 20% of a production unit, and—while that is lost—there is still a *net* gain of 30% of a production unit (50% gain minus 20% loss). In practice, both countries will want to gain some of the benefits of specialisation and trade; and that will entail a compromise exchange rate for oranges and lemons. The limits to variations in the exchange rate are set by each country, since Upland will want at least 40 lemons in return for 100 oranges (in order to maintain at least a pre-specialisation output level), while Downland will not be prepared to yield more than 32 lemons for 50 oranges, otherwise it, too, will be worse off than before specialisation. The actual exchange rate is therefore likely to be somewhere between 40 lemons for 100 oranges (Upland's *minimum* rate) and 64 lemons for 100 oranges (Downland's *maximum* rate, equivalent to 32 lemons for 50 oranges). The exact point of exchange will depend on a number of factors—some internal, such as the intensity of demand in both Upland and Downland for oranges and/or lemons, and some external, such as the overall world demand for, and supply of, oranges and lemons.

It is by means of the operation of the law of comparative costs outlined in the second example that we get the apparently absurd situation of a country importing a good which that country itself could make more cheaply. Politicians and parliamentary lobbyists are hot on this one; so take note when you listen to their speeches. The solution is merely that by not making that particular commodity resources are released for the *even more profitable* production of an alternative commodity.

The perfect operation of the law of comparative costs is very seriously hindered in practice by the existence of barriers. The least important barriers (least important because they can be overcome technically) are those of distance; though transport costs may indeed nullify production cost differences. The most important barriers, on the other hand, are those created by governments; they are the most important because they represent human will, and that is not so easily changed. Customs tariffs, exchange controls, trade quotas, and all sorts of other devices in fact are used by governments to influence the perfect flow of commodities. The controls may be imposed for a variety of purposes, such as to 'protect' infant industries which might otherwise never get started, and to 'protect' an area from the unemployment which might be created if cheaper goods were allowed in from another country. However good the intentions of a trade-controlling government, however, its actions are bound to thwart the achievement of those benefits which result from specialisation and trade. We will say more about this in section 14H. Another friction to the smooth operation of the law of comparative costs is that cost alone is not always the decisive factor in trade: design, delivery dates, after-sales service, and the provision of credit facilities are other factors of growing importance.

14B The terms of trade and the balance of trade

The expressions—terms of trade and balance of trade—are dissimilar in meaning.

The **terms of trade** represent simply the import-buying power of a unit of exports. If import prices fall in relation to export prices, then the terms or trade are said to have improved, since a unit of exports buys more imports (*or* fewer exports are needed to buy the same imports). For example, if an export unit of, say, 10 cars is needed to buy an import unit of 300 tons of wheat initially, and then subsequently only 9 cars are needed, the terms of trade have improved. Improved terms of trade are brought about whenever export prices rise faster than import prices, whenever export prices rise while import prices remain steady or fall, or whenever export prices fall more slowly than import prices. If the opposite conditions obtain, and a unit of exports buys fewer imports, then the terms of trade are said to have worsened.

The **balance of trade** is that balance achieved by the total value of goods exported measured against the total value of goods imported during a certain period (usually a month or a year). If the total value of goods exported is less than the total value of goods imported then there is a deficit balance of trade (or a *trade deficit*); and if the value of goods exported exceeds the value of those imported then there is a credit balance of trade (or a *trade surplus*).

The balance of trade is therefore one total quantity measured against another. The terms of trade, however, is a relationship between the prices of units of exports and imports, and has no connection at all with the total quantities of exports and imports. It is quite possible for a country to have improving terms of trade (a unit of exports buying more and more imports) and yet at the same time a colossal balance of trade deficit (the total value of imported goods exceeding the total value of exported goods).

14C The balance of payments

The balance of payments represents the total amount of money coming into the country measured against the total amount of money leaving the country. It is not the same as the balance of trade, which is concerned solely with the value of the *goods* exported and imported. The balance of trade (sometimes called the balance of visible trade, since the goods going out and coming in are visible to the eye) is an important component of the balance of payments, but it *is* only a component.

Money enters or leaves a country for other reasons than the export and import of goods, chief among them being the existence of an invisible trade in services, and the movements in and out caused by investment, borrowing, and lending. It is therefore possible to divide the balance of payments into its component parts:

1   The balance of visible trade, which accounts for about half the total amount of money involved.

2   The balance of invisible trade (i.e., services), which accounts for about a quarter of the total money involved.

3   The balance of capital account, which registers the outflow of funds for British investment abroad and the inflow of funds resulting from foreign investment in Britain.

4   The balance of monetary movements, which represents either borrowing from abroad or the setting aside of surplus to reserve, and which is designed to bring the whole balance of payments into final balance.

The first two components—visible and invisible trade—are grouped into what is called the balance of current account, to distinguish them from the third component—the balance of capital account. The fourth component is purely an accommodating or 'balancing' device, and its sole purpose is to achieve a final balance. The total balance of payments, indeed, must always balance; the balancing device sees to that. When people talk of a balance of payments deficit, they mean a deficit on current and capital accounts; and the deficit then has to be 'balanced' by borrowing from abroad. The usual sources of borrowed money to cover a payments deficit are the USA, the IMF, the World Bank, and the Group of Ten (the ten most industrialised trading nations of the free world). In time of supreme emergency, Britain might also sell some of its assets abroad (i.e., its foreign investments); and in lesser emergency it might use up some of its gold and foreign currency reserves. On those occasions when Britain has a payments surplus (on current and capital accounts), the surplus money might be used to build up the reserves, to pay off the debts incurred during times of deficit, to lend to foreign governments, and to add to investment abroad.

There is no reason why any individual component of the balance of payments should be in regular balance; all that matters to a country in the long run is that there should be an average overall balance. Britain, for example, normally runs a deficit on the first component, the balance of visible trade, though that deficit is usually more than covered by a credit on the balance of invisible trade to produce an overall credit on the current account balance. The balance of capital account is also usually in deficit, because British residents normally invest more money abroad than foreign residents invest in Britain, and that deficit therefore also has to be carried by the surplus on invisible trade. Invisible trade is clearly of great importance to Britain; it is the only component of the balance of payments which consistently yields a surplus. Even in 1964—one of the worst trading years in Britain's post-war history—the invisible trade balance was £138 million in credit, whereas the visible trade balance showed a deficit of £519 million and the capital account a deficit of £363 million.

The items included in the invisible trade balance are:

1   Government expenditure and receipts, for such things as the maintenance of British forces abroad, aid to foreign countries, and the upkeep of embassies abroad.
2   Merchant shipping carrying services.
3   Civil aviation services.
4   Travel abroad by British residents and in Britain by overseas residents.
5   Interest, profits, and dividends earned by British investment abroad, and paid out for foreign investment in Britain.
6   Private transfers, including all money transferred from Britain by emigrants and to Britain by immigrants.
7   Other services, which includes the balance of expenditure on a miscellany of services such as advertising, acting, banking, brokerage, higher education, industrial consultancy, insurance, and surgery.

Not all these seven items contribute to the overall credit on the balance of invisible trade. Government business, for example, invariably produces a deficit—and a growing one at that; shipping produces a surplus—but only just, and it is a declining surplus at best; civil aviation produces an increasing surplus; travel is nearly always a deficit item; interest, profits and dividends yield a large and growing surplus (and it is worth bearing in mind that the surplus on this item is produced out of the deficit on capital account, and that in general the surplus here is greater than the deficit on capital account); private transfers yield a growing deficit, particularly as the British emigrants have more money to transfer out than the bulk of immigrants have to transfer in; and other services produce a growing surplus. The largest items by value are the deficit on government business and the surpluses on interest, profits and dividends and on other services.

Occasionally, as during the entire mid-1960s in Britain, a country develops a persistent balance of payments deficit. While borrowing from international agencies is acceptable for short periods, it is likely in the long term to produce a crisis of international confidence in the ability of a nation to manage its financial affairs in a sound manner. The failing confidence is reflected in an unwillingness by foreigners to hold the deficit country's currency; the currency then steadily loses value in relation to other currencies (i.e., it *depreciates*) and as a result there is a tendency for exports to earn less and imports to cost more, thus further aggravating the problem of a payments deficit. The necessary steps to combat the problem are one or more of the following:

1   Internal deflation, designed to cut domestic demand and reduce imports. Unfortunately for Britain, its imports are largely foodstuffs and essential raw materials, both of which are in fairly inelastic demand. It is also unfortunate for Britain that—because of wage rigidity—deflation tends to produce unemployment (cutting production and exports) rather than generally lower wages (which would make exports cheaper and more likely in consequence to be sold abroad in larger quantities). On the other hand, merely a mild form of deflation—of the order of a credit squeeze—tends to produce a slow-down of imports for stockpiling; instead of importing to maintain stocks, producers use up some of their existing stocks—imports are cut, but the solution is inevitably short-term and self-cancelling in character since imports need to be increased at a future date in order to build up stocks again.

2   Import controls, designed to reduce the quantity of imports. Visible imports may be lessened by increasing tariffs, by quotas, by surcharges (attempts in 1964–65 without success), and by import deposit schemes, whereby importers have to post a returnable non-interest-earning deposit with the government in proportion to the value of the imports, thereby taking money out of circulation domestically (cutting purchasing power) and also acting as a disincentive to increased imports. Invisible imports (i.e., services which take money out of Britain) may be reduced by orders restricting the amount of foreign investment (this is of short-term use only, since foreign investment helps to create a surplus on invisible trade in the long run), limiting the amount of money British tourists can take or spend abroad (the notorious 'travel allowance'), blocking the transfer abroad of profits and dividends earned in Britain by foreign investors, and restricting the amount of money which can be taken abroad by emigrants. All these devices have been tried at one time or another, and all tend to arouse the hostility of other nations; some countries indeed even threaten to use retaliatory tariffs, and that doesn't do anyone any good. The use of import controls is in general a poor attempt at a solution, since all that is likely to happen is a reduction in overall world trade—and the benefits of international specialisation are lost.

3   Export incentives, designed to increase the quantity of exports. These form a much better approach to the problem of a payments deficit than import controls, since the overall effect is to augment world trade; the only qualification is that the incentives should not appear to take the form of a 'hidden' subsidy, which can be interpreted by other countries as unfair competition. Visible trade can be strengthened by a variety of measures, chief among them being: (a) increasing domestic productivity (more capital, better-trained labour, superior management, etc.) to cut unit costs of production in order either to make exports more profitable and so attract more firms into export-production or to lower export prices and so extend foreign demand; and (b) holding domestic inflation down to a rate slower than that being experienced in other trading nations, so that domestic prices, including costs of production, rise less fast than those of competitors, therefore rendering domestic exports more competitive in price in world markets. The purpose of the National Economic Development Council (NEDC or 'Neddie') and all the 'Little Neddies' (one for each major industry in Britain) is to achieve the first goal; and the purpose of the Prices and Incomes Board (PIB) was to achieve the second. The prolonged intractability of the problem, however, has caused many people to seek an explanation (and a remedy) in the host of fringe factors which affect world trade: slow delivery dates, inadequate overseas service facilities, advertising literature only in English, out-of-date design, inadequate export-credit facilities, lack of technical assistance, the belief of many producers that exporting is not profitable, lack of export-sales personnel, and the downgrading of export agents in the industrial hierarchy. It is interesting to note that about 60% of Britain's exports are produced by only 100 or so firms, and that as much as 80% comes from no more than about 600 firms. Many small firms make no effort at all to sell abroad, and in consequence the ICFC in May 1968 backed a new attempt—the British Organisation for the Development of Exports (BODE)—to increase the export interest of small and medium-sized firms. Meanwhile, invisible exports (i.e., services which bring money into Britain) can be increased by persuading more foreigners to take holidays in Britain, to make more use of the services of British carrying agents (ships and aircraft), to insure themselves with British companies, and to buy the products of foreign-based but British-owned firms so that greater profits can be remitted to Britain.

4   Devaluation, designed to lower the international exchange rate of a country's currency. The measure is permitted by the IMF when a country's balance of payments is in 'fundamental disequilibrium', i.e., if the measures just noted fail to provide a solution in a reasonable amount of time. What is 'reasonable'? The answer depends on the country concerned, its part in world trade, and the role of its currency in international finance. Two or three years might be 'reasonable' for a small country; a decade or two for a large country. The act of devaluation gives official recognition to the depreciation of a currency; Britain, for example,

devalued in 1967, changing the official exchange rate of sterling for US dollars from £1 = $2.80 to the lower rate of £1 = $2.40, so that Britons got fewer dollars and cents in return for their pounds. In England, the rate is expressed in terms of the £, but perhaps it makes sense more forcefully if you regard the change as being the equivalent of a fall in value of sterling from 35p needed to buy $1.00 before 1967 to 42p needed to buy $1.00 after 1967. The price of a dollar rose as the international value (purchasing power) of the pound fell. The immediate result of devaluation is to make imports costlier in terms of the domestic currency (e.g., having to pay 42p to obtain a dollar's worth of imports instead of having to pay merely 35p), and either to make exports cheaper in terms of foreign currencies or to give exporters a higher profit at unchanged foreign currency prices (thereby making exporting a more attractive proposition to firms in the devaluing country). The consequent tendency is for the devaluing country to import less (because imports cost more) and to export more (because of either cheaper exports or higher profits). However, the tendency is influenced drastically by the elasticities of demand for imports and exports. If domestic demand elasticity is low (i.e., inelastic) then imports continue to be brought in with little change of quantity, but at a greatly increased total cost, thus aggravating an already difficult situation. Further, if foreign demand for exported goods is also inelastic, then a lower export price does little to attract larger sales, even assuming that the devaluing country's economy has sufficient surplus capacity to supply additional goods for export. It is quite possible, indeed, that total revenue may actually fall. Another snag with devaluation—for Britain—is that many imports are incorporated into subsequent exports (e.g., raw cotton into cotton shirts); so that dearer imports are of necessity reflected in more costly exports (or at least less cheap exports). Still another snag—for Britain—is that many essential foodstuffs are imported, and as their price rises so does the pressure for wage increases (because of a higher cost of living). Any effective act of devaluation by Britain must, therefore, be accompanied by rigorous restrictions on cost-increasing wage increases; indeed, any inflationary tendencies (larger money supply, increased borrowing and spending, reduced savings) must be severely curtailed, otherwise rising factor costs will rapidly offset any advantages gained from devaluation, and increased domestic consumption will divert production from the all-important export markets. A final snag to a devaluation of sterling is that many foreign countries hold sterling as part of their gold and foreign currency reserves; and all such holdings are immediately worth less after devaluation than they were before. Foreign countries do not welcome this. And beyond the economic arguments, there is also the fact that whatever government is in charge when the pound 'falls' regards devaluation as a political loss of face; witness the British government's decision not to devalue in 1964, and the ensuing measures to avoid devaluation, until it was eventually necessitated in 1967.

14D The foreign exchange market

Outside the communist world, where most international trade is handled by government agencies, the bulk of trade is carried on by independent exporters and importers. The arrangements whereby the importers pay the exporters, using gold, dollars, sterling, some other trading currency, or the currency of the exporter, are known as the foreign exchange market. If a British exporter ships, say, cars to the USA, he will most likely receive payment in dollars; the dollars, however, are not acceptable as part of the domestic currency in Britain, and so they must be exchanged for an equivalent amount of sterling. The exporter's bank arranges this, issuing sterling to the exporter and sending dollars to the Bank of England to be added to the gold and foreign currency reserves of the nation. Conversely, if an exporter in the USA ships tobacco to an importer in Britain and requests payment in dollars, the British importer has to make arrangements with his bank to negotiate a release of dollars from the gold and foreign currency reserves at the Bank of England in return for an equivalent payment by the importer in sterling to the Bank. Many different banks operate in the foreign exchange market, but the chief types are the merchant banks and the commercial banks. They all charge a commission on these routine sales and purchases of foreign currency. Don't forget that all items entering world trade necessitate a reverse flow of funds; and that applies to invisible as well as to visible trade. When you go abroad for a holiday and seek some foreign currency from your bank, you are making an invisible import; you are also making use of the foreign exchange market.

Apart from routine sales and purchases of foreign currency for the purposes of existing trade, the foreign exchange market also engages in:

1 Arbitrage. This is the business of buying and selling currencies in one world market centre for sale or purchase in another in order to stabilise (and make a profit out of) any fluctuations which are pulling an individual exchange rate out of line in one centre only. For example, assume an initial equilibrium situation:

in London:	£1 = 20 kroner;	£1 = 80 escudos
in Oslo:	20 kroner = £1;	20 kroner = 80 escudos
in Lisbon:	80 escudos = £1;	80 excudos = 20 kroner

For some reason, the escudo-kroner rate in Lisbon changes to 100 escudos = 20 kroner. That rate now causes a disequilibrium situation to exist, and it is the function of the arbitrate dealers—or *arbitrageurs*—to restore equilibrium to the exchanges (that is not their prime purpose, however; their prime purpose is to make a profit for themselves). On seeing the disequilibrium situation, the arbitrageurs in London, say, buy 20 kroner for £1 and then sell the 20 kroner in Lisbon for 100 escudos. The 100 escudos gained in their transaction are then converted to sterling in either Lisbon or London to yield £1·25. So long as the disequilibrium situation exists in Lisbon, the increased supply of kroner (for conversion to escudos) in Lisbon, and the increased demand for escudos (for conversion to sterling) in Lisbon and London will operate to restore the initial equilibrium situation. In this way, a measure of stability is provided for the exchanges.

2 Forward exchange. Importers do not always want to obtain foreign currency immediately. There are many occasions when all they want immediately is a guarantee that a certain quantity of foreign currency will be available for their use at some time in the future. One of the tasks of foreign exchange dealers is to provide such a guarantee. However, contracts for future delivery inevitably contain an element of risk—perhaps depreciation or even devaluation of the domestic currency. Accordingly, the *forward* rate of exchange is usually less favourable than the immediate, or *spot*, rate. The difference may be regarded as the price the importer has to pay in order to preserve liquidity during the intervening period, as well the cost of insurance against the risk of excessive depreciation.

14E The gold standard

The complete—*gold specie*—standard had certain characteristics:

1 Full convertibility. The domestic standard currency unit (e.g., the £) was freely convertible at par into gold, and gold bullion was freely mintable into coin. Gold coins and convertible notes both circulated freely. The value of notes and coin together was equal to the value of the country's gold holdings.

2 Free export and import of gold. International trade was financed by the movement of gold from importers to exporters, if the exporters wished to receive payment in that medium. In practice, because gold was bulky and expensive to transport, the usual instrument of payment was a bill of exchange; however, bills themselves were risky if exchange rates fluctuated, and at times it was both safer and cheaper actually to ship gold. The exchange rate at which it became worthwhile for the importer to pay the exporter in gold was called the *gold export point*; the situation arose whenever the price of a foreign currency in terms of, say, sterling rose above the combined price of gold in terms of sterling and the cost of shipping that gold. It then became worthwhile for the importer to buy gold with sterling and transport the gold to the exporter. The *gold import point* was the exchange rate at which it became worthwhile for an exporter to demand payment in gold.

The immediate effects of the gold specie standard were twofold: first, the quantity of domestic currency was firmly regulated, since the amount depended entirely upon the value of the nation's gold holdings; and second, the foreign exchange market was given stable guidelines, since each domestic currency in the world was related to gold—in readily comparable quantities, moreover, since each currency's standard unit was fully convertible into a certain quantity of gold. For example, if one ounce of gold was worth £4 in England and $20 in the USA, then the pound-dollar rate was £4 = $20, or £1 = $5. Exchange rates based on this type of comparison were said to be at *mint par*.

The operation and success of the gold specie standard rested upon certain conditions: first, gold had to be able to influence the amount of currency inside a country, so that if a country increased its holdings of gold (through a payments surplus) then the quantity of its internal currency showed an equivalent rise, and if there was a loss of gold then the quantity of currency decreased; and second, gold had to be readily transferred from debtor countries (those running payments deficits) to creditor countries (those running payments surpluses). Given these conditions, the gold standard provided an entirely self-regulating basis for international trade. Debtor countries lost gold, and consequently suffered a reduction in the quantity of their internal currency, thereby enduring falling prices along with all the other phenomena of deflation; the lower prices resulted not only in lower-cost and more competitive exports but also in lower-profit imports, thereby encouraging exports and discouraging imports, and so tending to equalise the original trade imbalance. Conversely, creditor countries gained gold, which inflated the domestic currency and raised internal prices; exports were made less competitive and imports more profitable, and the tendency was to an equalisation of the original trade imbalance.

The chief troubles with the gold specie standard were that some countries —notably France and the USA—did not operate by the rules. They did not allow gold to move out freely when they were paying other exporters; nor did they allow their increasing holdings to inflate their internal currencies. In consequence, the debtor countries lost gold continuously—and accordingly suffered the worst effects of deflationary pressures (e.g., unemployment and unrest) without gaining any compensating potential advantages. A further disadvantage of the gold specie standard was that not enough new gold was being discovered and mined to keep pace with the growth in world trade. The last great gold rush was in 1898–99 in the Klondike, and since then the volume of world trade has vastly outstripped the slowly growing total supply of gold.

During the present century the gold standard has collapsed. The first world war marked the critical turning point; Britain—one of the world's greatest trading nations—abandoned gold, and, despite intense deflationary measures to restore pre-war price levels (see figure 13.2), never succeeded in getting back to the gold specie standard. A partial return was effected in 1925, but only to the gold bullion standard, whereby gold was not allowed to circulate internally—its use being restricted to the financing of foreign trade. The gold bullion standard failed to survive the Great Depression of 1929–31, and since 1931 Britain has had a completely government-managed currency, accompanied by government-controlled foreign exchange rates. The pound was tied to the US dollar at the rate of £1 = $4.03, but persistent visible trade deficits coupled with periodic overall payments deficits, the cost of a second world war, and the ambitions of governments both to found a welfare state and to maintain the relics of an imperial presence have caused two devaluations against the dollar: in 1949 to $2.80, and in 1967 to $2.40.

In 1968, even the remote prospect of a return to the gold standard was eliminated. The main trading countries of the world—France excepted— abandoned all pretence of a gold backing for trade and foreign exchange. They established a two-tier price system for gold, retaining the fixed (and nominal) rate of $35 an ounce for monetary gold, but deciding at the same time *not to use it*, and also freeing the price of non-monetary gold to seek its own equilibrium level. On the free market, gold then became a commodity like any other.

14F Purchasing power parity

During the initial stages of collapse of the gold standard in World War I the idea was introduced that exchange rates could be fixed by comparisons of internal purchasing power rather than by reference solely to gold. The idea of purchasing power parity is that exchange rates can be determined by comparing the domestic costs in different countries of a representative selection of goods and services; so that if a selection of goods cost £1 in Britain and $3.50 in the USA, then the exchange rate should be £1 = $3.50. The idea has been rarely reflected in actual practice, partly because many goods and services (e.g., roads and schools) do not enter world trade and are often not paid for directly even domestically, therefore upsetting price comparisons, and partly because exchange rates are artificially managed by governments. There are various devices of exchange management, chiefly:

1   Central bank support. If a currency is depreciating, the central bank will buy that currency on the foreign exchanges, using gold and foreign currency reserves or loans from other central banks for the purpose, in order to increase demand for the currency and so maintain its price (exchange rate). Britain has done this often.

2   International loans. Loans may be made by the USA, the IMF, the Group of Ten or any rich individual nation in order to help a central bank carry out support operations for its currency. The loans are usually made willingly, since depreciation (appreciation also, though more rarely) leads to speculative pressures on the foreign exchanges, aggravating an already troublesome situation. The latest idea for easing speculative pressure is that of 'recycling' speculative money; so that any country receiving money sends it back to the country of origin, thereby putting a counter-pressure on the exchanges in the hope of achieving stability.

14G Stable and floating exchange rates

Stable exchange rates are those whereby the domestic currency has a fixed foreign exchange price in terms of either gold or another currency, usually dollars. Floating exchange rates are those whereby the domestic currency has a variable foreign exchange price in terms of another currency, usually dollars. Note that floating rates are not related to gold; the operation of the gold standard requires that a domestic currency has a fixed or stable relationship with gold.

The operation of a gold-based stable foreign exchange rate means that domestic prices must vary up or down as a country gains or loses gold through the existence of a surplus or a deficit on international trade. The mechanism is self-regulating: a payments surplus brings gold in, thereby inflating the domestic currency, putting up prices, and so rendering exports less competitive abroad and imports more profitable to foreigners. A deficit has the opposite effect: gold leaves the country, deflating domestic price levels, and so making exports more competitive abroad and imports less profitable to foreigners. With a gold-backed system, therefore, external foreign exchange-stability is secured at the expense of internal price variability.

The operation of a freely floating exchange rate means that a country can pursue internal price stability, but only at the expense of external foreign exchange variability. If a country has a surplus on its balance of payments (perhaps because the rate of domestic inflation is less than elsewhere), then there will be a growing demand by foreigners for the currency of the surplus country in order that they might pay for their imports; the growing demand will cause the currency to appreciate on the foreign exchanges, thus making the exports of the surplus country more expensive abroad and rendering foreign imports to the domestic market more profitable, as the Canadian government found when it operated a freely floating exchange rate throughout the 1950s. A deficit has the effect of reducing demand by foreigners for the currency of the deficit country (foreigners do not need so much of it because they are not buying so many goods from the deficit country) as well as of increasing the demand by the deficit country for the currencies of other countries (so that the deficit country may be able to pay for all its imports). The result of a deficit, therefore, is depreciation of the domestic currency on the foreign exchanges; so that exports are effectively reduced in price abroad (thereby extending demand) and imports are made more expensive at home (thereby contracting demand). The effect of floating exchange rates is therefore to restore equilibrium, either by making exports less, and imports more, profitable in the case of a payments surplus or by making exports more, and imports less, profitable in the case of a deficit. The simple theory is, however, severely restricted in its practical application by the existing elasticities and inelasticities of demand. In the case of a deficit country, for example, foreign demand for reduced-price exports would have to be at more than unit elasticity if total revenue to the exporting country were to increase; and domestic demand for higher priced imports would have to be at more than unit elasticity also, if total spending on imports were to be reduced. An additional disadvantage of completely free rates is that they make the assessment of comparative cost advantages very difficult; and the difficulty would almost certainly be reflected in practice in both a diminution of world trade and a declining efficiency in domestic production. Deficit countries would, indeed, tend to opt for inefficient domestic production of those items which help to create the deficit by being more efficiently produced abroad. There is probably little long-term advantage to be gained, therefore, from freely floating exchange rates, as far as deficit countries are concerned.

Since abandonment of the gold standard, the current situation is largely one of exchange rates fixed in terms of another currency, usually dollars; so that Britain's foreign exchange rate is £1 = $2.40. However, the fixing is not rigid, and foreign exchange prices are permitted (by the IMF) to vary 2% between a floor and a ceiling; Britain's permitted range, for instance, is between $2.38 and $2.42. In this respect, the 'dollar parity' is similar to the gold (mint) parity with its permitted fluctuations between the gold import and export points. Within the permitted range the rate is managed by the government; if the rate falls to the floor, the central bank engages in support operations, and if the rate rises to the ceiling, the central bank pursues a recycling policy. Nevertheless, foreign exchange reserves coupled with international loans can go only so far in support of a currency troubled by persistent depreciatory pressures; sooner or later the downward pressures must be recognised (and relieved) by the act of devaluation. Upward pressures, conversely, can be relieved by the act of revaluation, as happened with the German mark in October 1969 after a brief period of flotation in order to ensure that the new pegged rate fairly accurately reflected true market conditions. At the time of writing (mid-1971), the Japanese yen is under considerable pressure for a revaluation, and the German mark (again) and the Canadian dollar have been unpegged and floated in order to ease similar upward pressures.

Because there is the assumption of so much political face in the maintenance of foreign exchange rates, devaluation and revaluation are used infrequently; their use is also limited by the unsettling effects which changes in rates have on world trade. On the other hand, the maintenance of rates in fundamental disequilibrium produces a wide variety of other undesirable effects: deficit countries face prolonged deflationary measures both to bring export costs and prices down and to reduce the tendency to import; while surplus countries face strong inflationary tendencies as the money supply increases through export earnings. Indeed, an excess of imports over exports has an in-built deflationary tendency, since the net balance of imports adds to the nation's real income while subtracting from money income (i.e., R is increased while M is reduced); a net balance of exports has the opposite—inflationary—tendency, since earnings (money supply) are increased while the quantity of goods and services available for purchase is reduced (because part of the quantity is sold abroad).

Two suggestions which have been advanced as means of avoiding the worst effects of both variable and fixed rates are those of the 'wide band' and the 'crawling peg'. The idea of the wide band is that the permitted floor and ceiling limits to variation be allowed to extend rather more than the current 1% on either side of the pegged (fixed) rate, so that a currency could tolerate a greater degree of variability in foreign exchange value before the domestic central bank had to engage in support or recycling operations. The crawling peg idea is that the rate be pegged on the basis of a moving average rate (say, a five year moving average; so that the current rate is the average of the previous five years' rates). The main argument in support of the crawling peg is that it makes due allowance for fluctuations in rates by ignoring the short-term speculative pressures and taking account only of the long-term depreciatory or appreciatory pressures. The main—and possibly overwhelming—argument against the crawling peg is that it makes the future more certain—and in consequence more aggravating to the present. For example, if a country faces persistent depreciatory pressures, then the exchange rate for its currency will be certainly lower in the future. The country's citizens know therefore that in, say, a year's time they will have to pay more for their imports and that their export sales might be larger. What would you do in these circumstances? The chances are that you would go on an import-buying spree and hold your potential exports off until next year. And you would thereby intensify the already-existing payments deficit, and add to the already-strong depreciatory pressures. Citizens of a persistent surplus country would face the opposite temptations: to sell as many exports now before they get dearer (and foreign demand for them is contracted) and to buy as few imports as possible, because they will be cheaper in the future. The crawling peg is therefore like a self-fulfilling prophecy; it aggravates rather than ameliorates. Nevertheless, in those cases where a currency has a history of periodic major devaluations, and there is little current confidence in the economy, there may well be a good argument for the use of the crawling peg: it would at least reduce speculation (since future losses of exchange value would be discounted on the forward exchanges) and it would avoid the worst features of the big periodic economic crisis. Brazil has employed the crawling peg since 1968. In the first 18 months of use, for example, the peg moved 13 times, bringing the cruzeiro down by over a quarter. Chile has also adopted the crawling peg.

14H Trade policies

The reality of 'One World' with trade guided solely by considerations of comparative costs does not yet exist. Individual nations pursue selfish policies based on military or social factors rather than on purely economic factors. The USA, for example, does not trade with the communist bloc; the Commonwealth runs its own (disintegrating) scheme of preferential tariffs; the European Common Market pursues an internal harmonisation policy; the communist world has its own satellite Comecon organisation; the Latin American states have their own free trade area (LAFTA); and so on.

The main trading policies throughout British history have been:

1 The Bullionist policy. The idea was common in the 14th and 15th centuries that the only real wealth was gold and silver. In consequence, trade was geared to the production of exports in return for gold; and the gold was simply stored in treasure-houses.

2 Mercantilism. During the 16th and 17th centuries the Bullionist policy was slightly modified to accept the need for imports. However, the aims of Mercantilism were still based on the notion that a favourable trade balance, supported by increased holdings of gold and silver, was in itself a worthy objective. Exports were accordingly encouraged by bounties, and imports restricted by tariffs; trade was channelled by treaty into those

fields which were most likely to yield surpluses; and colonies were forbidden the manufacture of potentially competitive goods. Since satisfaction of individual domestic wants did not figure at all in the aims of Mercantilism, there was a great deal of smuggling—ordinary citizens attempting deviously to obtain those items which were forbidden to them by tariffs.

3 Free Trade. Adam Smith and his followers fought hard and—eventually— successfully against mercantilist ideas. They argued that the true wealth of a nation rested in its ability to consume rather than in its ability to produce for others; that consumer satisfaction should be the ultimate aim of any trade policy; and that the pursuit of trade surpluses for their own sake was a mistaken policy. The ultimate achievement of Free Trade in the 19th century was marked by the scrapping of many tariffs and an approach to near-perfect trading conditions.

4 Protection. Protective tariffs came increasingly to be applied by British governments of the early-20th century. Despite the sound economic case for Free Trade there were many other arguments involving social and strategic factors which came eventually to prevail. Amongst the factors we may note:

(a) Unemployment in certain British industries, created by cheaper imports from more efficient (lower cost) foreign countries (the *unfair competition* argument).

(b) Reduced national security, caused by declining output from British farms as cheaper foreign foods were imported, so increasing Britain's dependence on overseas food supplies (the *national defence* argument).

(c) The inability of new and potentially efficient industries to get started when the domestic market was already flooded with comparable foreign goods (the *infant industries* argument).

For these reasons, British industry came to be increasingly protected by high tariffs (reaching a peak in the 1930s), and British trade came to be increasingly channelled to and from those countries generally sympathetic to Britain's needs (reaching a peak in the establishment of Imperial Preference tariffs under the Ottawa Agreement of 1932). During the 1930s —at the height of the protective movement—there were extensive *Buy British* campaigns, which would normally make as much economic sense as *Buy London* or *Buy West London*, or even *Buy Acton*, campaigns. The chief trouble with the arguments against Protection is that Protection is able to demonstrate immediate and obvious gains to a particular sector of the economy; if the cotton industry, for example, is suffering the effects of cheaper foreign competition, then the shutting out of that competition brings immediate and obvious benefits to the people in the cotton industry. Unfortunately for Free Trade, its benefits are diffused throughout the whole economy—and are rarely obvious to even a trained eye. Arguments for Protection, therefore, have an overwhelming *political* advantage. Economically, however, Protection helps one sector (the protected sector) a lot, but damages everyone else (the consumers) a little each.

5 Bilateralism. During and immediately after World War II Britain entered into a number of bilateral trading agreements with certain other countries; for example, with Argentina, so that Argentina supplied beef in return for British exports of machinery. Britain's main purposes were to secure supplies of certain necessary imports and to obtain guaranteed markets for exports; it was a secondary consideration that the supplies should be the cheapest available and the export markets the most profitable—the aim was the best compromise.

6 Multilateralism. The trading pattern which yields the greatest total satisfaction to consumers throughout the world is multilateral in nature. Multilateral trade means that a country sells in the most profitable market and buys in the cheapest market—making due allowances for transport costs. It is not necessary that exports from one country are balanced by exactly equivalent reciprocal imports. For example, if Britain buys tobacco from the USA, it is not necessary that the USA buys anything from Britain. It *is* necessary, however, that the USA buys something from a foreign country, in order to put dollars on to the world's foreign exchanges, and that Britain sells something to a foreign country, in order to earn the necessary foreign exchange to pay for its imports of tobacco from the USA. The foreign country need not be the same in both instances. For example, the USA may buy transistor radios from Japan, Japan in turn may buy iron from Australia, Australia machinery from Germany, Germany coffee from Brazil, Brazil wheat from Canada, and Canada sports cars from Britain. The USA has now spent money, and Britain has earned it, but the two acts are separated by a long line of intermediate transactions. Given the acts of the USA spending at one end of the line and Britain earning at the other, it does not matter very much to either Britain or the USA how many intermediate transactions there are. It matters to the intermediate countries, of course, since they can each get something they want out of the transaction. Indeed, the longer the line of intermediate transactions, the greater is the total amount of satisfaction derived by consumers the world over; and that should be the primary aim of all world trade. Under these conditions, Britain is likely to have a persistent deficit in its trade with the USA; but a deficit with any one country is of no importance whatsoever—all that matters is that there should be an *overall* balance with the rest of the world at large.

Since the period immediately after World War II it has been the aim of Britain—and other major trading nations—to achieve a fully multilateral pattern of trade. Progress towards that end has been laborious and slow, because of the entrenched nationalistic suspicions of most countries and the periodic crises which have shaken the major trading currencies. The problems of international liquidity (see the end of section 13B) are indeed intimately bound up with the problems of achieving truly multilateral trade, since universal acceptance of trading currencies is a paramount requirement. International co-operation is, however, making progress: the IMF has succeeded in securing a large measure of agreement about international liquidity; and the General Agreement on Tariffs and Trade (GATT) has worked successfully to obtain a great deal of international collaboration in reducing tariffs—spurred by the so-called Kennedy Round of the 1960s, which was initiated by the US Trade Expansion Act of 1962.

Section 15
Income

15A Definition of income

In essence, income is the return from work and ownership. Work is done by the factors of labour and enterprise, whose returns are commonly called wages and profits respectively, while ownership is applied to the factors of land and capital, whose returns are usually called rent and interest respectively. It is not one of the purposes of economics to investigate the sources of ownership; thus capital acquired by theft is treated the same way in analysis as if it were acquired by saving.

Possession of the factors of production may occur at three different levels. *Individual* possession yields personal income, so that a person may receive a return in the form of any one or more of wages, profits, rent and interest. *Corporate* possession yields company income, in the form of undistributed profits (see section 9C). Those profits which are distributed as dividend, on the other hand, are personal income to the individual recipients. Possesion may further be *social* or *national*, yielding local or central government income. It is absolutely essential to note, however, that government income is restricted solely to the return from its possession of production factors. Tax revenue is not in any sense income to a government, since the tax is already someone else's income, and the government is merely appropriating it for transfer. The main point to remember is that income arises only from the production of goods and services (see figure 6.4).

Income is often additionally characterised in one of the following ways:

1 Earned, i.e., gained as the return for work, in the form of wages and profits.

2 Unearned, i.e., gained as the result of ownership, in the form of rents and interest.

3 Nominal, i.e., expressed in money terms.

4 Real, i.e., expressed in terms of goods and services, the quantity of which may vary as the value of money varies, despite a possibly constant nominal income.

5 Notional (or imputed), i.e., that for which market-determined quantification is impossible. For example, a person owning and living in a house derives a notional income equivalent to what it might be expected that he should pay in rent if he did not own a house. He is, as it were, his own landlord, and his notional income is what he might be considered to earn (unearn?) as a landlord.

15B The national income

National income in Britain is currently about £30–35 thousand million a year. This means an average income of roughly £625 for each person in the country. How do we know this? And how can we increase the amount?

We know the amount because we can work it out in different ways. To start with, we know that income arises from production, since each £ spent on production goes to one or more of the production factors and forms in turn a £ of their income. And just as income equals production, so national income equals national production. In section 6L we noted that the total amount of production taking place within a country is called the Gross Domestic Product. Let us now say a little more about it. Britain's total output is not intended for consumption solely within Britain; some of it—about 13 to 14%—is destined for export. On the other hand, not all the products consumed in Britain are in fact made in Britain; some of them—about 15 to 16%—are imported. Britain's exports produce income for British people, but its imports yield income for foreigners. Accordingly, the income related to Gross Domestic Product is equivalent to total domestic consumption plus exports, but minus imports. An additional complication arises from the possible confusion which exists between Gross Domestic Product and Gross National Product. Gross Domestic Product does not include the so-called property incomes (rents, interest and foreign investment returns) which enter international invisible trade. Other invisible trade items (shipping, insurance and banking, for example) provide both work (product) and income directly for people in Britain—the suppliers of those services actually work in Britain—but holdings of foreign property provide income for people in Britain only indirectly. The work (product) provided by the property takes place abroad, but the income recipients live in Britain. Foreigners abroad also derive income from property which they own in Britain, and a net balance must therefore be computed by deducting the outflow of property income to foreign residents from the inflow to British citizens. The net balance for Britain is usually positive, and the amount is added to the Gross Domestic Product to produce the Gross National Product.

Another general qualification to observe before we examine the different methods of calculating the national income is that a portion of the gross product must be set aside for the eventual replacement of worn-out capital. If the portion set aside (reinvestment—see section 6L) is assessed in physical terms, then we are left with what is called Net National Product, and if in monetary terms, then with Net National Income. Both Net National Product and Net National Income represent the annual addition of wealth to a country. And, as we have already noted, they are both merely different ways of regarding the same thing: product is income, and income exactly reflects product. When we talk of national income, what we are really talking about is this annual addition of wealth: national income, therefore, equals Net National Income.

Let us now examine the three methods of assessing national income. The figures computed by each method should, of course, be identical, but inaccuracies of data collection preclude this. Nevertheless, allowances for inaccuracies, called balancing items, are made in order to achieve the logical necessity of equality.

The first method of assessment is that of adding the values of all products (goods and services). Market values are used, since not only are they the only values with any economic validity but they are also the only values expressed in nominal terms (and the national income is expressed in nominal terms). However, market values themselves require qualification, because they do not truly represent production factor costs. For example, many market prices are inflated by the existence of indirect taxes, which yield transfer payments. The value of the taxes must therefore be deducted from the market values, in order to obtain a true figure. Other market prices, conversely, are less than true factor costs, because of the existence of subsidies. Accordingly, the value of subsidies must be added to the market values in order to obtain a true factor cost.

In order to obtain the true sum of individual factor costs, care must also be taken to avoid the dangers of double-counting. Take, for example, the case of a simple production flow: iron mine—steel mill—tool maker. Assume that the iron mine produces and sells a quantity of iron for £10, that the steel mill buys, processes and then sells that iron for £25, and that the tool maker buys the steel and turns it into tools which he sells for £100. The total value of product appears to be £135 (£10 + £25 + £100), but you should note that the £25 selling price of the steel mill includes the £10 paid to the iron mine, and that the £100 selling price of the tool maker includes the £25 paid to the steel mill. There are two ways of computing the correct figure (i.e., that which avoids counting the same thing twice): first, to regard the £100 paid by final customers as including the other payments earlier in the productive chain, and therefore as the only price worth noting (the *final price* method of computation); and second, to add only the values created at each stage of the productive chain, i.e., the £10 created by the iron mine from inert resources, the £15 created by the steel mill by buying at £10 and selling at £25, and the £75 created by the tool maker by buying at £25 and selling at £100 (the *value added* method). The value added method is preferable, since it does not seek a limit to the productive chain; the final price method, additionally, is open to the major criticism that the end of the productive chain is not in fact always discernible.

Apart from the statistical snags in the assessment of national income by adding together the values of all products, there is also a major practical problem: all production which lacks a market value to start with is omitted. This means—on a major scale—that all the world's subsistence production is omitted (and perhaps about half the world's population lives on a subsistence farming basis), and—on a minor scale—that unpaid production by housewives, hobbyists, and members of religious orders is also ignored.

The second method of assessment is that of adding the values of all incomes. Personal incomes, which form the bulk of all income, can be fairly readily ascertained from income tax returns—provided, of course, that transfer incomes, such as state pensions, are excluded. Transfer incomes, indeed, involve us in the risk of double counting, since the money has already been counted as part of other people's gross income, taken from them by tax and then transferred to the pension recipients. Only those personal incomes which arise from production should therefore be counted—and these include wages, profits, rents and interest receipts. Company income has also to be added; but only—remember—the undistributed profits (the distributed profits form personal income to the shareholders). Government income should be included, but only insofar as it arises from production; for example, the net trading profits on state airlines, coal mines, railways, and electric power generation. Just as with the first method of assessment, gratuitous production is ignored, since no income attaches to such production. This means that if a householder decorates his own house, the national income total ignores the fact of decoration, but that if he hires (and pays) a decorator, the national income rises by the extent of the decorator's earnings.

The third method of assessing the national income is to add the values of all expenditures. Since, in the first method, all product values are regarded initially as market values, and since market values can be obtained only through exchange for money, then a count of all transaction values is logically identical with a count of all product values. Furthermore, the sum of monetary income assessed in the second method (less that set aside for necessary capital replacement—remember, we are dealing only with net national income and product) is equivalent to the combined amounts spent on consumption and set to net investment. Both consumption expenditure and net investment outlay represent the creation of additional wealth; and that is what we are concerned with. However, not all domestic expenditure can be recorded. The money spent on imports has to be subtracted, since that is income for foreigners, but all the money earned by exports has to be counted, whether the transactions take place domestically or not. In addition, care must be exercised to see that the total value of indirect—or outlay—taxes is deducted from the sum of total expenditure, since the taxes merely transfer income to the state; they do not create it. The value of subsidies, however, should be added, since they provide income to the producer of the exchanged goods; and that income is not reflected in the subsidised price of the goods. The true factor cost, indeed, is the market price plus subsidy, minus the indirect tax. The principles involved in the determination of (net) national income by the three different methods are outlined in figure 15.1.

A country's standard of living generally depends upon the size of its national income. Standards of living are measured by such ratios as the numbers of cars, TV sets, telephones, and washing machines per 1000 people. There is no single index; so national income figures are often used as a substitute. For example, in dollar terms throughout (the dollar is now the international standard of measurement), Kuwait and the USA have average per person national incomes of over 3000, and Canada, Sweden, and Switzerland of between 2000 and 3000; while at the other end of the scale nearly all the countries of south-east Asia and tropical Africa have average per person

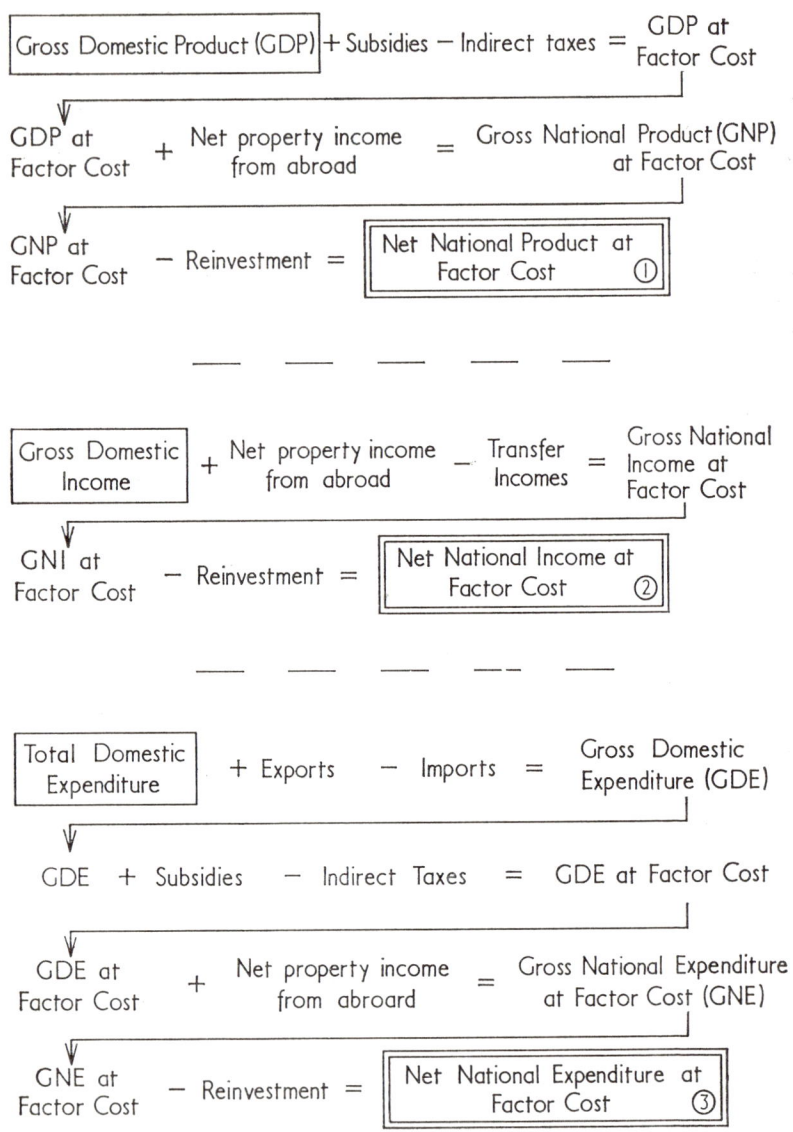

FIG 15.1 Methods of assessing National Income.

national incomes of under 100. There is an immensely complex variety of reasons for these differences in income levels. Among the most important are:

1 The quantity and quality of the natural resources.
2 The skill, energy and ambition of the people.
3 The production techniques available to the community.
4 The savings possibilities for capital formation by the nation.
5 The efficiency of factor co-operation.
6 The political equilibrium of the state, favouring or thwarting long-term investment.
7 The proportion of total work done for monetary return.

If you haven't yet done so, you should read Rostow's *Stages of Economic Growth* for a reasonably integrated approach to the problem.

The use of average national income figures for purposes of comparison is, however, a technique which needs considerable care. Comparisons between countries are, indeed, at best merely indicative, and at worst misleading. The chief and immediate snag is that a common unit of measurement must be used, in order to obtain any sort of comparison at all. Customarily, dollars are used, and each domestic currency is converted at its official dollar-exchange rate into a national income figure expressed in dollars. Since the official exchange rate is often pegged at an artificial level in relation to dollars, the conversion may produce a figure which is meaningless to start with. A second snag is that some countries rely on a great deal of concealed production—concealed in that it is done for non-monetary gain, and accordingly does not figure in the national income. A third point to watch is that some countries may need to enter into a certain amount of production merely to combat the harsher aspects of the physical environment; for example, irrigation schemes to combat drought, drainage works to combat flooding, domestic warmth to combat cold, air conditioning to combat heat, extensive transportation systems to combat distance, skyscrapers to combat lack of space, and so on. The making of such environmentally necessary products can be regarded in two ways: either as merely placing a country on an equal footing with those which do not face the particular problems or as posing a stimulus to further productive activity. A fourth disadvantage in the straight use of national income figures for comparison purposes is that countries distribute their national incomes according to different principles; so that in some countries (Sweden, for example) governments tax and redistribute personal income much more than they do in others (such as France).

Average national income figures per person may therefore be quite misleading. There will usually be a fairly close scatter about the average in those countries which have redistributed incomes, but in other countries there may well be huge disparities between the rich and the poor. Kuwait, for example, has immense differences in personal income, despite its high average figure. A fifth disadvantage arises when comparisons are made over a period of time, whether between different countries or not. Inflation—usually—plays havoc with comparisons based on money values. For example, if inflation is occurring at a rate of 3% per year, and national income is increasing at 8% per year, then the increase of national income is being artificially inflated by purely monetary considerations to the extent of 3% per year. The true growth rate, without inflation (i.e., at constant prices), is merely 5% per year.

Since about 1950 the true growth rate in Britain has been about 2–3% per year, which is a slow rate when compared with those of other countries with a broadly similar production structure. Japan, for example, has been outstanding with a 10–11% average annual growth rate; West Germany has had about 6% annual growth, Italy $5\frac{1}{2}$%, France 5%, Canada 5%, the USA 4%, and Sweden 4%. Britain's comparatively slow growth has been the cause of much concern, and while the problem is undeniably complex it has not lacked attempts at analysis.

In March 1968, Edward Dennison (*Why Growth Rates Differ*) attributed the causes of slow growth to Britain's relatively poor performances in (a) increasing the quantity of its factor inputs, especially capital, and (b) increasing the quantity of output per unit of input. Britain did not invest enough, and it did not make sufficient effort to improve its efficiency.

In the April 1968 issue of the National Provincial Bank Review, Graham Hutton (*The British Disease and Its Cure*) suggested that the reasons for slow growth were:

1   The large and ever-growing burden of generally non-productive public expenditure on the productive private sector.
2   The under-utilisation of both labour and capital, particularly as a result of restrictive practices on the part of organised labour.
3   The existence of a legion of organised incentives for waste and disincentives for economy, such as the quantity of bureaucratic red tape involved in planning.

The third, and most important, analysis (*Britain's Economic Prospects*) was published by the American Brookings Institution in June 1968. It detailed a number of contributory causes of slow growth:

1   The uncontrolled nature of public spending, despite often rigid measures against the private sector.
2   The inadequacy of capital investment, despite—by international standards—unusually large distributed profits.
3   The existence of diseconomies of scale, despite the existence of large firms, because of the over-differentiation of products.
4   The lack of sufficient net capital stock per worker.
5   The existence of collusive oligopoly and price-fixing arrangements.
6   The inadequate quality of management, not only in itself but also in its recognition of appropriately significant skills such as engineering.

7   The misdirected and inadequately financed educational system, which was not directed towards producing people with adequate managerial and technical skills.

8   The restrictive practices of trade unions, characterised by overmanning, wildcat strikes, and the serious underuse of capital.

9   The lack of satisfactory cost accounting procedures.

10 The inadequate road system.

11 The tendency of management to yield to strikers rather than to take the long-term view that a strike was the price of eliminating inefficient practices.

12 The availability of cheap subsidised public housing, which tended in fact to produce labour immobility rather than the intended mobility.

13 The multitude of non-selective welfare benefits, which were not only costly in themselves but also conducive to labour immobility.

14 The lack of a sufficiently large trading market to permit the gain of economies of scale (consistent with product variety).

Overall, the Brookings Institution reinforced Dennison's conclusions that not only was Britain not spending enough on investment but that it was also not making efficient-enough use even of the resources actually employed.

15C The business (trade) cycle

The average growth rate over a period of, say, 20–25 years is only what is called the long-term, or underlying, trend. It inevitably masks fluctuations which occur on the way. The fluctuations may be minor ones, occurring per-haps in a two to five year cycle, or they may be major ones, occurring in some-thing like an eight to ten year cycle. The minor ones are usually of the stop-go variety, induced by short-term measures to counteract inflation and deflation in turn. The major fluctuations, on the other hand, are produced by different causes, though short-term measures may play a contributory part. The name *business cycle* properly refers to the major fluctuations only.

The cycle is a continuous and progressively interlocking series of events, but for analytical purposes it is convenient to divide it into two phases.

The first phase is one of boom, prosperity or expansion. The essential characteristic of this stage is a short-term rate of growth in excess of the long-term trend. This is brought about by rapidly rising quantities of production, rising employment levels, increasing optimism, rising wages and profits, higher prices, and an increasing volume of borrowing for both investment and spend-ing. Eventually, because of wage drift, higher reinvestment costs, dearer material supplies, and increasing interest charges, the costs of production in-crease to a point where the concurrent slackening of growth of demand (higher prices, diminishing marginal utility of additional goods, more ex-pensive borrowing for consumption) causes a decline in entrepreneurial profits. At such a point, even though total demand may be still growing, the *slower* rate of demand growth reduces the need of entrepreneurs to allocate so much of their revenue to *net* investment. The demand for the products of the capital goods industries therefore falls, and there is, in consequence, a cutback in production in that field. The marginal firms cease production and the supra-marginal ones reduce their output. A quantity of variable production factors is thus rendered unemployed. Chief among these is labour, but power and raw materials also suffer a reduced demand; and as a result there is a related fall in the production of both power and raw materials, leading to further unemployment directly in those industries, as well as indirectly in the 'roundabout' supporting industries (for example, transport, generator equipment, mining machinery manufacture, and so on). In turn, the reduced demand for consumption goods exerted by the unemployed workers produces falling profits in the consumer industries, thereby forcing marginal firms out of business, creating more unemployment, further restricting overall demand, and so on. The tendency for a change of demand in any one sector of the economy to have repercussive effects throughout the rest of the economy is called the **multiplier**. The effects of changes in demand operate through the changes which occur in the income derived from satisfying that demand. Attempts to quantify the multiplier (rather spuriously, because of the neglect of both the long time-lags and the interlocking character of the process) rest on the use of the formula

$$\text{Multiplier} = \frac{1}{1-\text{MPC}} = \frac{1}{\text{MPS}}$$

where MPC = Marginal Propensity to Consume, and
     MPS = Marginal Propensity to Save.

Income is assumed to be either spent on consumption or set aside for saving (see section 6L); any additional (marginal) income is also similarly divisible. The desire to spend a certain portion of additional income is called the marginal propensity to consume; the marginal propensity to save is its reciprocal. If $\frac{9}{10}$ of marginal income is spent, then $\frac{1}{10}$ is saved; and so on. The multiplier in that case would be 10 (i.e., $\frac{1}{1/10}$), which means (spuriously) that an initial injection of an additional £1000 income would eventually produce an addition of £10,000 to the national income. And also—as a corollary—that a withdrawal of £1000 income at the start would eventually result in a decline of the national income by £10,000. An important (but unquantified) qualification to the perfect operation of the multiplier formula is what is called the 'Pigou effect' (after the British economist, A. C. Pigou), whereby the marginal propensity to consume is assumed to diminish as a person's total wealth increases, so that at a low income level as much as, say, $\frac{9}{10}$ths of a marginal £10 might be spent, but at a higher income level, as total wealth has increased, perhaps only $\frac{1}{10}$th of a marginal £10 might be spent. In the first phase of the business cycle, then, the multiplier initially augments the tendency to rapid growth, but subsequently begins to spread the inevitable effects of reduced demand throughout the economy as a whole—with a widening and cumulative impact.

The second phase of the business cycle is one of recession, contraction, slump or depression. As soon as the capital goods industries have begun to suffer a reduction in the demand for their products, the multiplier effectively spreads the results of that decline: total output falls; unemployment rises; wages, profits and prices fall (or cease to rise so rapidly as formerly); the amount of borrowing for investment and consumption decreases; and a general air of pessimism pervades the economy. Eventually, the costs of production fall (because of lower wages, lower investment costs, lower interest charges, and lower costs for materials) to such a level in relation to the slackened demand that increasing entrepreneurial profits become possible. At that level it is the aim of the entrepreneurs to induce the community to start spending more again. Many people will have hoarded money during the period of recession; the purpose of the entrepreneurs is to induce *dishoarding* (or to induce an increase in the propensity to consume). Prices may be cut in order to extend demand, new products may be marketed, intensive advertising may be undertaken; and the government might also help, by a public works policy designed to put more money into the hands of the unemployed workers. Once demand has begun to increase, reinvestment and—subsequently—net investment orders may be put to the capital goods industries; the multiplier will then bring about a cumulative return to growth and expansion.

Whereas the multiplier spreads the *effects* of changes in the demand for capital goods, the **accelerator** is responsible for the *degree* of change. The operation of the accelerator is based on the fact that consumer goods are produced by capital goods on a more than one-to-one basis. For example, 1000 tyres may be produced annually by a single tyre-making machine. Suppose that a tyre-making firm makes 100 000 tyres annually, using 100 machines for the purpose, and that each machine has a working life before replacement of 10 years. The tyre-making firm accordingly replaces 10 machines a year, thereby providing a regular market for the machine firm (the capital goods firm). Suppose now that during a boom the consumer demand for tyres rises by 20% to 120 000 tyres a year. In order to produce the additional 20 000 tyres, the tyre firm needs at once an extra 20 machines. The demand for machines thus rises from 10 a year to 30 a year, i.e., by 200%, compared with the 20% rise in demand for tyres. If the demand for tyres then becomes stable at 120 000 a year, the tyre firm will have a reinvestment need of only 12 machines a year; so the machine manufacturer has to cut back production from 30 to 12. The situation will be aggravated by the fact that the tyre firm has gained 20 new machines fairly quickly, and will not wish to amortise them immediately at the same rate as its original 100 machines. You can see here that (a) a relatively small change in the demand for consumer goods produces a disproportionate change in the demand for capital goods, i.e., the change is *accelerated*, and (b) a fall in the demand for capital goods is not necessarily caused by a fall in the demand for consumer goods. Indeed, the demand for capital goods may decrease merely because the demand for consumer goods fails to continue increasing at the same rate as formerly. Obviously, the accelerator is a powerful instrument of economic instability; coupled with the multiplier, its influence is pervasive.

The key to understanding—and control—of the business cycle lies in the relationship between aggregate consumer demand and the quantity of gross investment. Only if aggregate consumer demand is either stable or rising steadily will the capital goods industries be consistent in their production (and income-yielding capacity, via the multiplier). If consumer demand either falls or slows down its rate of growth, however, then the accelerator causes disproportionately large cut-backs in the production of the capital goods industries, and the multiplier spreads a diminishing income-earning ability throughout the economy. Indeed, if growth ever slows down, a recession is the result.

Unrestrained growth is to be avoided, however, since it contains the causes of its own recession. On the economic side, ever-increasing prices, wage drift and higher interest rates combine eventually to restrict the growth of consumer demand as well as the profitability of production, and on the physical side the availability of production factors (especially labour and land) is unlikely in practice to increase at the same rate as growth of output, thereby leading to the marginal employment of less efficient factors at a rising cost (assuming that the most efficient factors are employed first). Marginal product per unit of input therefore diminishes, and so, correspondingly, does marginal income and—in turn—marginal demand. The accelerator then sets the recession in motion, and the multiplier spreads the effects cumulatively.

In order to avoid the damaging effects not only of unemployment during recession but also of loss of exports (rising prices inducing a contraction of foreign demand) and increased imports (higher domestic prices yielding larger profit opportunities to foreign manufacturers) during boom, government control of a business cycle should be designed to produce a steady growth of the economy. This may be done through the use of techniques of *aggregate demand management,* by means of appropriate fiscal and monetary policies, and *investment management,* by means of appropriate fiscal, monetary and physical incentives and disincentives. It is not an easy task. Indeed, no country in the world has yet solved the problem satisfactorily. The best thing that can be said for modern economic management is that the vicissitudes which characterised the past, culminating in the great depression of the early 1930s, have been considerably damped down since 1945. And that is no mean achievement.

Section 16
Factor incomes

16A Factor prices

The costs incurred by producers in hiring units of production factors are at the same time the chief source of income to the owners of the production factors. Accordingly, an analysis of factor prices not only relates to costs of production, but also indicates the way in which the total national income is distributed among the different groups of factor suppliers. Wages, for example, are costs to producers but incomes to workers, and their levels not only affect output and prices from the supply side but also from the demand side. Indeed, all owners of production factors act in this way on both sides of the market: on one side they are suppliers, aiming to achieve the maximum return from their labour, capital or whatever, and on the other side they are consumers, hoping to buy at the lowest possible prices. However, as consumers they do not demand the provision of labour, capital and so on directly; they demand only consumption goods directly. The demand for labour, capital and other production factors is, in fact, an indirect demand, or *derived* demand, and comes from entrepreneurs in response to their assessment of final consumer demand.

Factor prices, then, are the result of an interaction between the demand for factor units by producers and the supply of factor units by their owners.

16B Factor demand

Entrepreneurs demand units of production factors in accordance with the need to achieve lowest average cost levels of output (optimum production under perfect competition or somewhere near optimum production under imperfect competition). They therefore seek to hire factor units in the lowest cost *combination*. As a result, the demand for a single group of factors is influenced not only by its own expected or desired return but also by the expected or desired returns of other factors which must be hired in conjunction. The demand for labour to work machines is, in other words, related inevitably to the cost affected demand for machines. The demand for a single group of factors is therefore not only a derived demand but also a *joint* demand. Further, it is also a *competing* demand (see sections 4F and 6M), since there are often strong possibilities of substitution between one type of factor and another. Machines may, indeed, be employed to replace labour if the price of labour rises too high for the producer to achieve lowest average cost output with the existing factor combination.

The extraordinarily complex nature of demand for any single group of production factors is necessarily simplified by the entrepreneur. The process of simplification rests on the use of money as a measure of value; and the entrepreneur has to ask himself in relation to factor employment whether the factor unit will pay for itself. The answer depends upon three things:

1 The cost of the factor.
2 The additional (marginal) physical product of the factor (MPP).
3 The additional revenue gained by the sale of that additional physical product.

The additional revenue gained by sale of additional physical product is called **marginal revenue product** (MRP), and though it is clearly related to marginal physical product (MPP) it is by no means dependent upon it. Marginal revenue product (MRP) will, of course, rise or fall as consumer prices rise or fall, even though marginal physical product (MPP) remains constant. MRP may also rise or fall with consumer prices even though MPP moves in the opposite direction, provided that consumer price changes are more than sufficient to offset opposed changes in MPP. On the other hand, MRP will also rise or fall as MPP rises or falls so long as consumer prices remain constant (or move to a less than offsetting extent in the opposite direction). In general, the entrepreneur will hire units of production factors up to the point where the outlay on the additional factors (the marginal cost of the factors) equals the revenue earned by sale of the additional physical product (the marginal revenue product of the factors). Beyond the point where the marginal cost equals the marginal revenue product, the additional factors cost more to hire than they produce in monetary revenue; and there is clearly no profit to the entrepreneur in hiring factors beyond that point.

As a general rule, the MPP of any single factor will tend initially to rise, since the early stages of production tend to be characterised by increasing returns consequent upon increasingly efficient factor combinations. In time, however, diminishing returns will characterise the productive process; and the onset of diminishing returns of MPP will be hastened in practice by the understandable tendency of firms to employ the available superior factors first and then only subsequently the inferior factors. Assuming a constant price level for the products of a firm in perfect competition, we find that there is an inevitable tendency (see above) for MRP to decline with MPP. In imperfect competition, the decline of MRP is even faster than that of MPP, since product prices must be lowered to clear the market of the increased supply. The normal tendency, then, is for the MRP curve to fall to the right, in much the same way as a normal demand curve (see figure 16.1). Indeed, the falling MRP curve forms the demand curve for a particular factor by a particular entrepreneur, since the entrepreneur's decision whether or not to employ that factor is guided ultimately by the factor's MRP.

Both in theory and in practice, however, it is enormously difficult to isolate the revenue returns accruing to any single type of factor. Production is a combinative function, and even though it is possible to posit in theory that all other things remain equal the calculations which are then designed to prove the point are invariably artificial and intended carefully to support the point

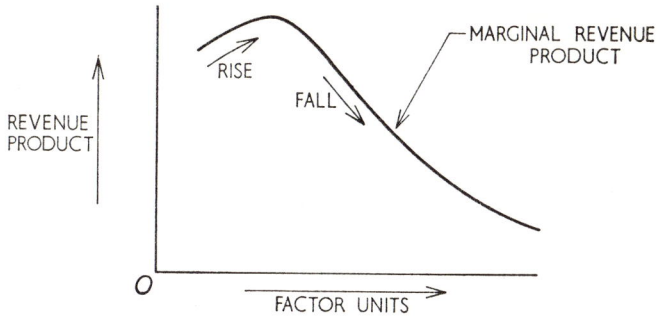

FIG 16.1 Marginal revenue product and factor demand.

being made. If real production is used as an example, then it ceases to be possible to keep all other things equal, and the difficulties commented on in section 1C become all too apparent.

Apart from the problems of isolating the MRP of any single type of factor, an additional difficulty in determining the demand by an entrepreneur for a particular type of factor is that the demand is competitive as well as joint. This means that the demand for a single type of factor is dependent upon more than just its own cost and MRP (assuming that it is possible for the moment to isolate its MRP). The demand is also dependent upon a comparison with the costs and MRPs of competing factors. The entrepreneur has in fact to decide whether or not the revenue return per unit of outlay on one factor exceeds the revenue return per similar unit of outlay on another factor, or (the other way round) whether or not, per similar unit of revenue return, the outlay on one factor exceeds the outlay on another factor. The ideal situation is reached when the outlay per unit of revenue return is the same for all factors; so that an additional £10 spent on one factor yields the same revenue return as £10 spent on another factor. The mechanism of factor substitution to the point of **equi-marginal revenue returns** is outlined in section 6M; it is worth reading the section again.

Remember, though, the very great problems of analysing factor demand:

1 The difficulty of isolating the MRP of any single factor.

2 The necessary comparisons between the MRPs of different types of factor.

3 The variable relationship between MRP and MPP.

4 The fact of almost universal permanent inflation, which renders cost and revenue comparisons difficult over any period of time.

5 The fact that not all firms seek in practice to maximise profits, and may therefore employ factors for other than maximum return reasons.

6 The fact that costs of competing factors change out of phase with each other.

7   The immense difficulties of assessing MRP for factors employed throughout the whole of tertiary industry, which itself is about half of all industry.

16C Factor supply

The supply positions of the individul factors were noted in sections 6C,
6H, 6L and 6M. You will remember that a high degree of short-term inelasticity characterises all the factors. The differences of character among the
factors were noted in section 6B, and it is only worth adding here that physical
capital is rather different from the other factors in the long term insofar as it
is produced by entrepreneurs on a profit-making basis, thereby gaining the
demand character of a consumption good, whereas the other factors are produced more or less independently of the monetary return. Not entirely, of
course, since labour, land and money capital supplies are all related to monetary return—but much less directly so in the long term than is physical capital.
It is interesting to remember here that it is the variations in demand for
physical capital which accelerate the growth and recession phases of the business cycle.

16D Factor price determination

The pricing of factor inputs has been based traditionally on the *marginal
productivity theory of income distribution*, which states—briefly—that factor
prices are determined by the attainment of equilibrium between the supply of
the factor and the demand for it, the latter itself being the product of an
equilibrium between the MRP and the marginal cost of the factor. There is
thus a cyclic quality to the theory: factor prices are determined partly by the
demand for the factors, and the demand is affected partly by the prevailing
factor prices.

    The matter is aggravated by the fact that individual factor prices are
difficult to analyse in isolation. They may exist in apparent isolation (e.g., the
price of a machine may not bear much apparent relationship to the price of a
man's time), but they are nevertheless inextricably linked. Even so, the principle of factor income determination by marginal productivity analysis may still
be illustrated by reference to two factors only. Assume that labour and land
are being employed in combination for the production of a particular item, and
that the demand and supply positions for labour are as shown in figure 16.2.
The intersection of demand (MRP) and supply curves yields the equilibrium
price of labour. You will notice that the wage rate (price) is lower than the
marginal revenue product of all workers except the last to be employed, and
that it is identical with the MRP of the last (marginal) worker. This is because
the employer does not have to pay a higher wage rate to the more productive
workers, since their supply exceeds the demand for them. Moreover, in practice, nationally negotiated wage rates tend anyway to have a standardising
effect on wages paid. Above the rectangle (*OWEL*) representing the total
return to labour there is a residual surplus; this is the return to land.

    Factor prices in real life do not accurately reflect the marginal pro-
ductivity theory basis. The closest correspondence is probably in the long-

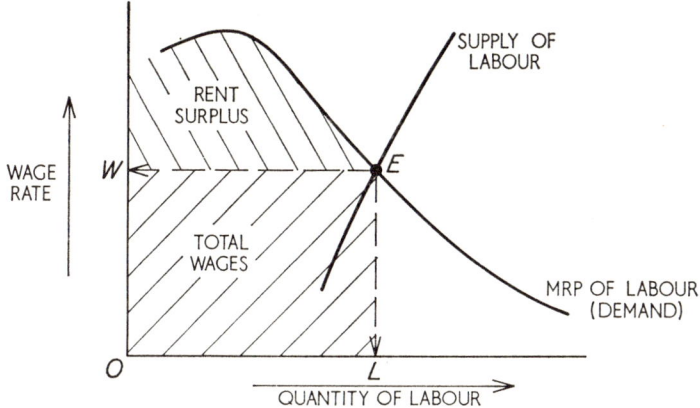

FIG 16.2   Determination of returns to land and labour by marginal
productivity and supply curves.

term money capital market (in the short-term money market government
policy has quite a distorting effect), and the greatest deviations are probably in
the labour market, where union bargaining often has a seriously distorting
effect.

16E Personal income equalities and inequalities

Personal income is usually gained by supplying a single type of production
factor, such as labour, but it **may** also be gained by supplying more than one
type of factor, such as labour and money capital together (though not necessarily in the same proportions). Other personal incomes again may arise not
from the supply of one or more of the production factors but from transfer:
for example, part of a person's factor supply income may be taken from him
by government tax and transferred to a non-supplier such as a university
student or an unemployed worker. However it is gained, personal income is
likely to vary greatly from one person to another, some people receiving very
high incomes and others very low incomes.

Even equal money incomes probably do not give their recipients equal
utility, because of differences in the costs of living from place to place and
from time to time. A person earning £20 a week in mid-Wales, for instance, is
in a superior position to a person earning £20 a week in central London
regarding the outlay of his income on real goods and services. And, similarly,
a person earning £20 a week in 1940 is not to be compared with one earning
£20 a week in 1970. Utility from equal money incomes also varies according
to the differences in tax deductions, the number of dependants to be supported, the sum of necessary outgoings, and so on. Farm workers in free cottages and coal miners with cheap fuel, for example, can economically 'afford'
to earn less than people without those benefits, since the other people have to
pay a certain amount of their income for these essential goods and services.

In any event, money incomes are usually different to start with. Variations in ability tend to produce differences in income, as also do variations in chance (winning the football pools, drawing a Premium Bond prize) and opportunity (benefiting by inheritance, having family connections). Differences in saving habits can also produce differences in income, since those who save most suffer a reduction in their initial spending ability, only to gain additional spending ability later as interest payments accrue.

The patent inequalities of income are justifiable on the grounds that the existence of high income opportunities forms an economically valuable incentive to those on low incomes or to those just starting out on a career, and that the existence of high incomes is necessary in a free economy for the creation of capital, since most of the necessary saving is carried out automatically by those with high incomes (the 'Pigou' effect). Other claims in support of income inequalities are that they reflect human inequalities which exist anyway, and that they do not matter so long as the poor do not actually starve.

On the other hand, however, a very strong and increasingly widespread notion that personal incomes ought to be very much less unequal than they are has grown over the last hundred years or so. Personal sentiment, social conscience, and political feeling are all inextricably mixed in the development of this notion, and it is now accepted by all political parties, though with varying degrees of vehemence: from concession to the apparently inevitable to a passionate belief in equality as a matter of principle. Other reasons for suggesting greater income equalisation are that excessive inequalities may lead to civil disorders and revolution, as well as to socially unfair production, insofar as yachts and country cottages may get produced to satisfy the concentrated demand of the high income groups while hospitals and schools suffer for lack of money. There is also an argument that income inequalities lead to the formation of social classes, but it is more likely that social classes would exist anyway, for many reasons other than income differences; as illustrated by the persistent attitudes of disdain by the established upper groups for the ever-present nouveau riche.

Once the idea of greater income equalisation is accepted, the problem has to be faced of how best to interfere with the working of the market economy. It is, of course, the operation of the market and the interaction of supply and demand that form the basis of income inequality, though the extent of inequality is increased by the existence of numerous frictions (such as labour immobility, which stops workers moving to higher-wage areas). The problem of interference with the imperfect market economy is aggravated by the wide choice of criteria: should the re-allocation of incomes to be each according to his individual needs or to each according to his social deserts or to each according to his economic effort? If needs form the basis of re-allocation, then what are needs? And how can the needs of one person be compared with those of another? If deserts are selected as the criterion, then who is going to decide on a measure of deserts? And if effort is chosen as the basis, then how is effort going to be measured unless MRP is used? Would it be a measure of the results obtained, or of the trouble taken? What of those people who try but fail? What of those who do not even try? And of those who are physically or mentally incapable of trying? An alternative and by-passing solution, of course, is to allocate incomes so that all receive the same; but then you have the problem noted at the beginning of this section—that even equal money incomes do not give equal utility to their recipients. And incentive would probably suffer a mortal blow. Not that money income is the only spur to economic activity—there are actions taken also for reasons of fame, patriotism, humanitarianism and so on—but money is certainly the chief spur to action.

Governmental efforts to equalise incomes have therefore not progressed to the stage where incomes are equal; nor is it acceptable policy that incomes should in fact ever be equal. Effort has been directed instead merely to reducing the extent of inequality: the poor receive supplementary and often hidden income in the form of 'free' welfare services and subsidised housing; the rich face high marginal rates of taxation on income and high and progressive death duties on inherited wealth. Strong emphasis has been given to programmes designed to reduce or eliminate poverty, and there has been much talk of guaranteed minimum incomes. The trouble with, say, minimum wages is that if actual wages have to rise to meet the minimum then almost certainly there will be a strong substitution effect: some labour may be indispensable, but *all* of it is not, and an indeterminate portion of it may well be replaced by machinery. There is certainly no easy solution to the problem.

Distribution: rent

17A Economic rent

The term *economic rent* is one of the most highly specialised in economics and yet at the same time one of the most widely applicable. Its meaning is completely different from the meaning of rent in ordinary everyday language. In its everyday sense, rent is a periodic payment for the hire or use of a good, such as a house, a car, or a TV set. Analysis of such rents would reveal, however, that they consist largely (though not necessarily always and entirely) of payments for management, maintenance, repairs, interest on capital investment, and profits to the entrepreneurs. In economics, the term has a totally different meaning. It means a payment to any factor of production *in excess of* the payment necessary to bring a sufficient supply of that factor to the market. The idea of economic rent in this sense has already been introduced (section 5A): excess or surplus profit accruing to an entrepreneur is—by definition—greater than the profit needed to create a sufficient supply of entrepreneurs (normal profit), and the surplus profit is therefore a type of economic rent. Note that the rent accrues to the entrepreneur and not to the good which is being produced, even though it is the sale of that good which yields the surplus profit. Note also that the amount of excess profit gained by an entrepreneur is governed by the price at which the good is sold in the market. The market price of the good, in fact, determines the surplus profit or economic rent. Rents indeed are entirely price-determin*ed*, not price-determin*ing*. They are not a cost of production. They are precisely those payments which are *not* necessary to bring about a sufficient supply of production factors.

17B Ricardo's theory of rent

In the still mainly agricultural economy of early 19th century England, there was a growing acceptance by economists after Adam Smith of the ideas of equilibrium pricing. The mechanism was applied intelligibly to consumer goods and acceptably (at the time) to labour; but the rents earned by landowners posed a special problem. The nub of the problem rested in the fact that landowners of similar-sized plots gained different returns. Ricardo traced the differences to variations in soil fertility; so that although farm products of a particular type all sold at the same price in the market they could be produced more cheaply on superior land than on inferior land, thereby yielding the farmers on the superior land a higher return and in consequence enabling the owners of that land to charge higher rental fees. This *unearned surplus* accruing to the owners of the superior land because of the inherent quality of that land was called economic rent by Ricardo; it was generally regarded as unearned because the owners had done nothing (except acquire the land) in order to gain the surplus return.

17C Modern rent theory

The emphasis has been shifted from variations in soil fertility to the more widely accepted economic notion of scarcity, and rent theory is now concerned to explain economic rents as the product of the ordinary supply and demand equilibrium mechanism. The supply of land, for example, is both fixed (inelastic) and free: it exists without any cost of production, and its quantity remains virtually the same whether the price is zero or extremely high. A supply curve for land would therefore show a straight vertical line. Under such conditions, the price of land is determined entirely by the nature of the demand for its use. Figure 17.1 illustrates how land prices may vary as demand conditions change: as demand increases, land prices inevitably rise, and as demand falls, prices fall.

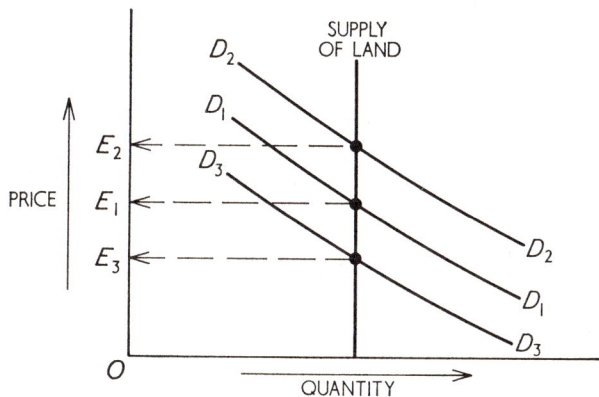

FIG 17.1   Demand changes and the behaviour of land prices.
NOTES:
1   If demand rises from D_1 to D_2, price rises from E_1 to E_2.
2   If demand falls from D_1 to D_3, price falls from E_1 to E_3.

Since land exists freely regardless of its price, the owners of land naturally take the view that any return on it is better than no return at all. They will, nevertheless, seek to obtain the highest possible return. If only one use is possible for a given area of land (an unlikely situation, since land is a very general factor), then the extent of user demand determines the land price that can be charged; and all the income is pure surplus, or economic rent, since the alternative is no use, and no return, at all. If, however, an area of land has a variety of alternative uses, then the owner will seek the returns from the most profitable use, forgoing the returns from the less profitable alternative uses. The second most profitable use yields what are called the **transfer earnings** of the land, since those earnings represent the alternative income to the owner if the use of the land were transferred from the most profitable use. Economic rent is in this case merely the *excess* of returns from most profitable over second most profitable use, since the supply of land for the most profitable use exists at *any* price level *above* that of the second most profitable use, but not at any lower price. For example, if a unit of land can be leased, because of the extent of derived demand for it, for £50 for growing fruit, £40 for growing wheat, £30 for building a house, and £20 for rearing sheep, then the owner of the land will clearly lease it (subject to the friction of planning permission) for fruit growing. His income from the unit of land will be £50, including an economic rent of £10: the transfer earnings of the land are £40, and the fruit-growing lease exceeds that sum by £10. If planning permission is given only for sheep rearing, and the alternative to that is to leave the land idle, producing no income at all, then the land will be let for sheep rearing and the whole £20 will be counted as economic rent. The cost of £50 to the fruit grower or £20 to the sheep farmer will be counted as a necessary cost of production by the producer concerned, but you should realise that his ability and desire to pay that sum are determined entirely (in theory) by the nature of consumer demand for his product.

The concept of rent as a pure surplus gain can be extended to other factors than land. Land, of course, has no cost price by definition, and therefore any income accruing to landowners (over and above the transfer earnings if there are alternative uses for the land) is obviously pure surplus. Other production factors, however, have a cost price: something has to be expended in producing them. The costs incurred in producing the other factors in sufficient quantities to meet the market demand for them, as well as the costs incurred in meeting the transfer earnings (if any) of land, are called **true costs**, or costs of production, and include, remember, normal profits. Any income which accrues to a factor over and above that needed to induce a sufficient supply of the factor may be termed economic rent. An element of economic rent exists in many different types of income. For example, suppose a shopkeeper finds his trade doubled as the result of a new housing-estate development. His original income was sufficient to cause him to supply a retailing service; the additional net income he gains as a result of the housing development is therefore pure surplus. It is precisely because of population shifts and changing spending powers that many shop leases are kept short: the land owner wants to avail himself of higher leasing charges if the earning power of the land increases, while the retailer wants to avoid committing himself to a certain level of charges in case the earning power of the shop declines. Another example of the rent element in income lies in the earnings of superior entertainers, whose very high incomes mask the often much lower transfer earnings that the entertainers might make in alternative employment. The excess of entertainment earnings over transfer earnings is economic rent. Still another form of economic rent accrues to those people who save regularly even at a low rate of interest; if the rate of interest rises for any reason then those people gain a surplus return (more than that needed to bring their particular supply to the market).

Surplus earnings of these types result from the fact of supply inelasticity. Entertainers, for example, are often unique: they are the sole suppliers of their particular commodity, and their earnings are geared entirely to the consumer demand for that commodity. If the consumers want The Beatles more than they want John Ogdon, then The Beatles earn more. Matters of social justice, support of the arts, artistic worth, and so on are utterly irrelevant to the pricing mechanism. It is a case of the consumer calling the tune.

Factor supply inelasticity also characterises capital goods in the short term. Although capital goods are produced in response to demand by firms, once the capital goods have been produced they exist independently of their cost of production: their supply in the short term is fixed (remember the distinction between fixed and variable factors in section 7A and the definition of the short term in section 7C?). This means that any return to capital, once the capital exists, is a form of economic rent, since the alternative of no use at all yields zero returns. In the long term, of course, capital must yield a return sufficient to cover renewal; so the economic rent is strictly a short-term phenomenon. The term **quasi-rent** is sometimes used to denote this particular type of short-term rent.

Section 18
Distribution: wages

18A Types of wage

Commonly, wages are what wage-earners receive weekly. However, in economics, the term is extended to include all that share of the net national income which is distributed to the factor labour, and in that context it means the remuneration (excluding any element of economic rent) of surgeons and entertainers and the salaries of teachers and industrial managers as well as the weekly wages of welders and shopgirls. Insofar as money actually changes hands in payment for labour services, such explicit wages account for about 65–70% of the net national income. However, there is also a wage element involved in the money many small private entrepreneurs (e.g., shopkeepers) think they are making as profit. If a small shopkeeper makes a certain trading gain on his retailing activities then part of that income is *implicit wages*—the money, indeed, that he should be paying himself for his work in the shop. If many small shopkeepers reckoned their trading gain in this way, and compared their implicit wages with what they could perhaps earn in alternative employment, there is a distinct possibility that many of them might close their shops. If all wages, explicit and implicit together, are counted, then the portion of net national income going to the factor labour is more likely to be in the neighbourhood of 75% or so.

The money returns gained by labour are nominal wages, and may be counted gross (i.e., the full sum) or net (i.e., after tax and other necessary deductions at source). In the assessment of true factor costs, wages should be reckoned gross; the various deductions merely represent forced contributions to a flow of transfer incomes. Nevertheless, to the wage earner it is the net figure which matters—his 'take home pay', as it were. It matters because he is concerned with what he has available for spending. The wage earner's concern with spending power is reflected in the interest economists attach to the subject of real wages. Real wages are, as we noted in section 2D, the wage earner's income in terms of the goods and services which he can actually buy with his nominal net wages. They are clearly governed by more than just the amount of tax deducted; for example, they may rise, even though nominal net wages remain stable, as the prices of consumer goods fall, or they may fall as the prices of, say, food and accommodation rise. Real wages are also influenced by differences in costs of living from place to place, by variations in costs of essential tools and clothing, and by the existence or not of various fringe benefits, such as the free use of a company car and the availability of luncheon vouchers. If a worker's money wages are doubled, then he gains nothing if the prices of all the goods and services he buys are doubled too. Indeed, he may well lose, since the country's export trade will suffer; but you can read all about that in the section (13J) on inflation.

18B Wages under perfect and imperfect conditions

Wages are the price of labour, and react to the supply and demand mechanism exactly as all other prices. Under absolutely perfect conditions, all units of labour are identical with one another and in infinite supply; and all products are identical with one another and have a common price. Wages under these conditions are also identical with one another, at a level determined by the interaction of total supply and total (derived) demand. In fact, of course, such a perfect model is absurd; units of labour are by no means identical with one another, nor are they in infinite supply; no more are products identical with one another and of uniform price. Wages patently differ, even allowing for the exclusion of the economic rent element (i.e., excluding those parts of income which are in excess of the sums necessary to ensure a sufficient supply of labour). The differences arise from the qualitative variability of the suppliers of labour.

Labour, indeed, does not really exist as a single type of production factor. There are quite literally thousands of different types of labour, and even within general groupings there are multitudinous varieties. This is not to imply that groupings are mutually exclusive of one another—that, for instance, doctors cannot become surveyors or that cotton spinners cannot become electricians—but it does imply a certain amount of exclusiveness. The matter of exclusiveness is a function of the cross elasticity of labour substitution—just how far, for example, coal miners can be substituted for bricklayers. There are high possibilities of substitution with many unskilled and semi-skilled jobs, since the jobs require little or no training and can be done by almost anyone. In such cases, the supply of labour is likely to be fairly elastic for any single job, though the total labour supply position is likely to be fairly inelastic for the unskilled jobs as a whole (see section 6H and figure 6.3). As labour becomes more and more specific, because of higher skills and abilities and longer training periods, there is a greatly diminished possibility of substitution, and the supply becomes more inelastic. The supply of surgeons, for example, cannot be increased in the short term either by substitution or by training, though the supply of surgical services can be increased slightly by surgeons working longer hours; even in the long term the supply is likely to be less elastic than that of, say, bricklayers because of the high cost (in time and money) and the scarcity of the high skills needed for the job. In general terms, therefore, we can say that the less skilled the work and the less specific the labour the greater is the elasticity of supply, and conversely that the more skilled the work and the more specific the labour the greater is the inelasticity of supply, and that in both cases the elasticity is greater in the long term than in the short term.

The demand for labour by an entrepreneur is based upon the marginal revenue product schedule of the particular type of labour required, and the MRP schedule is itself determined by the interaction of the marginal physical product (MPP) of the labour and the market price of the good produced (see section 16B). If we assume the goal of profit maximisation, then the entrepreneur will hire labour up to the point where marginal revenue product equals the cost (wage) of the additional workers. In perfect competition, the wage rate is fixed by the market, and therefore given for the individual firm; the entrepreneur's only decision in the matter therefore concerns the number of labour units to employ at the chosen scale of production. In imperfect competition, however, there is no such thing as a single market-determined wage rate; there is instead a wide band of rates, and within that band the individual entrepreneur is himself partly responsible for determining an actual rate offered to labour. The entrepreneur in imperfect competition therefore has to make two interlinked decisions (wage rate paid and numbers employed) instead of merely one (numbers employed). His decisions rest on consideration of two interrelated factors:

1   As he hires more units of labour, their MPP declines (unless he moves to a larger scale of production altogether, whereupon he may be able to gain economies of scale).

2   As he produces more goods for sale, their price falls in order to extend market demand.

Since the two factors occur concurrently, the MRP of the labour units declines even faster than either MPP or market consumer price. This is because MRP is the product of MPP and marginal revenue, and if both of these decline, then—for arithmetic reasons alone—MRP declines even faster. Ultimately, since the entrepreneur's decisions about the wage rate are geared to the concept of making his hired units pay for themselves, the producer will not willingly pay more than the MRP of labour. His decision rests therefore, in the end, on the same consideration as that of an entrepreneur under perfect competition. The difference is that the entrepreneur under imperfect competition has no standard single external wage rate to guide him; nor has he a stable market consumer price to help him determine MRP more accurately.

Since, under imperfect competition, the MRP curve is always steeper than the demand curve for the commodity produced (see figure 18.1), the inelasticity of demand for labour is always greater than that for the commodity. In the short term the tendency to demand inelasticity for labour units is increased by the difficulties of factor, especially capital, substitution. In the long term, however, labour and capital are more easily substitutable, and the demand for labour units is correspondingly more elastic (though still less elastic than the demand for the commodity produced).

The wage rate itself is determined by the intersection of the curves for (a) a particular type of labour demand, based upon considerations of MRP, and (b) the supply of that labour, based upon considerations outlined in section 6H regarding the conflict of interests between the desire of workers for income on the one hand and leisure on the other. The situation is illustrated in figure 18.2, and can be analysed in the same way as that used to analyse figure 3.4.

Demand and supply shifts from the initial position illustrated in figure

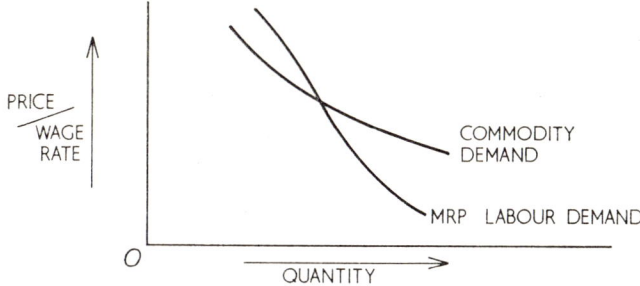

FIG 18.1   Elasticities of labour demand and commodity demand.

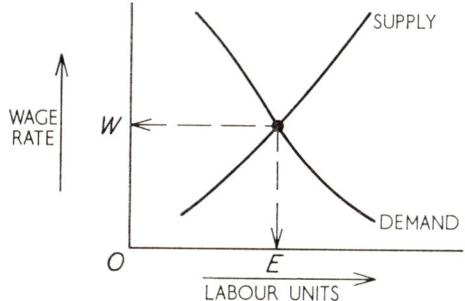

FIG 18.2   The determination of an equilibrium wage rate under perfect competition.

18.2 are caused most commonly by technological changes and population
growth respectively.

Technological changes are usually progressive (though not necessarily
gradual), and in any single industry usually tend to reduce the demand for a
particular type of labour by permitting the substitution of capital for labour,
thereby—assuming stable supply conditions—lowering the equilibrium wage
rate. The Luddites saw this simple relationship. However, in anything but
the very short term, the supply of labour for a reduced-wage job will also
tend to shift negatively, since the job will not attract many new entrants. In
time, therefore, the reduced supply of labour will tend to force a rise in the
lower equilibrium wage rate. If minimum wage legislation or effective trade
union resistance prevent the wage rate falling to its new equilibrium level,
then there is a strong theoretical likelihood of even greater unemployment
than would be the case under equilibrium conditions. Figure 18.3 illustrates
the point.

Population changes are also usually progressive (and much more gradual).
In the short term the increases are the result of immigration; and in the long
term they are the result of natural net population growth caused by either
declining death rates (as in 19th century England) or increasing birth rates (as

in post-1945 France). In either case the effect is to shift the total supply curve for labour to the right, though not necessarily the supply curve of labour for any particular job. The supply curve of labour for a particular job is more likely to be shifted to the right by inter-job transfers resulting from the superior attractions of higher wage rates over the general tendencies to immobility

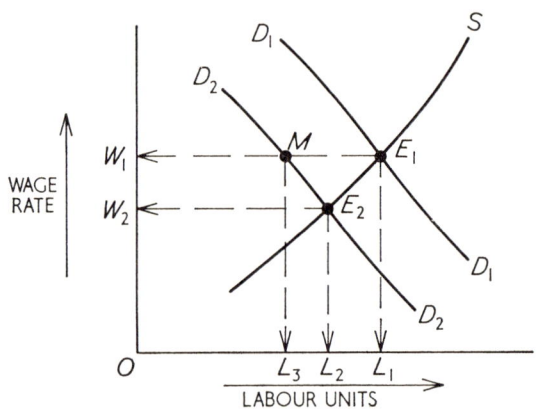

FIG 18.3   Maintained wages and unemployment.

NOTES:

1   At $E1$, wage is $OW1$ and employment is $OL1$.

2   At $E2$, wage would fall to $OW2$ and employment to $OL2$.

3   At M, wage is maintained at $W1$, but employment falls to $OL3$.

noted in section 6F. It should be stressed, however, that higher wage rates are not an automatic inducement to a worker to change jobs: quite apart from the matter of limited ability among the population as a whole for certain jobs (e.g., architect), there may be a strong disinclination even among those persons capable of doing the job actually to make the transfer. The disinclinations arise from such considerations as time involved in training, hours and conditions of work, community status, existing pension rights, and so on. In such cases the wage rate has to be that which will induce a sufficient number of persons to overcome their disinclinations. In some other jobs requiring immense skill (e.g., High Court judge), on the other hand, the equilibrium wage rate can be quite low, simply because of the great attractions the job offers in the form of non-monetary gain.

The last paragraph highlights some of the problems involved in a purely theoretical analysis of wage rates. Supply and demand conditions both change, often unpredictably; and a great many non-monetary (and therefore in a sense non-economic) factors enter into the determination of labour supply for any particular job. Real-life wage rates are indeed impossible to analyse fully on any strictly economic basis.

In general terms, however, one basic rule will be followed by both demanders and suppliers of labour: that of return maximisation. Demanders will in general attempt to obtain their factor supplies, including labour, at the lowest cost consistent with the necessary productivity to obtain maximum profits at the prevailing market price of the commodity produced. Suppliers of labour, on the other hand, will in general attempt to obtain the maximum wage for their labour consistent with their competing desire for leisure and their disinclination to mobility. In the early days of factory industrialisation, there was a tendency for suppliers of labour greatly to outnumber demanders, thereby placing demanders in a relatively oligopsonistic position (i.e., a small number of buyers in the market); in places, demanders even assumed a monopsonistic position, since they were often the only employers offering work in certain localities. Under such conditions, and given a certain amount of early-industrial unsophisticated immobility on the part of the labour suppliers, the employers were often able to hold the wage rate at an artificially low level. The root cause of this was, of course, the almost complete inelasticity of labour supply.

Trade unions developed partly in order to correct the apparent market imbalance. They sought to counter oligopsonistic and monopsonistic positions on the part of demanders by creating oligopolistic and monopolistic positions on the part of the suppliers. To a large extent, the development of these positions has meant that at the present time most wages are the product of what is called **collective bargaining**, rather than of pure untrammelled market conditions. The situation is one of oligopolists trying to attain an equilibrium position with oligopsonists.

The considerations influencing the two-sided collective bargaining procedure are very similar to those outlined in section 3A for the equilibrium price mechanism. The demanders of labour (the employers) hope to acquire the factor at the lowest cost, but are prepared to go above their lowest hopes. The first zone of consideration is up to the point where the MRP of labour equals the MRPs of the other employed factors, at which point it becomes possible for the employers to start thinking of substituting other factors for labour. At any labour cost above this point of equi-marginal revenue product (assuming that it can be identified), labour is replaced by other factors, and some unemployment occurs (the exact amount depending upon the elasticity of substitution). As far as the employer is concerned, therefore, the point of equality of MRPs is not necessarily the maximum wage that he will pay, even though substitution of some labour by capital will inevitably entail extra capital costs. A very strong trade union may push the employer beyond that point, but only at the cost of some unemployment for its members. It could be argued that only a foolish union would push wages so high, but such an argument ignores not only the fact that some American unions (e.g., the miners' union) have successfully pushed up wages at the cost of unemployment but also the possibility that the employer will raise consumer prices and so increase the MRP of labour, thereby effectively shifting the labour demand curve to the right. The real maximum wage as far as the employer is concerned is that which just allows him to gain a normal return on his investments, and so continue in business. However, most employers are unwilling to pay wages at this level unless they are forced to do so; more usually they have a lower maximum in mind, beyond which they will not go unless forced by a strike or a strike threat. This lower maximum may be regarded as the employer's negotiating maximum, or outer defences. On the employer's side of the collective bargaining procedure, therefore, we can distinguish three possible wage figures: a low figure which the employer hopes to be able to pay; a negotiating maximum; and a real maximum, which, if exceeded, will put the employer out of business. The employer's ideas on the real maximum are affected by his estimates of the consumer demand elasticity for his products if he raises their price (the greater the elasticity the less flexible will the real maximum be) and the chance of equivalent wage increases among his competitors (the more widespread the wage increases the more flexible will the real maximum be).

There are also three possible wage figures on the union side of the negotiations: the initial asking figure; the expected minimum; and the real minimum. The initial asking figure is usually pitched above the reasonably expected figure, if only because—in the event of arbitration—a compromise figure is commonly agreed. The expected minimum figure is the one which the union is prepared to fight over, even to the extent of a strike. It is based upon complex considerations, including such factors as the potential strength of union solidarity during a strike, the size of union reserves to support strikers during a strike, the wage increases actually being negotiated and agreed upon in other industries, changes in the cost of living since the previous wage agreement, the profit position of the negotiating firm, and the union's estimates of the firm's ability to pay increased wages. The real minimum is the figure which the union believes to be the lowest its members will accept without causing the disintegration of the union; any settlement figure lower than this minimum and the union members are likely to think that the union has failed them.

It often happens that the employer's negotiating maximum is lower than the union's expected minimum. In such a case, failing compulsory arbitration (which usually produces a compromise figure anyway), a strike is the inevitable result. The strike may appear to be over a relatively small difference only —a few pence an hour, say—and there is often therefore much public hostility towards the strikers. The public usually regards the losses incurred by the strikers as being far more than they could make up—even with the higher wages—over the foreseeable future; and so the public thinks that the workers are being silly or childish by going on strike. It should be realised, however, that most workers will not willingly sacrifice income for trivial reasons; and it should also be realised that the workers, for their part, regard the small difference as being the product of plain stubbornness by the employer, and that the employer is likely to lose more in cancelled orders and loss of goodwill than it would cost him to pay the small difference. In fact, of course, the strike is not just over the small final difference. The union believes that were it not for the threat of a strike the employer would probably never have been driven from his initial low offer, and that a threat—to be effective in negotiations—must occasionally be carried out. The employer similarly regards his resistance to a strike threat; he cannot, indeed, always yield, otherwise union demands are likely to be greatly increased in future negotiations. In this context, it is worth looking back on inflation in section 13J and remembering that inflation can be caused by employers giving in to excessive union demands; and also that the Brookings Institution's report on the British economy (section 15B) commented unfavourably on the common practice in Britain of management giving in to strikers rather than taking the long-term view.

The question whether unions have succeeded in raising wages or not is decidedly difficult to answer, since there is no basis of comparison. Wages have certainly risen over the last 100 years, even in real terms, but just how much of the rise is the result of union activity is impossible to say, since no one knows how wages would have behaved without unions. It is unfair to compare wage increases in non-union industries over a period of time with those in union industries, and say that the rises are similar, thereby implying that unions have had little or no effect, since the wages in non-union industries are intimately affected by those in union industries through the total labour supply market. Furthermore, many employers in non-union industries offer wage increases roughly comparable to those in union industries merely to avoid the growth of unions in their own industries.

In addition to working for higher monetary returns for their members, unions also work for better real wages; for example, improvements in pension plans, cheaper canteen facilities, longer paid holidays, and in-service training facilities. Strikes may arise out of these issues as well as out of purely nominal wage disputes.

The successful settling of a wage claim—by negotiation or strike—in a major industry tends to set a pattern for similar claims in other industries. Major settlements are indeed trend setters in the field of wages, and it is quite likely that one settlement may provoke claims by other unions on the grounds that their members must not appear to lag behind in the race for higher incomes. If the situation appears to the government to be getting out of control, then legislative action may be taken. The USA, for example, has given its government powers to enforce a 28-day 'cooling-off' period before a strike can occur legally, in the hope that last-minute arbitration procedures can work successfully. Despite this, the USA has the worst strike record of any country in the world (as well as the highest productivity per worker and the highest level of real wages per worker). By comparison, strikes in Britain are less than one-third as frequent in days lost per 1000 workers. West Germany, however, has an even better strike record than Britain, generally losing only one-sixth as many working days per 1000 workers as Britain. The absolute total of strike activity in Britain cannot therefore on its own be held responsible for Britain's periodic economic troubles; more likely, as the Brookings Institution reported, it is the wildcat nature of many of the strikers and their concentration in commercially important sectors of the economy (motors and docks, for example) that does more damage than the number of days lost would alone suggest. Partly because of this, and partly because of mounting public hostility towards the trade unions (either for supporting strikes or for failing to control unofficial strikes), there have been numerous attempts by British governments to bring a semblance of industrial order to the union/wage claim/strike picture of apparent anarchy.

The most significant attempt followed the statutory establishment in August 1966 (after the July 1966 sterling crisis) of the National Board for Prices and Incomes (commonly called the Prices and Incomes Board, or just the PIB). The PIB machinery had been set up in early 1965 to supervise a voluntary system of 'early warnings' of price and wage increases by employers and unions, with a target or guideline norm for income growth of some 3–3½% a year. However, by 1968, after prolonged economic trouble and sterling devaluation, the official line was that no one was 'entitled automatically to an increase in pay', and that an income growth of 3½% a year should be regarded as an absolute maximum. Through 1968, such a rate would have just about failed to keep pace with inflation. The conditions for governmental acceptance of a proposed wage increase were that it should, within the 3½% ceiling, reflect any one or more of the following:

1 Increases in productivity.
2 Adjustments to remedy a socially unsatisfactory standard of living.
3 Arrangements to get people to move into jobs where they are needed in the national interest.
4 The attainment of wage parity between different groups of workers who are doing similar work.

The application by the PIB of one criterion to one industry and another criterion to another industry led initially to a great deal of confusion, since different industries tended to think that they were somehow being treated unfairly (witness the eloquent complaints by university teachers in early 1969). Another problem faced by the PIB was that its chief purpose was designed to be a long-term restructuring of wages, and yet it was forced to operate in its early years almost entirely as a suppressive instrument because of the immediate urgency of Britain's short-term problems

18C Equal pay

About 35% of Britain's workers are women. However, their average income for their work is only about 60% of the wage levels attained by British men. Among the fully-employed women, one-tenth earned less than £6 a week at the time of the government's *Survey of Women's Employment* (published in 1968 after a survey in 1965). Only one-tenth as well earned over £16 a week—at a time when the *average* wage for men was over £20 a week. There are many possible reasons for this state of affairs:

1 The patriarchal nature of western society, and the typical and traditional granting of superior rights to men

2   The assumption by many women that a job is merely something to do until they get married or have children, and the similar assumption after marriage or child-raising that a job is merely a way of supplementing their husbands' incomes or of earning 'pin money'.

3   The assumption by many employers that women have made the above assumption, even when they patently have not (for example, married women are outnumbered—relatively—by spinsters in the ratio of 10:1 in the higher branches of the civil service).

4   The inadequate education allowed to many girls by parents, who often more readily pull a girl out of school at 15 or 16 than a boy.

5   The limited range of jobs open to girls compared with boys, and the consequent increase of supply in those jobs, with the likelihood of a lower equilibrium wage rate.

6   The observed fact that it is more difficult to get women to join trade unions than it is to get men to join, thereby lessening the collective bargaining power of many women (as Ramsay MacDonald, Britain's first socialist Prime Minister, once said, 'We must take these women by the scruff of the neck and force them into combinations.')

The European Common Market made legal provision in 1961 for equal pay for similar work done by men and women, and the USA did so in 1967; equal pay is also a government and TUC policy matter in Britain. It exists in a few jobs (medicine, teaching, civil service, for example), but it is far from realisation in most. Resistance to the concept of equal pay—let alone the practical implementation—is strong:

1   Many men feel that they are somehow superior to women, even when their economic productivity is the same.

2   Most men feel that they should be paid more because of their family commitments.

3   Many men fear that equal pay would result in a reduction of their own wage rates.

4   Not a few women, as well as men, argue that a woman's place is in the home.

On the other hand, proponents of equal pay contend:

1   That it would remove the intense discontent felt by many women at work.

2   That it is morally equitable.

3   That it would lead to more efficiently productive use of female labour, since women could no longer be regarded as cheap labour.

4   That standards of living would rise with the increased national productivity.

5   That even if many men have burdensome family commitments, requiring a higher real income, then any necessary adjustments should be made through tax allowances rather than through higher initial nominal wages.

Discounting the social and anthropological arguments, the plain economic argument that wage rates are determined ultimately by reference to the MRP of labour indicates that sex differences have nothing to do with wage rates: payment is according to product—and equal pay for equal work is a necessary corollary. There is only one qualification: social and anthropological arguments are strong—and in the real world they exist as established views and prejudices.

18D Wage systems

Once a level of wages has been agreed, a method of wage payment has to be established. The different methods are:

1   Time wages. These are payments over a period of time, e.g., so much a week or so much a year. They are the method employed whenever output is difficult to assess, as in service industries, or whenever unhurried and careful work is required, as in watch-making. The method offers a number of advantages:

(a) dispute over the amount of wages is impossible;

(b) the worker does not suffer if short emergency stoppages occur;

(c) quality need not suffer at the expense of quantity; and

(d) the workers are not so liable to strain (a debatable point, in fact).

There are also several disadvantages:

(a) higher output from more efficient workers is not encouraged;

(b) the employer has no immediate remedy against time-wasting by workers; and

(c) supervision or inspection is often necessary for the maintenance of standards.

2   Piece wages. These are payments for a certain quantity of output, e.g., so much per basket of fruit collected or so much per thousand bolts made. They are the method employed whenever output is repetitive and easily assessable. The advantages are:

(a) provision of incentive to the more efficient worker;

(b) fixed capital receives more intensive use, leading to a reduction of oncosts; and

(c) a possibly higher total national product.

The disadvantages are:

(a) resentment of the efficient by the less efficient workers;

(b) increases in accident risk and carelessness, necessitating quality control and safety supervision; and

(c) increases in strain felt by workers.

3   Bonus wages. These are different attempts to obtain the advantages of time and piece wages without getting the disadvantages as well. There are many varieties of bonus wage, but the two chief types are:

(a) a fixed time wage with higher overtime rates as the bonus; and

(b) a fixed time wage with bonus piece rates for any output over and above a set norm.

4 Sliding-scale wages. These are a form of time wage geared to the movements of the cost-of-living index.

5 Profit-sharing wages. These are a method designed to distribute some of the firm's profits to the workers. The usual device is a special share issue to the workers, so that the workers obtain a dividend in the manner of shareholders, as well as a wage. Part of the thinking behind this device is that employers expect that the workers will work harder and strike less if they have a personal stake in the firm's profits.

Section 19
Distribution: interest

19A The theory of interest

Interest is the price of a loan of money over a period of time. It is not just the price of money capital in particular, since interest must also be paid on loans for consumption, such as holidays, and still less is it the price of money in general, for money is its own standard of value. Holdings of money earn no income for the owners unless the money is lent to users: cash in hand or immediately available in a current account in a bank earns no interest. Only when the money is lent to a user does it earn a factor income for its owner, and establish a factor cost to its user. The determination of the price of a loan (the interest rate) depends, therefore, in the manner of all prices, upon the balance achieved between the supply of money for loan and the demand for it.

19B The supply of loan funds

The total supply of loan funds is clearly limited initially by the total supply of money in the country, and is therefore subject immediately to whatever restrictionist or expansionary policies are pursued by the suppliers of money in general (the government and the government-influenced banks). Within the ceiling imposed by the total supply of money, the supply of loan funds itself is the product of an interaction between the desire of the holders of money to retain it in convenient liquid form and the contrary desire to put it to some income-earning use. The holders of money may be (a) individual persons who have saved out of past income or who have current income surplus to their immediate needs, and (b) business firms which have built up reserve funds out of undistributed profits, and accumulated money to cover depreciation costs. Insurance companies and banks (apart from *bank money*—see section 13B) are not holders of money in the strict sense; they are merely guardians of other people's money, and channels whereby small sums may be collected into a larger reservoir of funds. The desire of the holders of money to retain it in liquid form is called *liquidity preference*—noted in section 13A—and is the result of what Keynes called the transactions, precautionary, and speculative motives. We could also add ignorance and distrust of the monetary institutions. Ignorance and distrust are illustrated most markedly by those people who stuff money into a suitcase under the bed; but even those people who keep large inactive balances in a current account are not entirely free of ignorance. The manner in which the holders of money accumulated their savings is of little direct concern to our analysis. It used to be thought that the interest rate was the necessary price to induce saving, but it is now widely accepted that saving by both individual persons and business firms takes place with only the slightest connection to interest rates (see section 6L on saving).

It might be thought at first that since money in liquid form earns no income for its owners, then any return on it is better than none, such return representing an economic rent. However, even though liquid money earns no income, it does offer the personally valuable convenience of liquidity. The desire for liquidity has to be overcome if any of the money is to be lent out. The rate of interest is the price which must be paid to the holders of money in order to induce them to sacrifice part of their liquidity. The equilibrium rate of interest is that which draws forth an exactly sufficient supply of loan funds to satisfy the demand.

19C The demand for loan funds

The demand for money as such is unlimited, since money represents a claim on goods and services, the long-term demand for which is insatiable. If money could be borrowed freely, then the demand for loan funds would also be unlimited, since in any society there would be enough people preferring to spend in the present rather than defer satisfaction of their wants to the future. The fact that an interest-price has to be paid to the holders of money in order to persuade them to overcome at least part of their liquidity preference, however, inevitably curtails the demand for loan funds. The interest-price, in fact, like all other prices, acts as a mechanism for allocating a scarce resource; in this case, the limited supply of loan funds. The existence of an interest-price, then, means that the demanders have to think about the purpose of the proposed borrowing, and make some assessment of its return. The normal economic measure of return value is money, and it is only in this manner that we can initially approach the topic; but it should be borne in mind that a return to the borrower does not have to be monetary in nature—some borrowers, for example, might feel that a health return or a status return more than justifies the poor monetary return on their borrowing. It is for such reasons that some people go heavily into debt when buying a house or a car, the return in social status more than justifying the poor economic return. Ignoring these non-economic motives for borrowing for the moment, let us now examine the monetary aspects.

The demand for loan funds arises from three primary sources: consumers, governments and business firms. The demand by consumers and governments is only *indirectly* productive (and therefore only *indirectly* income-yielding in the strict sense); the reason for this is that production in practice is only encouraged—and not directly caused—by the positive shifts which occur in total consumer demand for goods and services. The demand for loan funds by business firms, on the other hand, makes up the *directly* productive segment of total loan fund demand; and only interest paid on such loans constitutes a direct factor income. The demand for loan funds by a business firm derives from its demand for physical capital, and the demand for physical capital in turn depends on the marginal revenue product (MRP) of the capital. The revenue productivity of physical capital is therefore the ultimate determinant of the demand for loan funds by a business firm, and, since physical capital is subject to the law of diminishing returns, a normal negatively-sloping demand curve for loan funds can be produced. Such a demand curve shows that loan funds are in extended demand whenever the interest-price is low, and in contracted demand whenever the interest rate is high. For example, a farmer may borrow money at a high rate of interest in order to buy a single tractor, because the increase in income he enjoys from the use of a single tractor is sufficient to compensate him for paying the high rate of interest. He is likely to buy a second tractor with borrowed money, however, only if the interest rate falls, because the diminished marginal productivity of the second tractor is unlikely to be sufficient to produce enough income for him to be able to afford to buy it at the higher interest rate. The farmer's demand for loan funds to buy tractors therefore extends as the interest rate falls; and his decisions regarding the borrowing of money to buy tractors rest clearly on a comparison between the MRP of the additional tractor and the cost (interest rate) of the borrowed money. So long as the MRP of the capital item is above the interest rate (i.e., so long as marginal income exceeds marginal outlay), then the demand for loan funds is strong. The demand ceases at the point where the MRP of capital equals the interest rate, for at any point below this level outlay on interest exceeds income from marginal product, and borrowing is not undertaken (except for non-monetary gain).

The only way to compare the marginal products of additional units of, say, tractors, steel mills, ships and knitting machines is in monetary terms. This is why marginal *revenue* productivity rather than marginal *physical* productivity is used as the criterion; money—in a free enterprise economy— is the chief measure of value, although under other economic systems there may be other criteria (social or military need, for example). The use of money as a measure of value permits simple comparisons to be made: for instance, if £100 spent on additional knitting machines yields a marginal revenue product of, say, £10, then the return is 10%; and this is obviously superior to the return of £35 MRP gained from £500 spent on additional egg-packing machinery. If the actual interest rate is at all over 10%, then neither piece of machinery will be bought on borrowed money, since the outlay exceeds the return; at any interest rate between 7% and 10% only the knitting machine will be bought; and at interest rates lower than 7% both pieces of machinery will be bought. The qualification of 'borrowed money' requires amplification: clearly, if a firm has to borrow money at a certain rate of interest then that firm will undertake only those projects which offer a similar or higher rate of return—but what if the firm has its own reserves, and does not need to borrow? In that case, it might appear that since no interest has to be paid on money borrowed from itself then the rate of return is not a significant criterion. However, you should remember that by investing its own money in its own capital equipment the firm is forgoing the returns which that same money could have earnt if it had been invested elsewhere (the opportunity cost); and on that basis alone, any firm, whether it has to borrow money or not, must take note of the expected return on capital investment compared with the interest rate on loan funds. And, by doing so, a firm responds positively to the desire to buy capital equipment only when the expected return on that investment either exceeds or at least equals the rate of interest on the equivalent sum of money. A high rate of interest clearly favours only those investments which have a high marginal revenue product, i.e., the more profitable (efficient?) ones. In this way, interest rates act as a filter to investment decisions, encouraging the more profitable and discouraging the less profitable. Society benefits to that extent. However, it is one of the main arguments against the uncontrolled operation of the free market for loan funds that socially desirable capital investment may suffer, in so far as the manufacture of trivia may be more profitable (and certainly be seen to be more profitable by entrepreneurs) than the production of schools and hospitals.

19D The rate of interest

It is tempting to regard the interest rate as the equilibrium price balancing the supply of and demand for loan funds; and in a sense this is so. However, as you well know, there are in fact many interest rates in operation at any one time, ranging from, say, the interest on Post Office Savings Bank accounts to the interest on loans made by registered moneylenders. The reason for the existence of so many different interest rates is simply that the market for loan funds is very varied; there is indeed no such thing as a single market, but instead many separate—though often substitutable—markets. For example, if a firm wishes to borrow, then it may do so from the commercial banks, the merchant banks, the investment trusts, the public at large, the insurance companies, other firms, the shareholders, and, of course, its own reserves. In the same sort of way, any one of these sources may be used to supply funds to other borrowers. Despite the possibilities of substitution, there is nevertheless in practice a fairly well-established pattern of market segmentation. People who wish to borrow for house purchase rarely look outside the building societies and insurance companies; firms which wish to borrow for large capital projects rarely look beyond their own shareholders or beyond the possibility of acquiring new shareholders; firms seeking funds for small capital projects rarely go beyond their own reserves or their bank manager; and so on. On the supply side, people with small amounts of money for loan usually get it to market through the Post Office and Trustee Savings Banks, the commercial banks, and the insurance companies; people with larger amounts use the commercial and merchant banks, and their stockbrokers; and so on.

The different interest rates in existence reflect this segmentation of the market; and in each case the individual interest rate may be held to represent the particular equilibrium established within that segment of the market. The possibilities of substitution, however, inevitably mean that individual interest rates within the general spread cannot get radically out of line with the rest. If government bonds, for example, offer a markedly superior yield to that offered by other 'safe' investments (e.g., building societies), then loan funds will be switched from the lower return investment to the higher. Even though interest rates differ within the spread, then, they must still move up or down more or less sympathetically.

The imperfect elasticity of substitution does not on its own explain the *cause* of the differences in interest rates in the first place. Interest rates may be kept different by imperfect substitution possibilities, but why should they differ at all? Three interlinked factors help to explain the initial—and persistent—differences: duration, risk and liquidity.

In general, the longer the duration of a proposed loan, the greater will be the sacrifice of liquidity by the lender, and the higher the inducement needed to make him overcome his desire to retain liquidity. Long-term loans therefore tend to carry a higher interest rate than those taken out over the short term; compare the different rates, for example, quoted by the banks on 4th September 1969 for their loans on trade bills:

$$3 \text{ month bills} \quad 9\tfrac{1}{2}\%-9\tfrac{3}{4}\% \quad (9.50-9.75)$$
$$6 \text{ month bills} \quad 9\tfrac{3}{4}\%-10\% \quad (9.75-10.00)$$

The risk of non-repayment varies from borrower to borrower, and is the second cause of differences in interest rates. The government is the safest borrower, since it is also the country's ultimate monetary authority; and so interest rates for government borrowing are generally lower than others obtaining in the market (see also the end of section 13C). Other borrowers present higher risks, ranging from the 'first-class' risks of large joint-stock companies to the very high risks of those private individuals with a poor credit rating. The quoted interest rates for these different categories of borrowers reflect the degrees of risk incurred by the lenders. Banks, for instance, usually lend to large companies at a rate one or two percentage points lower than the rate quoted for even credit-worthy private customers. The higher rates quoted for the higher-risk loans therefore include an element of insurance against non-repayment. It used to be a common principle to deduct this imputed amount of insurance from the quoted gross interest in order to obtain a pure net interest figure; but if interest is regarded entirely as the inducement needed to secure a supply of loan funds from the suppliers then the problem of gross and net interest disappears, since the supply would not be forthcoming to high-risk borrowers at all unless the rate were correspondingly high.

The matter of liquidity, the third factor causing differences in interest rates, is of course crucial. It not only underlies the considerations regarding duration and risk, but also acts independently: long-term loans from the demand side may or may not in fact be equally long-term from the supply side. A great deal of government borrowing is long-term in character—some of it, indeed, is infinite in character (the funded debt)—but that does not necessarily invoke an equal long-term loss of liquidity for the lenders. By means of the Stock Exchange, the government is able to borrow long and individual lenders are able to lend short, simply by having the facility of transferring their rights to another lender. Whenever government bonds are bought and sold, other than at issue and maturity, the original lenders are simply regaining liquidity, and other lenders are making the sacrifice instead. It is the lender's ease of regaining liquidity which permits the government to offer fairly low rates of interest even on long-term and infinite loans. Where liquidity cannot be regained so easily, the interest rates on loans are higher; which is why commercial banks find it more profitable to make advances than to discount bills (see table 13.3).

So far, we have examined the various internal factors affecting interest rates: (a) the relationship between the sacrifice (sale) of liquidity and the marginal revenue product of the investment; and (b) the variations caused by differences in duration, risk, and ease of regaining liquidity. These are not, however, the only factors influencing interest rates. There are also two external factors: the government and inflation.

The government is able to exert a strong—even overriding—influence on market rates by means of its control of Bank Rate (see section 13G). Bank Rate dominates the discount market technically and the rest of the market traditionally; whenever it moves up or down, the other rates move in sympathy—partly, of course, because of the substitution effect in the market, but also because of the traditional esteem in which Bank Rate is held as an official guide to the market.

The effect of inflation, the last factor, is entirely unidirectional—upwards. Not only do governments raise interest rates in an attempt to counter inflation (see section 13J), but inflation itself also has an upward force on the rate. The lenders expect that under inflation they will be repaid less in real terms than the amount of the original loan; so they raise the supply price of the loan in order to offset the expected decline in purchasing power. A nominal rate of interest of 5%, coupled with inflation at a rate of 5%, obviously means a zero real return to the lender; inflation merely erodes completely the nominal return. Under such conditions, lenders request a higher price, simply in order to maintain a normal real rate; and borrowers are usually willing to pay it, simply because they expect for their part that their own incomes will at least make an offsetting rise. Inflation over a long period is almost always an advantage to the borrowers, since a rate high enough to compensate the long-term lenders in real terms would be socially unacceptable; which is why it usually pays house buyers to take out a mortgage rather than use cash, even if they have the cash.

Distribution: profit

20A The nature of profit

Even if you still believe that all the best things in life are free, then you probably at least accept that what you regard as necessities have some sort of cost.
And also that someone else in the community will have gone to the trouble of
building the house you live in, growing the food you eat, and making the
clothes you wear. You will expect these other people to require a return on
their efforts, sufficient to cover the inputs of labour, land and capital. Depending upon your political views, you might qualify those expectations by saying
either 'sufficient to cover *at least* the inputs . . .' or 'sufficient to cover *at most*
the inputs. . . .' If you are open-minded, then perhaps you will not make any
qualifications at all yet. Whether you make any qualifications or not, you
should now ask yourself why these other people have bothered to build your
house, grow your food, and make your clothes. And, above all, who made the
decisions regarding the type of house built, the quantity of food grown, and
the style of clothing made. You should also be rather curious about the
guesses some of these other people must have made regarding the type of
house you like to live in and the style of clothes you like to wear. What if the
guesses had been wrong? Or would you prefer that you didn't have much
choice in the matter, and that you had to wear what someone else had already
decided you should wear?

Since production of houses, clothes and most other goods must precede
actual consumption, then someone, somewhere, has to decide on the quantities and styles to be produced. Someone has also to hire labour, land, and
capital, and get production under way. That someone could be a state planner,
allocating resources of labour and so on to the production of commodities
which the government thought that the community needed or wanted. In
some countries, that someone is indeed a state planner. He may well receive
a high wage for his important task. In other countries, that someone is a
private individual, making his own estimates of what you are likely to want.
He, too, may receive a high return for his task—with one big difference: if he
guesses wrongly about your wants, then he gets no return at all. He loses his
job, in fact. The uncertainty which anyone faces regarding the future is borne
by the planning department in the first case, and by the private entrepreneur
in the second. In the first case, the cost of correct guesses is merely the probably high wage of the planner, and the cost of wrong guesses (assuming that
the community has a choice of consumption items) is higher taxes for all.
In the second case, the cost of correct guesses by the entrepreneur is what are
commonly called profits, and the cost of wrong guesses is the loss of a job to

the entrepreneur and his workers. It is not the purpose of this book to suggest which of the two systems is superior to the other; but it is a purpose here to examine the profit system in a little more detail.

In the last paragraph we noted that the returns to an entrepreneur (assuming for the moment that we can identify him—see section 6M) are what are 'commonly called' profits. The qualification arises because the word *profits* means different things to different people. To opponents of the profit system, it means all the revenue which is surplus to the immediate cost of the item sold; for example, if a TV dealer sells a set for £80, having paid only £50 to the wholesaler, then his profit is alleged to be £30.

An accountant looks at the situation differently. He regards profit as the net income accruing over a period of time, after all the explicit costs of operating the enterprise have been met; so that if a TV dealer has sold 10 sets during the week, an accountant will put total revenue at £800, and then from that sum deduct £500 as money paid to the wholesaler, as well as making deductions for the cost of running the shop (rent, hired labour, insurance, interest on loans, depreciation, and so on). The **operating profit** in such a case is likely to be well under the apparent profit of £300, since the deductions may take, say, another £200 out of the total. The accountant would then put the TV dealer's operating profit at £100 for the week, and, after making a further deduction for tax liability, arrive eventually at a **net income** figure of perhaps £60 for the TV dealer.

The economist has an even more stringent view of profits. He deducts from gross income not only the explicit and contracted costs, but also the various *implicit* costs. These are difficult to quantify, since they exist only by implication; but they do exist, and must be discounted. They include the elements of rent, wages and interest which exist in operating profit. If an entrepreneur owns his own land, for example, then an element of rent exists in his operating profit; the element is equivalent to what the land could earn if hired out to another user—its transfer earnings, in fact. By using the land himself, an entrepreneur is forgoing that amount of rent, and an equivalent sum should be deducted from operating profit in order to bring into closer focus the amount of pure profit. It is quite possible, of course, for an entrepreneur to be using land which, if hired out, would bring him a return even greater than his total operating profit; and that is clearly a very uneconomic way of using one of the scarce factors of production. But in real life it often happens that way; perhaps planning has a case here? The element of wages inherent in operating profit is the sum which the entrepreneur could be earning himself if he were employed by someone else; and that amount too may be greater than his operating profit. If so, it would reflect his desire for what he regards as independence, and being his own boss. Nevertheless, such an implicit amount has to be deducted from operating profit, since in no way can such a sum be regarded as economic profit; it is wages. Deductions also have to be made for implicit interest. Most entrepreneurs invest some of their own money in their business, even if only to the extent of buying some shares in a jointly-owned company, and a deduction has to be made of the interest which that money could have earnt if it had been invested elsewhere (in safe government bonds, for example).

Looked at in the economics sense, which is what we are concerned with, profits may therefore be regarded as **residual income**. They are what is left after all costs, including implicit or opportunity costs, have been paid. They should, of course, be positive—i.e., there should be *something* left over— otherwise why should the entrepreneur bother organising everything? In fact, they are not always positive; as we have already hinted, entrepreneurs may at times be better off financially by hiring out their land or labour to another user. Those entrepreneurs who put up with a negative economic profit do so for many reasons of their own; and those reasons, even though they can be noted, cannot be explained economically. They include such considerations as inheritance, desire for employer status, desire for power and control, a wish to be economically independent (as though that were possible), and a desire to make things (see also section 6M). Some entrepreneurs may even be ignorant of their negative economic profit; they receive a return which satisfies them, and are simply unaware that their labour and so on could generate a higher return elsewhere. Other entrepreneurs, on the other hand, guided primarily by a desire for high profits, will cease production if profits become negative; and it is they—rather than the ones who struggle along persistently on a negative economic return—who are the truly marginal entrepreneurs.

Economic, true, or pure profit, then, is a residual income. It is the return to enterprise. However, enterprise itself is a combinative function—partly planning and hiring, and partly bearing the uncertainty of the business. Planning and hiring, as under a state-run economy, can be considered a special form of labour, rewarded by an explicit or implicit wage; but uncertainty-bearing is a different sort of activity altogether, and represents the crux of the enterprise function. Pure profit is therefore the reward for uncertainty-bearing. Uncertainty itself arises simply because no one can accurately foretell the future, and all production of goods must occur in anticipation of future demand. No one *knows* just what the future demand will be; or how the supply of input factors will behave; or how prices of inputs will change. And yet someone has to make an estimate—based, where possible, of course, on market research and past experience—otherwise production will never be undertaken. Pure profit is the reward for bearing these uncertainties. It is important here to distinguish between the unknown future which can be insured against on an actuarial basis (the risks of fire and flood, for instance) and the unknown future which cannot be insured against at all. The insurable unknown is not an economic uncertainty; it is a cost of production, in the same way as money set aside for capital replacement. The uninsurable unknown is, however, an uncertainty; no one can ensure that his goods will be demanded in the future at the rate he now expects, nor can anyone ensure (or insure against the contrary possibility) that all relevant prices will remain stable. Some producers, of course, can make *futures* contracts (see section 11B), but they are then abdicating their uncertainty-bearing function. The various uncertainties are bound to exist in a dynamic economy—they are the product of change. In a perfect and known economy, there would be no uncertainty—and therefore no profit. The return to enterprise would merely be implicit wages for management and organisation. Profit is therefore a result of imperfect competition in the real world.

You should note very carefully that uncertainty is not the *cause* of profit. Pure profit is the residual income under conditions of uncertainty whenever sanguine expectations are exceeded by reality. All entrepreneurs hope for this state of affairs, and it is this hope which encourages their supply. Sometimes, the entrepreneurs are lucky, and they gain a pure profit; at other times they are unlucky (or simply inefficient), and they sustain a loss. Uncertainty *may* give rise to profit, but it may equally well give rise to a loss. The incentives to entrepreneurial success are therefore twofold: profit *and* loss—the carrot and the stick. Uncertainty-bearing, accordingly, offers both the chance of profit and the danger of loss; it does not automatically *cause* profit.

Earlier in the book (section 5A), we noted the existence of normal and surplus profits, and defined (a) normal profit as the minimum needed to draw a precisely sufficient supply of entrepreneurs into production, thereby forming an essential (or true) cost of production, and (b) surplus profit as any additional revenue gained by the entrepreneur over and above that needed to maintain his entrepreneurial function. Normal profit is—obviously?—a compound return, consisting partly of implicit rent, wages, and interest, and partly of pure profit. Surplus profit is, of course, entirely pure profit, since it contains no implicit or true cost element whatsoever. Pure profit is therefore some normal profit and all surplus profit. In so far as monopoly profit is surplus profit, then monopoly profit is pure profit too.

At this stage, you can probably see that pure profit bears a very strong resemblance to economic rent, in that both are pure surplus returns. In perfect competition, pure profit is impossible; even the small part in normal profit would cease to exist, since entrepreneurial omniscience, an essential characteristic of perfect competition, would eliminate the uncertainty-bearing function, and the return to entrepreneurs in the form of normal profit would consist entirely of implicit costs. In imperfect competition, however, in the real world, uncertainty certainly exists, and a return for bearing it is inevitably present even in the normal profits gained by entrepreneurs. Above that minimum amount of pure profit, however, the supply of enterprise is perfectly inelastic, and it is in this sense that pure profit is a surplus return comparable to economic rent. However, as you well remember, there is often an economic rent element present in wages too—and also in interest.

20B The function of profits

Profits have a twofold purpose. The first purpose—that of offering an opportunity of gain to entrepreneurs, in order to draw forth a supply of enterprise—has just been noted. It is a hotly disputed purpose, being vilified or justified in total according to the political and social view of the disputants, and in degree according to the definition of profit chosen (if a definition is chosen at all). Vilification, for example, is usually based on the notion that profits in real life are frequently excessive, i.e., greater than those needed to produce a sufficient supply of enterprise, and also on the supposition that individual risk-takers should not be able to benefit from (exploit?) the uncertainties which beset society as a whole. On the other hand, justification proceeds on the basis of individual freedom of action, in that if a person wishes to take risks or pioneer new lines then he should not only be allowed to do so as of moral right but also be encouraged to do so by the chance of financial gain. The penalty of financial loss is regarded as a sufficient deterrent to the production of unwanted items, and the existence of competition a sufficient safeguard against the taking of excess profits over a long period. There can be no economic reconciliation between these opposed views, since the topic is not entirely within the purlieu of the subject matter of economics. You can be taught what the economic system is, and how it works, but you cannot be taught what to think about it.

The second function of profits has a much wider measure of support. Indeed, both ends of the effective political spectrum pay attention to the discipline exerted by profits in determining the allocation of resources, even though the word *profits* may be replaced by such terms as **cost effectiveness** or **social benefit**. This second, disciplinary, function of profits is a result of the nature of production: maximum economic efficiency is achieved under any sort of political system whenever the real resources available to the community are combined in a manner which yields the lowest average production costs in real or monetary terms consistent with the satisfaction of the demands by that community, whether expressed collectively by the government or individually in the market. Profits are a test of such efficiency, and communist planners seek maximum social benefit just as much as capitalist entrepreneurs seek profits. The name may be changed, but the facts remain the same.

20C Variations in profits

Not all productive activities achieve the same level either of profits or of real-cost effectiveness. Returns, in fact, vary enormously. And they vary in both planned and free enterprise economies. The reason, of course, is that uncertainty about the future is not a political or an economic matter; it is a condition of life, and the plans and predictions of communists are neither more nor less likely to be accurate in the outturn than the profit-and-loss-inspired estimates of free enterprise businessmen. Khrushchev's virgin lands policy in western Siberia during the early 1960s was just as much a failure as the American dust bowl of the 1930s, and the Soviet space programme initially just as much a success as the American.

The variations in return—call it profit or real-cost benefit—are the result of variations in uncertainty. In some industries, the return is higher because the uncertainties are greater; so, of course, are the chances of loss. New-technology industries such as micro-electronics and computers offer many examples. Variations are also caused by differences in entrepreneurial ability, in access to production factors, in access to market, in the scale of production, and so on. There isn't any way in which any sort of economy can produce equality in all these fields. People and geography see to that.

Questions

1 'Economic laws may be defined as statements of tendencies.' Discuss this statement. *B*

2 What do you understand by 'economic planning'? *OA*

3 How, in a market economy, is the allocation of resources decided? *OA*

4 What can state planning do that private industry cannot do better? *OS*

5 How does the price mechanism allocate resources to different uses? *OA*

6 Explain the principle by which the entrepreneur will substitute one factor of production for another in order to maximise his profit. *B*

7 Under precisely what circumstances should railways be permitted to run at a loss? *OA*

8 Most market demand curves are depicted as sloping downward to the right. Why? *OA*

9 What factors determine the elasticity of demand? What is meant when it is said that the elasticity of demand is unity? *B*

10 Why do shops have 'sales'? *OA*

11 Why do cinema managers admit children at reduced prices? *OS*

12 Why do so many Governments raise a lot of revenue by taxes on alcoholic drinks, tobacco and petrol? Do you approve of such action? *C*

13 If purchase tax on cars were abolished and an equivalent sum raised from extra petrol duty, what would the consequences be? *OA*

14 Analyse the effects of an increase in purchase tax on the price of (a) new cars, and (b) second-hand cars. *C*

15 'Scarcity and production costs determine the shape and position of the supply curve; the prices and availability of substitutes determine the demand curve.' Explain and discuss. *OA*

16 Why do we normally draw supply curves sloping upwards to the right? *OA*

17 If the supply of petrol increases, what would you expect to happen to the price of motor cars? *OS*

18 Why do apples cost more per pound than do potatoes in most British markets? *OA*

19 Why does the price of tomatoes fluctuate more violently than the price of salt? *OA*

20 What is meant by redundancy of labour? Suggest ways of reducing it. *B*

21 'An increasing population is a most potent factor in promoting economic growth.' Consider this statement critically. *B*

22 Why does output increase much faster in some advanced economies than in others? *OS*

23 'If the British economy is to grow at 4% per annum it needs more investment; more investment can be generated only by reducing consumption; it follows that consumption today must be sacrificed if we want more consumption tomorrow.' Discuss. *OA*

24 'Nationalised industries are responsible to Parliament; Imperial Chemical Industries Ltd. is responsible to no one.' Discuss. *OA*

25 How would you calculate the cost of producing a pound of mutton? *OA*

26 What is meant by marginal cost? Explain how you would calculate the marginal cost of a short journey by car. *OA*

27 There are two modern ways of heating a house. In the first, using electric wires buried in the floor, the original installation costs are very low, but the running costs are fairly high. Secondly, from a gas- or oil-fired boiler hot water may be circulated through radiators: in this method, installation costs are high while running costs are low. How would you analyse the economic reasons for choosing between these two methods? *OA*

28 It is normally assumed that average costs rise as output increases. It is also assumed that technical progress reduces real costs. Are these two assumptions consistent? *OA*

29 Explain what is meant by *marginal*, *average* and *total* costs. Should a firm close down if it cannot cover its average costs? *LA*

30 The following table relates to an $8\frac{1}{4}$ acre small-holding in East Africa. The amount of the net income is related to the acreage under cash crops—pyrethrum and tea. But these crops increase the labour requirements of the holding. Work out (a) the average return per man, and (b) the marginal return

per man for each situation. Assuming that a worker can be hired for £30 a year, which situation will bring the greatest income to the farmer?

Situation	Acreage	Labour force (number)	Net income (excluding cost of paid labour)	
1	$3\frac{3}{4}$	3	323	
2	$5\frac{1}{4}$	4	427	
3	$6\frac{1}{2}$	5	525	
4	$7\frac{1}{4}$	6	605	B

31 'The advantages of large-scale production are so great that soon there will be no small firms.' Comment. — LA

32 The owner of a shop is considering expanding his business by buying the shop next door. What factors will influence his decision? — OA

33 What are the advantages of the joint stock form of company? — LA

34 There are many firms making clothes, but only a few which make soap. Why? — OA

35 'Low cost shops are bound to displace high cost shops; therefore small shops are bound to disappear.' Is this true of Britain? — OA

36 Distinguish between a joint-stock company and a co-operative society. — B

37 Should the state bribe firms to set up new plants in depressed areas? — OA

38 How does the British government attempt to induce firms to set up new businesses in one place rather than another? Do you agree with the principles on which it chooses the place in which it will encourage or discourage development? — C

39 There is plenty of spare labour in Northern Ireland but little in Coventry; why, therefore, do many firms protest when they are asked to place their new plants in Ireland? — OA

40 Make a case in favour of workers who strike in protest against threats of redundancy. — OA

41 'Declining industries should be killed off quickly, not supported in a long and painful old age.' Discuss with reference to not more than three British industries. — OA

42 Why are most new industries established in the south of England? — OA

43 Why are some types of retail shops increasing in number more rapidly than others? — OA

44 What conditions are generally necessary for an organised wholesale market to develop? — B

45 What principal services does the wholesaler perform? Would the elimination of the wholesaler tend to lower prices to the consumer? *B*

46 'Makers of household detergents have been criticised for spending too much on advertising. But the forces of supply and demand may be relied upon to ensure that no firm advertises more than the customer would wish.' Explain and discuss. *OA*

47 'Newspapers are financed more by advertising revenue than from income from sales; advertising revenue is greater when sales are larger; it follows that newspapers should be given away.' Discuss. *OS*

48 How would rational firms decide how much to spend on advertising? *OS*

49 'When the price of butter rises less is bought; therefore the price will fall again; therefore the price of butter can be expected to be steady through time, with only short term fluctuations.' Discuss. *OS*

50 Suppose that the selling price of motor cars is fixed by agreement amongst motor car producers. Who loses and who gains from such an agreement? *OA*

51 What is meant by the marginal cost of producing, say, motor cars? Are cars sold at marginal cost? For what reasons may cars or other products be sold at prices different from marginal cost? *OA*

52 'In the public interest, all firms should be made to charge prices that are equal to marginal costs.' Discuss. *OA*

53 'Monopoly is the reward for efficiency and hence should be encouraged.' Discuss. *OS*

54 'Not even a monopolist can simultaneously fix price and quantity sold.' Why then is monopoly said to be evil? *OA*

55 What is meant by price discrimination? Under what conditions is such discrimination possible? *B*

56 Who loses when a firm practises price discrimination between different markets? Who gains? *OS*

57 What explanations may be offered for the apparent stability of prices in oligopolistic markets? *J*

58 Why is a £5 note more acceptable in settlement of a debt than a diamond which is commonly bought and sold at about £5? *OA*

59 How does bank credit help to finance industry and trade? Explain how the lending power of the commercial banks is limited. *B*

60 Is there a relationship between the volume of bank deposits and the level of prices? *OA*

61 Would price rises be seriously inhibited if the monetary authorities took steps to prevent any increase in the volume of money? *OS*

62 How do banks make profits? *OA*

63 What problems does a Central Bank have to consider in its relations with:
(a) the Government;
(b) the banking and financial community;
(c) the general public? *B*

64 'It is increasingly difficult to tell the difference between banks and non-banks.' Discuss. *C*

65 By what methods does the Government control the banking system? How useful is such control? *OA*

66 What is meant by monetary policy, and in what circumstances is its use appropriate? *A*

67 What are the main instruments of monetary policy? Assess their efficacy as economic stabilisers. *J*

68 Would you expect a decrease in the volume of bank balances to be accompanied by a fall in the price level? *OS*

69 What are the effects of putting up Bank Rate? *C*

70 Explain how the clearing banks and merchant banks can provide finance for a U.K. exporter who is selling overseas on short-term credit. *B*

71 ' "Stop-go" policies are the only means available to the Government to offset "go-stop" cycles in our economic system.' Explain and discuss. *OA*

72 Why do almost all governments at times adopt 'stop-go' policies? *OA*

73 What measures can a government take to deal with inflation? *J*

74 What is a price index number? How is one calculated? *LA*

75 What do you understand by inflation and productivity? Would the rate of inflation be slower if productivity rose faster? *OA*

76 'Government expenditure is always inflationary.' Discuss. *OA*

77 Outline the chief problems involved in measuring changes in the value of money over time. *J*

78 How do changes in interest rates affect the economic system? *OS*

79 Why should Bloggs Ltd. (a public company) care if the price of Bloggs shares falls on the Stock Exchange? *OA*

80 Does a rise in the rate of interest on government securities have any effect on industrial investment? *OA*

81 What is the national debt? Should it be paid off? *OA*

82 Suppose that the Government decides that it must spend an extra £500 million next year. Discuss the alternative ways in which this money could be found. *OA*

83 Distinguish between the progressive and the proportional principles of taxation and outline the factors that affect the incidence of these types of tax. *B*

84 To what extent is the general level of prices influenced by government budgetary policy? *OA*

85 Analyse the expected effects of a reduction of a budget deficit on the growth of output, on the volume of bank deposits, and on the price level. *OS*

86 In what ways does the Chancellor of the Exchequer's Budget differ from the housewife's budget? *OA*

87 Why does Britain import machinery that can well be made at home? *OA*

88 Explain how changes in comparative costs between industries lead to changes in international trade. *OS*

89 Britain imports many machines for use in factories here, and exports many rather similar machines for use in foreign factories. Why does this happen? Is it consistent with the theory of comparative costs? *OS*

90 England imports cotton textiles from India, where the hourly wage rate is low, from America, where the hourly wage rate is high, in competition with her own Lancashire production, where the hourly wage rate is between the two. Why? *C*

91 Explain what is meant by the *terms of trade* and the *balance of trade*. What relationship exists between these two concepts? *J*

92 'The balance of payments always balances.' Explain and discuss. *LA*

93 Explain carefully the interaction between the level of aggregate demand within a country and the country's balance of international payments. *OS*

94 'If the U.K. generates a large balance of payments surplus this will impart a deflationary shock to the world trading community.' Explain and discuss. *OA*

95 Does it harm the economy if Englishmen buy castles in Spain? *OA*

96 'If a country is fully employed, but has a deficit on the current account of the balance of payments, the deficit can be wiped out only by reducing consumption and investment at home.' Explain and discuss. *OA*

97 Explain the following extract from *The Times* City page: 'Sterling drifted lower yesterday, to its lowest point for over 3

years. . . . The rate was pulled down by the Americans entering the market to offer the pound in the afternoon. . . . There may have been some official intervention to steady the rate. . . . The forward pound moved little, but spot sterling continued to fall. . . . Continental currencies nearly all hardened against the pound.' *B*

98 What is meant by the 'gold standard'? Should the world go back to gold? *OA*

99 Outline briefly the main factors influencing forward exchange rates, and also explain the meaning of 'premium' and 'discount' when used in connection with such rates. *B*

100 'Import duties (tariffs) are disruptive of trade and destructive of welfare.' 'Import duties are essential to protect the British balance of payments.' Discuss. *OA*

101 Should we make laws to prevent the purchase of imports from countries with low wages? *OA*

102 'Lancashire cotton is being ruined by cheap foreign labour.' Is this an argument against free trade? *OS*

103 Do all individuals and all countries necessarily gain by an increase in the freedom of international trade? Apply your answer to the current working of the Common Market. *OA*

104 The national income per head in Ruritania is one half of that in England. Does it follow that Englishmen are twice as prosperous as Ruritanians? *OA*

105 Describe the methods of calculating the national income. How far can the national income be used as a measure of economic growth? *B*

106 Outline the factors on which a nation's standard of living depends. *B*

107 Why are most Englishmen better off than most Africans? *OA*

108 Why is real income per head lower in Britain than in the United States? *OA*

109 'Denmark is rich without being industrialised; if India wishes to be rich, she should remain an agricultural country.' Discuss. *OS*

110 How is money national income calculated? Does money national income correspond exactly to the level of national welfare? *LA*

111 Explain how the national income is measured by the 'output method' and discuss the particular problems which are involved. *J*

112 If a country had increased its National Income by 50% in five years, what questions would you ask in order to decide whether this had been an impressive achievement? *C*

113 Suppose the Government next year spends £100 million more than this year, while tax receipts remain constant. What sort of effect is this change likely to have on the national income? *OA*

114 Define the multiplier. How is it related to the marginal propensity to consume? *LA*

115 'A low marginal propensity to save means a high multiplier; therefore, the higher the level of saving in our present situation, the less the risk of a slump.' Discuss. *OA*

116 Is it possible to reconcile the views that (a) savings are necessary for growth and (b) savings create unemployment? *J*

117 Discuss some of the chief determinants of the level of employment in the British economy. *OA*

118 What is a factor of production? How is its price determined? Give specific examples. *B*

119 What forces principally determine the distribution of income between personal earnings (wages plus salaries) and profits? Does Government tax policy influence the outcome? *OS*

120 What determines the supply of labour to an occupation? *LA*

121 What difficulties would be encountered in using national minimum wage legislation to help solve the problem of poverty? *C*

122 What forces determine the relationship between the pay of dockers and the pay of bricklayers? *OA*

123 Should coalminers be paid the same wage wherever they work? *C*

124 'Professors should be paid more only if their productivity rises.' Discuss. *OS*

125 Should inequality of incomes be reduced by state action? *OA*

126 What is meant by economic rent? Is the profit received by shareholders in British manufacturing firms a form of rent? Or is it a 'cost of production'? *OA*

127 If there were a sudden increase in the fertility of agricultural land what would happen to farmers' incomes? *C*

128 Do you think increases in land values should be especially heavily taxed? *C*

129 What are the principal factors underlying the determination of wages? *B*

130 'The inter-industry mobility of labour is essential if the marginal productivity theory of wages is to work.' Discuss. *OS*

131 What are the relative advantages and disadvantages of piece rates (i.e., payment by result) and time rates? *J*

132 Why are wages higher in industry than in agriculture? *C*

133 Why do women tend to be paid less than men for doing the same kind of job? Outline the economic arguments justifying 'equal pay for equal work'. *J*

134 Why are women often paid less than men for doing the same job? Would you favour removing such discrimination? *C*

135 Consider the economic forces that influence the level of interest rates. In which direction is each force likely to exert pressure? *B*

136 'The rate of interest is of greater significance to the poor than to the rich.' Discuss. *C*

137 What are the determinants of the rate of interest in a free enterprise economy? *J*

138 Use the concept of equi-marginal returns to explain how an entrepreneur would organise his business for maximum profit. *B*

139 What is meant by economic efficiency? How would you measure the relative efficiency of two economic systems? *OA*

140 In a modern joint-stock company, who maximises what? *C*

141 Make a case against economic planning. *OS*

142 If large size is evidence for efficiency, is there any case for controlling or nationalising large companies? *C*

143 'An incomes policy raises more problems than it solves.' Discuss. *C*

144 'The main case for an incomes policy rests on post-war experience suggesting that full employment, price stability and free collective bargaining are inconsistent policies.' Discuss. *B*

145 The government does not control the price of petrol; why should it control the price of foreign exchange? *C*

146 Suppose you wished to predict changes in interest rates on long-dated Government bonds during the next five years; what information would you seek and how would you use it? *OS*

147 'To relieve traffic congestion it is more logical to tax the motorist than to subsidise public transport.' Discuss. *C*

148 What would be the main economic implications of a shorter working week? *B*

149 Explain briefly the contrasts involved in any three of the following:
(a) direct and indirect taxation;
(b) perfect and imperfect markets;
(c) market price and normal price;
(d) total utility and marginal utility. *B*

150 What forces determine the amount of investment that businessmen plan to undertake at any one time? *OA*

151 Why does salmon cost much more than plaice in most British fish shops? *OA*

152 'Road space is rapidly becoming acutely scarce and should be priced as a scarce commodity.' Discuss. *C*

153 'The more parking space we provide, the more cars there will be; the solution is to provide *no* parking space at all.' Discuss. *OA*

154 Suppose the Government has available £500 million for the investment programme of the nationalised industries. On what principles should this sum be distributed among the different industries? *OS*

155 Why should a wise business firm seek knowledge of the intentions of other firms before making investment decisions? *OS*

156 Why is the government always anxious to predict investment expenditure by business firms? *OA*

157 What is the effect on the British economy of an American firm building a factory in Britain? *C*

158 Should the Government try to restrict either the price at which land is sold or the use to which land is put? *OS*

159 'A good home market is the necessary support of the export trade.' Discuss. *OA*

160 What main economic factors have influenced British industry in the last decade? *B*

161 In what ways can the government affect the level of aggregate demand in an economy? *J*

162 Are the same criteria of efficiency equally applicable to both private and public sectors of industry? *J*

163 Discuss alternative means of raising the growth rate of the United Kingdom. *LS*

164 'Growth depends at least as much on investment in human beings as on investment in physical capital.' Explain and discuss. *LS*

Index